NOT JUST NAMES

With best wishes

Paul

*This book is for
Andrew and Thomas*

NOT JUST NAMES

A Tribute to the Fallen of Cannock Chase

Paul Bedford

BREWIN BOOKS

First published by
Brewin Books Ltd, 56 Alcester Road,
Studley, Warwickshire B80 7LG in 2015
www.brewinbooks.com

© Paul Bedford 2015

All rights reserved.

ISBN: 978-1-85858-536-9

The moral right of the author has been asserted.

A Cataloguing in Publication Record
for this title is available from the British Library.

Typeset in Haarlemmer MT Std
Printed in Great Britain by
Hobbs The Printers Ltd.

Contents

	Introduction	vi
1.	Bridgtown	1
2.	Cannock	20
3.	Hednesford	90
4.	Chadsmoor	227
5.	Wimblebury	260
6.	Heath Hayes	264
7.	Norton Canes	289

Introduction

The Great War of 1914-18 has always held a fascination for me, and so there was a sense of inevitability that my second book would be about that conflict. I also wished to focus on the locality where I was born and where I have spent the majority of my life.

I have always been aware of the enormous sacrifice made by those who gave their lives during those four bloody years. I have attended many Remembrance Sunday services and have also visited graves, cemeteries and memorials in Belgium and France. The thought developed from this that I should like to try and write a fitting tribute to the men from the Cannock Chase area who fell in the Great War and whose names are found on the local War Memorials.

It is envisaged that there will be three volumes of this work. This, the first of the three focuses on the Memorials of Bridgtown, Cannock, Hednesford, Chadsmoor, Wimblebury, Heath Hayes and Norton Canes, all of which are found within what may be loosely termed as Cannock Chase. At the time of the Great War, these towns and villages were dominated by coal mining and a vast majority of the men who served and died made their living from the extraction of coal.

As a result of my research, it soon became clear that a large number of soldiers from Chadsmoor did not appear on local memorials. An initial meeting with Tom Walsh at Cannock Council set wheels in motion. The task was passed to Derek Davis who set up a committee to try and rectify this odd situation. As a result of tremendous hard work, on the 18th April, 2015, Chadsmoor will have a memorial dedicated to the memory of some 160 servicemen from the village who died in the Great War.

This book is the result of a tremendous amount of careful research from various sources. It began with trawling through the local newspapers of the time, carefully recording any information about soldiers who were serving in the armed forces. This research was underpinned with cross referenced checks using the Commonwealth War Graves Commission's Debt of Honour and the Soldiers Died in the Great War information. The census material found on both Find My Past and Ancestry has been used as a further way of double checking the information about each individual, in order to try and reconstruct their past.

An appeal through the local papers came in very useful and ensured that a more accurate version of certain soldiers' lives was possible. I would like to thank the Express and Star and the Cannock Chase Chronicle for their support in this search.

Indeed, no book could be written without the support of generous people who have given up their valuable time in order to help. The Library staff at Cannock have been helpful and patient. The Chase Project have been very helpful in providing material about the Cannock War Memorial which has helped unlock some of the mysteries. Lorraine Vernon and Trevor Green have been very generous with their support, especially about Pte William Vernon and Lt Col William Burnett. David Matthews provided useful information on Spr George Hughes which meant that errors on my part were avoided. Steve Dawes helped with Pte Arnold Bishop and Pte Norman Bishop, as did Ray Deakin on Pte Isaiah Jones. John Ashley was extremely helpful in sending pictures about L/Cpl Richard Timmins. Wal Kimber, who was a former teaching colleague got in touch and guided me through the life of Pte Frank Reynolds, as did Nora Rutter on her relative Dvr Herbert Price. Lynn Evans has also been an enthusiastic supporter throughout.

I would wish to make it clear that no matter how carefully the research is carried out, there will no doubt be mistakes in this book. If this is the case then please feel free to contact me via my publisher and I will do my very best to amend future reprints. If anyone has photographs of soldiers, then again these could be included in the future, as could any information about those who at the moment remain as just names on a memorial.

This book would not have been finished without the love and support shown by my family and in particular I would like to express my admiration for my wife Lynn, who despite having a very busy and stressful job as a Curriculum Leader, has always found the time to give encouragement and advice.

Paul Bedford,
Penkridge, Staffordshire
March 2015

Chapter One

BRIDGTOWN

Private Robert Beadle
CH/18536

This young man was only 18 years of age when he died of gunshot wounds to his shoulder on 19th July 1915. He had been wounded three days before and was being treated on the Hospital Ship, Grantully Castle. He was a native of Darlington, Co. Durham, where his parents, William and Jane lived at 31 Farrier Street. Robert was serving with the Royal Marine Light Infantry in the Chatham Battalion of the Royal Naval Division and had already seen service at Dunkirk between 20th September – 2nd October 1914 and the defence of Antwerp 3rd – 9th October 1914, suggesting that he may have lied about his age when joining up. There is no evidence to explain why he is remembered on the memorial at Bridgtown. Robert Beadle's name is also recorded on the Chatham Naval Memorial, Kent. It is more likely that this entry was made in error and that it should be Richard Beedles of Chadsmoor. (See Cannock Memorial)

Private Ernest Benton
11999

Ernest Benton had served in the Hednesford Territorials for two years before he then volunteered for the army two weeks before the war began in July 1914, serving with the 2nd Battalion, King's Own Scottish Borderers. He was despatched to France on the 19th September, 1914 and was one of the first from the Cannock area to be killed in action when he fell on the 29th October, 1914. He was aged 22 at the time of his death. He came from mining stock; his father

Arthur Benton was a collier until his death in 1905 at the age of 40. His widowed mother Mary Ann lived at 52, Walsall Road, Cannock. The couple had married at Cannock in late 1892. In 1911, Ernest was working as a labourer, filling coal tubs underground at Littleton Colliery and lodging with the Yapp family at 13 Company Buildings, Walsall Road, Cannock. He is remembered on the Le Touret Memorial, France.

Private Charles Edgar Bird
12037

Charles was a twin and was born in Cannock in 1886. His father Daniel was an engine stoker and later a farm labourer and the family lived at Rumer Hill in Cannock. Daniel had married Ellen Bedson at Cannock in the spring of 1892. Charles served in the 1st Battalion, South Staffordshire Regiment, being sent to France on the 17th December, 1914, and at the time of his death on 18th May, 1915 was 27 years of age. His brother, John Matthew Bird saw his brother's body buried and wrote home to inform the family of Charles' tragic death. After the war his body could not be identified and he is also remembered on the Le Touret Memorial, France. Like many men from this area, Charles was a coal miner before he volunteered for service.

Pilot Officer Cyril Brewe

Cyril Brewe rose from humble circumstances to become an officer in the Royal Air Force. He was born in 1886 at Burntwood, his parents having married in 1875 in Stafford. In 1891, John Brewe, his father, was earning his living as a farmer at Lea Bank, Burntwood. Later John and his brother, George were both employed as boat loaders on the canal, although John subsequently became a miner and moved to Heath Hayes, but Cyril began work as a general labourer in Whitehouse's Edge Tool factory in Bridgtown. The family then lived in Church Street. Cyril was keen to improve his prospects and joined the staff of the Cannock Chase Courier before enlisting in the Royal Marine Light Infantry at the age of 19, serving on HMS Prince of Wales. He rose to the rank of Corporal before the onset of the Great War, and was sent to France on the 27th August, 1914. Cyril saw action at Antwerp, Bruges and Gallipoli, when he transferred to the Royal Naval Air Service. By the time of his marriage to Annie Selina Parker on Christmas Day 1916 at St. James' Church, Norton Canes, he had risen to the rank of Chief Petty Officer based at the Isle of Sheppey. On the 1st April 1918, Cyril was transferred to the newly created Royal Air Force where he served in Mesopotamia, rising to the rank of Pilot Officer in 84 Squadron. He was killed on the 22nd June 1921, aged 35 and is buried in Basra Military Cemetery, Iraq. His widow lived at Lilac Cottage, Washbrook Lane, in Norton Canes.

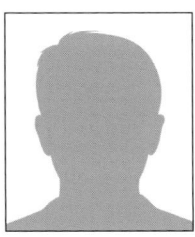

Lance Corporal Alfred Carpenter
18329

Alfred Carpenter was born in 1892 at Bridgtown. His father Harold, had married Elizabeth Lewis at Cannock in early 1886 and he was employed as an Edge Tool Polisher who also hailed from the village. By 1911, the family had moved to Bloxwich, living at 107 Station Street. Alfred had followed in his father's footsteps and also worked as an Edge Tool Polisher. When the war broke out Alfred volunteered and initially joined the Royal Scots (Regimental Number 22703), arriving in France on the 2nd October, 1915. He then transferred to the 6th Battalion, Machine Gun Corps (Infantry). Alfred died of wounds on the 7th October, 1917, aged 25, during the fighting around Ieper in the Battle of Passchendaele. His death occurred at the Casualty Clearing Station at Dozinghem, as the troops called it. (The two nearby CCS's were named Bandaghem and Mendinghem). He is buried at Dozinghem Military Cemetery, Belgium.

Private Frank Cascarino
136812

The Cascarino family had a colourful history. Frank's father, Domenico was born in Italy, and had been employed as an itinerant musician and a navvy, having moved from Stourbridge, where he had married Jane Adcock in the spring of 1888, to Chester, where Anthony was born and then back to Stourbridge in Worcestershire, where Frank and his brother Louis were born. By 1911, the family had moved to Bridgtown, living at 55, Bridge Street, where a further five children had been added to the family. Domenico was working as a boat loader at the coal wharf whereas his two eldest sons, Anthony and Frank, were horse minders down the pit. Frank was called up and joined the 6th Battalion Machine Gun Corps (Infantry), being sent to France on the 24th August, 1915. He was posted missing in action, following the fighting at Soissons in July 1918, news coming through that he had been wounded and taken prisoner and moved to Darmstadt in Germany. It was here that he finally succumbed to these injuries on the 18th September 1918, aged 22. Frank is buried in Niederzwehren Cemetery at Kassel in Germany.

Private George Henry Cryer
11967

In many ways the Cryer family show the changes in working practice that were taking place at the time. In 1891 and 1901, the father James Cryer was a shepherd at Pillaton, near Penkridge, having married Hannah Morgan at Lichfield late in 1883. Within ten years, he and his family had moved to Rumer Hill, Cannock where he worked as a general farm labourer, whereas his eldest son, James was a colliery surface labourer, whilst George had followed his father and also earned his living as a farm labourer. By the outbreak of the Great War, George worked for Cannock Urban District Council. George answered Lord Kitchener's call in 1914, joining the 9th Battalion, South Staffordshire Regiment, a Pioneer Battalion raised for labouring duties at the Front. He was accidentally killed on 21st May 1916, Captain Walter P. Bradshaw taking the trouble to write to his parents informing them that George's death had been instantaneous without any suffering. He was only 24 years of age and is buried at Bois-de-Noulette British Cemetery, Aix-Noulette, France.

Private John Dainty
3449

John Dainty had joined the Army in 1914, initially in the Royal Army Medical Corps, which was not surprising as he had been a member of the Cannock and Leacroft Colliery Ambulance Company. However, he had then transferred to the 1/6th Battalion South Staffordshire Regiment in the Machine Gun Section. Before the war broke out John had been employed as a blacksmith at the colliery. He was on leave just two weeks before he was killed, when the grateful folk of Rumer Hill had presented John with an address book and a cigarette case. On his return to the Front, he was killed by a shell whilst digging a shallow trench in No Man's Land, on the 24th June 1916, aged 22. His body was buried in "a pretty little cemetery behind the lines". John's body now lies in Foncquevillers Military Cemetery, France. His grieving parents, John and Elizabeth had married at Cannock in the spring of 1883, John earning his living as an engineer fitter.

1. Bridgtown

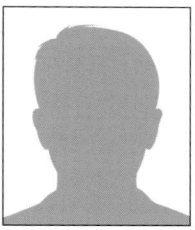

J. T. Duckhouse

This is an entry on the war memorial that may well remain a mystery. There are only three men with the surname Duckhouse who were killed in the Great War. These were Leonard, Samuel and David Thomas. Only the last named has any connection with the area, as Sergeant David Thomas Duckhouse resided in Cannock and is remembered on the memorial in the town centre. I can only assume that the entry on the Bridgtown memorial has been confused with this Cannock soldier. Intriguingly though, there is a reference to T. Duckers of Bridgtown being wounded in action in the Cannock Chase Courier of 28th October 1916.

Private Thomas William Dutton
56225

Thomas Dutton was born at Fair Oak, Rugeley in 1881 and again came very much from mining stock. He was 5 feet 5 inches tall and weighed 138 lbs according to his service record, suggesting with a 37 inch chest measurement, a stocky build. Dutton was a family man, having married Emma Edwards at St. Luke's, Cannock on 1st March, 1903. The couple had six children, born between 1905 and 1915. They had moved to Hemsworth near Wakefield in Yorkshire between 1908 and 1911 but by the outbreak of war Thomas and Emma lived at 57 Longford Lane, Bridgtown. On the 23rd February 1915, Thomas Dutton joined the Army, attesting at Hednesford, where he was posted to the Royal Army Medical Corps as a private, being granted 5th rate corps pay on the 5th June, 1915. Thomas Dutton was serving on His Majesty's Hospital Ship Galeka Castle when it struck a mine on the 28th October, 1916. He was drowned at sea in this tragedy, aged 34. He is buried at Ste. Marie Cemetery, Le Havre, France.

Sapper William Fellows
112554

William Fellows was born in Bridgtown on 13th October, 1886, being the eldest of a large family born to John and Mary Anne Fellows, and living in Church Street. John hailed from Dudley and was a coal miner, although he had married Mary Anne Howarth at Cannock in late 1883. His eldest son worked in a brickworks, as a labourer and then as a fireman, before joining the Royal Navy as a stoker, serving on a number of vessels between the 14th August 1906 and the 18th August 1911, when he was discharged. His conduct was described as either good or very good until the final year of his service when he found himself in the cells on no fewer than four times. The Navy decided not to place him on the reserve list. William was married to Elizabeth Lewis at St. Luke's, Cannock on the 30th May 1914. In the Great War, William decided to join the Royal Engineers and his place of residence is given as Chelsea, although he actually enlisted at Cannock. He was posted to the 175th Field Company, R.E. serving as a Sapper until the 14th November, 1915 when he was killed in action aged 29. William is buried in Maple Copse Cemetery, near Ieper in Belgium.

Private Benjamin Fellows
22695

Benjamin Fellows was also born in Bridgtown, in 1889, being the 3rd youngest son of Francis and Amelia Fellows. Once again the father made his living as a coal miner and was the older brother of John Fellows. Francis had married Amelia Woodall at Dudley in the summer of 1893. The family then moved to Bridgtown and lived at 20, Park Street. It was at Bridgtown that Francis died in 1906. Following what had become almost a family tradition, Benjamin, also worked at Hawkins' brickworks as a brickmaker, alongside his brothers John and Thomas. Benjamin joined the 4th Battalion, South Staffordshire Regiment and was killed in action on the 24th March, 1918 at the age of 31, during the retreat forced by the German Spring offensive. His body was never recovered and he is remembered on the Arras Memorial in France.

Private John Felton
31525

John Felton was born in Bridgtown in 1894 and was one of eleven children born to John and Elizabeth Felton. Both parents hailed from the Black Country, John from West Bromwich and Elizabeth from Wolverhampton, where the couple had married in 1881, yet with the exception of George, all of their children had been born in Bridgtown. John junior worked as a labourer in an iron works, rather than following his father's trade as a wood turner. When war broke out in 1914, John joined the South Staffordshire Regiment, on the 28th August, 1914 seeing service at Ieper, Armentieres and the Somme where he was gassed and sent back to Canterbury to recover. He saw further service from October 1916 in Italy before being discharged from the Staffordshires on the 22nd January 1919. He then joined "B" Company, 2nd Battalion, the Seaforth Highlanders in May 1919. John had completed five years service in the Army, surviving the carnage of the Great War, and so it was exceptionally sad that this soldier succumbed to influenza on 11th October 1919 at the Military Hospital in Inverness, aged 25. A funeral service was held at Inverness where John was given full military honours, before his body was returned to Bridgtown. John Felton lies at rest in Cannock Cemetery.

Sapper Richard George
121660

The George family had an interesting history, the father of the family James, was born in Wolverhampton, whilst his wife, Jane was born in London, and had been married before she met James, having three children from that marriage. In 1891 the family of nine was living in Cheslyn Hay. Her second husband died in 1895, and this brought about a move to Bridgtown, where her sons James and Richard found jobs as edge tool strikers. Richard married Sarah Ann Westwood in Cannock in 1907 and by 1911 they had four children and were living at 32 Park Street in Bridgtown. When war broke out, Richard volunteered for service and joined the Royal Engineers in one of the newly formed Tunnelling Companies, attesting in Hednesford on the 13th September, 1915, and being posted to the 184th Company, in France on the 27th September. Richard saw service at Ieper where he died from pneumonia on the 6th March 1916, at the age of 31. He is buried in Wanquetin Communal Cemetery, near Arras in France.

Private George Frederick Homer
19889

Although George's father, James, a hard solder plater, was born in Birmingham, the family were very much from Walsall, where James had married Ann Hawkes in 1882, George being born in the town in 1886. In 1901, George was a fifteen year old grocer's assistant and the family were living at 94 Rutter Street, Walsall. In 1908, George married Alice Neville in Walsall and by 1911, the family had moved to Ash Tree Street in Pelsall, where George had become a Grocer's

Manager. By the outbreak of the Great War the Homers had moved to Bridgtown, where George was a Grocery Manager employed by H.W. Parker. However, George joined up in August 1914, electing to join the 9th Battalion, South Staffordshire Regiment, a Pioneer battalion. He was sent to France in March 1915 and served until the 13th June 1916, when he was killed in action, aged 31, leaving a widow and three children. George Frederick Homer is buried in Railway Dugouts Burial Ground, near Ieper in Belgium.

Pioneer Ernest Henry Hulme
130343

The Hulme family were local to the area with Ernest's father, Thomas coming from Little Wyrley and his mother, Clara being born in Hednesford, although they had married at Walsall in 1889. The family had moved to Bridgtown by 1891, according to the 1911 census, Ernest was an errand boy and other family members were involved in brick making, although Thomas had continued to ply his trade as an axle maker. During the Great War, Ernest had at first joined the King's Shropshire Light Infantry, but then transferred to "F" Special Company of the Royal Engineers. Ernest was seriously wounded in 1918 and was taken to the Base Hospital at Boulogne where, sadly, he died of his wounds on the 6th June, 1918, aged just 22. News of his death came to his parents at Watling Street, Bridgtown, around a week later.

Private William Henry Hulme
242539

William Hulme was an example of the many young men who joined the Army during the Great War who were under age. He was born in 1899 in Bridgtown, although his father, also William Henry, a gas engine driver and gas fitter, came from Stockport, where he had married Fanny Winsor in 1895. William's mother, Fanny, was more local, having been born in Norton Canes. The family lived for a time in Lancashire, Bridgtown and in Cheslyn Hay. Prior to enlisting, William worked in the Edge Tool works of Whitehouse's at Bridgtown and resided in Broad Street, although his mother now lived in Chase Terrace. William joined the 1/6th Battalion, South Staffordshire Regiment, and was sent to France on the 5th March, 1915, which would suggest that he enlisted in the autumn of 1914. William was twice wounded during the war. He was home on leave three months before he was killed in action, aged 18 on the 23rd April, 1917, although his age is given as 21 in the Cannock Advertiser. William's body was not recovered after the war and he is remembered on the Arras Memorial in France.

E. Haynes

E. Haynes may well remain one of the soldiers of the Great War about whom we know nothing, yet whose name appears on the memorial at Bridgtown. The only reasonably close reference that I have found is to Private George Edward Haynes, 10th Essex Regiment, who was born in Brewood and who was killed in action on 21st April, 1918, aged 24.

Private Haydn James Jones
22965

Haydn Jones was born in Bridgtown in 1896, the same year that his father, George, died at the age of 32, leaving his widow, Emma, with a young family. She married Ernest Alfred Savage in Cannock in 1902 and the family continued to live in Bridgtown at 32 Union Street. By 1911, the couple had six children living with them and Haydn, the youngest son, was a labourer aged 15. Haydn volunteered for the Army in August 1915, at Hednesford, electing to join the 3rd Battalion, Royal Scots (Lothian Regiment), but was transferred to the 2nd Battalion on 1st October, 1915. Haydn was 5 feet 7 inches tall and weighed 126 lbs. Like many soldiers in the war he suffered from trench foot and spent two months in hospital at the beginning of 1916. Haydn was also wounded, suffering a gun shot wound to his arm, spending five days in hospital at Etaples, in July 1916. He was posted missing in action on the 13th November, 1916, believed to have been badly wounded. Incredibly the death of Haydn Jones was not confirmed until November 1919, when his body was recovered and buried in Serre Road Cemetery No. 1 which is on the Somme battlefield in France. Haydn was only 21 at the time of his death.

Private John Jones
19752

The Jones family epitomised those who followed the work around. The father and main breadwinner, Joseph, was born in Ocker Hill, in the heart of the Black Country. He was a miner and with the demise of the Black Country mines had moved first to Hamstead, then to Daw End in Rushall and finally to Bridgtown. His family had grown to include his wife Fanny and six children by 1911. Perhaps mining had taken its toll, as he had become a boat loader, whilst his eldest son, John, was helping the family coffers by working as a ripper underground at the age of 14. With the onset of the Great War, John volunteered for the Army on the 4th August, 1915, joining "A" Company, 8th Battalion, the South Staffordshire Regiment. He was sent to France on the 4th January, 1916 and he was killed in action on the Somme, in the battle to seize Delville Wood on the 10th July, 1916, aged 20. Sadly, John's body was one of the many not recovered, and he is remembered on the Thiepval Memorial on the Somme in France.

Lance Corporal Alfred Benjamin Kendrick
13415

Alfred Kendrick was born in 1891 in Wolverhampton, the son of Alfred and Helen Kendrick. The family had moved around the country living in Manchester, Birmingham and Wolverhampton before settling down at 45, Union Street, Bridgtown. Alfred died of wounds on the 30th July, 1916, aged 25, whilst serving in the 7th Battalion, East Lancashire Regiment, having enlisted in Manchester. He had been sent to France on the 18th July, 1915. Yet the rest of the family history remains a puzzle, as no reference can be found to them on either the 1901 or 1911 census. Alfred is buried in Dartmoor Cemetery, Becordel-Becourt on the Somme in France.

Private Frank Layton
R4/089872

The story of Frank Layton is one of intense fascination. He was born in Andover, Hampshire in 1876, the eldest son of Robert and Eliza Layton. They had married in Islington, London in 1867, with their first three daughters being born in Whitechapel. The family had then moved to Andover where they had set up a general merchant's business. By the age of 18, he was working as a butcher's assistant in his home town. Yet within ten years, he had moved to Cannock and was living and working for D.W. Clarke as a carter. He married Emily Ellen Holloway at Dudley in 1904, which in itself is interesting, as she came from Bath in Somerset, where she was living with her mother in 1901. By 1911, the family were living at Rumer Hill, where Frank was now a roadman at the Mid-Cannock

Colliery. Frank volunteered for service in 1915 and served in the Army Service Corps, 30th Remount Squadron at the 5th Base Remount Depot. He died from illness on the 23rd January, 1918 at the Base Hospital in Calais, leaving his widow and four children. Frank was aged 42 at his death and is buried at Les Baraques Military Cemetery, Sangatte near Calais in France.

Private William Lewis
8200

William Lewis was born in Jackfield, near Broseley, Shropshire in 1895. The family originated from this part of the world, his father John being born in the village, whilst his mother, Elizabeth (nee Sargent) came from nearby Broseley. The couple were married in Madeley in 1887, although residing at Jackfield, where John worked as a general labourer. By 1901 the family had just moved to Littleworth in Hednesford, where John was now employed as a roofing tile setter. By 1911, the Lewis's had moved to 17, New Street, Bridgtown, where John was a brickyard labourer and William a 16 year old general labourer. William had joined the Hednesford Territorials where he served for three years, winning the Colonel Smith prize for being the best shot. At the outbreak of the Great War, William volunteered for service with the 1/5th Battalion, South Staffordshire Regiment, being sent to France on the 5th March, 1915, seeing service at Ieper and Armentieres, and lost his life on the 13th October, 1915 at the battle of Loos, during the attack on the Hohenzollern Redoubt, aged only 19. His body was not identified after the war and he is remembered on the Loos Memorial in France.

Sapper John Lockett
1467

The Lockett family were native of Cheslyn Hay, and had earned their living from bricklaying, the father of the family, William being a bricklayer, along with Thomas, one of the sons, whilst William jnr, Joseph and John acted as labourer's to them. This position had changed by 1911, as William had retired, William jnr had become a clay miner, with Joseph and John now employed as miners, leaving only Thomas as a bricklayer's labourer. On attesting on the 8th September, 1914, John gives his residence as Norton Canes, but there is no obvious link to Bridgtown. He was sent to France on the 1st March, 1915. John was killed in action at the battle of Loos on 13th October, 1915, whilst serving in the 1/2nd

North Midland Field Company, Royal Engineers. He was aged 33, and was only 5 feet 5 inches in height. His body was never identified after the war and he too is remembered on the Loos Memorial in France.

Driver George Lloyd
241344

The Lloyd family were bakers and grocers by trade. Daniel Lloyd was originally from Market Drayton in Shropshire, whereas his wife came from West Auckland in County Durham. They had settled in Birmingham for a time before moving to Bridgtown around 1887, where they had set up a successful grocery business. Daniel had died at the young age of 45 in 1904. Ralph, one of the sons, had migrated to Canada in the early years of the twentieth century and married there. In the Great War he served with the Canadian contingent. George enlisted in July 1917 with the Royal Field Artillery, serving as a cook with the 121st Brigade Head Quarters. In late 1918, George contracted pneumonia and died at the Base Hospital at Etaples on the 24th October, 1918, aged 28. George was a married man having wed Hannah Maria Croft at St. Luke's on the 23rd June, 1913. George's body was buried at Etaples Military Cemetery in France.

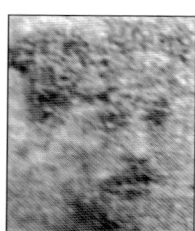

Private William Henry Hughes
22441

Although William's father, Thomas, was born in Dudley, the rest of the Hughes' were born in Bridgtown. William was a willowy 5 feet 8 inches tall and had been employed as a butcher's assistant and latterly as a van driver for the Cannock Co-operative Society, before he decided to join up on the 10th February, 1916, where he was classed as grade "B", presumably due to a slight heart murmur and a varicose vein in his right leg. He was held in reserve until the 23rd February, 1917 when he was recalled as Private 67194 with the Durham Light Infantry, being posted the following day. An insight into the discipline in the British Army of the time was shown when William was given two days field punishment number two for eating his iron rations. Shortly after this William was transferred to the Labour Corps, on the 14th May, 1917. It was whilst serving with the Labour Corps on the 26th June, 1917, that he was severely injured in the head, when a gunshot wound fractured his skull. He died of his wounds at 2 Casualty Clearing Station on the following day, aged 24. His medals were sent to Mrs.

Henry Hughes who lived in Southport, Lancashire, although his parents lived at 58, North Street, Bridgtown. William's body was buried in Bailleul Community Cemetery Extension (Nord) in France.

Private Sidney Charles Evans
36914

The father of the family Evans, George, originated from Dawley, Shropshire, whereas his wife came from Bradley in Staffordshire. The children were all born in Cheslyn Hay, although in 1901 they were residing in Wolstanton, Staffordshire, where George was a brick and tile maker. By 1911, the family had moved to Bridgtown and were living in Bridge Street. There had been a clear change in circumstances, as George had risen to managerial status in a brick works, and his daughter, Nellie, was a school teacher, whilst one son, Francis was a colliery clerk. Intriguingly, Sidney spent the first two years of the Great War in Russia, returning to England in 1916, when he enlisted in the 2/6th Battalion, South Staffordshire Regiment. He served in France until the 21st March, 1918, the first day of the German Spring Offensive, when he was posted as missing in action. His family had to endure a wait of twelve months before he was presumed to have been killed on that day. Sidney's body was not recovered after the war and he is remembered on the Arras Memorial to the missing in France. Sidney was 21 at the time of his death.

Private Ernest Mears
8202

In 1901, the Mears family were living on the Watling Street in Bridgtown. The father of the family, William, was a coal miner, which meant that they had moved frequently between Bloxwich, Churchbridge and Bridgtown. However, this happy existence was turned into turmoil in 1906, with the early death at the age of 43, of their mother Caroline. The family were split up between friends and relatives. In 1911, Ernest was living with James Tench and his widowed sister Agnes Williams at 21, Longford Lane, Bridgtown. He was employed as a grinder. By the outbreak of the Great War, Ernest was living in North Street with his married sister Ada and her husband George Whitehouse. He volunteered in 1914, joining the 1/5th Battalion, South Staffordshire Regiment, and being sent to France as a Signaller with his Battalion. He was killed during the battle of Loos on the 13th October, 1915, when he died of wounds after a charge of the German trenches.

Ernest was only 20 years of age. The news of his death was passed on to his sister by Signaller E. Martin in a letter. He described Ernest as "popular with the chaps" and gave his final words as "Goodbye Mart, you have been a good pal to me. I'm done." Ernest had spent 3 years with the Hednesford Territorials and was employed at the East Cannock Colliery. Ernest's body was buried in the Loos British Cemetery in France.

Sergeant Frederick Moore
7048

The Moore family originated from Oxfordshire, but had moved to Staffordshire in the mid 1880s. The children were all born in the Cannock area, with Frederick being born in Norton Canes. His father, Frederick was employed as a Corporation Carter and in 1901, they were living in Francis Street, Walsall. By 1911, the family had moved to Hollyhedge Lane with Frederick junior employed as a bran packer in a mill. He had spent 9 years with the colours, serving with the Royal Army Medical Corps in India from January 1902 and being placed in the reserve. Later in 1911, Frederick married Rosa Mary Hudson at Lichfield and had also changed his job, being employed as a carter by F. J. Cowern. This also necessitated a move to Watling Street in Bridgtown. The couple had two children, the second, Dorothy, being born towards the end of 1915. Frederick was recalled to serve during the Great War, initially helping to train troops on Salisbury Plain, before being sent to France on 1st July 1915. At Festubert he was one of only 5 officers and N.C.O.'s in his regiment, the Royal Welsh Fusiliers who returned alive from the battle. Frederick was also engaged in some of the heavy fighting between the 1st and 9th July on the Somme. Frederick was a popular soldier, but was killed in action at Bazentin on the 24th July, 1916, at the age of 34. His body was buried at Flatiron Copse Cemetery, Mametz in France.

Private John William Morris
40051

The Morris family were Staffordshire people, and the children were all born in the Cannock area. John Morris senior worked as a coal miner and latterly as a labourer above ground. His son John William worked as a labourer in a Tilery. During the Great War, John served in the 4th Battalion, Worcestershire Regiment and was wounded in September 1918, dying of these wounds at Bandaghem Casualty

Clearing Station on the 29th September, 1918, aged 23. His body was buried in the nearby cemetery, Haringhe (Bandaghem) Military Cemetery in Belgium.

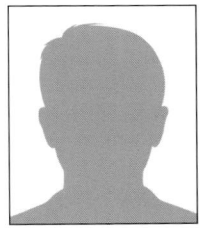

Private Harry Read
22702

Harry Read was born in Bridgtown in 1897, the family living initially in Churchbridge, but then moving to Watling Street by 1911 and finally to Walsall Road. His father, Alfred, had been an edge tool striker but had then opted for mining, becoming a rockman. Harry worked as a polisher at Whitehouse Brothers. Harry answered his nation's call in 1915, joining the 2nd Battalion, Royal Scots on the 15th August and being sent to France in September. He was posted as missing in action on 3rd May, 1917, and then confirmation of his death on that day being passed on to his parents in Bridgtown. Harry was only 20 at the time of his death and sadly his body was not identified at the end of the war. He is remembered on the Arras Memorial to the missing in France.

Gunner Howard Richards
74779

Howard's father Charles Richards came from Herefordshire and his wife Annie from Burton-on-Trent, but all of the children were born in Bridgtown, Howard being the second eldest. He followed his father, becoming an axle hardener in a cart manufacturer. The family lived at 38 Watling Street, Bridgtown, before moving to 116 in the same street. In the Great War, Howard served with the Royal Garrison Artillery, 139th Siege Battery and he was badly wounded, being taken back to the base hospital at Boulogne, where he died on the 12th April, 1917. Howard was buried near the hospital in Boulogne Eastern Cemetery in France. He was only 20 at the time of his death.

Lance Corporal Frank Rowley
16495

The Rowley's were a Staffordshire family and like many earned their living in the mining industry, between Burntwood, Cannock and Hednesford. Frank married Helen White on 11th July, 1909 at St. Peter's, Hednesford, their first child

Gwendoline being born in 1910. During the Great War, Frank served in the 1st Battalion, South Staffordshire Regiment and died of wounds on the 28th March, 1917, aged 32. He is buried in St. Leger British Cemetery in France.

Sapper William Shelley
102801

William Shelley had moved to Bridgtown by 1901 and was working as a carter/haulier, living as a lodger of the Curnow family in Mill Street. On the 21st April, 1907 he married Mercy Winfer at St. Luke's Parish Church and they lived with her family at 45 Longford Lane, Bridgtown. The couple had three children, Annie born in 1909, Ethel born in 1911 and William born in 1912. William senior worked as a miner at the Leacroft Colliery. In the Great War, William volunteered for service with the Royal Engineers in 1915, being sent to France on the 26th June of that year. He then transferred to the 180th Tunnelling Company, engaged in mining under the enemy lines. On the 28th March, 1918, after more than three years' service, William was killed by a shell. His remains were buried in Ribemont Communal Cemetery Extension on the Somme in France. He was 31 years of age when he met his death.

Private James Henry Sutton
5960

James Sutton was a veteran of the Boer War who volunteered for extra service in 1914. He was born in Balsall Heath, Warwickshire in 1881, the son of George and Mary Sutton, his father being a butcher. Both James and his brother George were employed as upholsterers. By 1908, James had moved to the Cannock area and indeed was married to Martha Willis at St. Luke's on the 7th June of that year. On the 1911 census, the couple were living on the Walsall Road, Great Wyrley and had a son, Frank Eric. Martha's brother Harry was also lodging with them. James was now employed as a colliery labourer, above ground. Before the War, the family had moved to Wedges Mills and had been blessed with two more children, Ethel born in 1913 and James born in 1914. James joined the 2nd Battalion, South Staffordshire Regiment and was posted to the Western Front. On the 13th March, 1915, Martha received a postcard from James saying that he expected to be sent home on furlough in the next two weeks. Four days later, she received a letter from Matron M. M. Blakeley telling her that her husband had died from his wounds at Boulogne. He had been very badly wounded, without much chance of recovery. He had been unconscious just before he died and had not suffered too much. Not surprisingly a very distressed Mrs. Sutton sent a telegram to the Matron asking for confirmation. Her husband's death was confirmed by return. James Sutton was 33 at the time of his death and was buried in Boulogne Eastern Cemetery in France.

2nd Lieutenant Cyril Duncan Whitehouse

Cyril Whitehouse was one of the ten children of Haydn and Fanny Whitehouse. Cornelius Whitehouse, Haydn's father had founded the very successful Edge Tool Company of Messrs Whitehouse which was the major employer in Bridgtown. The Whitehouse family lived at "The Poplars" in Bridgtown. Cyril attended Queen Mary's Grammar School in Walsall, and held a certificate from the Officers Training Corps. Cyril was an articled clerk to Mr. George Brown, Auctioneer of Rugeley. In 1916, Cyril was commissioned into the Household Battalion, Life Guards but was then attached to the 1st Battalion, Welsh Guards, being sent to France in October, 1917. Cyril was initially posted as missing in action on the 24th May, 1918, but his death on that date was later confirmed. The 21 year old 2nd Lieutenant's body was not identified after the war and he is remembered on the Arras Memorial to the Missing in France.

Sergeant Richard Wilson
9005

The Wilson family was much travelled and somewhat intriguing. The father of the family, Richard senior, on the 1901 census gives his place of birth as Castleford, Yorkshire, with 236 New Bole Hill, Treeton, Yorkshire as the address. Ten years later, the address is 17 Longford Lane, Bridgtown, yet Richard's place of birth is given as the United States of America. His sons earned their living from the local Cannock pits with Herbert a colliery ropeman and Richard junior and Vincent both horse drivers, at the Coppice Colliery. Richard junior must have joined the army before the outbreak of war as his service record indicates that he travelled with his Regiment, the 1st Battalion, South Staffordshire from South Africa, disembarking in France on 4th October, 1914. He rose from Private to Sergeant and was wounded on no fewer than four occasions during the war. Amazingly, he was only allowed one period of sick leave. Both brothers served during the Great War as well, Herbert in the Royal Army Medical Corps and Vincent in the Royal Field Artillery. Their father also served in the Royal Engineers before being given a medical discharge. Two sisters worked in munitions factories, clearly showing the total involvement of the family to the war effort. Sergeant Richard Wilson was killed in action on the 12th May, 1917, aged 26. Sadly his body was not identified after the war and he is remembered on the Arras Memorial to the Missing in France.

Lance Corporal Robert Winfer
102800

The Winfer family were born and bred in the Cannock area. Robert's father and his eldest son were both born in Shareshill. Robert senior was a coal miner, whereas his sons both earned their living at a Tilery, although Robert junior later became a miner, working at the Old Coppice Colliery. Robert was a well known local sportsman, playing football for Bridgtown Amateurs and later, for Cannock Town. On the 27th September, 1903, he married Daisy Young at St. Luke's Church. Between 1904 and 1913, the couple had five children. Despite being in a reserved occupation, Robert volunteered in February 1915, electing to join the South Staffordshire Regiment, although later in the war, he transferred to the Royal Engineers, serving in the 253rd Tunnelling Company. In 1917, Robert came home on leave with the news that he had just been promoted to Lance Corporal. This cheerful soldier was killed in action on the 27th September 1917 when he was hit by a shell. Significantly, he died with his habitual smile on his face, perhaps thinking about his wife on what was their fourteenth wedding anniversary. Robert Winfer was buried at Mendinghem Military Cemetery in Belgium; he was aged 33 at the time of his death.

Private Samuel Alfred Smith
15514

Samuel Smith was born in Cannock in 1896. His parents, Richard and Harriet had been married at Stafford in 1888, and the family had settled in Bridgtown, living on Walsall Road. Richard earned his living as a coal miner. By 1911, Samuel was working as a mine engine driver, whilst his older brother, Frederick was employed as a grinder. Samuel volunteered for service in 1915, firstly with the Cheshire Regiment and then transferring to the 8th Battalion, Prince of Wales'

Volunteers, South Lancashire Regiment. In 1916, Samuel was very badly wounded in action, and was returned home to be with his parents at 5, Church Street, Bridgtown. It was here that he died from his wounds on the 11th September, 1916, aged just 20. Samuel was buried at Cannock Cemetery with full military honours. His brother Frederick was badly wounded in the foot during the war.

Private Charles Thomas Onions
M2/193380

The fortunes of the Onions family were somewhat varied. Charles married Emily Jane Smith at Cannock in 1895. By 1901, they were living at Saredon, where Charles was employed as a colliery carter. They had a daughter, Frances Mary who was born at Hatherton. However, ten years later, Charles was now a boarder with the Bedward family at 33, Longford Lane, Bridgtown. His wife was a housekeeper to Thomas Reeves, an edge tool grinder from Cannock, living at Elmore Green Road in Bloxwich, with her son Thomas Charles Onions. Their daughter, Frances Mary was a general domestic servant working for Ellen Harvey, a shopkeeper from Churchbridge. For whatever reason, Charles decided to join up, enlisting with the Army Service Corps, despite being over the age for service. He was taken ill and died on the 29th March, 1917, aged 47. His body was buried at Lijssenthoek Military Cemetery in Belgium.

Chapter Two

CANNOCK

Private Albert Henry Ansell
19090

The Ansells were a local family, with the father, James, heralding from Bridgtown, whilst his wife, Phoebe, came from Wednesbury. The seven children were all born in Huntington, and James earned his living as a coal miner. The couple were married at Cannock in 1895, but in 1901, Phoebe and the children were living in Cannock, whereas James was working in Gedling, Nottinghamshire as a pit sinker. By 1911, he had returned to Cannock and was a coal miner. The family lived at Gladstone Place, on Stafford Road. Albert was the eldest of the children and in 1911 was employed as a fifteen year old nipper in Littleton Colliery. In the Great War, Albert volunteered and joined the 8th Battalion, Northumberland Fusiliers, where after initial training, he was attached to the Machine Gun section of the battalion, being sent to France on the 25th November,1915. Albert was killed in action on the 26th September, 1916, aged 20. His body was buried in Regina Trench Cemetery, Grandcourt on the Somme in France, in the village of Courcelette.

Acting Bombadier Albert Addison
48857

Albert Addison was born in 1889 at Bradley, Staffordshire. His mother, Emma Jane Addison remarried, marrying Enoch Stonehouse at Walsall in 1897 following the death of her first husband, Richard, four years earlier. In 1901, the Stonehouse family were living at Stubbers Green, Aldridge, with Albert aged 12 and presumably at school. Albert joined the Army at Lichfield on the 25th August, 1909 electing to join the South Staffordshire Regiment, and after some minor misdemeanors, was promoted to Lance Corporal. He bought himself out of the Regiment on the 9th July, 1914. On the 16th October, 1910, Albert married Lizzie Morris at St. Luke's, the groom giving his address as Longford Lane. A son Albert R. Addison was born in 1912 but this was followed by tragedy in 1913 when a second son, Richard was born but died shortly afterwards. After leaving the Army, Albert was employed at Littleton Colliery, but was one of the first to volunteer for the Army on 28th September, 1914, joining the Royal Garrison Artillery, 15th Siege Battery. He was sent to France in June 1915, and served without incident or injury for over two years, despite not enjoying any leave since November 1916. On the 20th September, 1917, the left section of the Battery was being heavily shelled. Addison and Sergeant Pollard refused to leave their gun. The gun was hit by a shell, which killed Addison and also wounded Pollard. This information was passed onto his widow by Lieutenant Dell. At the time of his death, Albert Addison was 28 years of age. He was buried at Heudicourt Communal Cemetery Extension, Somme, France.

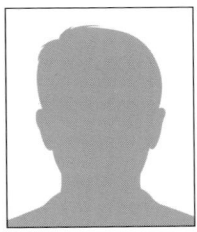

Private William Edwin Benton
783

Edwin Benton, William's father was a boot maker from Cannock with the business being located on the Walsall Road. The parents had married at Cannock in 1886 and had initially set up their business in Mill Street. Edwin was assisted in his shop by his wife Emily. In 1911, William was employed as a clerk in a factory, but went on to find employment as a clerk in the offices of the National Insurance Company in Birmingham, and was well respected. William decided to enlist at the outbreak of the Great War, joining the 16th Battalion of the Royal Warwickshire Regiment, being sent to France on the 21st November, 1915. William was killed in action on the 2nd September, 1916 at the age of 27. This information was passed on to his father by his cousin Lance Corporal Christopher Wootton of Bloxwich. William's body was buried in Guillemont Road Cemetery, Guillemont, on the Somme in France.

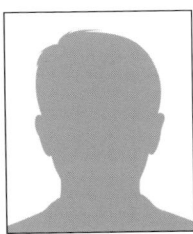

Private Ernest William Benton
11999

In 1901 the Bentons were a settled family living at the Malt Houses, Shareshill. Ernest's father, Arthur was a coal miner and his eldest brother, John Henry a tool grinder. Arthur had married Mary Ann Worsey at Cannock in 1892. By 1905, however, the family was turned upon its head with the sudden and unexpected death of Arthur. This meant the disintegration of the family unit, as by 1911, the children were living apart from each other, with Ernest working as a tub loader underground at the Littleton Colliery, and boarding at 13 Company Buildings, Walsall Road, Cannock, with the Yapp family. Two weeks before the outbreak of war, in July 1914, Ernest decided to join the Army, enlisting with the 2nd Battalion, King's Own Scottish Borderers. He had already served for two years with the Hednesford Territorials, and so was reasonably used to Army life, and hence was sent to France on the 19th September, 1914. This young man (he was only 22 at the time of his death) was killed in action on the 29th October, 1914, one of the first to die from the Cannock Chase area. His body was never recovered and Ernest is remembered on the Le Touret Memorial to the Missing in France. The news was conveyed to his widowed mother in Cannock.

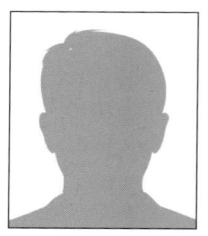

Lance Corporal Alfred Ernest Benton
7827

It will remain a mystery how a colliery labourer from Prince's End, Staffordshire and a young woman from Sleebourne, Northumberland, met and married. These were Arthur and Elizabeth Benton, the parents of Alfred, who were married at Gateshead in late 1893. The children were all born in Cannock and the family lived at Old Fallow Road before moving to 6, Summer Terrace on the Hednesford Road, Cannock. Alfred earned his living in 1911, as a horse driver below ground and later as a coal miner at the East Cannock Colliery. Alfred was also a member of the Hednesford Territorials, serving for four years, which probably explains his promotion to Lance Corporal at the age of 20. On the commencement of the war, Albert joined the 1/5th Battalion, South Staffordshire Regiment, being sent to France on the 5th March, 1915. He was killed in action on the 13th October, 1915, when part of a bombing party, at the Battle of Loos. His body was not identified after the war and he is remembered on the Loos Memorial to the Missing, France.

Private Richard Beedles
20120

The Beedles family were used to travelling around the country. Natives of Shropshire, where Richard's parents were married in 1896, by 1901 the family were living in Wigan, Lancashire, where the father, Richard senior was a labourer in a coal mine.

2. Cannock

By 1911, they had moved to Walsall Road, Cannock with Beedles senior, a coal miner and his namesake son a 14 year old door minder at Littleton Colliery. Richard junior then found employment in a munitions factory in Birmingham. Richard enlisted on the 13th September, 1915, joining the 1st Battalion, South Staffordshire Regiment. He served in Jersey for six months before being sent to France. He was at the Front for only two months before he was killed in action, being badly wounded in the leg by a rifle grenade, and dying just a few hours later. This former Sunday school teacher at the Weslyan Chapel at Bridgtown was only 19 when he died. His parents, now living at Nantghwilt House, Beech Tree Lane, in Cannock were told of their son's death in a letter from Corporal A. Needham. Richard's body was buried at the Citadel New Military Cemetery, Fricourt on the Somme in France.

Private Albert Edward Barnes
35777

Albert Barnes was the son of a grocer's porter, one George Barnes who hailed from Pensnett in the Black Country. His mother, Elizabeth came from Holly Hall in Worcestershire, and the couple had married at Stourbridge in late 1895. Albert was born in 1898, also in Pensnett, as were his sister Hilda and his brother John. The family had moved to Hednesford by 1911 and Albert had managed to find a job as a 13 year old errand boy. He later worked for the Cannock and District Co-operative Society. Albert was called up on the 3rd January, 1917 and joined the Training Reserve Battalion, before being transferred to the 6th Battalion, King's Own Yorkshire Light Infantry, arriving in France on the 29th March, 1917. He was killed in action on the 16th December, 1917 at the age of 19. His body was not recovered at the end of the war and he is one of some 34,000 soldiers whose names appear on the Tyne Cot Memorial to the Missing, just outside Ieper in Belgium. His parents were informed of his death by telegram just before Christmas, having moved to Victoria Street, Cannock.

Private Alfred Baker
39510

Alfred Baker was born in Wem, Shropshire in 1883, the eldest son of Joseph and Elizabeth Baker. His father was a stone mason, the family living at Shrewsbury and at Hoole in Cheshire. In 1911, he was lodging with the Bradbury family at

8, New Street, Bridgtown and was employed as a tile setter, by Lewis Tileries. He must then have moved to Birmingham according to his Army records, as he gave this city as his residence and joined up at Great Barr. Yet he was the nephew of Alfred and Emma Sellman of 46, Newhall Street, Cannock, who had married at Cannock in 1883. Alfred was killed in action on the 6th March, 1918, aged 34. His body was buried at Mory Abbey Military Cemetery, Mory, France.

Private Herbert Baker
GS/84063

Herbert Baker was somewhat intriguing. He married Mary Gallear on the 10th April, 1898 at St. Luke's, Cannock, both giving their age as 19. The couple were living in Mill Street, Cannock in 1901, with Herbert earning his living as an edge tool forger. Yet in 1911, Herbert, now 32, was employed as a roadman at Leacroft Colliery and was living at 33, Stafford Road with his father and mother, George and Ann Elizabeth Baker. Herbert gives his status as married, yet his wife is not living with him. The family had a boarder staying with them, who was a clerk at the Post Office; her name was Gertrude Baker, 33 and single, born in Stoke-on-Trent. Herbert joined up on the 27th May, 1915, enlisting in the 8th Battalion, King's Royal Rifle Corps, army number R/13795. He was sent to France on the 12th September 1915 and was wounded after only a month. On recovering, he was transferred to the Royal Fusiliers, serving with the 2/4th Battalion, London Regiment. Herbert was killed in action by a shell on the 1st September, 1918, aged 39. His body was not identified after the war and he is remembered on the Vis-en-Artois Memorial to the Missing in France. His address was given as 63, Newhall Street, Cannock.

Private Joseph Henry Bird
1182

Joseph's parents, Arthur and Mary Bird had lived in the Cannock area for over 30 years when their son was killed in 1916. They had married at Cannock in the spring of 1887, living at Stafford Street, Heath Hayes and on the Cannock Road, Heath Hayes before moving to Cannock. Here they lived at Sunnyside, Paddy's Lane, Cannock and all of their children were born and raised locally. Arthur was a coal miner, and in 1911, his second son Joseph was employed as a 14 year old horse driver underground at Cannock and Leacroft Colliery. Joseph enlisted in the 1/5th Battalion, South Staffordshire Regiment on the 17th September, 1915, being sent to France in January 1916. At the age of 19, Joseph was blown up by a German mine explosion on the 2nd April, 1916. This information was passed on to his grieving family by Lieutenant Frank Rowe, who informed them that his body had not yet been recovered. Indeed, Joseph's body was never found and he was remembered after the war on the Arras Memorial to the Missing in France.

Private Edward Bickley
17783

Edward Bickley in some ways proves to be something of a mystery. He was born in Hatherton in 1891 and according to the 1901 census, was living at 2, Railway Street, Cannock, with his widowed mother Ann, four other siblings, a nephew and a niece. Yet, the family seem to have disappeared ten years later. However, it is definite that Edward was a miner working at Littleton Colliery and that he volunteered for service in the Army in 1914. Edward joined the 2nd Battalion, South Staffordshire Regiment, seeing service in the ill fated Dardanelles campaign. Edward was then sent to France, where he was killed on the 30th June, 1916 when he was shot by a sniper. Edward was aged 26 and was buried in Cabaret-Rouge British Cemetery at Souchez in France. The news of his death was passed on to his mother at 125, Hednesford Road, Cannock.

Private William Bickley
17214

One thing that is known is that William was Edward's older brother. He was born in 1878 at Bushbury and married Agnes Thornley at Cannock in late 1898. The couple had seven children and lived at 15, Railway Street, Cannock. Like many men at the time in the area, William was a coal miner working at Leacroft Colliery, but decided to answer his country's call on the 27th January, 1915, enlisting with the 7th Battalion, South Staffordshire Regiment. William also saw service in the Dardanelles campaign, as did his brother, but William was also posted to Egypt before being sent to France in 1916. William was badly wounded in the back and brain by shrapnel on the 29th September, 1916. After initial treatment at a Casualty Clearing Station, William was transferred to No.1 General Hospital, Etretat, France where he died from his wounds on the 7th

October, aged 39. The Matron Miss A.P. Wilson wrote to his widow, with the comforting news that her husband had "died the death of a brave man". His body was buried in Etretat Churchyard, near Le Havre, France, a cemetery used by the hospital.

Able Seaman Harry Bland
176208

According to his Navy records, Harry was born on the 22nd October, 1877 in Burton-on-Trent. However, census evidence would indicate that he was born some two years later in 1879. This would suggest that when he joined the Navy in October 1893, he was only 14 years of age. His father and mother both came from Northamptonshire, with the family moving to Oundle, Burton-on-Trent and later to Cannock because of John's trade as a cooper. Tragically, John Bland died in 1892, perhaps hastening his son's decision to run away to sea. Harry enjoyed his new life, staying in the Navy for 14 years of exemplary service. He travelled the world and saw service during the Boxer rebellion in China, being awarded the China Medal. Harry came out of the Navy in 1907, returning to Cannock and working at the East Cannock Colliery. In 1912, however, he re-enrolled for service in the Navy, joining HMS Ocean on the 18th March, 1912. In 1915, Harry's ship was part of the fleet in the Dardanelles and the ship was sunk by torpedo on the 18th March. Harry was transferred to HMS Albion and it was while serving on this vessel that he was killed in action by a shell on the 19th June, 1915, aged 37. His body was buried at Lancashire Landing Cemetery, Gallipoli, Turkey. News of his death was received by his sister, Mrs. Mary Ann Kent who lived at 8a Wolverhampton Road, Cannock.

Sergeant Frank Boult
1418558

Frank Boult was born in Cannock on the 8th February, 1884, the second son of John and Amelia Boult, of Church Street. His father was a Colliery Secretary and in 1901 the family was living at Great Wyrley Hall, whilst Frank was now articled as a surveyor to W.E. Rogers of Rugeley. Sadly his mother died, aged 60, in 1910 and his father remarried in 1911, with Sara Anderson becoming his second bride. In 1914, Frank decided to migrate to Canada, where he settled and married in Winnipeg, Manitoba. His wife was named Mary Violet and the couple had one child. Frank continued as an architect and had managed to secure a position in the offices of the Grand Trunk Railway. On the 13th September, 1915, Frank volunteered for service with the Canadian Expeditionary Force, joining the 90th Battalion, Winnipeg Rifles but then transferring to the 78th Battalion. Frank was 5 feet 10 inches in height, with brown eyes and brown hair, and a fine physique. He also had a tattoo of a twig with leaves and flowers on his right arm. Frank sailed on the Empress of Britain and disembarked at Liverpool on the 30th May, 1916, being appointed as acting corporal the very next day. He arrived in France on the 13th August, 1916, being confirmed as a corporal on the 24th of that month. Just before Christmas 1916 Frank was admitted to hospital for one day suffering from laryngitis. Frank became a sergeant on the 1st March, 1917 but was killed in action on the 9th April, 1917, aged 33. His body was not recovered after the war and he is remembered on the Vimy National Memorial in France. His widow in Canada and his father in Cannock were both told the sad news.

Rifleman Walter Henry Buck
42030

Walter Buck was born at Cannock in 1884, and was the second son of William Buck, a coal miner born at Hednesford and his wife Mary Ann who hailed from Darlington, County Durham. In 1891, the family were living in Caxton Buildings, Cannock, where his mother helped the family finances by dressmaking. He left England after 1901 and settled in New Zealand. Perhaps he felt that he might better his prospects, which as a coal pit labourer at Littleton Colliery were not that great. If so he may have been disappointed for when he enlisted in the 3rd New Zealand Rifle Brigade, he was still a labourer. His next of kin was his mother, who was living at 10, Paddy's Lane, Cannock, but he also included Mrs. Huxtable of George Street, Te Kuiti as a friend. Walter was 5 feet 4 inches, with grey eyes and fair hair and was classed as perfectly fit for service, despite wearing upper and lower dentures. He joined the Army in Hamilton on the 4th December, 1916. Walter sailed from Wellington on the 14th March, 1917, arriving at Devonport on the 21st May. He was sent to France on the 1st June, 1917 and served with his unit, being admitted to hospital for the treatment of boils in March, 1918. Walter was wounded with a gunshot wound to his left leg in May 1918 and from there was transferred to the 1st Battalion. Walter was sent on leave for two weeks on the 14th August 1918, and presumably went to see his mother and family in Cannock. He was wounded in the right hand in September 1918, a slight wound as he was back with his unit after one day. Walter was killed in action on the 4th November, 1918, aged 34, just one week before the Armistice was signed. His body was buried at Romeries Communal Cemetery Extension near Valenciennes, France.

Private Lewis Bird
95079

Lewis Bird was Cannock born and bred. His father, also named Lewis was also born in the town and worked as a labourer in an iron works for all of his life. In 1862 he married Elizabeth Talbot at Penkridge, with the couple having three daughters, Sarah, Lucy and Elizabeth and Lewis. It appears that they lived at the same address, Stoneyfields, Cannock for over 30 years. Lewis became an axle turner for carts and coaches, and continued to work in this field until 1915. He married Elizabeth Violet Thomas at the Congregational Church, Cannock on the 18th June, 1910, with a daughter Marjorie being born on the 1st September, 1911. On the 9th December, 1915 at the age of 37, Lewis joined up. He was 5 feet 9 in height although fairly slightly built and opted to serve in the Royal Army Medical Corps Number 5 Convalescent depot, attesting at Bridgtown. Interestingly, he was then held in reserve until the 16th October, 1916 when he was posted to 8 Company RAMC at York and then to the 69th General Hospital at Blackpool. On the 29th June, 1917 Lewis embarked for Salonika from Southampton, arriving on the 15th July. Within three weeks the poor man was admitted to hospital with malaria. Lewis was then in and out of various hospitals with recurring bouts of malaria, bronchitis and neurasthenia all through the rest of 1917 and well into 1918. With the end of the war almost in sight, this unfortunate soldier died from pneumonia, aged 40. His body was buried at Kirechkoi Hortakoi Military Cemetery, Greece. His widow remarried and migrated to Canada.

Lance Sergeant Charles Beech
S/12791

Although a native of Tong in Shropshire, Charles Beech spent most of his life in Cannock, being brought up by his widowed aunt, Sarah Fletcher and her family at Stoneyfields. In 1911 he was still at school, but it would appear that he later found employment as a shop assistant. On the 7th June, 1915 Charles joined up at Stafford, making it very clear that he wished to join the Rifle Brigade, being posted to the 6th Battalion of that Regiment on the 12th June, 1915. He also declared that he was 19, when in fact he was only 17 at the time of enlisting. Charles was sent to

France on the 24th November, 1915, joining the 8th Battalion of his Regiment. Nevertheless, his rapid promotion would suggest that he was responsible and efficient, being made corporal and then sergeant in less than two years. He was wounded in August, 1916, being returned to his unit within one month. On the 4th April, 1918 Charles was listed as wounded and then missing in action, before finally the Army posted him as being killed in action, at the age of 19. His medals were sent to his father in Tong, yet the scroll was delivered to his sister, Elizabeth Sambrook, at Beech Tree Lane, Cannock. Sadly her request for her brother's personal effects was met with the official claim that there were none. This brave young man's body was never identified and he was remembered on the Pozieres Memorial to the Missing on the Somme in France.

Private Joseph Brown
19747

Joseph Brown came from a Midlands family and was born at Cannock, Staffordshire in 1895. He was the second son of Thomas and Emma Brown, a couple who had married at Wolverhampton in 1873. Thomas was born in Darlaston and worked as a coal miner, whilst his wife came from West Bromwich. In 1881, the family were living at Brewer's Cottages in Wednesfield, but by 1891, they had moved to the Five Ways Road at Wimblebury. Tragedy struck the family in 1904 when Thomas died at the age of 55. His widow moved to Bridge Street, Smethwick. In January, 1915, Joseph joined the Army, enlisting with the Royal Welsh Fusiliers and being sent to France on the 29th June, 1915. Joseph served until the 27th August, 1916 when he was killed in action on the Somme at the age of 21. His body was not identified after the war, and Joseph is remembered on the Thiepval Memorial to the Missing on the Somme in France.

Gunner William James Brindley
204901

William James Brindley was another local man who joined the Army in January 1917. He was born at Cannock in 1898, the eldest son of William Thomas Brindley and his wife Elizabeth, the couple having married at Cannock in 1897. By 1911, the family of five were living in Longford Lane, Hatherton, having moved there from Shareshill, where William Thomas was a coal miner, whereas his son was an errand boy for a local grocer. William James decided to join the Royal Field Artillery, serving in "D" Battery, 113th Brigade. He had married Alice Fellows at Walsall in 1916, and the couple lived at "Leamore" 57, Cope Street, in Bloxwich. William was sent to France in June 1917 and was killed in action on the 31st July, 1917 when a piece of shrapnel hit him under the left armpit, whilst he was working in his gun detachment. This was the first day of the Battle of Passchendaele, and this 19 year old Roman Catholic was buried at Dikkebusch New Military Cemetery, Belgium. Before enlisting William James had worked at the Littleton Colliery. His mother and father resided at 30, Mill Street, Cannock and his father William Thomas also served during the Great War in a Tunnelling Company in the Royal Engineers.

Gunner Francis Richard Bailey
28307

Frank Bailey came from a Cannock family, with his father, Thomas Bailey hailing from the town and all of the children also born there. Frank was born in 1888, with the family living at Stoneyfields. In 1901, Frank was working at one of the local edge tool factories, having decided not to follow in his father's footsteps as a railway clerk. However, by 1911, Frank had joined the Army, and was serving with 88 Company Royal Garrison Artillery, at Victoria Barracks, Hong Kong, where he had risen to the rank of Corporal and was an instructor. When he came out of the Army he stayed on the Reserve list and volunteered for duty in the Great War, rejoining the Royal Garrison Artillery, but with the 114th Trench Mortar Battery. He was badly wounded on the 24th July, 1917 when his gun received a direct hit, killing the rest of the gun team outright. Frank was taken to the Dressing Station but died shortly afterwards from his wounds. This information was conveyed to Frank's brother William Horton Bailey who lived with his wife and child at 167, Wolverhampton Road, Cannock and who was also employed as a railway clerk. Frank was 30 years of age at his death and his body was buried at Lijssenthoek Military Cemetery, near Poperinghe, Belgium.

Sapper Thomas Brough
112557

Thomas Brough was born at Calf Heath in 1868. He was the second son of William and Sarah Brough, with the family residing in Cheslyn Hay. Thomas married Amanda Groves at St. Luke's Parish Church on the 28th October 1889, with the couple setting up home at John Street, Chadsmoor. By 1901, the growing family, Thomas and Amanda having had seven children, had moved to Church Street, Chadsmoor. By 1911, the family had moved yet again, this time to reside at Huntington Terrace in Chadsmoor. Thomas had been employed as a coal miner and a colliery fireman all of his working life, spending 25 years at the East Cannock Colliery. In the Great War, the Government asked for miners to volunteer in a Headers and Tunnellers Battalion. Despite being over the maximum age and the father of seven, Thomas stepped forward, joining the 175th Tunnelling Company, Royal Engineers on the 13th August, 1915 and being sent straight to France. His eldest son George was also serving with the Northumberland Fusiliers and Thomas had three brothers in the armed services. On Christmas Day 1915, Thomas was shot by a sniper, being killed instantly. He was 47 years of age and his body was buried at Railway Dugouts Burial Ground, just outside Zillebeke in Belgium.

Private Walter Bayley
13712

The war memorial in Cannock lists a William Bailey, but it is my belief that this is an error and that the soldier referred to was Walter Bayley. His father Samuel was born in Cannock before marrying and moving to Burton-on-Trent where Walter was born in 1896, along with his sister Eva in 1898. In 1901 the family were living at 25 Brizlincote Street, Stapenhill, where Samuel earned his living as a brewery labourer. By 1911, the Bayleys had moved back to Staffordshire where Samuel was employed as a wood sawyer at Cannock Wood, whilst his eldest son was 15 and unemployed. However, before the outbreak of war, Walter had managed to find a job at the Cannock and Rugeley Colliery. Walter enlisted on the 4th September, 1914, answering the call of Lord Kitchener, and joined the 9th Battalion, Royal Welsh Fusiliers, being sent to France on the 15th June, 1915. It was with this Battalion that the 22 year old was killed on the 22nd March, 1918. His body was never recovered and he is remembered on the Arras Memorial to the Missing in France.

Private Frederick Cooper
24195

Frederick Cooper was born in Walsall in 1875 and came from a large family, having four sisters and four brothers. The family earned its living in the iron industry with his father John being an iron caster, a trade followed by all of his sons by 1891.

Frederick married Lily Adeline Sargeant at St. George's Church, Walsall on the 26th April, 1896 and on the 31st October, 1897 a son Frederick was born, followed by a daughter Eliza on the 24th September, 1902. Frederick was now employed as a stone quarryman and the couple were lodging with his wife's relations at Stafford Road, Cannock. By 1911, they were now living by themselves on the Stafford Road and Frederick was now working as a colliery cleaner at Littleton Colliery. Frederick volunteered for the Army at Whitsun 1915, joining the 3rd Battalion, Royal Welsh Fusiliers before being posted to the 9th Battalion on the 16th October, 1915. Frederick was killed in action on the 3rd February, 1916 at the age of 42. A letter from the Chaplain attached to the Regiment was read out at the Chapel, including this poignant line "…something comforting about the death of a gallant soldier on the field of battle". His body was buried in Ovillers Military Cemetery in France.

Private Charles Carter
17796

Charles Carter was born at Hednesford of mining stock in 1889. Charles was the second son of William Carter and Selina Bradford, who had married at Cannock in 1881. He had six siblings and they lived at John Street, Chadsmoor, before moving to 35, Old Fallow Road. By 1914, Charles had moved to Mansfield in Nottinghamshire where he worked as a miner at Shirebrook Colliery. He joined the Army in 1915, joining the 9th Battalion, Sherwood Foresters, being sent to the Balkans on the 31st December, 1915 before returning to the Western Front in time for the Big Push on the Somme in 1916. The 27 year old Charles was killed in action on the 26th September, 1916, at the same time as his brother William was recovering from serious wounds in a Base Hospital at Boulogne. Charles' body was never recovered after the war and he is remembered on the Thiepval Memorial to the Missing on the Somme.

2nd Lieutenant Bernard Melville Carpenter

The story of the Carpenter family is quite fascinating. George Carpenter, the father of Bernard was an industrious man, working as an engine driver at a local brick and tile works, and also as a shop keeper, selling provisions at Watling Street, Cannock. By 1891, the shop had been moved to the Walsall Road in Cannock, but by 1901, George was employed solely as an engine driver.

Indeed, by 1911 he was unemployed. Both he and his wife Harriett saw the value of education, resulting in the eldest son Frederick working as a warehouseman, William as a commercial clerk and Alec as an invoice clerk. Bernard attended Queen Mary's Grammar School at Walsall, where he had become a student teacher before gaining a degree at Oxford University in June 1914. He then returned to Queen Mary's where he became a History Master. Bernard joined the Army in April 1916, being offered a commission in the 6th Battalion, Middlesex Regiment, on the 21st November, and was gazetted on the 1st December, before being attached to the 19th Battalion. He was severely wounded in the left thigh in March 1918, and was transferred to the Base Hospital at Etaples where he died from his wounds on the 3rd April, at the age of 25. His body was buried in Etaples Military Cemetery in France.

Private David Chandler
5/9604

David Chandler was born in 1882 at Broadway in Worcestershire. His father, William, an agricultural labourer, was some twenty years older than his mother, Sarah Ann and died in 1893 at the age of 65. David was the only son of a marriage which produced six children and a step-daughter from Sarah Ann's previous marriage. By 1901, David had moved to London where he was working as a railway porter and was living at 22, Crowndale Road, St. Pancras, whilst his widowed mother was working as a charwoman in Evesham. In 1911, David was living in Mill Street, Cannock with his widowed mother, and earning his living as a bill poster. On the 19th March, 1912, David married Margaret Ann Cross, a divorced woman with two children from her failed marriage, in Prestwich Register Office. The family moved back to Cannock and a third child, Catherine Alice, was born on the 9th December, 1915. In the meantime, David's mother had moved back to Evesham to live with her married daughter Emily Goodall. David was called up to serve in the 5th Battalion, (Training Reserve) Yorkshire Regiment on the 1st February, 1917, reporting for duty at Rugeley Camp on Cannock Chase. On the same day he contracted a cerebral-spinal fever which saw him admitted to the Military Hospital, where after three weeks he died on the 25th February, 1917, aged 35. His body was taken to Evesham where he was buried with full military honours.

Private Francis James Chilton
300359

The Chiltons were a mining family from Cannock. Elijah, Francis' father was born in the town whereas his wife Alice came from Tipton in the Black Country. The couple were married at Cannock in 1882 and had six children, with Francis being the eldest of four boys. They had settled in Walsall Road and by 1911, Francis was a tub loader and his brother Arthur a horse driver. Very little is known about Francis' Army service, other than he joined the 1st battalion of the Staffordshire Yeomanry and then the Corps of Hussars, being sent to Egypt on the 21st November, 1915. Francis was killed in action on the 17th April, 1917, aged 26, and his body was buried at Gaza War Cemetery. His brother Arthur served in the Royal Army Medical Corps as a cook and survived the war.

Private William Thomas Craddock
201690

In 1891, Alfred Craddock, a miner from Cannock, married Agnes Smith, two years his senior and born at Measham in Leicestershire. They had two children, Harold the eldest and William Thomas. The family settled down to life in Cemetery Road and by 1911, Harold had become a bricklayer and his brother an augur maker at Churchbridge. William was also a well known local preacher at Cannock Congregational Church. In 1915, William volunteered for service, joining the 2/5th Battalion, South Staffordshire Regiment and seeing service in France. William was killed in action during the Battle of Passchendaele on the 23rd September, 1917 aged 23. Like many of the young men killed in this battle, his body was never found and he is remembered on the Tyne Cot Memorial to the Missing. A memorial service was held for William at the Congregational Church.

2nd Lieutenant Barnabas Tom Wilcox Davenport

The Davenports had become a relatively prosperous family with John Davenport and his son Hezekiah working as Colliery Agents. Hezekiah had married Catherine Wilcox at Madeley, Shropshire in 1887 and the couple had had three children, Catherine Grace, Archibald and Barnabas. The family lived at "Fairmount" on the Walsall Road in Cannock, and in 1911 Archibald was a Builder and Contractor whilst Barnabas was still at school. Barnabas was on the staff of the Cannock Urban District Council Surveyor's Department until he joined the Royal Warwickshire Regiment in October 1914 at the age of 17 and was wounded on the 27th August, 1916. On the 27th March, 1917 the 19 year old Barnabas was commissioned as a temporary 2nd Lieutenant in the Royal Warwickshire Regiment, before being attached to the 1/4th Battalion, Norfolk Regiment, being posted to Egypt. The 20 year old was killed in action near Jerusalem on the 15th December, 1917 and his body was buried in Ramleh War Cemetery.

Corporal Edward Ernest Devall
28202

Edward Devall came from a large family, having seven brothers and sisters. He was the third son and was born in 1892 at Bridgtown, although both of his parents, James and Bertha came from Colton. The family moved from Bridgtown to live on the Hednesford Road at Cannock and then to the Walsall Road. His father was a drayman and Thomas, the eldest son, followed his father into this trade. Edward became a miner, working at the Old Coppice Colliery at Cheslyn Hay, which probably prompted the change of address. On the 4th May, 1913 Edward married Minnie Parsons at St. Luke's Church, with a son named Ernest being born on the 27th September. With the onset of war, Edward, who had served for four years in the Hednesford Territorials, volunteered for service in January 1915, firstly with the Royal Army Medical Corps and then transferring to the 10th Battalion, Cheshire Regiment after just five months with the RAMC. He had risen to the rank of corporal by the 6th December, 1915, seeing service in Egypt and France. His wife and son meanwhile had moved from Cannock and were living at 229 Antrobus Road, Handsworth in Birmingham. On the 28th July, 1916, only one week after arriving in France, Edward was killed in action on the Somme, aged 24. His body was buried at Knightsbridge Cemetery at Mesnil-Martinsart in France. His widow, Minnie received 15 shillings and sixpence per week as a pension from the Government. An intriguing post-script ends this story. On the 4th July, 1921 Minnie and her seven year old son left the port of Liverpool on the Dorset, bound for Auckland, New Zealand. She wrote to the War Ministry to register her change of address and to ask for her husband's war medals and memorial plaque. She was informed that these had been sent to her previous address in Birmingham on the 30th March, 1922 and that they had a receipted card signed Mrs. M. Devall. After initially disclaiming any responsibility, the War Office instructed the factory to issue a new plaque. The medals were not included in this agreement.

Corporal Edward Richard Doughty
802019

It would appear that the Doughty family had a somewhat colourful history. Edward's father, Thomas Richard Doughty was born in Penkridge in 1858. He married Sarah Keeling at Wolverhampton in 1879, with their first child, Alice being born a few months later. Thomas was at the time a Police Constable, and the couple were living at Ford Street, Wolverhampton. Indeed it was at Wolverhampton that Edward was born in 1880. By 1891, the family had moved to Lower Rushall Street, Walsall where Thomas had changed career, having become a confectioner. His wife died in 1894, but Thomas soon remarried, tying the knot with Amy Williams at Birmingham later in the same year. The family then moved to Cheslyn Hay, where Thomas now earned his living as a carpenter. Meanwhile, Edward had moved in with his uncle James Doughty in Cannock and was employed as a wood loader. His father died in 1909 and on the 14th September, 1910, Edward and his wife Annie embarked on the SS Virginia at Liverpool bound for a new life in Canada. They lived in London, Ontario where Edward was employed as a carpenter. On the 18th November, 1915 Edward volunteered for service in the 135th Battalion, Canadian Infantry. He arrived at Liverpool on the 30th August, 1916 before being sent to France on the 11th February, 1917 having been transferred to the 116th Battalion. On the 31st March, 1917, Edward was stopped £1 12 shillings for cutting his great coat, yet on the following day he was promoted to the rank of corporal. Edward was reported as missing in action on the 23rd July, 1917 with his death on this date being confirmed some four months later. His wife returned to Cannock after his death and his pension and bonus payments, together with his medals were sent to her at 9, Victoria Street in the town. Edward was 37 at the time of his death and his body was never found after the war. He is remembered on the Canadian National Memorial at Vimy Ridge in France.

Sergeant David Thomas Duckhouse
15512

David Duckhouse came from Aldridge, where he was born in 1893, the eldest son of Samuel and Eliza Duckhouse. His father also hailed from Aldridge, although his mother came from Darlaston. David had five sisters and two brothers, all of whom, with the exception of the youngest, Winifred were born in Aldridge. Winifred was born in Shelfield. The family had moved to Cannock by 1911 and found a house in Cemetery Road, where Samuel was employed as a coal miner and his son as a labourer at Littleton Colliery. David enlisted in the Army on the 3rd September, 1914, with Fred Lockley. Both men chose to join the Cheshire Regiment, before transferring to the South Lancashire Regiment, David to the 2nd Battalion and Fred to the 8th Battalion. David was married in 1915 to Florence Emma Lockley, the sister of Fred, at Hartley Wintney in Hampshire, shortly before David was posted to France, although he did come home on leave for one week from the 30th December, 1915 to the 6th January, 1916. On the 29th April, 1916, David was wounded in the left cheek and left eye by shrapnel. He was taken to a Casualty Clearing Station, then to a General Hospital and from there to a Base Hospital, before being transferred to England on the Hospital Ship, Brighton. In 1917, the couple had their one child, a girl named Winifred after David's sister. After recovering from his wounds David spent some time as an Instructor before being sent back to France on the 1st April, 1918, rejoining his unit on the 10th April. Sadly this brave soldier was killed in action just two days later on the 12th April, 1918. His body was not recovered after the war and he is remembered on the Ploegsteert Memorial in Belgium. David was aged 25 at the time of his death. One intriguing mystery about David Duckhouse is that on his Army record his height is given as 5 feet 4 inches whereas in the report of his death in the Cannock Advertiser, his height is given as 6 feet 1 inches.

Private Harold Dyke
10327

In 1885, at Cannock, John Dyke married Clara Lucy Brookes. They set up a home at Blackfords in the town where John earned his living as a coal miner. By 1901, John and Lucy had six children and had moved to Stoneyfields, where John was now a grocer and beer house keeper. By 1911, John had set himself up as a general haulier, in which he was helped by his second son Harold. His eldest daughter, Emmy was a domestic servant, as was Clara his youngest daughter, whilst the eldest son John jnr, was a colliery clerk. Harold volunteered for the Army in 1915, joining the 7th Battalion, South Staffordshire Regiment. Harold was sent to the Dardanelles, where on the 22nd August, 1915 he died from his wounds aged 23. His body was not recovered and he is remembered on the Helles Memorial at Gallipoli.

Private Sidney Emberton
57872

Tracing the ancestry of the Embertons is a complex task. William Emberton was an 18 year old soldier in the 38th Regiment at Whittington Barracks on the 1881 census. Ten years later, he was married to Lizzie, having four children, and working as a groom, with the family living at Calais Street, Leicester. By 1901, Lizzie was now calling herself Elizabeth Dale and stated that she was a widow, working as a charwoman. There were now six children, including Sidney Emberton, living in Durham Street, Leicester. William Emberton was listed as living at the same address, but as a boarder whose marital status is given as single. In 1911, Sidney Emberton was living in Cannock, working as a horse driver, along with his brother Frank and step brother Charles. His mother was given as the wife of William Henry Hadley, although no record of a marriage can be traced. On the 9th November, 1914, Sidney turned up at the Drill Hall in Hednesford to volunteer for the Army. He joined the Northumberland Fusiliers as Private, number 15284. On the 18th November, Sidney was posted to the 15th Battalion, before being transferred to the 1st Battalion on the 28th July 1915. On this day, Sidney went to report feeling unwell, complaining of dropsy, vomiting and headaches. This was diagnosed as Trench Nephritis. On the 13th September, 1915 he was transferred back to the Depot in England and was discharged as being physically unfit on the 3rd June, 1916. Initially an address of 40, Mill Street, Cannock was given, and a pension of 12 shillings and 6d was awarded, although Sidney's address was now given as c/o Mrs. H. Hope, 113, Ada Road, Cape Hill, in Smethwick. Despite receiving a pension, Sidney must have been recalled for service with the 3rd Battalion, Devonshire Regiment, attached to the 2nd Infantry Labour Company. Whether his nephritis recurred is not clear, but Sidney died on the 3rd April, 1917 at the age of 22. His body was buried at Plymouth (Efford) Cemetery.

Private George Roland Edwards M.M.
19568

The Edwards' were from the Herefordshire/Worcestershire area, with Arthur Edwards earning his living as a farm labourer, and in 1891 living with his wife Jane and their sons, Henry and George at Rockford in Worcestershire. By 1901, the family had grown to six, and they had moved to Broseley in Shropshire. Yet in

1911, Arthur was living in Bridgtown, Cannock, earning a living as a waggoner on a farm, whilst George was a miner at Littleton Colliery. Arthur's wife Jane was a housekeeper in Penkridge with Walter and Archie living with her. Both declared themselves as married, although it is odd that they are living in two locations. In January 1915, George joined the 7th Battalion, South Staffordshire Regiment, seeing service in Gallipoli and in France. He was a brave soldier and was awarded the Military Medal, and was then transferred to the 52nd Infantry Brigade Head Quarters. It was here, working as a linesman that he was killed by a shell on the 19th November, 1917, aged 27. He was described in a letter to his father as "cheerful, bright and always ready to do his duty". George's body was not recovered after the war and he is remembered on the Arras Memorial to the Missing in France.

Private Leonard Charles Evans
G/62984

This is the story of two families, the Evans' and the Harrisons. In 1879 at Cannock, Isaac Evans, a miner from Tipton, married Eliza Wilkinson. They lived at Walsall Road, Bridgtown and began a family which by 1891 numbered five, including Leonard, born in 1890. John Harrison, a licensed victualler manager from Brownhills, married Mary Jane Roberts, at Brownhills in 1884. In 1890, the family moved to Chadsmoor, living on the Cannock Road. They had had three children by 1891 and lived in reasonable comfort with two domestic servants to do the daily chores. However, late in 1897, John Harrison died, and the following year, Eliza Evans also passed away. On the 14th December, 1899 Isaac Evans married Mary Jane Harrison at St. Luke's at Cannock. The suddenly enlarged family moved to Newhall Street in Cannock. However, by 1911 Isaac and Mary had moved to 103, Wolverhampton Road in the town where Ernest Harrison and Esther Harrison, were the only children still living with them. Leonard, now a 21 year old fitter and metal turner in an edge tool works, lived with his married sister Mary Ellen Prime on the Hednesford Road in Cannock. Mary Ellen had married Samuel Prime at Cannock on the 5th December, 1909. Leonard was certainly in no rush to join the Army and he was not called up until the 23rd April, 1918. Initially he was with the North Staffordshire Regiment but was transferred to the Duke of Cambridge's Own Middlesex Regiment, the 7th London Regiment. Leonard embarked for France in August 1918 and was killed in action just a few weeks later on the 23rd August, 1918 at the age of 28. His body was not recovered at the end of the war and he is remembered on the Vis-en-Artois

Memorial to the Missing in France. At the time of his death, Leonard's address was given as 10, New Street, Cannock

Private Ernest William Farmer
24364

Ernest Farmer was born in Small Heath, Birmingham in 1884, the second son of Henry Farmer a brass founder and his wife Mary Farmer. The couple had married at Birmingham in 1880, and in 1891 they were living at 110, Lombard Street, Deritend. In 1901 the family of five lived at 116, Osbourne Road, Yardley, where the 17 year old Ernest was employed as a shop assistant. By 1909, Ernest had moved to Church Street, Cannock and on the 31st October, 1909 at St. Luke's he married Marion Mintern, who came from Bristol but had moved to Birmingham. Ernest was now the manager of Altham's Tea Stores in the town, and the family soon set up a new home at 87, Wolverhampton Road. The couple had three children, William George (b.1910), Albert Henry (b.1912) and Mabel Victoria (b.1913). On the 17th April, 1916, Ernest joined the 1st Battalion, South Staffordshire Regiment, being sent to France in July 1916, as reinforcement for the Big Push on the Somme. Ernest was killed by a shell on the 31st August, 1916, the same shell also killing Private Albert Marston of Hednesford. Ernest was 32 years of age at the time of his death, and like many others who fell on the Somme, his body was not identified after the war. Ernest is remembered on the Thiepval Memorial to the Missing on the Somme in France.

Private Percy Fellows
57265

Joseph Fellows, Percy's father was born in Willenhall, but the family had moved to Union Street, Bridgtown, Cannock, by 1881. In 1890, Joseph married Amy Paddock, a girl from Penkridge, at Cannock and moved to live in New Street, Bridgtown where later that year a daughter, Clara Evelyn was born. Joseph had always been employed in the mining industry, starting as a labourer but then becoming a coal miner and by 1901 this was still the case. The family had increased to seven and had moved to Rose Cottages on the Old Fallow Road. Percy was born in 1900 and at that time was the youngest. In 1911, Percy was at school, with his older brother Reginald, whilst William, the eldest son was a horse driver at Littleton. The youngest member of the family was now Hilda who was born in 1902. Before the war broke out Percy had also become a miner at Littleton, whereas Reginald had found employment with his father at West Cannock Colliery as a shaft repairer. Percy enlisted for service in April 1917, joining the 11th Battalion, Lancashire Fusiliers. He went missing in action on the 28th May 1918, and his death was confirmed by the Army twelve months later in 1919. Percy was only 18 at the time of his death and his body was not recovered. He is remembered on the Soissons Memorial to the Missing in France.

Private Reginald Sylvester Fellows
S/26743

Reginald was the older brother of Percy and he did not join up until March 1918, electing to join the 1/6th Battalion, Seaforth Highlanders. He was sent to France in August 1918, and lost his life on the 25th October, 1918 at the age of 20. His body was buried in Maing Community Cemetery Extension in France.

Private Frederick Ferneyhough
19584

Frederick Ferneyhough was born in 1887 at Fradswell near Lichfield. His father was William Ferneyhough, a carpenter from Kings Bromley and his mother was Mary Jane Ferneyhough who came from Birmingham, the couple having married in the city in 1874. In 1891, the family of five was living at St. Paul's Street West, Burton-on-Trent. In 1891, the family of seven was living at 4, Gresley Row, Lichfield, although three of the five children had been born in Burton-on-Trent. However, in 1894, Mary Jane died and four years later, William remarried. His second wife was Maria Harris who had three children from her first marriage, and the couple set up home in Kings Bromley. Frederick had left home and in 1901 was working as a milk boy on Blakelow Farm at Swynnerton. By 1911, Frederick, now 24, was a cowman at Cophurst Farm, Lightwood near Stone. Frederick must have decided that agriculture did not have a long term future, and so he decided to move to Cannock, where he worked at Littleton and later at East Cannock Collieries. In 1915, Frederick married Florence May Smallman on the 13th June, at St. Luke's. The couple set up home at 15 Lloyd Street, Cannock, and in 1916 a daughter Iris M. Ferneyhough was born. Frederick enlisted for the Army at Hednesford on the 5th December, 1915, joining the 7th Battalion, South Staffordshire Regiment where he saw service in Gallipoli and in France, mostly as a servant to Lieutenant

Proctor. On the 10th June, 1917, Frederick died from his wounds, incurred during the Battle of Passchendaele. His body was never recovered after the war and Frederick is remembered on the Menin Gate Memorial to the Missing at Ieper in Belgium. Frederick was 29 at the time of his death.

Private Joseph Foster
13722

The Fosters were a large family, with no fewer than eight children. Thomas Foster, the father, came from Darlaston, whereas his wife Eliza hailed from Tipton. The couple had married at Dudley in 1877. They lived at Lichfield Road, Walsall in 1881 where Thomas was a miner, but between 1891 and 1901, the family lived at Occupation Road, Walsall Wood, the village where most of the children were born. By 1911, the family had moved to Cemetery Road, Cannock, where the 15 year old Joseph had found employment as an electrician's boy. In September 1914, Joseph volunteered for the Army, joining the 9th Battalion, Royal Welsh Fusiliers, being sent to France on the 19th July, 1915. At the Battle of Loos, Joseph was badly wounded when a bullet passed straight through his body, and he died of these wounds on the 26th September, 1915 aged just 19. His body was buried at Chocques Military Cemetery in France.

Stanley Fisher

Sadly there is no information about this man. It would appear that he will remain a mystery as there is nothing to connect anyone of this name to Cannock. There is, however, a mention of Stanley Fisher on a memorial in Newhall Street in the town.

Private Francis David Green
18072

David Green was born at Chesterfield in Derbyshire and his wife Elizabeth came from Tipton, yet the couple were married at Penkridge in 1874. By 1881, they had set up home at Cannock, on the Walsall Road, and remained there from then on. Francis was born in 1880 and was the second eldest son. He went to school in the town and by 1901 had become an edge tool improver. Early in 1910, Francis married Sarah Smallman at Cannock and the couple set up a home at 170, St.

John's Road. Francis was now a coal tub loader at Cannock and Leacroft Colliery. The couple had one child, a son, born in 1912 and named Howard Francis Green. Francis decided to enlist in the Army in April 1915, joining the 2nd Battalion, South Staffordshire Regiment and embarking for France on the 2nd October of that year. Francis was badly wounded in November 1916, dying on the 16th, aged 36. His body was buried at Contay British Cemetery, Contay, France.

Private Frank Gorman
19581

The Gormans were a coal mining family, with the father of the family Frank snr hailing from Tipton and his wife Sarah Ann, also coming from Tipton. By 1901 they were living at Pelsall, where indeed the four sons were all born. The family then moved to Clarendon Street, Bloxwich before settling at 17 Lloyd Street Cannock about the time of the Great War. In 1909, Frank jnr married Florence Brough at Cannock, with the couple moving to 173, Station Road, Cheslyn Hay, where Frank was employed as a coal miner. A son, Stanley was born at Cannock in 1913. Frank volunteered for service in the 1st Battalion, South Staffordshire Regiment on the 19th August, 1915, being sent to France on the 8th December of the same year. There was a report in the local press that Frank had been wounded in August 1916, and this was then amended to missing in action on the 31st August. It was not until 1919, that the Army stated that Frank had been presumed to have been killed on that date, aged 20. His body was not recovered and Frank is remembered on the Thiepval Memorial to the Missing on the Somme. At the time of his death, Frank Gorman was living at 17, Lloyd Street, Cannock.

Private George Getley
16995

George Getley was born at Seighford, Staffordshire in 1880, the second son of Joseph and Fanny Getley. The family came from a farming background, with Joseph employed as a farm labourer on Kingwood farm at Leacroft in 1881. The family was a large one, numbering eight children. By 1901, George, now 21 was working as a colliery labourer, lodging with Richard and Harriet Eden at 5 King Street, Cannock. On the 16th February, 1902 George married Fanny Hood, a local girl from Churchbridge, at St. Luke's, Cannock. The couple set up home at Bridgtown where George and Frederick were born, before in late 1910, they decided to move to Mansfield in

Nottinghamshire. They moved with the Morgan family, with Fanny Getley and Susannah Morgan expecting babies, in both cases their third child. The two families shared 6 Howard Road, Mansfield. The Getley family moved back to Cannock after a short stay in Mansfield and Fanny gave birth to their fourth child in 1914. George answered the call to arms in 1915, joining the 2nd Battalion, Northumberland Fusiliers, and was sent to France on the 1st June, 1915. Just four months later, on the 1st October, 1915, George died from illness, aged 36. His body was not recovered after the war and he is remembered on the Loos Memorial to the Missing in France.

Gunner Albert Handley
103979

In 1866, Edward Handley married Emma Eccleshall at Stafford. He was a blacksmith, a trade which he followed for his entire adult life. The family lived for a time at Ranton which was where Edward was born, but by 1881 the growing family had moved to Market Place in Cannock. The Handleys had nine children, with Albert being the fifth of the six sons. The family then moved to Mill Street and by 1901, the 20 year old Albert was working as a boot maker, a trade which he also followed for his working life. His mother died in 1910, leaving Edward living with his daughter Lucy, Albert and Ernest. Albert took an active part in the community being Vice-President of Cannock F.C., being a noted billiards player and was a member of Royal Oak Bowling Club. He was also a member of the Cannock Liberal and Labour club and was a member of the Ancient Order of Buffaloes. Albert enlisted on the 21st February, 1916 joining the Royal Garrison Artillery, being mobilized on the 16th July and posted to Dundee for training. He was transferred to the 192nd Siege Battery on the 29th July 1916 making his way to France. Albert was sent on leave in October 1916, returning to the Front in November. On the 4th July, 1917 Albert was posted to the 5th Siege Battery and just a month later, he was killed in action by a shell and was buried with two comrades at Bard Cottage Cemetery near Ieper in Belgium. At the time of his death, Albert was 37.

Private Russell John Haycock
325498

Russell Haycock was born at Albrighton in Shropshire in 1895. His father was Jasper Jeremiah Haycock who was a coachman at Ingestre and later at Upper Penn. Jasper married Agnes Russell at Newport, Shropshire in 1893. The couple had three children,

Celia Jane, Russell John and Arthur Thomas. On the 1901 census his wife and three children were living with Agnes's widowed mother at Forton in Staffordshire, due to Jasper's employment as a coachman at Rookery Lane, Upper Penn. However, by 1911, they were reunited, living at 140 Wolverhampton Road in Cannock. Jasper was now a chimney sweep, with Celia a confectioner's assistant and Russell a butcher's apprentice. In the Great War, Russell decided to join the Worcestershire Yeomanry, before transferring to the Corps of Hussars. He was sent to Egypt on the 23rd April 1915 and was killed in action exactly one year later at the age of 21. His body was not recovered after the war and Russell is remembered on the Jerusalem Memorial to the Missing in Israel.

Sapper George Hughes
112555

In 1891, George Hughes, aged 7 was living in Cannock, the town of his birth, with his mother Jane, and three brothers, Harry, Sydney and Ernest. Ten years later, George was living with William, his married older brother, and was working as a tool stamper. His father, also named William was a bricklayer from Shropshire, and he and his wife were living together again in 1901 on the Walsall Road where Sydney worked as his father's labourer. The couple were still living there in 1911, having taken on a lodger, William Wall to eke out their pension. However, by 1911, George had joined the 1st Battalion, Grenadier Guards and was at St. James' Park Barracks where he was a cook. Late in 1911, George married Louisa Carter at St. Pancras in London, with their first child Minnie being born there in early 1912. The family then moved to Cannock where a second daughter, Emily was born in 1914. Yet in the Great War, George did not rejoin his old Regiment, choosing instead to enlist with the 175th Tunnelling Company, Royal Engineers. George was sent to France on the 25th August, 1915 and this 32 year old sapper died on the 18th September, just one month later. His body was buried at Poperinghe New Military Cemetery in Belgium.

Private Harold Percy Hall
112624

Harold Percy Hall was born at Cannock in 1892, the eldest child of Thomas Hall, a labourer and coal loader, and Sarah Hall, who had married at Cannock in 1891. They were a Cannock family and lived on the Hednesford Road, where 6 children were born, the exception being Frederick who, according to the 1911 census was born at Witton in Birmingham, although ten years earlier his town of birth is recorded as Cannock. By 1911, Harold and his brother William were working as horse drivers down the pit, whilst Frederick was a colliery labourer at Mid Cannock Colliery. Harold married Cecelia Belcher on the 26th November, 1911 at Rugeley with their first child, Alfred being born at Cannock on the 25th February, 1912. A daughter, Gladys was born in 1913 and a second son Stanley in early 1916. On the 29th August, 1914, Harold tried to enlist in the South Staffordshire Regiment, claiming that he had served for five years previously in the Regiment. He was discharged only 56 days later because of poor eyesight, despite having passed a medical at Hednesford. However, Harold was determined to serve his country and in August, 1915 joined the 175th Tunnelling Company, Royal Engineers. He was sent to France on the 26th August, 1915 and served as an efficient and well liked soldier. Harold was killed in action on the 9th October, 1916 when he and two comrades were killed by a shell. Sappers Harding, Hollingmode, Marklew, Shaw and Ray took the trouble to write to his widow, who had moved from the Old Penkridge Road to live in Bridgtown, that her husband had been "a good man, loved by his comrades". Harold's body was buried at Ecoivres Military Cemetery, Mont St. Eloi in France. He was only 24 at the time of his death.

Private Alfred Hickinbotham
19746

Alfred Hickinbotham was born at Bridgtown in 1884, being the eldest child of Thomas and Harriett Hickinbotham, the former from Penkridge and the latter from Brocton. The family lived on the Old Fallow Road, and Alfred had five other siblings. In 1901 he was employed as a horse driver at Littleton Colliery working alongside his brother George, whilst his father was a miner at the same pit. On the 2nd February, 1909 Alfred married Mary Ann Lockett at St. Luke's Church and the couple had one child, setting up home on the Stafford Road. His father, Thomas died at Cannock later that same year. Alfred had worked at the same pit for ten years, when he decided to enlist on the 12th January, 1915, choosing to join the 8th Battalion, Royal Welsh Fusiliers. After just eight weeks Alfred was sent to the Dardanelles, as part of the ill-fated attempt to knock Turkey out of the war. Alfred was killed in action on the 7th August, 1915 at the age of 32. His body was buried at Shrapnel Valley Cemetery in Turkey.

Rifleman Herbert William Jellyman
5859

Herbert Jellyman was born at Cannock in 1890, the youngest son of Abraham and Martha Jellyman, a couple who had married in West Bromwich some ten years earlier. They had moved to John Street, Cannock by 1881, where Abraham worked as an iron moulder. He was industrious and by 1901 had worked his way up to foreman, with the family having moved to the Walsall Road in Cannock. His wife sadly died at the age of 54 in 1909. His eldest sons Alfred and Ernest were both mechanical engineers, but Herbert showed himself to be a good scholar, winning a place at Queen Mary's Grammar School at Walsall. Herbert was also independent minded and was one of the leading lights in the controversy as to whether Q.M. students should smoke in public whilst wearing the school cap. After attending Q.M., Herbert then went to Westminster College to train as a teacher, and then worked for Birmingham Education Committee, before returning to Cannock, where he worked for ten years at the Walsall Road School. Herbert volunteered for service in London on the 1st December, 1915, electing to join the 1/9th Queen Victoria Rifles, London Regiment. He was sent to France in July 1916 and at the age of 26 he died of his wounds on the 24th September. His body was buried at Grove Town Cemetery, Maulte, France.

Corporal John Jones
34978

John Jones hailed from the Yorkshire town of Barnsley where he was born in 1894, the youngest son of John Frank Jones and his wife Charlotte. John's father came from Oldbury in the Black Country, but the rest of the family, three sons and two daughters were all born in Barnsley. Charlotte died in 1903, but John senior carried on as a widower, bringing up his children whilst continuing his work as a miner. His youngest sons followed him down the pit, but George the eldest had married and moved to Oldham where he worked as a piecer in a cotton mill. Around the time of the Great War, John Jones junior made the decision to move to Cannock, presumably because of perceived better prospects in the area. When war broke out, John joined the South Staffordshire Regiment, but was then transferred to the 5th Company Machine Gun Corps, where he rose to the rank of corporal. At the age of 22 John was killed in action on the 13th November, 1916. His body was not recovered after the war and he is remembered on the Thiepval Memorial to the Missing on the Somme in France.

Private Tom Jackson
6042

Tom Jackson was born at Cannock in 1887, the third son of James and Elizabeth Jackson. James was an edge tool grinder, who died at the relatively early age of 49 in 1897, leaving a widow and four sons. John, the eldest became Clerk to Cannock Urban District Council, whilst James the second eldest became a motor mechanic. Tom found employment as an edge tool warehouse boy by the age of 14. Tom was a noted footballer, playing for Cannock Juniors, Cheslyn Hay United and Cannock Central. Elizabeth Jackson died in 1909 and this is probably what triggered Tom's and his brother William's, decision to leave England. On the 5th August, 1910 the two of them boarded the Osterley, bound for Brisbane in Australia. They moved to Melbourne and became involved in dairying. On the 21st March, 1916, Tom joined the Australian Imperial Forces at Geelong, being placed in the 14th Battalion. He left Melbourne on the 1st August, 1916, arriving at Plymouth on the 25th September. From there he was despatched to France on the 12th December and went to be toughened up at Etaples between the 13th and 21st December, from where he joined his unit. On the 21st February he was hospitalised with abrasions to his foot which turned septic and developed into an abscess, not rejoining his unit until the 17th May, 1917. Tom was transferred to the Machine Gun Section and on the 19th August he was badly wounded, dying on the next day at the age of 29. His body was buried in the Messines Ridge British Cemetery in Belgium. It took over five years before officialdom sorted out his effects and will, as confusion meant that items were sent to England which should have been passed to his brother William.

Rifleman Herbert Jeffery
R/13793

Herbert was the third son of John and Alice Jeffery, and was born at Cannock in 1876. His father who hailed from Longton was initially a farm labourer, but like many men who moved to the Cannock area, he later became a miner. His sons were also coal miners and the family had lived in the town for over thirty years, moving from the town to Chadsmoor and then finally to Broomhill, settling down at 28, Victoria Street. John Jeffery sadly passed away in 1901 at the age of 58. Despite being in a safe job at West Cannock Number 4 pit, on the 28th May, 1915, Herbert volunteered for service, joining initially the 15th Battalion, Kings Royal

Rifle Corps at Hednesford. He was transferred to the 12th Battalion before being sent to France on the 30th December, 1915, spending the next 24 days enduring the infamous Bull Ring at Etaples. Herbert then became part of an Entrenching Battalion for three months, before finally joining his unit on the 21st April, 1916. Some four months later, on the 30th August, 1916, Herbert was killed in action when he was hit by a shell. At the time of his death, Herbert was 40 years of age. His body was never recovered after the war, and Herbert is remembered on the Thiepval Memorial to the Missing on the Somme in France.

Lance Corporal William Richard Jones
109

William Jones was born at Cannock in 1894, the second born son of Richard Jones a Shropshire miner and Maria Jones. The family settled in Cannock somewhere around 1888, after marrying in the town, living in Wolverhampton Road to begin with, before moving around the corner to Victoria Street. William, who was a leading choir boy, did not follow his father down the pit, but instead became a clerk in the offices of the Birmingham Waterworks Company. William enlisted in 1914, joining the 14th Battalion of the Royal Warwickshire Regiment, and being despatched to France on the 21st November, 1915. He had been serving in France for nine months when he was posted as missing in action on the 23rd July, 1916. It was later assumed by the War Office that William had indeed been killed on that day. At the time of his death, William was 22 years of age, and his body was recovered after the war, and was buried in Caterpillar Valley Cemetery at Longueval in France.

Guardsman William Gallear
22537

William Gallear came from a very large family, having nine brothers and sisters. His father, George Gallear was a Shropshire miner and his wife Eliza also came from the same county, but all of their children were born at Chadsmoor. The couple had married at Cannock in 1889, and two years later were lodging with the Millington family at Moreton Street, Chadsmoor. In 1901, the family of nine had moved into their own home in Moreton Street. The Gallears, by 1911, were living at 145 John Street, where no fewer than 15 people shared the house, including the in laws, Mark and Ellen Millington. William had spent some time in the South Staffordshire

Regiment and had also worked down the pit. On the 17th August, 1914, William joined up. He elected to serve in the 2nd Battalion, South Staffordshire Regiment, passed the medical, as expected from a man who had already served for 4 years with the colours, but was then surprisingly discharged on the 31st October, 1914, as not likely to become an efficient soldier. William, however, was determined to serve and on the 1st February, 1915, this 5 feet 9 inch miner joined the 2nd Battalion of the Grenadier Guards. On both occasions, William had joined up at Hednesford, and it may have been a surprise to Dr. Holton who had passed him fit on both occasions. William was sent to France on the 27th October, 1915 and served there for 11 months before he was killed in action on the 15th September, 1916, at the age of 24. His body was not recovered at the end of the war and William is remembered on the Thiepval Memorial to the Missing on the Somme in France. William's two brothers, George and Thomas both served in the Great War.

Corporal William Garbett
R/12254

In 1882, Thomas Garbett married Mary Goalby at Cannock. Their first born was a son named William who was born in 1884 at Chadsmoor. The couple had four more children, and lived at John Street at Chadsmoor. By 1901, William was a horse driver in a local mine, and on the 20th April, 1908, he married Ellen Bishop at St. Luke's Church. The couple had four children, Evelyn Maud, born in 1909, Elsie May, born 1910, Gertrude, born 1912 and William born in 1915. Gertrude sadly died from pneumonia in 1917. The family had moved to live at 235 Cannock Road in Chadsmoor, and William was by now a stallman at the Cannock and Rugeley Colliery. On the 19th April, 1915, William enlisted in the Army at Hednesford, joining the 15th Battalion, King's Royal Rifle Corps, being appointed as unpaid Lance Corporal on the 30th July of that year. He was posted to the 8th Battalion on the 12th September, 1915 in France, with his promotion being confirmed with pay on the 5th December. On the 5th August, 1916 William was promoted to Corporal, but just 19 days later, William was badly wounded by a sniper and died of his wounds on the same day, aged 32. His body was not found after the war and William is remembered on the Thiepval Memorial to the Missing on the Somme in France. Just before he was killed he had written home saying how much he was looking forward to his first leave as they were having a tough time of things with very heavy fighting. His widow, Ellen wrote to the War Office asking for her husband's watch, photographs and letters, but was told that there were no personal effects.

Private John Josephs
29075

John Josephs' father, Thomas Josephs was a coal miner from Shropshire, whereas his wife Elinor was born at Llansanfrydo in Montgomeryshire. The couple lived in Wrexham, which was where John was born in 1881. By 1891, the family had moved to Cannock, living at Caxton Buildings in Railway Street. In 1901, the Josephs were living on the Walsall Road, and John was earning a living as an edge tool striker. Thomas Josephs died in 1904, and his widow and son continued to live on the Walsall Road, with John now the bread winner. John was called up for service, firstly in the South Staffordshire Regiment, but was then transferred to the 49th Company, 10th Labour Battalion, the Lincolnshire Regiment. At the age of 37, John died on the 3rd January, 1918, and was buried at Mendinghem Military Cemetery in Belgium. His widowed mother died in Cannock just one year after her son.

Private George Henry Keeling
2695

James Keeling married Frances Rowley in Cannock in 1879. He was a native of Rugeley and she came from Willenhall. In 1881, they were living at Bradbury Lane, Hednesford with their new born daughter Caroline. James earned his living as a railway shunter. By 1891, James was now a contractor with the East Cannock Colliery Company, and the family had moved to Hill Street, Hednesford. More children had been born, Emily, Eliza, George and Elsie. However, in 1899 at the age of 43, James died. By 1901, his widow and family had moved to Hednesford Road, Cannock. Frances was making ends meet with dressmaking, while George was a pit bank labourer. In 1911, the family were living at Leacroft House, Cannock and George was now a boiler fireman, his brother Joseph a colliery banksman and the youngest Arthur a pony driver on the colliery surface. On the 27th March, 1913 George and Arthur sailed for Sydney, Australia. When war broke out, George enlisted in the 55th Battalion, Australian Infantry and was sent to France. He was wounded in action and died at Rouen on the 6th May, 1917 at the age of 30. His mother had moved to live in Lloyd Street, Cannock. Her son was buried in the St. Sever Cemetery Extension at Rouen.

Private John Kinsell
18908

John Kinsell was born in 1885 at Brierley Hill in Staffordshire. He came from a canal family, his father William being employed as a steerer on the canal, his elder brother William was a labourer on the canal, as was John. William Kinsell had married Priscilla Pugh at Dudley in 1858. The family had lived at Kingswinford and Brierley Hill. In 1903, John married Dinah Bedford at Stourbridge with the couple moving into the house in which his parents had lived before they died. John was now a steerer as his father had been, and between 1905 and 1910 they had three children before deciding to move to 65, St. John's Road, Cannock, where a fourth child, Ernest was born in 1913. A fifth child Alfred was born in 1915. John now worked at East Cannock Colliery as a miner, but in May 1915, he decided to enlist in the 1st Battalion, South Staffordshire Regiment, being sent to France on the 16th December of that year. John was severely wounded in the back, legs and left eye and was invalided back to England. Dinah visited her husband at Woolwich on the 24th July, 1916 and he died on the next day from his wounds, at the age of 31. His body was taken back to Brierley Hill where it was buried with full military honours.

Alfred Charew

It is my belief that there was no such person as Alfred Charew, and that his name appears on the memorial in Cannock as a result of error. (See Alfred C. Lerew).

Private William Henry Lloyd
29792

William Henry Lloyd was born in 1898, the son of Deborah Lloyd, a 22 year old seamstress, who was the daughter of George and Caroline Lloyd, who lived on the Walsall Road at Cannock. George was a tailor and the couple had lived and worked in Cannock since the 1880s. On the 24th November, 1901, Deborah married Francis Gray Davis, a bricklayer from Darlaston, with the family setting up home at 197, St. John's Road, Cannock. Before her marriage, she had worked as a servant to Hodgkinson's the grocer on the Walsall Road in the town. The couple had three children, but also offered a home to William Henry and his uncles, William and Henry Lloyd and his aunt Emma Lloyd. William Henry was called up in 1917, joining the 2/6th Battalion, Sherwood Foresters and was sent to France just before the German Spring Offensive in 1918. On the first day of the Offensive, the 21st March, 1918, William Henry was killed in action at the age of 20. His body was not recovered after the war and William Henry is remembered on the Arras Memorial to the Missing in France.

Sapper Harry Lloyd
79268

Harry Lloyd was the uncle of William Henry Lloyd, born at Cannock in 1887 and he worked as a coal miner, horse driver and then as a miner at Cannock and Leacroft Colliery. He enlisted with the South Staffordshire Regiment in October, 1914 and then transferred to the 184th Tunnelling Company, Royal Engineers. Harry was killed in action on the 30th November, 1915 at the age of 28. His body was buried at Cerisy-Gailly Military Cemetery in France.

2nd Lieutenant Charles Edward Holden Loxton

The Loxtons were one of the prominent families of Cannock. Charles' grandfather, Samuel Loxton was an architect and surveyor, who had moved the family from Wednesbury between 1871 and 1881. His maternal grandfather, Edward Holden had been the M.P. for Walsall. Charles' father, Charles Adshead Loxton was a solicitor, born in Wednesbury, and he also moved with the family to Cannock, where they took up residence at The Poplars on the Penkridge Road. Charles senior became Clerk to Cannock Urban District Council. Charles Edward was born in Walsall on the 3rd June, 1892 and was schooled at Mr. Royle's Preparatory School in Stanmore, and then at Harrow School, where he preferred to be called Edward. Charles then went up to University College, Oxford where he read classics. He rowed for Oxford before appendicitis cut short his involvement in this activity, although he did engage on a yachting tour with Noel Chavasse, the son of the Bishop of Liverpool, and in the Great War, the only man to be awarded two Victoria Crosses. Charles was 6 feet tall and had a genial disposition and possessed an attractive personality. He came down from Oxford in 1914, and on the 26th August, 1914, Charles was gazetted as a 2nd Lieutenant in the 5th Battalion, Prince of Wales' North Staffordshire Regiment, being sent to France almost immediately. Charles had a reputation as a strict but fair officer who was idolised by his men. He refused to tell his parents where he was fighting as this information would be crossed out if included in letters written by his men. He was described by a Sergeant in his Battalion as "more like a brother than a master". On the 23rd May, 1915 2nd Lt. Loxton was supervising his men on a wiring party at night at Wulvergem in Belgium. No Man's Land was suddenly lit up by lightning, and Charles Edward Loxton was shot in the groin and badly wounded. He was placed on a stretcher and taken to a Casualty Clearing Station but died there from his wounds. This popular and well liked officer was only a few weeks short of his 23rd birthday. His body was buried in a private grave in Nieuwkerke Churchyard in Belgium. A memorial glass window was paid for by the grieving family and placed in St. Luke's Church at the east end of the south aisle, with this inscription, "until the day breaks and the shadows flee away".

Private Ernest Adshead Dudley Loxton
2067

Ernest Loxton was the son of James Stokes Loxton, who was the brother of Charles Adshead Loxton. James was educated at Albion Villa School at Audley, and had then become a chemist's assistant to John H. Toone at 2, Granby Street, Leicester. By 1888, James had set himself up as a chemist and druggist in Surrey and in that year, he married Ada Constance Baldwin, the daughter of Henry and Jane Baldwin. Henry was a rope merchant and the family originated from Stepney. In 1889, Ernest was born at Teddington in Surrey and the family appeared to be well set. In 1894, following the birth of a second son, the family left England for Capetown in South Africa. It would appear that the marriage did not work out for in 1907, Ernest's mother re-married, when she wed Francis Stratton, an agent from London and by 1911, they had moved 3, Beverley Gardens at Barnes. Little is known of Ernest at this point, but it would appear that on the 21st July, 1911, he set sail for Brisbane in Australia, where he found work as a station hand on a sheep farm. On the 6th April, 1915, Ernest volunteered for service with the 9th Battalion, Australian Infantry, as part of the Australian Imperial Forces. He was sent to serve in Gallipoli, as part of the ANZAC forces sent to try and bring an early end to the war. Ernest was admitted to hospital on the 18th September, 1915 initially diagnosed as suffering from influenza, but was then sent to Mudros and then to Malta, where his illness was found to be enteric fever, and was finally sent back to England in order to recover. Ernest was considered fit to return to his unit in France in August 1916, but after a brief time in France he was re-admitted to hospital with colitis, again being sent back to England. He did not recover until October, 1916 and was returned to his Battalion in March, 1917. During overseas training a different side began to appear, when he was fined for using obscene language on parade and lost pay for a number of absences without leave. He did not return to France until the 4th December, 1917, but was sent to hospital for 33 days on the 12th to be treated for venereal disease. Ernest rejoined his Battalion again on the 23rd January, 1918 but just three months later, he was badly wounded by shrapnel in the left shoulder, which led to the perforation of his lung. Ernest died as he was admitted to the Casualty Clearing Station, at 6.30am on the 24th April, 1918. He was 28 at the time of his death and his body was buried at Caestre Military Cemetery in France.

Lieutenant George Guest Lomas

George Guest Lomas was born at Stechford, Worcestershire in 1894, being the only son of George and Eleanor Lomas. George Lomas senior was an intriguing character, who was the son of Thomas Lomas, a Birmingham cabman. By the age of 16, he was a clerk, living in the residence of Joseph Guest, Ashted House, Aston in Birmingham. In 1891, George and Eleanor were living at Droitwich, Worcestershire and by 1901, the family had settled at Wilmslow in Cheshire, where George had opened a business as an oil and produce merchant. Amazingly, by 1911, George had become a Church of England vicar and had a parish in Burton-upon-Trent in Staffordshire. He moved to become Vicar of Cannock around the outbreak of the Great War. His only son, George Guest was sent to St. Oswald's College, Ellesmere, whose motto was "Dimicans Pro Patria" – (fighting for the Fatherland). George junior was captain of the school and held a commission with the Officer Training Corps. As a result of this in February 1915, George was commissioned as a 2nd Lieutenant in the 2/6th Battalion, Manchester Regiment, being sent to France in April, 1917. He was sent on leave for two weeks in November, 1917 before returning to France. On the 22nd March, 1918, George was shot in the forehead whilst in the trenches. Lt. Colonel Melvil wrote to George's father to tell him that his son's death had been "instantaneous and painless". This letter arrived on the 9th April, 1918, on what would have been George Guest Lomas' 24th birthday. After the war, George's body was not recovered and he is remembered on the Pozieres Memorial to the Missing in France.

Corporal Howard Frank Lockley
PO/14211

The Lockley family were a long established Cannock family, with Howard's grandfather, George being a bricklayer from the town, and his father Frank, a railway warehouseman, also being born there. Howard was born in Cannock in 1889, and by 1901 was a 12 year old grocer's apprentice. However, in 1907 at the age of 18, Howard had joined the Royal Marine Light Infantry, signing on for eleven years. He was serving on the cruiser HMS Black Prince at the Battle of Jutland in 1916, when the ship's captain made a fatal error, turning towards ships on the horizon, thinking that they were British ships. In fact it was the German Fleet and Black Prince was blown out of the water, sinking with great loss of life. One of those killed was the 28 year old Howard Lockley, who went down with the ship on the 31st May 1916. Had Howard survived until August 1916, his terms of engagement would have led to his release from the forces. Howard is remembered on the Portsmouth Naval Memorial.

Lance Corporal Frederick Lockley
15516

If the loss of Howard had been difficult to bear for the Lockley family at 17, Newhall Street, Cannock, it must have been almost unbearable with the loss of their second son just six weeks later. Fred was also from Cannock and was born in 1893, and like his older brother Harry, he went into mining, with both working at Littleton Colliery, first as electric motor drivers and then as miners. When the war broke out, Fred joined up in 1914, initially with the Cheshire Regiment, but then transferring to the 8th Battalion, Prince of Wales' Volunteers, South Lancashire Regiment, and was sent to France in September 1915. On the 10th July, 1916, Fred, aged 23, was shot through the head on the Somme, dying instantly. The news was conveyed to his grieving parents in a letter from Private Harry Ash of Paddy's Lane, Cannock. The letter arrived on the 21st birthday of Fred's fiancée. Fred's body was buried at Pozieres British Cemetery, Ovillers-La Boiselle.

Private Percy Mears
203334

Frederick Percy Mears to give him his full name was born at Bridgtown in 1891, the first born of Frederick and Alice Mears. The couple had married in Cannock early in 1891. Frederick senior was a butcher and in 1891 the newly married couple lived at North Street. By 1901, the ten year old Percy, as he was usually known was living with his uncle and aunt, William and Selina Morgan at 136, Penkridge Road, whilst the rest of the family remained at Bridgtown. In 1911, the family were back together, but were living as boarders at Manstey Farm, Penkridge, owned by J.W. Adderley. Percy was now a grocer's apprentice and was 19 years of age. Percy joined the Army in 1916 and was sent to France with the 8th Battalion, King's (Liverpool Regiment). On the 20th November, 1917, Percy was posted as missing in action, and his death was later presumed to have taken place on this date, he was 26 years old. His conduct was described as "exemplary" by Captain W.T. Ball in a letter to Percy's parents. Percy's body was never recovered after the war and he is remembered on the Thiepval Memorial to the Missing on the Somme in France.

Private Ernest Mears
8202

See the entry for the same soldier on the Bridgtown memorial.

Private Enoch Marsh
12763

In 1896, at Dudley, Joseph Marsh married Sarah Brettle, and within a year the couple had had a child, Enoch, followed by a second boy, Thomas in 1900. Joseph was a coal miner and the family lived at 40b New Street in Sedgley. By 1911, the family had increased to six children and they had moved to Cannock, living at 41 Coronation Terrace, Blackfords. Enoch was now 14 and had started work, as a driver at East Cannock Colliery before becoming a dataller at the same pit. The family moved again, this time to 25 Heath Gap Road, whilst Enoch had become a member of the Blackfords Mission, after previously attending the Sunday school. Indeed, Enoch afterwards became the Secretary to the Mission. In 1914, after the outbreak of war, Joseph Marsh was reading the paper and observed that Lord

Kitchener's appeal mentioned that "every young man should be serving". Enoch observed, "That includes me Dad". His father agreed and the following morning, Enoch went to the Recruiting Office in Cannock and signed up to serve in the 2nd Battalion, South Staffordshire Regiment, being sent to France on the 10th March, 1915. Just two months later, on the 18th May, Enoch was posted as missing in action, which was later confirmed as killed in action. A memorial service was held at Williamson's Memorial Chapel, with an address given by Councillor W.E. Boot, whilst Mrs. Taylor played the Death March at the end of the service. Enoch was only 19 at the time of his death and his body was not recovered after the war. He is remembered on the Le Touret Memorial to the Missing in France.

Private John May

There is no record of a John May having been born in Cannock around this time, nor is there any mention of a John May living in Cannock at this period. Therefore it is quite possible that this soldier will remain just a name on a memorial.

Private William Meredith
19088

William Meredith was born at Broseley, Shropshire in 1882, the third son of Thomas and Thirza Meredith. Thomas Meredith was a tile maker by trade and the family had moved to live in Much Wenlock. 1901 saw William living in Aldridge, Staffordshire where he was working as a miner's labourer, and living with the Cotton family at Stubbers Green. In 1903, William married and he and his bride Sarah continued to live in the town until 1910, by which time they had had three children. In 1910, they moved to live in Cannock, moving to 58, St. John's Road, where two more children had been born by 1913, and where William had found employment at Littleton Colliery. On the 6th April, 1915 William enlisted in the 8th Battalion, Northumberland Fusiliers and saw service in the Dardanelles and in Egypt before being sent to France. He had been on the Western Front for only one month when he was killed in action on the 9th August, 1916, at the age of 34. His widow received a letter from Captain F.M.M. Carlisle, who told her how proud he had been of William Meredith. He had been a cheerful, good soldier, and had been sleeping peacefully on the firestep when an aerial torpedo had exploded, killing him with a lump of shrapnel in the head in the early hours of the morning. William's body was buried at Wailly Orchard Cemetery in France.

Gunner John Nickless
118423

John Nickless was the adopted son of John and Emily Nickless and whose name was recorded as Thomas on the 1901 and 1911 censuses, perhaps because the family preferred to use a different first name to that of his adopted father. Although his father had been born in Shrewsbury, the family had lived for a number of years in the Cannock area, at Broomhill, Huntington and finally at Pye Green. John junior, worked as a horse driver and then a miner at Number 3 Pit, West Cannock Colliery where his father had been a fireman, but had then reverted to a colliery labourer. John joined the Army on April 7th 1916, and was wounded twice whilst serving with the 92nd Battery, 17th Brigade, the Royal Field Artillery. The 23 year old Gunner died at the Military Hospital, Boyden Camp, Wiltshire, on the 29th January, 1918. His body was returned to Cannock, where it was buried with full military honours.

Private James Ward Onions
28668

The Onions family originally came from Shropshire, with Reuben and Ann Onions having been born and raised in the county. Reuben was a miner, and the family must have moved to the Cannock area around 1880. Their eldest son was James Onions, who like his father had been born at Madeley, but had met and married Ann Maria Ward at Cannock in 1894, when the Onions family were living at 46, John Street, Chadsmoor. James was a coal miner, and he and his wife had twin boys, William and James Ward, who were born in 1897. Two more boys followed the twins, Reuben in 1901 and Albert in 1908. James was a religious man, and worked at Chadsmoor Primitive Methodist Sunday School, where he was the Registrar. He was also an active member of the Christian Endeavour movement and indeed was on the executive of the Cannock and District Christian Endeavour Union. His son James Ward Onions volunteered for service in the Army in May 1916, joining the South Staffordshire Regiment to begin with, but he was transferred to the 2nd Battalion (Garrison), Lincolnshire Regiment and it was whilst serving with this unit that James was admitted to the Military Hospital in York, where he died on the 5th February, 1917 at the age of 20. His body was returned to Cannock where it was buried with full military honours.

Stoker 1st Class James Padmore
SS/108624

George Padmore married Mary Thursfield at Penkridge in 1872. In 1881, the couple were living in Gladstones Buildings on the Stafford Road in Cannock and had one child, a son named William. George was earning his living as an agricultural labourer. Ten years later, George was now employed as a coal miner, the family having moved to Huntington. William, also a coal miner, now had a sister, Ida Annie and a younger brother, James. In 1901, the family were living at Water Works Cottages, Littleton Terrace on the Stafford Road, with George was employed as a coal banksman, while William was now a carpenter. The family had increased to include George and Frank. By 1911, James had joined the Royal Navy as a stoker and was serving with the 5th cruiser squadron at Gibraltar. He was transferred to HMS Broke, and it was while serving on this vessel that he was killed in action on the 31st May, 1916 during the Battle of Jutland. At the time of his death, James was 26. His name is remembered on the Portsmouth Memorial to the Missing.

Rifleman Edwin Pee
R/11796

Frederick Pee was born in Dudley in 1856, and by 1881 had moved to the Cannock area, where he was lodging with his uncle Samuel Pee and his family at Bridgtown. Later that year Frederick married Mary Hannah Stokes at Cannock and within ten years the couple had moved to Union Street, Bridgtown and had a family of some five children. By 1901 they had moved to New Street, Bridgtown, and had added two more children to the family, including Edwin who was born at Bridgtown in 1896. The family then moved again, this time to 65, Blackfords in Cannock, and by 1911, both Edwin and his older brother Albert had followed their father down the pit, at West Cannock Colliery. When the Great War broke out, Edwin joined the Army in 1915, choosing to enlist with the 12th Battalion, King's Royal Rifle Corps. Two of his brothers were also serving in the Northumberland Fusiliers, but this did not stop some disturbing attacks on Frederick Pee's house. A post card was received addressed to Count Von Pee, and then on Thursday, 28th January, 1915 the kitchen windows were smashed. On the following day the sitting room windows suffered similar damage and on Saturday 30th January, whilst the police were watching the rear of the house, an iron fence was hurled through the parlour window. Edwin was sent to France on the 4th September, 1915, but on the 7th October, 1916, Edwin was killed in action. He was described as "always cheerful as a comrade and brave as a soldier. A man on whom you could rely upon to do his duty and a good influence on those not quite so stout hearted". Edwin's death was instantaneous and his body was carried back under shellfire in order to give it a decent burial. However, after the war Edwin's body was not found and he is remembered on the Thiepval Memorial to the Missing on the Somme in France. Edwin was only 21 at the time of his death and had still been living with his parents at the time of his enlistment.

Private James Penton
15298

James Penton was born at Norton Canes in 1894, being the second son of Thomas and Sarah Alice Penton. The couple had a large family, some 11 children being born between 1888 and 1906, all of whom survived. Thomas Penton was a Check Weighman at Littleton Colliery and he was followed into the mines by his three eldest sons, Thomas junior, James and Harry. The family had moved from Norton Canes to St. John's Road, Cannock, firstly at number 27 and then 33. On the 2nd September, 1914, James decided to enlist at Hednesford, joining the 8th Battalion, Prince of Wales' Volunteers, the South Lancashire Regiment. He was sent to Bournemouth for his training and showed a skill as a boxer, winning a Cup and Gold Medal. He was a clever boxer with a good reach and a strong left hook and took Lloyd a well known boxer of the time to 15 rounds. James was sent to France on the 28th September, 1915, serving in the Armentieres sector, and it was here on the 14th January, 1916 that he was shot through the neck by a sniper and killed instantly. He was described by Sergeant W.B. Jackson as "courageous and cheerful, a comrade and brother". James was buried with a service and with an inscribed cross on his grave. He was only 21 at the time of his death and after the war his body was reburied at Rifle House Cemetery, in Ploegsteert Wood, just outside Ieper in Belgium.

Sapper George Henry Pointon
179798

John Pointon had married his wife Elizabeth in 1883 and was at that time a farmer, with the family setting up a home at 31, Church Street, Rugeley, although George, their first child was born at Lichfield in 1880. In 1891 the family had increased to three, with the arrival of Eva in 1890 and Minnie in 1891. Yet, in 1901, John is described as a carter at a tannery and as a widower, but the family had increased to four with the birth of William in 1894. George was still living at home and was earning his living as a painter and plumber. Mystifyingly, in 1911, John and Elizabeth are living together, still at 31, Church Street, Rugeley, with William still living at home. George had married Lucy Bradbury at St. Luke's, Cannock on the 7th December, 1904 and the couple had set up home at 4, Victoria Street. Children soon followed with the birth of Wilfred in 1906 and Robert in 1908. George had worked for 12 years as a painter for John Stokes of Mill Street, Cannock and had been in the North Staffordshire Regiment Volunteers for three years. He had then changed his trade completely, working as a motor mechanic for Walter Bird at his Penkridge Road garage. George was also a member of the Rugeley (Foresters' Home) Court of the Ancient Order of Foresters Friendly Society. George enlisted voluntarily under the Derby Scheme in June 1916, enlisting in the 152nd Field Company, Royal Engineers, and spent twelve months training in England before being sent to France. On the 6th October, 1917, George was killed in action at the age of 38. George's eldest son Wilfred was at Walhouse School at the time and had just won a scholarship to attend Rugeley Grammar School, the family having moved to live at 22, Old Penkridge Road. George's body was buried at Larch Wood (Railway Cutting) Cemetery just outside Ieper in Belgium. George's brother William was also killed in the Great War, in 1916 whilst serving with the Grenadier Guards, and his name is found on the Rugeley Memorial.

Lance Corporal Percy Hartland Powis 240599

In the summer of 1882, at Cannock, George Powis a schoolmaster from Audley married Agnes Elizabeth Morris also a school teacher. In 1884 the couple celebrated the birth of their first child, Percy, followed by May in 1886, Agnes in 1887 and Morris in 1890. It would seem that the Powis' were finding four children and teaching somewhat challenging, for in 1891, Percy and May were staying with their grandparents at Whites Hill on the Hednesford Road, Cannock whilst the rest of the family were living at Clifton Villa on the same road, with the help of a servant and a nurse. In 1901, Percy having spent 5 years at Stafford Grammar School, had won a scholarship to Denstone College, and it was here that he is recorded on the census. The rest of the Powis family had moved to the Belt Road in Hightown, as this was closer to the Elementary School where George and Agnes worked. On the 6th October, 1909, Percy and his brother Morris embarked at Liverpool bound for the Gold Coast in West Africa, as they had accepted posts at the Cairo School to teach English. George Powis was now Head

Teacher of the National School and was helped by his daughter Agnes, with the family now living in Allport Road, Cannock. In the summer of 1914, Percy was back in England on a three month holiday when the Great War broke out. He volunteered straight away, joining the Non Manual Company of the South Staffordshire Regiment at Wolverhampton in September 1914, being sent to France on the 5th March, 1915. Percy then transferred to the 1/6th Battalion of the same Regiment. On the 25th May, 1917, at the age of 33, Percy was killed in action. His body was buried at Maroc British Cemetery, Grenay in France.

Private George Poole
29443

George Poole was born at Stafford in 1895, the son of George and Sarah Poole. In 1891, the couple were lodging at 6 Middle Friars, Stafford while their daughter Caroline was living in Lichfield with Henry and Harriett Gaskin, Mrs Gaskin being the child's aunt. In 1901 the family were living at 2b Tesslen Banks in Stafford. George senior was a general labourer, with Caroline, who was also born at Stafford, now living with the rest of the family. By 1911, the family had moved to 512, Stafford Road, Cannock where George senior had become a coal miner, and George junior was an electric motor driver at the West Cannock Colliery, although they both became road repairers in the same colliery. George's sister, Caroline had married George Husselbee from Penkridge and they were also living with her parents along with their two year old son, Sydney. During the Great War, George junior enlisted to serve in the Army, first of all with the Notts and Derbys Regiment and then transferring to the 13th Battalion, Alexandra, the, Princess of Wales' Own Yorkshire Regiment. At the age of 22, George was killed in action on the 26th July, 1917 during an enemy raid on the trenches. In a letter to the grieving family, a Captain from the Regiment wrote that he was "sorry to lose him, as he was cheerful, hard working and died doing his duty for King and Country". George's body was buried at Fins New British Cemetery, Sorel-le-Grand, on the Somme in France.

Private Edward Price
46457

John Price, a coal miner from Cannock married Selina Plant from Shropshire at Cannock in 1883. They lived at Old Fallow in the town and between 1895 and 1904 the couple had some 14 children, nine of whom survived. Edward was the second eldest boy and was born in 1891. In 1911, the family had moved to 97 Hawthorne View, Blackfords with Edward now 20 and working as a coal miner in a local colliery. With the onset of the Great War, Edward volunteered shortly after the start, initially joining the Royal Welsh Fusiliers, being sent to France on the 2nd August, 1915. Edward was then transferred to the 11th Labour Company, Lincolnshire Regiment, and it was while serving with this unit that Edward died on the 6th April, 1917 at the age of 26. Edward's body was buried at Fouquieres Churchyard Extension, in France.

Corporal Arthur Price M.M.
200230

Arthur Price was the younger brother of Edward, and was also born at Cannock in 1893. Like his father and brothers, he too made his living from the coal mines in the area, working with his father at Number 3 pit, West Cannock Colliery. Arthur too, was an early volunteer and joined the 1/5th Battalion, South Staffordshire Regiment, being sent to France on the 5th March, 1915. Arthur showed he was able to accept responsibility and was promoted from Private to Corporal. He was also a brave soldier and was awarded the Military Medal for showing courage during the war. Arthur was killed in action on the 28th April, 1918, at the age of 24, and his body was buried at Beuvry Communal Cemetery Extension in France.

Lance Corporal Arthur John Reynolds
250992

Arthur Reynolds was born at Cannock in 1897, the eldest son of Arthur Reynolds senior and his wife, Elizabeth, but was the second eldest child as the couple already had a daughter, Ethel Mary. Arthur Reynolds senior, was an iron moulder, and he too came from Cannock. The family lived on the Stafford Road before moving to Stoneyfields, where a second son, William was born in 1902. Arthur began his working life as a butcher's errand lad, but he later worked for the Co-op at Hednesford. Arthur enlisted on the 4th April, 1916 with the 3/8th Battalion, Durham Light Infantry, before being posted to the 6th Battalion and was sent to France on the 27th December, 1916, being posted to the 15th Battalion. Arthur was badly wounded on the 28th October, 1917 and was sent back to Dundee War Hospital to recover. Whilst in England he absented himself twice, receiving 7 days confined to barracks and 10 days loss of pay for the first offence and 168 hours detention with 7 days loss of pay for the second. Arthur was also given leave from the 15th November to the 26th November, 1917. Once his wounds had healed he was sent back to France on the 20th July, 1918. On the 5th October, 1918, Arthur was badly wounded, being transferred to the Base Hospital at Rouen, where he died from his wounds on the 15th October, aged 21. Arthur's body was buried at St. Sever Cemetery Extension at Rouen in France.

Private Samuel Reade
27576

Samuel Reade was born at Cannock in 1892, the second child but eldest son of Sampson and Ellen Reade, both natives of the town. His parents had married in 1889 and initially lived at Stoneyfields before moving to Rumer Hill. Sampson was a banksman at a local colliery, and his two sons, Samuel and Frederick also earned their living from mining. In 1911, Samuel was a tub coupler and Frederick a tub runner on the surface at a mine. The family had then moved to Longford Lane, Hatherton. Edith, the eldest of their four children earned her living as a waitress. With the onset of the Great War, Samuel decided to enlist with the South Staffordshire Regiment, before being transferred to the 1st Battalion, Royal Warwickshire Regiment, and it was while with this unit that he was killed in action. Samuel was 24 at the time of his death on the 11th October, 1916 and his body was never recovered. He is remembered on the Thiepval Memorial to the Missing on the Somme in France.

James Richards

Sadly this is a soldier who it seems will remain a name on a memorial as there is nothing to link any soldier of this name to the town of Cannock. It is, however, quite possible that this is a reversal of Richard James who also appears on the memorial.

Corporal John Rogers
9622

John Rogers was born at Cannock in 1894, and was the fourth son of George and Dinah Rogers. George was a general surface labourer at a local pit, and hailed from Dudley, whereas his wife came from the Cannock area, where they had married in 1885. In

1901, the family lived at Newhall Street, Cannock but by 1911 they had moved to Hatherton Lane. John was by now 18 and was working as a colliery clerk, while William, two years his senior was a horse keeper in a colliery. During the Great War, John served with the 10th Battalion, Royal Fusiliers, City of London Regiment. He was killed in action on the 8th October, 1918 at the age of 25. His body was buried at Bois-des-Angles British Cemetery, Crevecoeur-sur-L'Escaut in France.

Private Francis Bernard Rogers
260241

Francis Rogers came from Worcestershire, having been born near Stourport in 1892. His father William Rogers was a clerk at an iron founders, as was his third son, Jesse. His mother, Mary Ellen also came from Stourport and Francis had two more brothers, Horace and Archibald. By 1911, Francis was an assistant teacher living at Evesham, and it would appear that he came to Cannock before the outbreak of the Great War. He then moved to Somerset and it was here that he enlisted with the Somerset Light Infantry before transferring to the 2/6th Battalion, Royal Warwickshire Regiment. Francis was killed in action on the 6th December, 1917 at the age of 26. His body was buried at Fifteen Ravine British Cemetery, Villers-Plouich in France.

Private John Roberts
7039

John and Jane Roberts were both born in North Wales, at Llanfyllin in Denbighshire, but had moved to Shropshire in order to find work. John was an agricultural labourer, and the couple settled to begin with at Weston. It was here that five of their children were born, Alice, Sarah, Frances, John and George. The family then moved to the Baschurch area, where three more children, Thomas, David and Mary were born. Meanwhile, John and George had left home to find work and both were working on a nearby farm owned by John Reece, with John Roberts working as a cowman and George as an under waggoner. In 1902, John decided to join the Army and served for three years with the King's Shropshire Light Infantry, afterwards being on the reserve list for nine years. He then worked as a Police Constable at Dawley Bank in Shropshire, before settling in Cannock as a miner. He lived on the Wolverhampton Road in the town and worked at the East Cannock Colliery. John obviously stood out from the crowd as he was described as being "somewhat unusual in his style". In August 1914, John was recalled to serve in the Army, just two days before his nine years on the reserve list expired, and was once again posted to the 1st Battalion, King's Shropshire Light Infantry, being sent to France on the 9th September, 1914. John was killed in action on the 23rd September, 1914 at the age of 31. His body was not recovered after the war and his name is remembered on the Ploegsteert Memorial to the Missing in Belgium. John was one of the first soldiers connected to the town to be killed in the Great War.

Private Harry Stephens
8268

In 1890, John William Stephens, a house decorator from Redditch in Worcestershire, married Margaret Goodall Stanton, from Coseley at Lichfield. The couple moved to New Street, Cannock and it was here in 1891 that William was born. By 1901 they had moved to the Cannock Road in Chadsmoor, and the family had grown with the births of Harry, Samuel and Ethel. John Stephens had also become active in local politics being a socialist. In 1911 the family were now living at Cemetery Road, and John had changed trade to that of plumber, although William was a painter, whilst Harry was a bricklayer and Samuel a moulder. Harry had also joined the Hednesford Territorials, with whom he served for four years, and by the outbreak of the Great War, he had moved to Church Street, Cannock and had become a miner, working at the Littleton Colliery. Harry was mobilized as soon as war was declared, serving in the 1/5th Battalion, South Staffordshire Regiment and being sent to France on the 5th March, 1915. On the 5th August, 1916 Harry was killed when a shell fragment struck him in the back. His father, who was by this time the Labour member of the Cannock Tribunal, received the information in two letters, one from the Reverend W. Rice and one from Private Price of Blackfords. In Harry's pocket was found a picture, carried by many soldiers in the Great War, entitled "The Great Sacrifice". The body of the 22 year old Harry was buried at Berles-au-Bois Churchyard Extension, near Arras in France.

Captain Charles Edgar Holton Smith

Charles Edgar Smith was born on the 5th June, 1884 at Banbridge, Co. Down and was the eldest son of Charles and Ellen Smith. Charles Smith was an engineer and the couple were married at Hackney in 1881. The bride, nee Holton was the sister of Richard Holton who was a medical Practitioner at

Hednesford and who conducted many medical examinations on soldiers who volunteered for the Army. Charles as an engineer, worked for a time in Germany and whilst there, Charles Edgar was educated at the Moravian School on the Rhine, before returning to England to attend Chigwell School in Essex. Here he won colours for football, with an assessment of his skills noting that he had "hardly been a success at half back, rather rough in his methods and careless to where he places the ball. Works hard but is too impetuous and he does not exercise judgement". He also won prizes for running, finishing second to Hewett in both the three miles road race and the mile open. Charles Edgar was also a noted swimmer and won prizes for his efforts. His brother, Peter de Safforie Smith also attended the school and captained the football team, before marrying Eleanor Holton, the daughter of Richard Holton on the 4th November, 1914 at Hednesford. Charles Edgar went on to Aberdeen University from Chigwell, where he too qualified as a doctor. He was the Second Surgeon at the British Red Cross Hospital at Tripoli during the Italo-Turkish War. In 1912, Charles Edgar married Ethel Bertha Terry at Cheltenham and the couple moved to High Green, Cannock in 1913, where Charles Edgar had set up a General Practice. The couple had two children, and the practice was proving a success, but on the outbreak of the Great War, Charles Edgar volunteered for service in the Royal Army Medical Corps. He was sent along with 24 other doctors to Serbia for six months before returning briefly to England. He was then posted to France and promoted to the rank of Captain. However, on the 16th September, 1916 Charles Edgar was one of four people killed by a stray shell as he was making his way to the trenches. Charles Edgar was 32 at the time of his death, and his body was buried at Adanac Military Cemetery, Miraumont, on the Somme in France. Chigwell School mourned at the news of his passing. His son Charles Warwick Bowman Smith R.N. was killed in action on the 5th March, 1942.

Private Charles Edward Smith
G/6073

In early 1896 at Burton-on-Trent, Frank Smith from Edingale married Elizabeth Thorpe from Haunton. Frank was a boiler stoker and by 1901 the couple had moved to Shuttington, living at 36 Alvecote Buildings. In the five years since their marriage they had had three children, Charles, Frank and Elsie, all born at Burton. Ten years later the family, now numbering six children, Gladys, Cyril and Harold having been born, had just moved to Stafford Road, Cannock. Frank senior had found work again as a boiler stoker, this time at Littleton Colliery, whilst Charles was a 13 year old coal screener at the same pit, later becoming a miner. When the Great

War broke out, Charles decided to enlist and was posted to the 9th Battalion, Royal Sussex Regiment, being sent to France on the 31st August, 1915. Charles was badly wounded on the 1st June, 1916 and died a few hours later, at the age of 18. His body was buried at Bailleul Communal Cemetery Extension (Nord). After the war his grieving parents returned the medals to which their son had been entitled to the War Office. In 1923, Mrs. Smith requested that the medals be sent again to their home at 186, Stafford Road, Cannock.

Private Percy Shorter
G/63039

Joseph Shorter, a coal miner from Cannock married Martha Ann Haddaway from Shropshire at Cannock in 1894. Their first son, Joseph was born in Shropshire, but the couples' second son Percy was born at Cannock in 1898. The family were living on the Hednesford Road, Cannock in 1901, but by 1911, they had moved to Huntington Terrace. A further two boys had been born in the meantime, Leonard and John, with Martha's brother Abner also living with them. Percy soon followed his father and brother down the pit, working for the West Cannock Colliery Company. Percy was called up in April 1918, joining the North Staffordshire Regiment, before being posted to the 7th Battalion, Middlesex Regiment, the Duke of Cambridge's Own. Percy was sent to France in August 1918, and just one month later was badly injured, dying from his wounds on the 8th September, 1918 at the age of 20. His body was buried at Peronne Communal Cemetery Extension in France.

Private Leonard Sheldon
42179

In 1876, John Sheldon, an agricultural labourer from Church Eaton, married Mary Ann Eggington at Wolverhampton. In 1881, they were living at Railway Street, Cannock and had three children, William, Elizabeth and George. However, by 1891 there were clear problems with the marriage. John, now a miner, was living at Stoneyfields, Cannock with William, George, Alfred and Leonard, whereas Mary Ann was living at 1, Cox Street, Birmingham with Elizabeth, Albert and Florrie who was only 8 months old and who was born in Warwick. John died in 1895 at Cannock, which prompted a move back to the town for the rest of the Sheldons. In 1898, Mary Ann married Henry Dean, a miner from Norton Canes, and they set up home at 33, Stoney Lea Road with William, now a miner, Leonard unemployed and Albert at school. Fred meanwhile, aged 19, was working as a farm labourer at Hatherton Farm. By 1911, Fred had joined his brothers at Stoney Lea Road, and was a miner, as was Albert, but Leonard had become an edge tool polisher at Cornelius Whitehouse and Sons, Bridgtown. Leonard attested for the Army under the Derby Scheme on the 27th February, 1916 and was put on the reserve list until required. He was mobilized on the 15th April, 1918 at Walsall, posted to the 3rd Battalion, North Staffordshire Regiment, before joining the 8th Battalion in France on the 13th August. On the 24th August, Leonard was compulsorily transferred to the 7th Battalion, Norfolk Regiment. On the 18th September, 1918 Leonard was killed in action, aged 33 at the Battle of Epehy. His body was buried at Epehy Wood Farm Cemetery, Epehy, near Peronne in France.

Sapper Frederick Sheldon
96836

Fred Sheldon was the older brother of Leonard and was born at Cannock in 1883. Having experienced life as a labourer at Hatherton Farm, he decided to follow his step-father and older brother and worked as a miner. During the Great War, Fred joined up in 1915, electing to serve in the 178th Tunnelling Company, Royal Engineers, being sent to France on the 25th August, 1915. At the age of 36, Fred died at Chatham on the 3rd June 1918, being buried at Fort Pitt Military Cemetery, Chatham.

Private Edward Arthur Smith
16242

Edward Smith was born at Newcastle-under-Lyme in 1898, his mother being Ellen Smith who had been born at Shepreth, Cambridgeshire, and who had been a servant for Colonel Arthur Haig in London. She had returned to Staffordshire for the birth of her child, staying with her parents, Frederick and Mary Smith, who were living at 5 Webster Street, Newcastle-under-Lyme. In early 1900, Ellen married Myles Boon, a locally born coal miner at Wolstanton, and by 1901 they were living at 26 Allen Street, Stoke-on-Trent, with Edward, recorded on the census under the surname Boon, and their five month old second son, John. It would then appear that some sort of family disagreement must have occurred, for Edward was brought up by his grandparents in Newcastle, under the surname Smith, whilst the Boon family moved to Hednesford in 1908, living on Wood Lane, before moving to 99, Old Fallow, Cannock. Edward was brought up as a Roman Catholic and was a member of the Roman Catholic Boy's Brigade where he played the bugle. At some point before the outbreak of the Great War, Edward moved to Cannock and lived in his mother's house, taking a job as a waggoner, but on the 14th August, 1914 Edward enlisted with the 3rd Battalion, North Staffordshire Regiment, before being transferred to the West Riding Regiment, serving with both the 2nd and 3rd Battalions. Edward was badly wounded on the 12th June, 1915 with gunshot wounds to his abdomen and back, being admitted to the 14th Field Ambulance on the 13th. From there he was taken to 13 General Hospital, Boulogne where he died from his wounds on the 24th June at the age of 19. His body was buried at Boulogne Eastern Cemetery and a requiem mass was held at Cannock. Interestingly, the death notice was sent to his grandparents and they also received the pension paid by the Army. In 1921 his grandfather Frederick Smith was informed that the money from Edward's will would be paid to his mother, along with the war medals. Following a letter from Mrs. Boon in 1922, the Plaque and Scroll were also sent to her. Yet the dead soldier's effects had been returned to his grandparents in October, 1915.

Private Harry Smallwood
16428

Henry Smallwood was born at Chatwell in Shropshire in 1848 and married Mary Titley at Shifnal in 1870, she hailing from Cannock. By 1871 they had moved back to Railway Street in her home town and in 1871, a son Thomas was born, followed two years later by a second son, Harry. Henry was a colliery banksman, but by 1911, he had become a labourer at a colliery, as had Harry, whilst Thomas was a colliery clerk. In October, 1914, Harry volunteered for service with the 2nd Battalion, South Staffordshire Regiment, being sent to the Dardanelles on the 11th April, 1915. He was invalided home from Gallipoli after contracting dysentery, receiving treatment initially at Alexandria. Harry was treated at Leeds and was then sent to Newcastle before being returned back to his unit, now on the Western Front. Harry was badly wounded on the Somme and died at a Casualty Clearing Station from these injuries on the 2nd August, 1916, aged 33. His body was buried at La Neuville British Cemetery, Corbie in France.

Stoker First Class Roland Smalley
K/19401

Roland Smalley was born at Alrewas in 1895, the son of Harry and Florence Smalley. The couple did not marry until 1898 at Aston in Birmingham, and by 1901 they had set up a bakers and confectionery at North Street in Bridgtown, where another child, Constance was born in 1900. It would appear that Roland was brought up by his grandparents, Joseph and Elizabeth Smalley, who also had a bakers and confectionery business on the Stafford Road in Cannock. In 1911, Harry had moved back with his parents, along with Roland, now a 16 year old errand boy in the business. Florence meanwhile, had set up a costumiery, with her sister Ida Sambrook on Somerset Road in Handsworth. Roland had been educated at the National School on the Penkridge Road and he was also a member of the Parish Church Choir. In 1913, at the age of 18, Roland decided to join the Royal Navy, serving first of all on HMS Victory at Portsmouth and then on HMS Black Prince, where he was attached to the Warrant Officer's Mess. He had not found life on the Black Prince to his liking and served two spells in the cells. On the 31st May, 1916 the Black Prince was sunk during the Battle of Jutland and the 21 year old Roland was one of the many young men who lost their lives on the vessel. He is remembered on the Portsmouth Naval Memorial.

Sapper William Spooner
112505

William Spooner was the third son of Benjamin and Maria Spooner. Benjamin came from Wednesbury, but his wife was born at Hednesford and the couple were lodging with the Ray family at John Street, Chadsmoor in 1881, where William's eldest brother, John Thomas had joined his father as a miner. By 1891, John Thomas had married and both William and his brother James had also gone down the pit. In 1895 at Cannock, William married Jane Barratt, and by 1901, they were living on the Cannock Road at Chadsmoor, and Jane had given birth to their first child, also named William after his father. William was still a coal miner, and his wife was a draper, suggesting smart business acumen. Yet by 1911, there had been a complete change of direction for William and his wife. He was now a licensed victualler in charge of the Roebuck Inn, 54, Stafford Road, Cannock where he was helped by Jane and her sister-in-law Katie Spooner. William's brother, John Thomas was now the Relieving Officer at the Cannock Union Workhouse on Wolverhampton Road. In

August 1915, William decided to enlist in the Army, despite at the age of 45, being over the maximum age for joining up. He was posted to the 177th Tunnelling Company, Royal Engineers and was sent to France. William was wounded in 1916, being sent back to a Base Hospital for treatment before rejoining his unit. On the 28th April, 1915 William Spooner relieved Sapper Jarvis of Station Road, Hednesford. Jarvis had only moved a few hundred yards away when a shell landed where he had just left. The shell blew the 46 year old Spooner to bits. His widow and three children received this news in a letter written by Jarvis, although the eldest child was serving in the Staffordshire Yeomanry. William Spooner's remains were buried at the Royal Engineer's Grave, Railway Wood, just outside Ieper in Belgium. There are only twelve soldiers remembered on the Cross of Sacrifice.

Sapper James Stringer
488101

James Stringer was born at Norton Canes in 1885, and was the third son of James and Maria Stringer. His father was a coal miner born at Walsall, whereas his mother came from Dawley in Shropshire. In 1891, the family of seven children were living at Jackson's Buildings on the Watling Street at Norton Canes. James senior died in 1900, and his son James was now working as a horse driver down the pit. In 1906, at Walsall, James married Amy Doody, a girl from Walsall Wood, with the couple soon moving to live at 14, Old Penkridge Road, Cannock, where their first child Florence Amy was born in 1910. The family then moved to 54, Paddy's Lane, Cannock where they celebrated the birth of a second child, James T. Stringer in 1912. On the 6th September, 1914, James enlisted in the Army, joining the 466th Field Company, Royal Engineers. James was sent to France on the 1st March, 1915 and had served for three years when he was taken ill with double pneumonia, dying on the 23rd March, 1918, at the age of 33. His body was buried at Lapugnoy Military Cemetery, near Bethune in France. It is interesting to note that James had four brothers who all served in the same Company of Royal Engineers.

Private Frederick Hyde Sutton
G/63045

In 1892, at Stoke-on-Trent, Nathan Sutton married Mary Jane Shore. The groom came from Cannock whereas his bride was born at Bradeley. The couple lived in the Potteries and in 1894 their first child, Susan was born at Shelton. However, within a couple of years, the family had moved to Cannock where Nathan managed to get a job as an edge tool handler at Messrs Whitehouse at Bridgtown. Meanwhile Thomas had been born in 1896, Frederick in 1899 and Nathan junior in 1904. By 1911, Susan was a tailoress and Thomas a Motor Driver in a colliery, with Frederick and Nathan at school. Frederick finally followed his father and worked at Whitehouse Brothers Edge Tool Works in Bridgtown. Frederick was conscripted into the Army in April 1918, initially with the North Staffordshire Regiment, but later being transferred to the Middlesex Regiment, the 7th Battalion, the London Regiment. Frederick was sent to France in August 1918, and was posted as missing in action on the 9th September 1918, at the age of 19. It was later presumed that Frederick had died on this date, and as his body was never found, he is remembered on the Vis-en-Artois Memorial to the Missing in France.

2nd Lieutenant Joseph Smith

Joseph Smith was born at Essington in 1895, being the third son of Joseph and Sarah Jane Smith. Joseph senior hailed from Wednesbury and Sarah Jane came from Uttoxeter, and all told the couple had eight children. Joseph Smith senior appears to have been an interesting character, being described as living on his own means in 1891, working as a coal loader on the pit surface in 1901 and employed as a colliery clerk in 1911. He was also a local councillor for Essington, where the family lived for over 30 years. Indeed, the Smith family made a living from Holly Bank Colliery with William, Harold and Joseph junior also employed as colliery clerks. With the outbreak of the Great War, Joseph Smith enlisted straight away, joining the South Staffordshire Regiment and being wounded on the 13th October, 1915, before accepting a commission in December, 1916. He was transferred from the 6th Battalion to the 1/5th Battalion, and on the 14th March, 1917, at the age of 21 Joseph was killed in action. Lt. Colonel J. M. Llewellyn wrote to his mother at 86, High Green to tell her that her son had "met his death at the head of his men, with fearless determination" and that his body had been recovered and buried with full military honours. Joseph's body was buried at Foncquevillers Military Cemetery, near Arras in France. Joseph's elder brother George P. Smith also served in the Great War in the Royal Marines.

Lance Corporal Henry Oliver Sansome M.M.
40081

In 1889, at Dudley Frank Sansome the 23 year old second son of a police sergeant hailing from Nottingham, married Elizabeth Dainty Mantle, a 19 year old spinster from Dudley. In 1891 the couple were living at 23 Vicar Street, Dudley with their new baby boy, William. Henry was born in 1892, and life seemed to be going well for the Sansome family with Frank working as a carter. However, in early 1900, Frank died at the age of 34, and a year later his widow was living at 10, Bond Street, Dudley with Henry and Edward Joseph McGuire, a 37 year old mineral water carter from Wednesbury and Sidney Briggs, aged 23 who was employed at the same firm as McGuire and who was originally from Ipswich. In the summer of 1901, Elizabeth married Edward McGuire, again at Dudley. William Sansome at this time was recovering at Oldwinsford Hospital and Sanitorium. By 1903 the family had moved to 66, St. John's Road, Cannock, and by 1911, William was a horse driver in a local colliery, whilst Henry was employed as a miner endless rope worker. In January 1916, Henry enlisted with the South Staffordshire Regiment, being sent to France in August of the same year. He was then transferred to the 4th Battalion, Worcestershire Regiment, and it was after this that Henry was invalided to St. Alban's Military Hospital with an illness. On recovery he was sent back to his unit in France, and then he was awarded the Military Medal for rescuing a wounded comrade from No Man's Land, whilst under fire. On the 15th June, 1918, Henry was badly wounded and died from his wounds at the age of 27. In a letter to his mother, Lieutenant E.W. Booth spoke of her son's bravery. Henry's body was not recovered after the war and he is remembered on the Ploegsteert Memorial to the Missing, near Ieper in Belgium.

Private John Sherratt
20798

According to the 1911 census, John Sherratt was born at Brindley Heath in 1895, the second son of Enoch Sherratt, a coal miner from Silverdale and his wife Sophia who was born at Shilton. The family had lived in the Potteries for some years as Emma and Enoch were born there, and the couple had married there in 1887, but by 1895 they had moved to Arthur Street, Chadsmoor. The family also lived in Wimblebury and finally settled at 99, Blackfords, Cannock and by 1911 had grown to eleven children, the youngest of which, Winifred was born in 1909. John became a miner, working at Littleton Colliery, but on the 8th January, 1915, he volunteered for the Army, joining the 2nd Battalion, Royal Welsh Fusiliers. He was stationed at Wrexham and Llandudno before being sent to Egypt. On the 21st April, 1916, John died of an infectious disease in hospital at Cairo, at the age of 21. His body was buried at Cairo War Memorial Cemetery.

Private John Horace Spencer
78370

In 1882 at Tamworth, Thomas Spencer married Emily Worwood, he being a 20 year old coal miner from Weeford and his wife, also 20, a shepherd's daughter from Bentley, Warwickshire. The couple had nine children in total, but three died in childhood, including their eldest son Thomas Henry. John Horace Spencer was born at Whateley, Warwickshire in 1899, and was the couples' only son. In 1901 the Spencers were living at Sunny Side, Kingsbury where Thomas was employed as a coal miner, but in 1911, they had moved to Burntwood Road, Norton Canes, where Thomas was a colliery labourer and John was at school. John enlisted in the Army in 1917, joining the 19th Battalion, Durham Light Infantry, and was sent to France being wounded twice whilst serving. He had also been twice absent without leave in 1917. His parents had moved by this time to 71, Cannock Road, Blackfords and it was here that a letter was sent by Lieutenant Cunliffe, telling Thomas and Emily that their only son had been killed in action on the 14th October, 1918. "We had practically gained our objective when your son fell, victim of a German sniper. His death was instantaneous and he is buried in a village. He was always cheery." The 19 year old John Horace Spencer was buried at Dadizeele New British Cemetery, near Ieper in Belgium.

Leading Signalman John Snell
219213

John Snell was born at Bloxwich in 1886, the eldest son of John H Snell a painter from Bloxwich and his wife, Mary who came from Darlaston. The family of five lived at Stafford Street, Walsall. John was educated in the town, attending Blue Coats School. By 1901, the family was still living at Stafford Street and John had become a pit labourer, although he then joined John Boys and Sons on the Pleck Road in the town. At the age of 18, John decided to join the Royal Navy, and was serving abroad in 1911 on HMS King Alfred. Whilst on leave in 1915, John married Elizabeth Armishaw at Cannock, and the couple set up a home at Stoneyfields in the town. Meanwhile, John returned to his ship and was taken ill whilst the ship was docked in Sierra Leone, dying on the 11th January, 1917 from appendicitis. His body was buried but was later deemed to be unattainable, and hence, he is remembered on the Freetown (King Tom) Cemetery Memorial. At the time of his death, John was 30 years of age.

Private Alfred John Titley
29211

Alfred Titley was born in 1895 in either Wheaton Aston or Lapley in Staffordshire. His father Arthur Titley was a farm labourer from nearby Blymhill, whereas his mother Lucy hailed from Bishop's Wood in Staffordshire. He had a sister, Bertha, born in 1893 and a brother, Christopher born in 1894. In 1901, the family lived on the High Street in Lapley. Ten years later, Arthur had now become a bricklayer's labourer living at The Pavement in Brewood, with Lucy, Bertha and his 78 year old mother Sarah. Christopher was working as a farm labourer in Wheaton Aston for the Trevitt sisters, whilst Alfred was living with Frederick Holland and his housekeeper at The Hawthorn, Wheaton Aston. Both Alfred and Alfred Knowles were butcher's apprentices. Alfred was also a well known and successful cyclist. Before the Great War, Alfred moved to Cannock to work as a butcher for Harry Lloyd at Blackfords, living at New Street in Cannock. In 1916, Alfred decided to enlist, joining the Army Service Corps, but later transferring to the 7th Battalion, East Yorkshire Regiment. On the 27th March, 1918, Alfred was badly wounded and was taken to a Casualty Clearing Station for treatment but did not recover and died on the 1st April, 1918 at the age of 24. His body was buried at Doullens Communal Cemetery Extension Number 1, in France.

Private Ernest Samuel Tomlinson
14517

Ernest Tomlinson was born at Cannock in 1892, the eldest child of Samuel and Florence Tomlinson. Samuel was born at Cannock and his wife at Wolverhampton, with the family settling in Cannock on the Stafford Road. Samuel worked as an auger polisher at Gilpin's, Churchbridge. Florence died in 1903, and four years later in 1907, Samuel married Jane Dawson, the widow of William Dawson the publican of the White Hart Inn. The couple continued to run the pub with the help of Jane's daughter Edith Dawson and Samuel's daughter May Tomlinson. Yet Samuel continued to work at Gilpin's and was joined there by his step son Albert Dawson, with Ernest choosing to work as an iron moulder at a foundry, but later joining his father and step-brother at Gilpin's. Ernest was a skilled footballer, playing for Cannock Town, Hednesford Town and Blackfords. He was also a member of the Church Choir. In September, 1914 Ernest joined up, choosing to serve in the 9th Battalion, Royal Welsh Fusiliers, and being sent to France on the 5th September, 1915. This was the last his family saw of him, as he received no leave and on the 25th July, 1916 he was killed by a shell, whilst in the reserve line, aged 25. The same shell killed two other soldiers, one of them being Isaiah Jones of Hednesford. The three of them were all part of the same machine gun team. In a letter written to Ernest's parents, Lieutenant Broomhall described Ernest as "brave, one of the best". Ernest's body was not recovered after the war and he is remembered on the Thiepval Memorial to the Missing on the Somme in France.

Private John Turnock
13087

John Turnock was born at Cannock in 1897, and on the 1901 census was living on the Stafford Road, Cannock with his aunt Annie Turnock and his brother Thomas and sister, Evelyn. It would appear that his mother, Catherine Turnock, was living in the same house, having married Samuel Wall in 1901. Interestingly she gives her place of birth as Tredegar, Glamorganshire. In 1911, the family had moved to 518, Longford Lane, Cannock. Samuel Wall was a miner and Thomas worked as his loader. John was also down the pit, working as a motor driver and later as a miner at the Mid Cannock Colliery. In the meantime, Samuel and Catherine had had five children of their own. John enlisted in 1914, joining the 7th Battalion, Ox and Bucks Light Infantry and being sent to France on the 21st September, 1915 but the Battalion was posted to Salonika in November 1915, and John was trained as a sniper. On the 9th May, 1917 during fierce fighting, John rescued an officer who was wounded and rolling towards a precipice. On returning to the assault, John was killed at the age of 20. His body was not recovered after the war and he is remembered on the Doiran Memorial in Greece.

Private Daniel Turner
20821

Daniel Turner, born at Walsall Wood in 1896, was the third son of William and Jane Turner. The couple had ten children in all, five boys and five girls, with all of them born in Walsall Wood, with the one exception of Charles, the eldest, who was born at Rushall. William was a coal miner, and in 1901 the family were living at Hall Lane in Walsall Wood, with the eldest sons, Charles and William being employed as colliery labourers. In 1911, William senior described himself as a licensed victualler and coal miner, whilst Daniel was a colliery labourer above ground. The family were running the Royal Oak Inn, on Green Lane, Walsall Wood. By the outbreak of war, Daniel had moved to Cannock, living at 123, Newhall Street, and working at Littleton Colliery. He enlisted in the Army in January 1915, joining the 14th Battalion, Royal Welsh Fusiliers, and being sent to France on the 2nd December, 1915. On the 6th October, 1918, Daniel died from wounds at the age of only 22. His body was not recovered after the war and he is remembered on the Vis-en-Artois Memorial to the Missing in France. Daniel's younger brother also served during the war seeing action in Mesopotamia.

Telegraphist William Henry Toms
Bristol Z/3366

William Toms was born at Merthyr Tydfil in South Wales on the 25th October, 1895, being the youngest of three children born to John and Sarah Ann Toms. The family were living in Wales at the time, but they originated from Cannock. Indeed, Elizabeth and Percy, the other children were born at Cannock. By 1901, the family had returned to their home town and were living on the Old Penkridge Road, with John working as a miner. The family were devastated by the death of Percy in 1910 at the age of 21, but a year later, Elizabeth married Arthur Barker, a 24 year old miner on the 9th May. The two were near neighbours, as the Toms family had moved to Paddy's Lane in Cannock. On the 12th November, 1915, just after his 20th birthday, William joined the Royal Naval Volunteer Reserve, serving as a telegraphist on HMS Victory. He was invalided out of the service on the 8th March, 1917 with pulmonary tuberculosis and remained at home until his death on the 26th July, 1918. He was described as studious and hard working and he was buried at Cannock Cemetery with full military honours.

Private William Vernon
12061

William Vernon was born at Chadsmoor in 1887, being the second son of William and Mary Vernon. His father was a miner from Gnosall and his mother came from Burslem, and indeed that was where the family lived until 1885, when they moved to Huntington Terrace in Chadsmoor. By 1901, John the eldest had become a labourer down the pit and Catherine the eldest girl was an assistant dressmaker. Ten years later, the family had moved to Allport Road, Cannock, and William and Charles had followed their father and brother down Littleton Colliery. Life must have been lively in the Vernon household at this time as there were six Vernons, two adopted children and four lodgers, three of whom were part of a travelling circus. William was also a member of the Sacred Heart Church Choir and was the cross bearer at St. Mary's school. In 1914, William volunteered shortly after the outbreak of war. He joined the 8th Battalion, South Staffordshire Regiment and was sent to France on the 1st August, 1915. When on leave in late 1915, William married Emma Jarman at Tavistock in Devon, a child Leslie, being born early in 1916. William was badly wounded on the 30th, December, 1916, being taken back to a Base Hospital at Rouen. A letter to this effect was received by his wife, followed by one a week later saying his condition was improving, but on the following Monday a telegram said that William had relapsed and died on the 7th February, 1917, aged 33, leaving behind a widow and one child. William's body was buried at St. Sever Cemetery Extension in Rouen, France.

Private Thomas Bradley Williams
300719

Thomas Williams provides a little mystery when trying to find his ancestors. He was born at Cannock in 1899, and his father was James Williams, a labourer on the surface of a coal mine. In 1901, he was living with his father in his grandparents' house on the Old Penkridge Road. Thomas and Isabella Williams had eight children also living with them, ranging in age from 23 to 1. By 1911, James and Thomas were boarding with Joseph and Mary Ann Pearce at 37, Mill Street, Cannock. James was now a grocer's coachman and Thomas is described as being at school in the high grade, suggesting ability above the average. There is no mention of a mother, however, and yet the Commonwealth War Graves Commission gives

James and Emma Williams as Thomas' step parents, and their address as 195, St. John's Road, Cannock. Despite academic promise the harsh realities of life meant that Thomas found his way down Littleton Colliery as a miner, before in 1915, at the age of only 16, volunteering for the Army. He joined the Staffordshire Yeomanry, before transferring to the Queen's Own Royal Regiment of Cavalry, and was sent to Egypt on the 10th November, 1915. Thomas was described as a bright intelligent trooper who was very popular with his comrades. At the age of just 19, Thomas was killed in action in Palestine on the 1st May, 1918. His body was never recovered and he is remembered on the Jerusalem Memorial in Israel.

Private William Williams
31633

William Williams was born at Bridgtown in 1890 being the eldest son of Elijah and Sarah Ann Williams. Elijah was from Broseley in Shropshire and his wife came from Cheslyn Hay. The couple set up home at Cross Street, Bridgtown where Elijah was employed as a brick burner, but by 1901 they were living at the Walk Mill Tile Works, where Elijah was the foreman. The family now consisted of six children and by 1911 this had increased to nine, with their married daughter Miriam, her husband Harold Sneyd together with their new baby boy, as well as a niece and a nephew all living together at 102, Watling Street, Bridgtown. The four sons William, Elijah, Frederick and Ernest all followed after their father and worked at the tilery. William married Annie Clarke at Cannock in 1913. A son, William B Williams was born in 1914. In August, 1916 William joined the Army electing to serve in the 7th Battalion, South Staffordshire Regiment and being sent out to France after very little training. He served through heavy fighting at Ieper and on the Somme. He was very badly wounded on the Somme and died from these injuries before he could be sent to hospital on the 15th October, 1918. William was aged 29 at the time of his death and his body was buried at Duisans British Cemetery, Etrun near Arras in France.

Sergeant John Ernest Williams
18036

John Williams was born at Leominster in 1876 and was married to Charlotte. In 1901, the couple were living at 10, Guildford Street in Leominster and he was a market gardener. Ten years later the couple had moved to Stretton Sugwas near

Hereford and John was now working as a domestic gardener and they now had four children. At what point the family moved to the Cannock area is not known. John joined the 8th Battalion, South Staffordshire Regiment and rose to the rank of Sergeant before he was wounded and died from his injuries on the 6th February, 1918 at the age of 42. His body was buried at Rocquigny-Equancourt Road British Cemetery, Manancourt, on the Somme in France.

Lance Bombardier James Garratt Watson 28691

James G. Watson was born at Cannock in 1887, being the second son of John Barr Watson and his wife Charlotte. The couple married at Woolwich in London in 1871, John was born in Scotland and Charlotte, although a British subject was born in America. John was a station master which meant that the family moved around the country. Their eldest children, John and Rosa were born in Warwickshire, Charlotte and Emily at Pelsall and James and Thomas at Cannock. In 1891, John Barr Watson committed suicide at the age of 44, just four years after he had become station master at Cannock. John Watson junior moved to London where he worked as a viewer of warlike stores, before moving back to Cannock, finding employment as a machinist. James had found work as a fitter at Bumstead and Chandler's iron works at Hednesford, before joining the Army and serving in the Royal Garrison Artillery in India. The Regiment was transferred to France on the 5th March, 1915 and became part of the 59th Siege Battery. James was wounded in April 1918 but recovered from his injuries and returned to his Battery, but on the 1st September, 1918 he was killed in action at the age of 32. An officer wrote of his "unfailing devotion to duty and the valuable service Bombardier Watson had always rendered". James was buried at Tigris Lane Cemetery, Wancourt near Arras in France.

Private William John Weaver 19745

Jack Weaver was born at Tinsley, Lancashire in 1879, being the eldest child of Joseph and Eliza Weaver. Joseph was born at Hanley, his wife coming from Shipton in Gloucestershire. Joseph was a horse keeper and carter and while the couple had spent some time in Lancashire, they had moved to Cannock by 1901 when they were living on St. Luke's Road. At this time Jack was working as a coal horse minder, and was also a member of St. Luke's Brass Band. He had joined the local Ambulance Corps under Dr. J.D. Butter. In 1902, Jack married Minnie Lavinia Thompson, a Rugeley girl, and the couple set up their first home in Cemetery Road, Cannock. By this time Jack had become a miner at Littleton Colliery. They had two children, May born in 1903 and Frank born in 1906. The family then moved to live at 137, Pye Green Road. Jack volunteered for the Army in December, 1914 enlisting in the 1st Battalion, Royal Welsh Fusiliers. His unit was posted to France on the 29th June, 1916, before being transferred to the Italian Front. On the 11th June, 1918 Jack died in hospital at Genoa from double pneumonia, aged 39. His body was buried at Staglieno Cemetery in Genoa.

Private Vincent Royden Witts
2706

Vincent Witts was born at Cannock in 1897, and was brought up by his grandparents John and Agnes Yates, who lived at 16, Old Penkridge Road. John Yates was a coal miner from Cheslyn Hay and they had four children of their own. John was still working down the pit in 1911 at the age of 60, when Vincent had just left school at the age of 13. He found employment as a draper, working for FWS Cope at Cannock, but in 1914, soon after the outbreak of war, Vincent enlisted. He joined the Non Manual Battalion, South Staffordshire Regiment, before transferring to the 1/6th Battalion. On the 1st July 1916, Vincent was posted as missing in action during the attack on Gommecourt. It was later assumed that he had been killed in action on that day. Vincent was only 18 at the time of his death, and had only been 16 when he enlisted. Vincent's body was never recovered and he is remembered on the Thiepval Memorial to the Missing on the Somme in France.

2nd Lieutenant John Daniel Williamson

In 1895 at St. Luke's Parish Church, Cannock, a society wedding took place between John Thomas Williamson a 40 year old mining engineer from Eastwood in Nottinghamshire and Margaret Jane McDowell, aged 34 and who was born in Kingston, Jamaica. The couple lived on the Penkridge Road in Cannock, and their first child, Isabelle was born in 1896, followed a year later by their first son, John Daniel. Robert was born in 1899, William in 1902 and finally, Grace in 1904. John was educated at Rugeley Grammar School and Solihull College where he joined the Officer's Training Corps. He was commissioned into the 1st Battalion, South Staffordshire Regiment as a 2nd Lieutenant, before being attached to the 4th Battalion on Thursday June 8th 1916. John was involved in the advance on Mametz Wood between the 1st and 5th July and on the 14th July, he led his men in an attack on High Wood. He was wounded in the hand but pushed on with his men, until he received a second more serious wound to the neck. John was carried back to the British lines by a wounded soldier, but died. The 19 year old was buried behind the lines but his body was not identified after the war and John is remembered on the Thiepval Memorial to the Missing on the Somme in France.

Gunner Herbert Walker
83860

Herbert Walker was born at Cannock in 1897, being the second child of Thomas and Sarah Ann Walker. Thomas was a coal miner born at Chadsmoor, whereas Sarah Ann was born at Burntwood. The couple were married at Cannock in 1893, with their first child Annie being born a year later. The couple's third child, Gladys May being born in 1904. The family set up residence at Broomhill, before moving to Spring Street around the outbreak of the Great War. Herbert found employment as a baker working at Taylor's bakery in Cannock, although as a youth he had found work as a bat picker on a colliery bank. On the 4th February, 1916 Herbert enlisted in the Royal Garrison Artillery, serving in the 181st Siege Battery. He was mobilized on 20th May and was sent to France on the 13th October, 1916. He was admitted to hospital on the 7th February, 1917 but was discharged and rejoined his unit after three days. However, on the 18th June, 1917 Herbert was digging a new gun position when shrapnel from a bursting shell hit him in the head. Herbert was taken to 10 Casualty Clearing Station but died later that same day. The 20 year olds' body was buried at Lijssenthoek Military Cemetery near Ieper in Belgium. His effects were listed as a pocket book, a letter, a card, a note book and two tins. The tins never made it back to his grieving family at 23, Spring Street, Cannock.

Corporal James Frederick Walker
20599

James Walker was born at Cannock in 1893, being the third son of Samuel and Annie Walker. The Walker family lived at Broomhill in Cannock for over forty years and during that time Annie gave birth to fifteen children, six of whom died. In 1901, there were only four children still living at home, Samuel junior, who like his father was a miner, John, James and Florrie. By 1911, John had moved to live a few doors away, Samuel had just got married and Florrie had married in 1908. James was a horse driver down the pit, and later became a coal miner. On the 28th February, 1914 James married Alice Ingram at St. Luke's Parish Church at Cannock. Her father, George Ingram was the sexton at the cemetery. The couple had one child, Frances, born in 1915. By this time, James was in the Army, having volunteered earlier in that year, serving with the 8th Battalion, Northumberland Fusiliers. He was posted initially to the Dardanelles on the 10th November, 1915, but after evacuation his Battalion was sent to France. James was mentioned in despatches and was also promoted to full corporal, being very popular with the Battalion. The 24 year old was killed in action on the 14th June, 1917 and as his body was never recovered after the war, he is remembered on the Ieper (Menin Gate) memorial to the Missing in Ieper city centre.

Private Philip Herbert Windsor
42309

Bert Windsor was born at Uttoxeter in late 1898, and was the second son of Alfred and Elizabeth Windsor. His father was a baker from Shifnal in Shropshire and his mother also came from Shropshire. In 1901, the family of four children were living at Eaton Terrace, Uttoxeter, but shortly afterwards moved to Cannock. In early 1902, Elizabeth died at the young age of 36, and her husband remarried in 1907, when at Newcastle-under-Lyme, Mary Ann Coombs became his second wife. The family continued to live in Cannock and in 1911 Alfred is described as a baker and confectioner journeyman. The eldest son Thomas was a blacksmith at a local colliery, whilst Bert was still at school. Due to his age, Bert was not called up until 1917 and was first posted to the North Staffordshire Regiment, before being transferred to the 1/23rd Battalion, East Surrey Regiment. At the age of 20, on the 18th December, 1918, Bert died in a hospital in France. His body was buried at St. Pol British Cemetery, St. Pol-sur-Ternoise, near Arras in France.

Private Joseph Harold Yates
202773

Joseph Yates was born at Cannock in early 1895, and was the youngest of five children born to Joseph and Alice Yates. Joseph senior was born at Cheslyn Hay and was a coal miner and later a roadman in a colliery. Alice and all of the children were born at Cannock, and the family lived on the Walsall Road in Cannock, before moving to 42, Newhall Street. The eldest child, Beatrice married Joseph Nourse at St. Luke's on the 2nd September, 1907, whilst James the eldest son had married Sarah Elizabeth Bradbury at Cannock the previous year. In 1911, only Charles, a bricklayer, Francis, a motor mechanic and Joseph, a boot repairer were living at home. Joseph worked for Bradbury's at Cannock and also for Whitehouse at Bridgtown. Joseph joined the Army on the 6th November, 1916, electing to enlist with the 2/5th Battalion, South Staffordshire Regiment and served in France. He was killed in action on the 22nd April, 1917 when hit by a shell with two comrades who were all buried together. This information was passed on to his parents by 2nd Lieutenant G. E. Bradbury, who lived on the Penkridge Road. The 22 year old Joseph was buried at Tincourt New British Cemetery near Peronne in France. Joseph's older brother Francis, served as a sergeant with the Army Service Corps during the war. Joseph was a former choir boy at St. Luke's Parish Church, Cannock.

Private William Young
15246

William Young was born at Cannock in 1884, and was the third son of George and Mary Ann Young, both of whom were born at Wolverhampton. The couple had married at Wolverhampton in 1871, but by 1879, they had moved to Hightown where their first child, Elizabeth was born. Samuel, the eldest boy, was by 1901 a coal miner like his father, whilst George junior, William and Edward were all horse drivers in a colliery. John and Thomas were both still at school at this time. Ten years later, Samuel was a banksman's labourer, whereas William, Edward and Thomas were miner's loaders. George had married Lizzie Williams and had two children of his own and John had also married Dinah Wootton, and she had just given birth to a baby daughter. William had established himself as a sportsman, being a clever footballer at half back for Hednesford Vics, Bridgtown, Hednesford Town and West Bromwich Albion. He was described as having a strong kick, being a smart tackler and a judicious "feeder". William was also a useful batsman playing for Cannock Central Cricket Club. He also gloried in the nickname of "Cree". On the 1st July, 1912, William married Mary Ellen Hickinbotham at St. Luke's Parish Church. The couple had three children, Ernest, born in 1912, Ethel born in 1914 and Dorothy born in 1916. William was now a miner at East Cannock Colliery and the family lived at 520, Stafford Road, Cannock. William enlisted for the Army in November, 1914 joining the

7th Battalion, South Staffordshire Regiment. The Battalion was sent to the Dardanelles on the 3rd October, 1915, and afterwards to Egypt and then to France. William was wounded in action in September, 1916, but was then returned to his unit. On the 6th September, 1917, William was badly wounded in the head by a bullet, but he failed to recover from this injury, dying on the 12th September 1917, at the age of 33. The news was conveyed to his widow on the 27th September. William's body was buried at Tincourt New British Cemetery, near Peronne in France.

Private Alfred Charles Lerew
265696

Alfred Lerew was born at Windsor in Berkshire in 1894, the second son of George and Elizabeth Lerew. George was an auctioneer's clerk from London, whilst Elizabeth was born at Richmond in Surrey. They had an elder son, William, who was employed as a mechanical engineer. The family were living at 1, Rose Place in Slough in 1901. William migrated to the United States, leaving from Glasgow in 1908. By 1911 Alfred was 17 and working as a junior clerk in a surveyor's office, whilst the family had moved to Greville Martin Road in Slough. Just before the outbreak of the Great War, Alfred moved to Cannock to take up a position as a clerk in the surveyor's office. Alfred enlisted on the outbreak of war and joined the 1/1st Battalion, Ox and Bucks Light Infantry. He served under the assumed name of John Lerew, presumably to avoid parental disapproval. He was sent to France on the 30th March, 1915 and served for two years before, on the 18th April 1917, he died from wounds at the age of 22. A letter of condolence was sent by Cannock Urban District Council to his parents and the passing of the young man was noted in the Council Minutes. Alfred's body was buried at Peronne Communal Cemetery Extension in France. Interestingly his 1915 Star was forfeited due to him being charged with fraud on the 21st December, 1915.

Lance Corporal Richard James
488294

Richard James was born at Coven, Staffordshire in 1876. He was the third son of Thomas and Elizabeth James, who were born in Church Eaton and Haughton respectively. The couple were married at Wolverhampton in 1870, and moved to the village of Bradley where Thomas was employed as an agricultural labourer. By

1881, the couple had had four sons, Arthur and Thomas both born at Bradley, with Richard and Freeman born at Coven. Three girls were also born, Mary, Annie and Martha between 1882 and 1892, with all three being born at Bradley. By 1901, Thomas senior was now a farmer, at Grove Farm, Bradley, but it would appear that this life did not appeal to his sons, with only Freeman continuing to work on the farm. Thomas junior was a plate layer on the railway, and Richard had moved to Cannock, where he was lodging with Frederick and Susan Whitehouse at Newhall Street. He was by this time a carpenter, and was employed by Charles Linford. By 1911, only Annie and Martha were left to help run the farm. Richard was now working for Thomas Parker of Cannock, and was boarding with the Bradshaw family, at 42, Spring Street. Richard was a keen supporter of Cannock Town F.C. He joined the Army in 1915, enlisting with the 469th Field Company, Royal Engineers, and was sent to Ireland as part of the force to put down the Rebellion. After this, he was sent to France in January 1917. On the 19th April, 1918 Richard died from wounds at the age of 42. His body was buried at Mendinghem Military Cemetery in Belgium.

Lance Corporal Joseph Walker
15404

Joseph Walker was born at Cannock in 1893, and was the third son of William and Julia Walker. Both were locally born, William from Great Wyrley and his wife from Burntwood, and the couple had married at Cannock in 1888. The couple set up home at West Chadsmoor, where Florence, the first of six children had been born in 1886. By 1901 the family had moved to live on the Old Fallow Road, and ten years later, they had moved again to Victoria Street, Broomhill. William had always been employed as a coal miner, and his sons followed him down the pit, with Thomas and John and Joseph all working below ground. Before the onset of the Great War, the family moved once more to live on the Pye Green Road at number 227. Shortly after the outbreak of war, Joseph enlisted in the 7th Battalion, South Staffordshire Regiment and was sent to the Dardanelles on the 21st July, 1915. He rose to the rank of Corporal, and was a good platoon leader, always looking after his men and being cheerful and of good courage. On the 12th October, 1915 the 21 year old Corporal was killed in action. In a letter to his parents, Private Frank Yardley said that "I am thoroughly convinced that he died like a brave soldier, happy and trustworthy. I have sadly missed his companionship". Joseph's body was not recovered after the war and he is remembered on the Helles Memorial, Gallipoli, Turkey.

Private Alfred James White
38903

Alfred White was born at Longton, Staffordshire in 1886, being the second son of Enoch and Sarah White. Enoch was a coal miner from Pelsall, whilst his wife was born at Fenton, and the couple had married in the Potteries in 1884. Their first child, Percy was born at Longton in 1885. By 1901, the family had increased to eight children, with Percy a miner like his father and Alfred earning a living as a 14 year old brewer's lad. At this time the White family were living at Spring Garden Road in Longton. Just after the birth of their youngest child, James, the family moved to Cannock. On the 1911 census, Enoch and his wife were living at Cedar Cottage, Green Heath, Hednesford, where they had set up a business as licensed hawkers. They still had six children living with them, but Harold had married in 1910, and was living with his wife and two children at Ivy Cottage, Green Heath. Meanwhile on the 26th December, 1908, Alfred had married Louisa Priscilla Parker at St. Luke's Parish Church. The couple moved to 65 Brindley Heath, where a daughter, Margaret was born in 1910, with two other daughters, Lily born in 1914 and Ethel born in 1915, completing the family. Alfred worked as a coal miner but was also a talented artist. He had been awarded a gold medal for helping to rescue a colleague whilst working in the pit. It would appear that Alfred and his family moved to Cannock during this period, and in 1915 he enlisted in the Army, joining the 4th Battalion, South Staffordshire Regiment. He served in France and was badly wounded at Bucquoy, when trying to help a wounded colleague during an attack on Adinfer Wood. Alfred died from his wounds on the 27th March, 1918, aged 31. His body was buried at Caberet-Rouge British Cemetery at Souchez, near Arras in France.

Chapter 3

HEDNESFORD

Driver Frederick Henry Adams
143053

Harry Adams was the eldest of eight children and was born at Hednesford in 1897. His parents were Harry Adams from Wolverhampton and Eva Adams, nee Taylor who were married at Cannock in 1896. The couple lived at 11, Rawnsley Buildings in 1901 and Harry senior earned his living as a boat gauger. By 1911, the family had moved to Guys Buildings at Littleworth and the 14 year old Harry junior was now an errand boy, whereas his father now earned his living as a clerk. Little is known as to when Harry joined the Army. He enlisted with the Royal Field Artillery, before being seconded to the Army Service Corps, serving with the 63rd Divisional Mechanical Transport Company. Just before the Armistice, Harry was badly wounded and died from these injuries on the 11th November, 1918, the day on which the Armistice came into effect. At the time of his death Harry was 21 years of age and his body was buried at Etaples Military Cemetery in France.

Private Walter Allen
40956

Walter Allen was the fourth son of Frederick and Elizabeth Allen. Frederick was born at Church Broughton, Derbyshire in 1842 and his wife came from Rushall and was born in 1855. Frederick was a pork butcher by trade and for a time the couple set up home at Gloucester, where Frank and Harry were born, before moving to Hednesford where Tilley was born. The family then moved to Brook Square, Rugeley where Trevor, Walter and Hugo were born. In 1890, Elizabeth died but within a year

Frederick had married Emma Halls and the family set up their business at Market Street, Hednesford. By 1911, it was clearly a thriving family business, with Frederick and Emma still working, Frank was head shop man, whilst Harry specialised in beef butchery. Trevor was the slaughterman and Walter and Hugo ran the family farm which supplied the meat. Only Tilley had a business interest outside butchery, and she earned her living from dress making. Again, little is known of Walter's involvement in the Great War. He most probably enlisted in 1916, and was sent to France where he served with the 1st Battalion, Royal Dublin Fusiliers. He was killed in action during the Battle of Passchendaele on the 4th October, 1917 at the age of 30. His body was not recovered after the war and Walter is remembered on the Tyne Cot Memorial to the Missing near Ieper in Belgium.

Private Arthur Archer
9560

Arthur Archer was born in late 1895 at Hednesford, being the second child and eldest son of Thomas and Caroline Archer, both of whom were born in the town. The couple had married in 1891. Between the years 1893 and 1915 the couple raised nine children but also knew the heartbreak of losing three other children who all died in infancy. Alice, the eldest daughter was by 1911 working as a servant to Matthew and Mabel Foggo at Chasetown. Matthew Foggo was a colliery manager and he and his wife had married at Birkenhead in 1907. Their first child, John Mowbray Foggo had been born at Hednesford in 1909. Arthur was living with his parents at Cecil Street, Chadsmoor, and like his father was a colliery labourer, Thomas above ground and his son below ground. When the Great War broke out, Arthur was one of the first to enlist, joining the 2nd Battalion, South Staffordshire Regiment. He was sent to France on the 8th February, 1915 and served until the 24th November, 1915 when at the age of 19 he died from wounds suffered in battle. Arthur's body was buried at Chocques Military Cemetery, near Bethune in France.

Sapper Thomas Archer
102066

On the 30th March, 1891, at Hednesford Thomas Archer a miner's labourer married Caroline Garbett. Both were born in the town and they set up a home at Barton's Building, Church Hill, in Hednesford. The couple had nine children who survived infancy, the last of whom, Florence Evelyn May was born on the 21st June, 1915. The couple moved to Cecil Street in Chadsmoor and finally to 82, Brindley Heath at Hednesford. In 1915, a Government plea for miners was answered in most mining areas. The plan was to create a number of Tunnelling Companies to mine under the German trenches. Thomas Archer, giving his age as 40, was one of the first to put forward his name. In fact Thomas was 46 and his eldest son Arthur was already serving in France. He passed his medical at Hednesford, given by Dr. Richard Holton before enlisting at London on the 31st May, 1915. Thomas joined the 171st Tunnelling Company, Royal Engineers and was paid the tunneller's rate of 2 shillings and 2 pence per day. He was sent to France on the 4th June, 1915 and his Army service lasted 16 days before he was killed by shrapnel on the 20th June, 1915. His last child was born the day after his death. There then followed an unseemly exchange of letters and certificates between Caroline Archer and the Pension Office at Chatham. The Pension Office queried the birth of Florence and indeed only offered initially a pension allowance for three of the five children still at home. This debate was not resolved until the 10th January, 1916 when the War Office agreed to pay 27 shillings a week for Caroline and her five children. Meanwhile, she had had a further shattering blow with the loss of her eldest son, Arthur. Thomas's body was buried at Larch Wood (Railway Cutting) Cemetery, near Ieper in Belgium.

Private Ralph Joseph Baker
53061

Ralph Baker was born at Hednesford in 1899, and was the second son of Joseph T. Baker and Esther E. Baker. Joseph was born at Sedgley and was a miner and his wife was born at Gentleshaw. They had married at Wolverhampton in 1891. In 1901 the couple lived at 19 Green Lane, Wolverhampton with their five children, Gertrude, Christopher, Annie, Ralph and James. Tragedy struck the family in 1902 with the death of Annie at only 4 years of age, and again in 1903 with the death of Esther at the age of 27. Joseph decided to return to Cannock and he moved in with his parents, Ralph and Sarah Jones, at Bradbury Lane, Hednesford. In 1911, Ralph Jones was a colliery surface man, whilst his son, Joseph was a roadman, and his grandson Christopher a colliery surface man. Ralph and James were still at school. When the Great War broke out, Joseph, who had remarried, marrying Louisa Jane Sockett on the 13th October, 1911, volunteered for service with the Royal Engineers in a Tunnelling Company on the 3rd August, 1915. His son Ralph tried to join the Royal Naval Division on the 16th December, 1915 giving his date of birth as 21st February, 1897. However, this untruth was discovered and he was discharged for being under age on the 6th February, 1916. However, he then joined the 2/5th Battalion, Lincolnshire Regiment and was sent to France where on the 15th April, 1918 he was killed in action. Ralph's body was never discovered after the war and he is remembered on the Ploegsteert Memorial to the Missing in Belgium. Joseph Baker survived the war and was discharged in 1919.

Private Albert Ball
64716

Albert Ball was born at Hednesford in 1881, the third son of William and Mary Ball. William, a coal miner hailed from Sedgley, although he also gave Gnosall and Shropshire as birth places, whereas his wife came from the heart of the Black Country, having been born at Lower Gornal. The family had moved to the Hednesford area by 1881, living at Platt's Building at Hightown, but by 1891 they had moved to Stafford Lane and remained there for over 30 years. The family consisted of nine children who made it through infancy, although two others died before the age of five. The sons, David, William, John and Albert all followed their father down a colliery as miners. Joseph on the other hand, also worked in a colliery but on the surface railway. By 1911, only William and Mary were still at home, with their daughter Mary, a domestic servant and Thomas a horse driver down the pit. Albert had moved to South Wales where he was still employed as a coal miner, and boarding with the Morgan family at 86 Aber Rhondda Road, Porth. With the onset of the Great War, Albert volunteered in the first few weeks, joining the Welsh Regiment, before being transferred to the 21st Battalion, Machine Gun Corps (Infantry). In late 1916, when recovering from wounds incurred on the Somme, he married Catherine Nicholls at St. Asaph. On the 30th March, 1917, Albert was killed in action at the age of 35. His body was buried at London Cemetery Neuville-Vitasse, near Arras in France.

Private George Ball
42022

George Ball was born at Hednesford in 1890, and was the third son of William and Harriet Ball. William, a coal miner stallman was born at Blythebury, whilst his wife came from Stafford. The couple, who had married at Stafford in 1876 set up home in the town, where their first three children, William, John and Sarah Ann were born, although by 1891, the family had moved to 56, Mount Street in Hednesford, where both George and his younger brother James were born. By 1901, William junior and John had followed their father down the pit, working respectively as a roadman and horse driver. Ten years later, William junior had married and was living at 4, Heath Street with his wife and daughter, and was working as a miner. John was also a miner and also married, living at Albert Street, Church Hill, with his wife, daughter and son. George and James were both underground colliery labourers, whereas their father was a colliery labourer on the surface. Sarah Ann was still at home and working as a domestic servant. On the 11th December, 1915, George volunteered for the Army, joining the 2/5th Battalion, West Yorkshire Regiment, being sent to France on the 16th April, 1916. George had married Gertrude Barnett at Cannock just before he was posted, the couple living at 218, Littleworth Tileries. He was wounded but returned to his unit, and was killed in action on the 28th March, 1918 at the age of 28. George's body was buried at Bienvillers Military Cemetery, near Arras in France.

Private James Ball
30831

James Ball was the younger brother of George and was born at Hednesford in 1893. He joined the Army on the same day as his brother, the 11th December, 1915 but was not mobilized until the 8th December, 1916, embarking for France on the next day. Despite being unable to read or write, James joined the 7th Battalion, South Staffordshire Regiment and served on the Western Front until the 26th July, 1917 when he was badly wounded in the right arm. He was returned to England where his wounds were treated for five months when he was discharged on the 4th April, 1918 as no longer physically fit for service. James was awarded a pension of 27 shillings for four months which was then reduced to 16 shillings per week. In 1921, James died at the age of 27, but his service and wounds meant that he was included on the War Memorial at Hednesford.

Private Joseph Edward Barnett
15076

Joseph Edward Barnett was born at Wolverhampton in late 1891, and was the eldest child of Thomas and Hannah Barnett. Thomas came from Willenhall, whereas his wife hailed from Wolverhampton, where they had married in 1880. In 1881, the newly weds were living at 10, Middle Gardens, Willenhall where Thomas was employed as a general labourer. By 1891 the family were living at Ghost Row, Littleworth, Hednesford, where Thomas was employed as an engine stoker. By 1901, they had moved to Blakeman Street in Hednesford and Thomas was now a tile and quarry loader, whilst Joseph was a brickyard labourer. His younger brother, John had followed in his father's footsteps and was a brick and quarry maker. In 1911, Thomas was now a labourer in a brickyard whilst his sons were both miners, and the family were living at Littleworth Tileries at Hednesford. With the outbreak of the Great War, Joseph volunteered in the first few weeks, joining the 7th Battalion, South Staffordshire Regiment, and being sent to Gallipoli on the 21st July, 1915. He died from wounds on the 1st December, 1915 at the age of 34. Joseph's body was buried at East Mudros Military Cemetery in Greece.

Private Ralph Barton
116054

The history of the Barton family is fascinating, but at the same time frustrating with many unanswered questions. Ralph's grandfather was Robert Barton, a builder from Burslem, and his grandmother, Mary Barton came from Madeley in Shropshire. In 1891, the couple were living at Hall Drive, New Street, in Hednesford with their eight children, including Edward Robert Barton, Ralph's father, then aged 21. He like his two older sisters had been born at Peckham, Surrey, whilst the other five children had been born at Hednesford. Also living in Hednesford, on Church Hill were Abner, David and Miriam Craddock, who were brothers and sister born at Brereton. In 1891, Edward Robert Barton married Miriam Craddock at Shardlow in Derbyshire, although the couple moved back to Hednesford. In the late spring of 1892, their first child, Robert was born, and on the 3rd November, 1893 a second son, Ralph came into the world. Both were born at Hednesford, and life seemed to be going well for the young carpenter, his wife and children. However, in early 1895, Edward Robert Barton died in Birmingham at the age of 26. His widow took up a job as a boarding house keeper at Anglesey Street, and in 1901 she was living there with Ralph, John William Favill, a grocer from Clayworth in Nottinghamshire and Walter M. Jones, a provision hand from Welshpool. Robert, the eldest son was inexplicably at the Royal Orphanage, Goldthorn Hill in Wolverhampton. Miriam Barton married John William Favill later in 1901, and the couple had three children of their own, Cyril, Miriam and Christian, all born at Hednesford between 1904 and 1910. On the 27th December, 1910 the 17 year old Ralph

Barton boarded the Highland Corrie at London, bound for Buenos Aires in Argentina. From there he made his way to Canada, where he found employment as a teamster. On the 29th March, 1915 at Vancouver, Ralph enlisted with the 11th Battalion, Canadian Mounted Rifles, giving his mother, Miriam Favill as next of kin. The Favill family had moved to Worcester where John was a grocer manager, and where Robert was an assistant in the business. Ralph was drafted to the 7th Battalion at Cheriton Camp on the 13 October, 1916, having arrived in England on the 25th July, before being sent to France on the 31st October. On the 8th April, 1917 he was reported as wounded but this was amended the next day as being killed in action. Ralph was 23 at the time of his death and his body was buried at Nine Elms Military Cemetery at Thelus, near Arras in France.

Driver George Baugh
T/24521

George Baugh was born at Dawley, Shropshire in 1881, probably the son of Thomas and Emma Baugh, who were both born at Dawley in Shropshire. In 1891, Emma was a 48 year old widow, working as a charwoman and with two of her children, Elizabeth and George reduced to begging on the streets. They lived at the Elephant and Castle Buildings on the High Street in Dawley. In 1901, George was living with his now married sister, Elizabeth, at Woodhouse Lane, Dawley and working as a coal miner. Shortly after this, George joined the Army, serving in the Army Service Corps, and was then placed on the Reserve list. He must have moved to the Hednesford area on leaving the Army and in early 1914, he married Annie Tudge at Cannock, the couple setting up home at 131 Clifton Terrace, Littleworth. As a Reservist, George was called up to serve on the 5th August 1914, being sent to France on the 5th October of that year. In September, 1914 a son, George was born to Annie Baugh after her husband had joined up. Sadly George never saw his son, for on the 17th April, 1915 his body was found in the River Lys at Merville in France. George was aged 33 when he died and his body was buried at Merville Communal Cemetery in France.

Private Alfred William Bayliss
18684

Alfred Bayliss is another who provides a challenge when investigating his history. According to the census, he was born at Hednesford in 1884, yet the only person of that name was born in 1879 according to the BMD register. On the 1881 census, John Bayliss, a shoe and clog maker was married to Fanny Bayliss, a woman some 35 years younger than her husband. The couple were living at 6, Elmore Row, Walsall. In 1890, Fanny Bayliss married Frederick Augustus Fraser at Walsall, and in 1891 they were living at 9, Green Lane, Walsall, with their 7 year old son Alfred W. Fraser, born at Hednesford. Frederick was employed as a railway porter, and came from Inverness in Scotland. By 1901, the family had moved to live on the Rawnsley Road in Hednesford, where Fred was a general labourer and Alfred was employed as a blacksmith. On the 26th December, 1910 at St. Peter's Parish Church at Hednesford, Arthur William Bayliss Fraser married Mary Jane Bethell Beard. He gave his age as 25, and his address as Stafford Lane, she was 19, and from High Town. Alfred gives his father as William Bayliss, a deceased boot manufacturer. The 1911 census confirms that Fred and Fanny Fraser were living on Stafford Lane, where the 61 year old was living off an Army pension and working as a colliery horsekeeper. Alfred meanwhile had set up a home with his new wife at 3, Belt Road, High Town, in Hednesford. A son, also named Alfred William Bayliss was born to the couple at Hednesford in early 1912. Alfred joined up in 1915, enlisting with the 1/5th Battalion, South Staffordshire regiment and he was sent to France on the 24th September, 1915. In 1917, he was wounded and captured by the Germans, and died from his wounds as a prisoner of war, on the 11th December, 1917. His body was not recovered after the war and the 32 year old is remembered on the Loos Memorial to the Missing in France.

Able Seaman Enoch Beddow
Bristol Z/3659

The Beddow family had lived in the Hednesford area since 1879, when John William Beddow, a 23 year old coal miner from West Bromwich married Emily Haycock, a 23 year old spinster from Brownhills. By 1881 they were living at John Street, Wimblebury where Henrietta, the first of their six children was born in 1880. In 1891, the family had increased to five children, with John William junior, Emily, Minnie and Enoch having been born, and they were still living at John Street. By 1901, they had moved to Hill Street, where John junior was also down the pit as a horse driver and Emily was a tailoress. On the 25th December, 1902 Henrietta married James Rowley at St. Peter's Parish Church, and Minnie had also left home. Emily Beddow died at the age of 49 in early 1908. By 1911, John senior was now a roadman, whilst John junior was a miner. Emily was acting as housekeeper, Enoch was a horse driver and Catherine the youngest, was a tailoress, with the family living at 4 Hill Street, Hednesford. On the 17th January, 1916 Enoch enlisted in the Royal Naval Division, deciding that this was better than being a general labourer. He was posted to the 1st Drake Battalion, arriving in France on the 1st August, 1916. After this, Enoch's service record shows that he was in and out of hospital, before being seriously wounded on the 23rd April, 1917 and was invalided back to England. He was not fit enough o return to his Battalion until the 5th June, 1917, but was readmitted to hospital between the 2nd and 17th October, 1917. Having returned to the Front, he was wounded again on the 23rd March, 1918, and after recovery rejoined his unit. Enoch was wounded for a third time on the 11th May, 1918. He was returned to England for treatment and was sent on leave, and whilst on this leave, Enoch married Gertrude Blanche Johnson at St. Peter's Parish Church on the 26th August, 1918. He returned to the Front on the 19th October, 1918, and was admitted to hospital with diarrhoea on the 28th October, before rejoining his unit on the 7th November. Enoch was demobilized on the 17th January, 1919 but on the 27th, he was admitted to the Cannock Chase Military Hospital suffering from pneumonia, and he died at eleven fifty five on the 28th January, 1919. Enoch's body was buried at St. Peter's, Hednesford, he was 28 at the time of his death.

Private John William Beddow
17601

John William Beddow was the elder brother of Enoch Beddow, and was born at Wimblebury in 1882. He worked as a coal miner before enlisting in February 1915 at Hednesford, choosing to join the 2nd Battalion, South Staffordshire Regiment. John was sent to France on the 29th September, 1915 and saw action at Armentieres and at Cambrai, where he was killed in action on the 8th January, 1918 at the age of 35. John's body was buried at Rocquigny-Equancourt Road British Cemetery, Manancourt, France, between Peronne and Bapaume.

Sergeant George Benn
5522

Joseph and Hannah Benn were married at Market Bosworth in Leicestershire in 1867, and in 1871 were living at Higham on the Hill in Leicestershire, where their first child Frederick was born. By 1881, the family, now numbering six children had moved to live at Station Road, Hednesford and Joseph continued to work as a colliery labourer. By 1891, Hannah and Joseph junior had left home but there were still six children with the birth of Emma in 1882 and George in 1884, whilst Fred had joined his father down the pit. In 1901, only John, a carter at a tileries, Abraham, a plasterer's labourer and George, a boiler mender at a tileries, were still at home, with the family still living at Station Road. By 1911, Joseph, Hannah and George were living at 5, Eldorado Terrace, Mount Street, with John, his wife Emily and their three children living next door at 6, Eldorado Terrace. Abraham had also married, but his wife Ellen and their four children had moved to live and work at Nuneaton. George had become a miner roadman as had his father. In the Great War, George joined the Middlesex Regiment before transferring to the 50th Company, Machine Gun Corps (Infantry). He rose to the rank of Sergeant before he was posted as missing in action in May 1918. George had in fact been wounded and taken prisoner, and he died from these wounds on the 5th June, 1918 aged 33. George's body was buried at Niederzwehren Cemetery, near Kassel in Germany.

Private Henry Birch
9793

In late 1880, Henry Birch, a labourer in an iron works from Pelsall, married Fanny Sperry, from Brownhills. By 1881 they were living at Heath End, Pelsall and their first child Mary had been born. In 1891, they were living at Barnett's Building, Railway Bridge, Pelsall and Henry was now an engine driver. The family had grown and the couple now had five children, including Henry junior who had been born at Norton Canes in 1885. Sadly Fanny Birch died in 1897 at the age of 38, by which time both Henry senior and his namesake son had become coal miners. In 1901, the family had moved to live at New Road, Walsall Wood. Shortly afterwards, Henry junior, decided to join the Army and enlisted with the 2nd Battalion, Sherwood Foresters, and in 1911, he was serving with the Battalion at Deccan in India. When he came out of the Army, he was placed on the Reserve List and came to live and work in Hednesford. He worked as a miner and lived at 4, Heath Street, Hednesford. In 1914, with the outbreak of war, Henry was recalled into his Battalion on the commencement of hostilities and was sent to France on the 8th September, 1914. He served until the last year of the war, when he was taken ill and sent back to England, where he died in hospital in Exeter on the 24th April, 1918, at the age of 33. Henry's body was buried at Exeter Higher Cemetery.

Private Oliver Birch
42145

Oliver Birch was born at Hednesford in 1898, being the youngest child of Joseph W. Birch, a coal miner born at Walsall, and Mary Birch from Wombourne in Staffordshire. The couple had had thirteen children, ten of whom survived to reach adult hood. However, in 1899 Mary was left a widow when her husband died at the age of 43. It appears that the family moved between the Kettering area of Northamptonshire and Hednesford, but they had settled on the Chase by 1891, and were living at George Street in Hednesford. In 1901, they had moved to Blakemore Street, where the eldest children, Sydney and Oscar, were working respectively, as a steam ploughman and a horse driver. By 1911, the family had moved again to the Middle Block, Church Hill, with Oliver still at school, while Sydney and John were loaders under ground. Gertrude was a 19 year old domestic servant and the family were being visited by Rose Gale, Mary's married daughter, with her four children. Oliver left home at the time of the Great War, to live and work in Walsall, and it was from here that he joined the Army, firstly enlisting with the North Staffordshire Regiment before transferring to the 7th Battalion, Norfolk Regiment. Oliver was killed in action on the 21st September, 1918 at the age of 20. His body was buried at Epehy Wood Farm Cemetery at Epehy in France.

Private Arnold Bishop
13065

In 1886 at Cannock, Charles Bishop a coal miner from Tividale in the Black Country married Selina Aldridge from Oldbury. The couple settled in Hednesford, living at Abbey Street, Green Heath and started a family. By 1891, they had had three children, all born at Hednesford. By 1901, the family had grown to eight children, including Arnold who was born in 1895, whilst the eldest, Ernest had begun work in a colliery as a horse driver. In 1911, the family had moved to Cross Street, Green Heath with nine children still living at home, Ernest having married Florence Elizabeth Smith at St. Peter's Parish Church on the 3rd August, 1909, with their first child Evelyn Maud being born in 1910. Meanwhile, Arnold had managed to find a job as a miner at West Cannock Colliery, and when the Great War began, he was one of the first from Hednesford to enlist in the Army, joining the 1st Battalion, South Staffordshire Regiment. Arnold was sent to France on the 23rd March, 1915 and saw action at Neuve Chappelle, Loos and

Ieper. On the 1st July, 1916 the 1st South Staffords were part of the attack on Mametz, and it was during the first few minutes of the assault that Arnold Bishop was killed in action. At the time of his death he was only 21 and his body was never recovered after the war. Arnold is remembered on the Thiepval Memorial to the Missing on the Somme in France.

Private James Bond
5318

Tracing the ancestors of James Bond has proved to be somewhat challenging. According to the CWGC his father was Thomas Bond who was born at Newport, Shropshire. In 1871, he, his wife Sarah and two children were living in West Bromwich. By 1881, the family had moved to live in Cannock on the Old Fallow Road. James had joined the army by 1901 and was serving with the Shropshire Artillery, although he was a prisoner in York Castle. On the 1911 census, James appears, aged 34 and living at Pye Green, Hednesford with his wife Kathleen Edith, who came from Petersfield in Hampshire. The couple had three children George aged two and twins James and Marion who in 1911 were just six months old. Two other children followed, Kathleen in 1911 and Walter in 1914. The couple had married at Petersfield in 1907, and must have moved to Hednesford shortly afterwards. What is known is that James enlisted at the outbreak of the Great War, joining the 2nd Battalion, King's Shropshire Light Infantry and was sent to France on the 18th February, 1915. James was killed in action just two months later, on the 29th April, 1915 at the age of 38. His body was not recovered after the war and he is remembered on the Ieper (Menin Gate) memorial to the Missing.

Corporal Thomas Frederick Bennett Borton
806075

In 1891, Thomas Henry Borton from Aynhoe in Northamptonshire married Bertha Bennett from Pensnett near Dudley at Stourbridge. Shortly afterwards the couple moved to Church Villas, Church Hill, Hednesford where Thomas had taken up a position with the Cannock and Rugeley Colliery Company as Chief Clerk. In 1892 their first child Thomas Frederick Bennett Borton was born, to be followed in 1898 with the birth of Ellen Gertrude Borton. The Bortons saw the value of education and by 1911 Thomas Frederick was an articled mechanical draughtsman with Bumsted and Chandler of Hednesford, whilst his sister was at a private school. Thomas Frederick then took up a position with the Shelton Iron, Steel and Coal Company in north Staffordshire. When the Great War broke out, Thomas Frederick joined up on the 4th September, 1914, enlisting with the 296th Brigade, Royal Field Artillery. He was sent to France and rose to the rank of Corporal, but in July 1917 he was badly wounded. Shrapnel fractured his knee and leg and he was taken back to a Base Hospital and then invalided back to the City of London Military Hospital. Thomas Frederick died from these wounds on the 27th September, 1917 at the age of 25. His body was taken back to Hednesford where it was buried with full military honours, with thousands lining the streets as the gun carriage went past on its way to St. Peter's Parish Church, the Church where Thomas Frederick had been a chorister.

Private Eli Bott
23528

In 1886 at Cannock, George Bott married Mary Ann Cadman. He was a boat loader from Cannock and his wife came from Heath Town. The couple set up home at 19, Hill Street, Hednesford, with the first of their nine children John Thomas Bott being born in 1889. Eli was the second eldest and was born in 1892, with the family it would appear struggling to send any of the children to school. In 1909, Mary Ann Bott died at the age of 48, leaving George to look after the children, and in 1911 there were still seven of them living at home with a grandchild George also under the family's roof. The boys had all gone down the pit, as had their father, whilst Alice was keeping house at the age of 19. When the Great War broke out, Eli was working as a miner at Old Hednesford Colliery but in July 1915, he decided to enlist, joining the 10th Battalion, Northumberland Fusiliers and after four months training was sent to France. Eli was killed in action on the 18th July, 1916 at the age of 24. His body was never recovered after the war and Eli is remembered on the Thiepval Memorial to the Missing on the Somme in France.

Corporal Frederick Ernest Bourne
G/2386

In 1883 in the Parish of Wolstanton in Staffordshire, George Bourne married Mary Jane Thorneycroft. Both were born at nearby Chesterton, and by 1891 they were living on the London Road at Chesterton where George had set up a grocers business. The couple had also had five of their nine children by this time, including Frederick who had been born in 1887. In 1901 the family had moved to live at Littleworth in Hednesford, where George was now employed as a foreman at the brickworks, whilst Fred was an errand boy at a boot stores and Edward his older brother was an assistant electrician. On the 2nd March, 1908 Beatrice, Fred's older sister married Ernest Nield, a manager of a fruit importers' from Holmes Chapel in Cheshire. The couple moved to live on the Audley Road, Alsager and Fred moved to live with them, working as a salesman for the firm. The rest of the family remained at Hednesford, although they had moved to live at 8, West Hill Avenue. By 1914, Fred was now manager of a new branch of the fruit importers' working in Leeds, but in September, 1914 he enlisted in the Army, joining the 4th Battalion, Royal Fusiliers, being sent to France on the 6th March, 1915. Fred rose to the rank of Corporal, but on the 16th June, 1915 at the age of 28, he was killed in action, after being bayoneted in the thigh. Fred's body was not recovered after the war and he is remembered on the Ieper (Menin Gate) Memorial to the Missing in Belgium.

Bombardier Thomas Albert Bradnock
33936

Edwin Winsper married Alice Bradnock at Lichfield in 1895, he was a 26 year old coal miner from Kingsley in Staffordshire, and she a 21 year old domestic servant from Birmingham. She already had a child, Thomas Bradnock who was born in 1892 and the newly married couple had added to their family with the birth of Frank at Chadsmoor in 1896. By 1901 the family had moved to live on the Rawnsley Road in Hednesford. By 1911, the family had increased to five children, although Frank had moved to live with his grandparents at Albert Street, Church Hill. Thomas had now started to use the surname Winsper and at the time of the census was on leave from the Army, the family having moved to live at 33, Cross Street, Hazel Slade. It would appear that Thomas was not placed on the Reserve List, but he was called up to serve in 1917, being posted to serve in the 58th Siege Battery, Royal Garrison Artillery. At the age of 26, Thomas Bradnock was killed in action on the 20th October, 1918. His body was buried at St. Hilaire Les Cambrai British Cemetery, near Cambrai in France.

Private William Albert Brookes
58986

William Brookes was born at Great Wyrley in Staffordshire in 1882 being the eldest child of James and Susannah Brookes. James was a coal miner, also born at Great Wyrley, Susannah came from Langley in Worcestershire. The couple lived on Bradbury Lane in 1891, but by 1901 had moved to Pye Green which was where they stayed. James and Susannah had ten children and in 1911 there were still eight of them living at home. William, Albert and Herbert followed their father down the pit, whilst Harold was a 14 year old errand boy for a grocer. On the 18th April, 1911 William married Lily Allman at St. Luke's Parish Church. They set up a home at Platt Street, Hightown, in Hednesford and between 1912 and 1918 had five children. William was called up to serve in the Army in late 1917, enlisting with the 1/5th Battalion, West Yorkshire Regiment and was captured by the Germans in 1918, being taken back to a prisoner of war camp at Poznan. It was here on the 16th September, 1918 that he died from meningitis at the hospital in Szczypiorno aged 28. His widow was informed in a letter from Lt. Colonel Imply, the Secretary for the Central Prisoner of War Commission. William's body was buried at Poznan Old Garrison Cemetery in Poland.

Private Frederick Brown
14356

In 1887 at Cannock the wedding took place of Andrew Brown a coal miner from Shifnal in Shropshire and Fanny Eccleston a servant from Clapton in London. They set up a home on Station Road, Hednesford and by 1891 they had two children, John born in 1889 and Frederick born two years later. By 1901 the family had swelled to five and they had moved to 322 Pye Green Road. Percy had been born 1893, Lois in 1895 and William in 1900. By 1911, Alfred had also been added to the household, and John and Fred had begun work as horse drivers down the pit. Fred was known locally as a goalkeeper with Green Heath Albion, Cannock Central and Cannock Town. By 1914, Fred had become a miner but decided to enlist shortly after the outbreak of war, joining the 11th Battalion, West Yorkshire Regiment. He was sent to France on the 26th August, 1914 and was wounded in 1916 but sent back to the Western front once he had recovered. Frederick was killed in action on the 20th September, 1917 during the Third Battle of Ypres, aged 26. His body was buried at Tyne Cot Cemetery, near Ieper in Belgium.

Lance Corporal Percy Brown
13017

Percy Brown was the younger brother of Fred Brown and was born at Hednesford in 1893. Like his brother he became a miner and he also decided to enlist in the Army in 1914 just after the outbreak of the war. Percy joined the 1st Battalion, South Staffordshire Regiment and was sent to France on the 26th January 1915. Percy saw action at Ieper, Hill 60, Houge, Gommecourt and Arras before he was wounded on his return to Ieper. He returned to the Front once he had recovered and was killed in action at Bullecourt on the 12th May 1917. The 24 year olds' body was not recovered after the war and Percy is remembered on the Arras Memorial to the Missing in France.

Lance Corporal Howard Brown
14925

In 1892 John Thomas Brown, a coal miner born at Birmingham, married Martha Ellen Winters from nearby Handsworth. The couple set up a home in the area and began a family with Thomas being born at Handsworth in 1892 with his brother Howard following in 1894. The family then moved to High Town in Hednesford where Rebecca was born in 1897 and William in 1900. A move was then made to 43, Bradbury Lane where Sophia was born in 1902. By 1911, Thomas and Howard were working for the West Cannock Colliery Company, whilst Rebecca had found employment as a machinist. On the 8th September, 1914 Howard volunteered to serve in the Army, enlisting in the 12th Battalion, Royal Scots. He was sent to France on the 11th May, 1915 and rose to the rank of Corporal. He was noted as being kind and cheerful and was well liked by everyone. Howard came home on leave in June 1916 but returned to the Front to take part in the Big Push. On the 15th July, 1916 Howard was killed in action on the Somme at the age of 22. His body was not recovered after the war and Howard is remembered on the Thiepval Memorial to the Missing on the Somme in France.

Private Thomas Buckley
12564

Thomas Buckley was born at High Town in Hednesford in 1897, being the fourth son of Edward and Mary Ann Buckley. Edward a coal miner came from Hanley and his wife hailed from Cheadle. The couple had lived for a time at Great Haywood where Albert, John and Ellen were born, before moving to live at 54, Bradford Street, High Town. By 1901, the family had increased to seven children, with Edward, Albert and John all earning their livelihood from mining. Mary Ann died at the age of 48 in 1909, and by 1911, John was married, and was living with his wife and two children. Albert was also married but had moved to live on Stafford Lane, and Ellen had also left home. Jonathon and Thomas were also down the pit, but Edward was now earning a living as a scavenger for the Council. In 1915, Thomas married Elizabeth Wilkes at Cannock and the couple set up a home at Rose Cottage, Hawkes Green. Shortly afterwards Thomas was called up and served in the 9th Battalion, South Staffordshire Regiment. On the 14th October, 1917 at the age of 20, Thomas died from wounds that he had incurred earlier that day. He was buried at the Menin Road South Military Cemetery at Ieper in Belgium. A letter to his wife from Captain Browning described him as "a good man who led a good life. He died for his country and for his home and for those who loved him".

Lieutenant Colonel William Burnett DSO

William Burnett was born at Tatenhill near Burton-on-Trent in Staffordshire in 1881. He was the son of Andrew and Mary Elizabeth Burnett. Andrew Burnett was the land agent and farm manager to Lord Burton. William was educated at Solihull Grammar School and in 1889, moved to live in Hednesford where he had taken a position as Mineral Surveyor to the Cannock and Rugeley Colliery Company, later becoming the Underground Mine Manager. In 1906 at Walsall he married Agnes Ellen Robinson, the second daughter of William and Lydia Robinson of Sutton Road, Walsall, he being a printer in the town. Their only child William Andrew Burnett was born at Hednesford in 1908. William Burnett was well known in social spheres in the area. He was an officer at Bloxwich Territorials before taking over from Sergeant Major Holton at Hednesford, raising the efficiency of the force to new levels. William was also chairman of Hednesford Town Football Club, and Captain and

3. Hednesford

leading batsman at Cannock and Rugeley Cricket Club. He also found time to attend each year the Cannock and Rugeley Colliery Workmen's Horticultural Show. With the outbreak of the Great War, William was placed in charge of the Hednesford Territorials who made up part of the 1/5th Battalion, South Staffordshire Regiment, and who made their way to France as one of the first group of reinforcements. On the 13th November he was promoted to Lt. Col. and placed in charge of the 6th Battalion, North Staffordshire Regiment. He was also mentioned in despatches and was awarded the DSO, before preparing his Battalion for the Battle of the Somme. On the 3rd July, 1916 William Burnett had been observing his Battalion, and on returning to his car, he was hit by a shell. He was taken to a Casualty Clearing Station, but died from his wounds later that day at the age of 36. William Burnett was a very popular officer, loved by his men and his body was buried at Walincourt Halte British Cemetery at Saulty on the Somme with full military honours. A memorial service was held at St. Peter's in Hednesford which was fully attended.

Private William Charles Byford
3032489

William Byford provided a challenge when tracing his family history. In 1877 at Lichfield, Charles Byford married Emma Evans. He was a coal miner originating from Essex, whereas his wife was born at Willenhall. They lived for a time at Rugeley, where Mary F., Annie, Mary E., and William were born, whilst Herbert was born at Walsall Wood in 1890. Tragically, Emma died at the age of 33 at Walsall. By 1901, Charles had met Emily Birchall and they were living at High Mount Street, Hednesford with four children of their own, although they were not married until 1902 at Aston. The children from the first marriage had all left home, with William working as an agricultural labourer at Moreton Farm at Colwich, a farm owned by James Lewis. By 1911, Charles and Emily Byford were living at Pye Green but only one of their children, Alfred was still at home. At some point between 1901 and 1911, William Byford left Britain to make a new life in America, settling in New York and working as a fireman. He shared a room at 851, West 181st Street with Charles Shatia. On the 4th January, 1918 William enlisted with the 3rd Battalion, Canadian Infantry at New York, giving his date of birth as the 12th July, 1891 and his place of birth as Walsall. This was a fabrication as he was born at Rugeley in 1887 and he gave his next of kin as Charles Shatia his housemate. Another mystery is that William did not serve under his own name, but called himself James Lewis. On the 30th August, 1918

William Byford was killed in action at the age of 31. His body was buried at Faubourg D'Amiens Cemetery at Arras in France.

Private Walter Henry Caddick
39612

Walter Caddick was born at Hednesford in 1892, and was the fourth child of Isaac and Sarah Caddick, he a coal miner from West Bromwich and she from Gloucester. By 1891 they were living at West Hill, Hednesford where the first of their children were born, Isaac in 1878, Flora in 1887 and William in 1891. In 1901 the family had moved to 23, Mount Street, and in the meantime Walter had been born in 1892, John the following year, Eliza in 1895, Ellen in 1898 and finally Gertrude in 1900. Isaac junior was now a miner like his father and Flora was a domestic servant. However, in 1905 Isaac senior died at the age of 57, which meant that in 1911, the widowed Sarah was living at home with William, Walter, Nellie and Gertrude. Both William and Walter were down the pit, although Walter had joined the Hednesford Territorials. Walter married Mary Elizabeth Loverock on the 8th March, 1914 at St. Peter's Parish Church in Hednesford. The couple had one child Edith F. Caddick, born in 1914, but shortly afterwards Walter enlisted with the South Staffordshire Regiment, being placed on the Reserve List to await mobilization. When Walter was posted in 1916, he found himself transferred to the 2nd Battalion, Worcestershire Regiment and was sent to France as part of the Big Push. Walter was killed in action on the 1st November, 1916 at the age of 24. His body was not recovered after the war and Walter is remembered on the Thiepval Memorial to the Missing on the Somme in France. Walter was one of the relatively rare men who was entitled to the Territorial Force War Medal.

Private William Arthur Calladine
27662

William Calladine was born at Mexborough in Yorkshire in 1891 and was probably the son of Emma Calladine. She was the daughter of Lewis and Clara Calladine nee Scattergood, who had married at Basford in 1863. They had had five children before the untimely death of Lewis in 1876. This left Clara to bring up the children with the help of her parents and by her taking a job as a charwoman. The family lived at Clayfield Road, Mexborough and by 1891 Clara's children had begun to work in the pits of the Denaby coalfield. In 1901, William Calladine was living with his grandmother at her house on 120, Church Street, Mexborough and in 1911, he had moved in with his uncle and aunt, Allen and Frances Calladine at 7, Hewitt Street, Mexborough, and was working as a pony driver in the pit. At some point before the outbreak of war in 1914, William moved to Hednesford to work, and lived at 485, Littleworth Road. He must have been in one of the first batch of volunteers in 1915, joining the King's Own Yorkshire Light Infantry, before being transferred to the 9th Battalion, Lancashire Fusiliers, being sent to Egypt on the 3rd December, 1915. He was then posted to France, and it was here on the 29th September, 1916 that William died from wounds incurred earlier. He was 25 at the time of his death and William's body was buried at Wimereux Communal Cemetery, near Boulogne in France.

Private George William Cathcart
75657

George Cathcart was born at Penshaw, County Durham in 1897, being the first son of Frederick and Rebecca Cathcart. Frederick was from Bocking, Essex whilst his wife was born at Wheatley Hill, Durham. Rebecca Fowler had married Frederick's brother Henry in 1882 and in 1891 they had had two children, Louisa born in 1889 and Sarah born in 1890. Frederick was living with them at Quarry Head, Painshaw, County Durham, where he and Henry worked as miners. A third child Catherine, was born to the couple in 1882, before Henry died at the young age of 33. Rebecca married Frederick Cathcart in 1896 and George was their first child, quickly followed by Lena in 1899 and Thomas in 1905. By 1901 the family had moved to live at 22, Barrack Row, Shiney Row, Fencehouses, County Durham and they continued to live at this address. In 1911, George had started his working life down the pit with Lena and Thomas still at school. On the 14th April, 1915 George volunteered for the Army, joining the 16th Battalion, Durham Light Infantry before being transferred to the 1st Training Reserve Battalion at Rugeley Camp. It was here that he met Jane Pagett, who lived at 34, George Street, Hednesford. The couple were married at St. Peter's Parish Church on the 4th June, 1917 and the following month George was promoted to Lance Corporal but lost his stripe in September, 1917 due to misconduct. He was transferred to the 8th Battalion, Durham Light Infantry and was sent to France as a Bandsman on the 18th December, 1917. George was killed in action on the 27th May, 1918 at the age of 21. His body was not recovered after the war and he is remembered on the Soissons Memorial to the Missing in France.

Private John Clarke
10213

John Clarke was born at Pershore in Worcestershire in 1880, the last of four sons born to John and Matilda Clarke. The couple had married in 1862 when the 24 year old agricultural labourer from Wyre Piddle in Worcestershire had married the 16 year old Matilda Harding from Bishampton in the same county. All told the couple had ten children born between 1864 and 1890, and they lived in villages around Pershore over this period. John died just after the census was completed in 1891 at the age of 53, and in 1901 Matilda, Lily and John were working as labourers in a market garden in Pershore, the rest of the family having left home. John decided to join the Army shortly after this, joining the Worcestershire Regiment and serving in India, where he was in 1911 and Egypt. By the outbreak of the Great War John had settled in Hednesford where he was a miner, living at Chapel Street, Hazel Slade. As soon as the war began, he joined up again with the 1st Battalion, Worcestershire Regiment and was sent to France on the 5th November, 1914. John was back in Hednesford at Christmas 1914 suffering from frost bitten feet, but returned to the Western Front shortly afterwards. John died bravely on the 10th March, 1915 at the age of 35. A letter from a girl named Alice was found in a pocket in his tunic and news of his death was sent to her address. John's body was not recovered after the war and he is remembered on the Le Touret Memorial to the Missing in France.

Private James Clarke
580

In 1890, William Clarke a miner from Pershore in Worcestershire married Elizabeth Grice from Norton Canes in Staffordshire. Within a few months the newly weds had moved to South Yorkshire where their first child, named William after his father was born in 1891 at South Elmsall. Alice was born in 1894 and James was born at nearby South Kirkby in 1898. The couple then decided to move back to Staffordshire and in 1901 they were celebrating the birth of John at 75, Brindley Heath, Hednesford. The family then moved to 23, Chapel Street, Hazel Slade where their last child Christopher was born in 1904. James followed his father and older brother down the pit and had also joined the Hednesford Territorials. He enlisted for the Army in 1915, joining the 3/5th Battalion, South Staffordshire Regiment, and was sent to Grantham to complete his training. However, he was taken ill and died in hospital on the 21st January,

1916 at the age of 18. His body was brought back to Cannock and James was buried with full military honours, at Cannock Cemetery, with a firing party from Rugeley Camp shooting three volleys and a bugler playing the Last Post. The Reverend G.J. Johnson conducted a service at the Primitive Methodist Church.

Private George Cook
9292

Tracing the antecedents of George Cook has been problematic. He was born at Dudley in 1884 and appears on the 1901 census as George Hammonds, living at 1 Court, Porters Street, Dudley. His father and mother are given as Israel and Edith Hammonds who were not married until 1898 at Dudley. She was married under the name of Ada Cook, and in the household were Katie, Florrie, George, Willie and Elizabeth. Israel Hammonds made his living as a coal miner. By 1911, the family had moved to Burgoyne Street, Hednesford, where Israel was now employed as a colliery surface labourer. George had now reverted to the surname Cook and was Israel's step son. The couple had had four children in the meantime, Isabella, Edith, Phoebe and Joseph. George was also employed down the pit as a horse driver. When the Great War began, George was one of the first to enlist, choosing to join the 1/5th Battalion, South Staffordshire Regiment and he was sent to France on the 5th March, 1915. George was killed in action on the 13th October, 1915, at the age of 21, in the Battle of Loos when his Battalion tried to storm the Hohenzollern Redoubt. George's body was not recovered after the war and he is remembered on the Loos Memorial to the Missing in France.

Sergeant Francis Cooke DCM
28000

Francis Cooke was born at Cannock Wood in 1876, the eldest son of George and Mary A. Cooke, he a miner from Chorley, Staffordshire and she from Cannock Wood. Mary had been married before to Arthur John Cheswell and she had two children from that marriage, one of whom Ann, married Thomas Hobson and went to live in Ashton-under-Lyne in Lancashire. In 1891, the Cooke family were living at Church Hill, Hednesford at the back of the Church, and where Francis was working as a 15 year old coal miner. By 1911, Francis had left the Midlands and was living and working at Ashton-under-Lyne. He was employed as a coal miner and was living with his sister Ann Hobson at 311, Katherine Street, Ashton-under-

Lyne. When the Great War started, Francis enlisted at the end of 1914 and joined the 1st Battalion, King's Liverpool Regiment. He was sent to France on the 1st June, 1915 and rose to the rank of Sergeant and was awarded the DCM for bravery in the face of the enemy. Sadly this brave 39 year old was killed in action on the 8th August, 1916. His body was not recovered after the war and Francis is remembered on the Thiepval Memorial to the Missing on the Somme in France.

Rifleman Henry Cooksey
R/13294

In 1877, at Dudley Annie Jones married Joseph Cooksey, she was from Bilston in Staffordshire and he was a miner from Dudley. Their first child Joseph was born in 1878, and then the family moved to live at New Street, Chadsmoor where David, Elizabeth, Florence and Harriet had been born by 1891. In the following ten years, Harry, Ada, Bertha and Annie were born, but in 1900 Joseph died at the age of 50. Annie married for a second time at Cannock in 1903, with another coal miner William Barratt becoming her husband. The family moved to 62, Bradford Street, High Town, Hednesford, where Rose Barratt and Sarah Ann Barratt were added to the household. Harry Cooksey was a horse driver down the pit and later became a miner. On the 4th April, 1914 Harry married Florence Owen at Cannock Register Office and the couple moved to Back 55, Station Road where on the 22nd October, 1914 Ada May Cooksey was born. On the 21st May, 1915 Harry joined the Army, enlisting with the 15th Battalion, King's Royal Rifle Corps. Harry was posted to France on the 12th September, 1915, when he was transferred the 8th Battalion. He was briefly attached to the 177th Company, Royal Engineers and while with this unit was stopped two day's pay for idleness on the 5th February, 1917. On the 29th September, 1917 Harry was transferred again to the 11th Battalion KRRC and on the 30th November, 1917 he was posted as missing in action, which was later confirmed as the date of his death. The 25 year old Rifleman was buried at Honnechy British Cemetery, near Le Cateau in France.

Lance Corporal Richard Cooksey
8082

Richard Cooksey was born at Hednesford in 1889, the illegitimate child of the seventeen year old Charlotte Hodgkiss, who originated from Wolverhampton but who was then living with her widowed mother at New Street, Chadsmoor. On the

25th December, 1892 she married John Cooksey at St. Luke's Parish Church in Cannock, and the couple had two children, Priscilla and Thomas before John tragically died at the age of 25 in 1896. On the 2nd April, 1899 Charlotte married Job Mason, again at St. Luke's with the family setting up a home at Blencowe's Buildings on the Stafford Road at Huntington, before moving again to Burgoyne Street, High Town. Job and Charlotte added to the family with Mary Jane, John Job, Sarah Ann and William Mason being born between 1900 and 1910. However, for Richard life was beginning to turn sour for at the age of ten he was sent to the Certified Industrial Boys School at Caverswall, Stoke-on-Trent. This was in essence a special school for serious young offenders. When he completed his sentence, Richard joined the Army, enlisting with the 1st Battalion, Bedfordshire Regiment, seeing service in India, Aden and Egypt where he was a keen bandsman. Richard's battalion was sent to France on the 4th January, 1915 and on the 28th April, the family received a postcard saying that all was going well. Just two days later, Richard suffered a gunshot wound to the head, and was taken to Number 2 Casualty Clearing Station where he died at the age of 25. Richard's body was buried at Bailleul Communal Cemetery Extension (Nord) between St. Omer and Lille in France.

Private Thomas Cooksey
18563

Thomas Cooksey was born at Hednesford in 1895 and was the brother of Richard Cooksey. By 1911, the sixteen year old was working underground at a colliery as a horse driver, and when the Great War broke out, Thomas enlisted in early 1915, joining the 1st Battalion, South Staffordshire Regiment. His Battalion was sent to serve at Gallipoli on the 11th September, 1915 before being transferred to France in 1916. On the 3rd September, 1916, Thomas was killed in action on the Somme at the age of 21. His body was not recovered after the war and Thomas is remembered on the Thiepval Memorial to the Missing on the Somme in France.

Private Joseph Cosby
23076

Joseph Cosby was born at Longton, Stoke-on-Trent in 1877, being the fifth son of Edward and Ellen Cosby. Joseph was one of twelve children and his father was a boot and shoe maker from Rugby, Warwickshire and Ellen a dressmaker from Bury in Lancashire. The children once they had grown up went into the pottery making industry, rather than following their father's trade. By 1899, Joseph had left the Potteries and was working as a bricklayer's labourer in Walsall Wood, and on the 25th May, 1899 he married Sarah Ann Burgess at St. John's Parish Church, Walsall Wood. Two years later the couple were boarding with John and Emma Pritchard at Ogley Hay and the first of their six children had been born, Mary Ellen Cosby. Yet in 1911, Sarah had taken the children back to the Potteries where she was working as a transferer and living with the Brown family at 3, Ford Street, Longton. Joseph was working as a miner's labourer and was boarding with the Powell family at 65, Brindley Heath, Hednesford. The family would appear to have got back together, for on Joseph's attestation papers, he gives his address as 73, Brindley Heath and lists his wife and six children. Indeed, Joseph joined the Army on the 1st August, 1914, when he signed up with the 4th Battalion, North Staffordshire Regiment, but after 286 days service he was discharged at Guernsey on the 11th June, 1915, as no longer being fit for service. Not to be deterred, Joseph then rejoined the Army on the 31st July, 1915, enlisting with the 3rd Battalion, Yorkshire and Lancashire Regiment. Between the 30th October, 1915 and the 14th February, 1916 he was forfeited pay on four occasions for absence, and on the 31st March, 1916 he was discharged for a second time as no longer being fit for service. Joseph died at the Military Hospital Cannock Chase on the 6th March, 1918 from a "disease contracted on commencing war service". At the time of his death Joseph was 39 years of age and he was buried at Cannock Cemetery.

Private Jonas Craddock
29218

Jonas Craddock was born at Gentleshaw in 1873 and was the eldest son of David and Catherine Craddock. David was born at Brereton and Catherine came from nearby Longdon, the couple had married at Stoke-on-Trent in 1856. A second son David was born in 1875, and in 1881 the family were living on the Rugeley Road at Chase Terrace. By 1891, the family had moved to live at Cannock Wood, where all three men were employed as coal miners. In 1899, at Cannock, Jonas married Eliza Caroline Hall and in 1901, the couple and their baby daughter, Catherine were boarding with Jeremiah Craddock, a 62 year old widower at The Spinney, Burntwood. By 1911, they had moved to live at Rawnsley Old Buildings at Hednesford and their family had increased to five children. These were Catherine, George, Rose, Charlie and Abner. Another son, Jonas junior was born in 1912. Jonas volunteered for the Army in early 1915, joining the Sherwood Foresters, and being sent to Gallipoli on the 7th November, 1915. Just before the end of the war, Jonas was badly wounded and was sent back to England where he died on the 5th March, 1919 at the age of 45. Jonas's body was buried at St. Peter's Churchyard, Hednesford.

Private Albert Edward Crutchley
393094

Albert Crutchley was born at Slitting Mill, Rugeley in 1898, being the son of Albert and Margaret Crutchley. Albert senior was a railway wagon examiner from Brereton and his wife came from Yoxall. On the 1901 census he is recorded as Robert Crutchley for some reason, and the couple were living at Slitting Mill with Albert junior and May who was born in 1900. However, tragedy was to strike in 1902 with the sudden death of Albert senior and Margaret at the age of 35 and 26 respectively. As a result, Albert was brought up by his grandparents, Fred and Mary Ann Crutchley, who had moved from Fair Oak, Rugeley to live at 21, Chapel Street, Hazel Slade. Albert did not join the Army until 1917, when he joined the 9th Battalion, Royal Scots. After the Armistice, Albert was waiting to be demobilized when he was taken ill with influenza and died at the Base Hospital at Etaples on the 28th February, 1919 at the age of 20. Albert was buried at Etaples Military Cemetery in France.

Private Edwin Cund
G/63087

Edwin Cund was born at Wolverhampton in 1898 and was the third son of John and Sarah Ann Cund. The couple had married at Dudley in 1880 and in 1881 were living at Brickkiln Street Willenhall, where John worked as a locksmith. The couple produced nine children, and by 1901, they had moved to 38, Powell Street, Heath Town, Wolverhampton where John and his eldest son, John junior were employed as locksmiths. In 1911 the family had moved to live on the Cannock Road, Wolverhampton where Edwin was at school, with his sister Clare Maud, whilst another brother, David had started work as a presser. Edwin left school and moved to Hednesford where he lived at 10 Abbey Street, Green Heath and where he worked as a miner. Edwin enlisted in 1917, to begin with in the North Staffordshire Regiment, but was transferred to the 7th Battalion, Middlesex Regiment and served in France with the Battalion until the 27th August, 1918 when at the age of

20 he was killed in action. Edwin's body was not recovered after the war and he is remembered on the Vis-en Artois Memorial to the Missing in France.

Sapper Ernest Haydn Dando
96863

In 1866, at Dudley, Alfred Dando a miner from Dudley in Worcestershire married Ann Hotchkiss from Netherton. The couple lived on the High Street at Dudley and by 1871 had had two children, Frederick and John. Sadly John died but other children were born, Joseph and Richard while the family were living at Dudley, before the family moved to New Street, Cannock where Ester and Alfred were born. In 1882, Ann died at the age of 33, and within a year Alfred had married Emily Ann Sargeant and they too had children of their own, Ernest Haydn, Haydn, Francis and George. In 1901, Emily was living at New Invention, Short Heath with the children, but Alfred was nowhere to be found. However, by 1911 the family were back together, living at 78, Brindley Heath. Alfred was 65 and had no work, but Ernest was a coal miner driver, Haydn a coal miner and Francis was also a coal miner driver at West Cannock Colliery. On the 1st September, 1914 Ernest enlisted in the Army, joining the Royal Welsh Fusiliers and was posted to the 9th Battalion on the 7th September. Yet on the 21st October, 1914 he was discharged from the Army due to his suffering from syphilis. Not to be daunted, Ernest volunteered for a second time, this time joining the 175th Tunnelling Company, Royal Engineers and being sent to France on the 1st June, 1915. Indeed Mrs. Dando received a special letter from King George V, as she had six sons serving in the Army. However, on the 10th January 1916, Ernest died from gas poisoning at the age of 28. Lieutenant Wannich sent a letter to Brindley Heath where he said that Ernest died from "gas poisoning on January 10th. Artificial respiration was to no avail and he was buried at Zillebeke on the 11th January. Ernest was a good workman and a good soldier". After the war Ernest's body was not recovered and he is remembered on the Ieper (Menin Gate) Memorial to the Missing in Belgium.

Private Henry Davies
9592

In 1878, Martha Poole who was a 23 year old unmarried girl from Dawley Bank in Shropshire gave birth to a son named Jabez. Three years later, she married Isaiah Davies, a coal miner, also from Dawley Bank at Wellington in Shropshire.

The couple had another child, Isaiah whilst they were living at Dawley Bank, before they moved to live at Station Road, Hednesford where John, Edward and William were born. By 1901 the family had moved to George Street, and Henry and Matilda had been born in 1894 and 1897 respectively. In 1911, the family was still living at George Street but only Henry and William were still at home, with Henry a surface labourer and William a coal miner like his father. Henry had joined the Hednesford Territorials before the Great War and as a result he enlisted straight away, electing to join the 2nd Battalion, South Staffordshire Regiment and being sent to France on the 27th December, 1914. On the 25th September, 1915 at the Battle of Loos, the 21 year old Henry was killed in action. Henry's body was not recovered after the war and he is remembered on the Loos Memorial to the Missing in France.

Private Thomas Richard Davies
13716

In 1881 at Cannock, Richard Davies a miner from Bilston married Lucy Jane Cox from Hednesford. The couple set up home at 33, Chapel Street, Hazel Slade and in 1893 their first child named Thomas Richard was born. He was soon followed by Emily, William, Alice, Charles and Lucy. Before 1911, the family had moved a few doors down the street to live at 10, Chapel Street and Thomas had also become a miner like his father. In early 1915, Thomas enlisted in the Army, joining the 9th Battalion, Royal Welsh Fusiliers and he was sent to France on the 19th July, 1915. He served on the Western Front until the 21st November, 1916 when at the age of 23 Thomas died from wounds. His body was buried at Etaples Military Cemetery in France.

Private Alexander Dawes
7579

Alexander Dawes was born at Hednesford in 1884 and was one of fourteen children born to Robert and Lydia Dawes between 1878 and 1910. The couple married at Penkridge in 1876 and in 1881 were lodging with the Cartwright family at Cannock. George and Sarah Ann Cartwright had four children of their own and Robert and Lydia had two children, with two lodgers also staying in one house. By 1891, the Dawes family had moved to 54, Wood Lane, Hednesford, where Robert worked as a coal miner and three of the six children were at school. In 1901, Herbert and

Alexander had joined their father down the pit, with both working as roadmen. At this point there were still nine children living at home. In 1904, Alexander joined the Army, enlisting with the 1st Battalion, North Staffordshire Regiment, serving for three years and then being placed on the Reserve List for nine years. Therefore when the Great War began, Alexander was called up from his job as a miner on the 4th August, 1914 being sent to France on the 10th September, 1914. He was involved in the retreat from Mons and saw action on the Marne and the Aisne, before he was killed in action by a shell in Belgium on the 12th March, 1915 at the age of 32. After the war, Alexander's body was not recovered and he is remembered on the Ploegsteert Memorial to the Missing near Ieper in Belgium. Perhaps the best way of remembering Alexander is to include a poem that he sent back to his mother shortly before he was killed.

The Kaiser's dreams are all going dead
His schemes are all being knocked on the head
As we all advance upon Berlin
Every man John Bull within
For England's sake we risk our lives
And then return to our children and wives

Gunner Samuel Dawes
203872

Samuel Dawes was the younger brother of Alexander, and he was also born at Hednesford ten years after his brother in 1894. In 1911, Samuel was working as a waggoner when aged just sixteen years of age for Mr. W. Shaw of Station Road, Hednesford a job he continued with until his call up in 1917. Indeed, Samuel was conscripted on 15th January, 1917, joining the Royal Field Artillery. He was sent to France in July of the same year and was killed in action by a shell on the 12th October, 1917 at the age of 23. A Captain wrote to his widowed mother, her husband Robert having died in 1911, to say "I liked your son very much and had great admiration for his pluck and bravery. He was badly hit and when a Major tried to help him, Dawes told the Major to leave him and help the others. The Major stayed with him but he died". Samuel's body was buried at Vlamertinghe New Military Cemetery near Ieper in Belgium. Three other brothers also served in the Great War, William Herbert and Thomas with the Royal Army Medical Corps and George who was wounded four times serving with the Northumberland Fusiliers.

3. Hednesford

Sapper John Deakin
96866

In 1879 at Stafford, Charles Deakin a railway wagon repairer from Hopton, married Alice Podmore from Salt. Within two years the couple had moved to 67, Station Road, Hednesford and their first child Edward John was born in 1881. Charles and Alice Deakin had 14 children in total, but only five of these survived to adulthood. By 1911, there were four children still at 67, Station Road, Edward who was a blacksmith striker, John born in 1890, who was a gripping on haulier in a colliery, and Ada and Alice who both worked in a clothing factory. In late 1914, John volunteered for service in the Army, joining the Royal Engineers and being sent to France on the 1st June, 1915. He was badly wounded and discharged from the Army on the 15th September, 1916. Sadly just two years later in 1918, John died at the age of 28 from the effects of these wounds. He was buried at St. Peter's Churchyard, Hednesford.

Private John Henry Degg
18935

John Henry Degg was born at Hednesford in 1879, being the first child of Henry and Agnes Degg, who had married at Cannock a year previously. At that time the family was living at New Street, Cannock along with Henry's brother John. Both Henry and John came from the Potteries and were working as miners, whereas Agnes came from Stonnall. In 1891, the family had moved to live at Platt Street, High Town, where Henry and Agnes's family had increased to four sons and John Degg was still living with them, along with his children, having been married and widowed. On the 25th December, 1900 at St. Luke's Parish Church, John Henry Degg married Agnes Minnie Picken. The couple began life at Platt Street, living just a few doors from his parents, but by 1911, they had moved to live at 80, Bradford Street, High Town. John Henry and Agnes had seven children born between 1902 and 1916. John Henry was a coal miner, working at the East Cannock Colliery, but in May 1915, he enlisted with the 1st Battalion, South Staffordshire Regiment, He was sent to serve on the Western Front in time for the Battle of the Somme and was killed on the 1st July, 1916 at the age of 38. His body was buried at Dantzig Alley Military Cemetery at Mametz on the Somme in France. A memorial service was held for him at High Town United Methodist Chuch, the service taken by the Reverend F.A. Steele. Mr. Gains Dando was the organist and the Communion set was donated by Mrs. W. Dando of West Hill.

Private Frederick Dennis
19545

In 1893 at Mile End, London James Dennis married Mary Ann Woodley. James worked as a labourer at a dye works and the couple lived 9, Church Terrace, Hackney, and by 1901 had had four children, Rose, Frederick, Ellen and Florence. In 1911, the family had just moved to live at Burgoyne Street, High Town where James was working as a bricklayer's labourer. Frederick was a grocer's assistant and Ellen was working as a finisher in a clothing factory. Frederick went on to work for the Star Tea Company at Hednesford, but on the 15th July, 1915 he enlisted with the 1st Battalion, South Staffordshire Regiment, being sent to France on the 31st December. He served until July 1st, 1916 when he was badly wounded and failed to recover from his injuries, dying on the 4th July, 1916 at the age of 20. Frederick's body was buried at Daours Communal Cemetery Extension, on the Somme in France. His parents had by the time of their son's death moved to live at Cannock Road, Chase Terrace.

Gunner William Douglas
143602

William Douglas was born in 1883 at Hednesford, being the third child and only son of Hope Hunter Douglas and Catherine Adams Douglas. The couple had married at West Bromwich in 1880, and Hope Douglas had set up a Hat and Clothing business in Hednesford. They had five children, Mabel, Catherine, William, Eleanor and Mary. In 1896, Hope died at the age of 43, but the business continued and in 1901 William was assisting in the shop on Market Street, and by 1911 he and his mother had also branched out into tailoring. On the 3rd August, 1913 William married Anice Kate Marston at St. Peter's Church in Hednesford. Her parents ran a boot and shoe business in the town, and the couple had their one child, a boy named William after his father in 1914. William senior was a well known sportsman, being a boxer and footballer, noted for his fine physique. He captained Hednesford Thursday Football Club and was also an excellent billiards player. William was a member of the Hednesford Tradesmen's Association. In May, 1917 William was conscripted into the Army, joining the Royal Garrison Artillery, 261st Siege Battery. He had only been at the Front for five weeks when he was wounded by shellfire and died from these injuries on the 16th August, 1917 at the age of 34. William's body was buried at Bard Cottage Cemetery near Ieper in Belgium.

3. Hednesford

Private George Albert Dowding
24822

George Dowding was born at Hednesford in 1891, and was the second child and eldest son of Alfred and Elizabeth Dowding. Alfred was a colliery boiler minder from Bilston and his wife came from Cannock. The couple had gone to live in America for a short time and whilst they were there, their first child, a daughter named Alice was born at Pennsylvania. George was born just after their return and the family were living at West Chadsmoor. In 1901, the family was to be found at 57, Brindley Heath, and Samuel, Agnes and Alfred had been born in the intervening period. By 1911, they had moved again to live at 129, High Mount Street, Hednesford, when George and Samuel had started work down the pit at Littleton Colliery. On the 27th May, 1912 George married Agnes Illsley at St. Peter's Parish Church, Hednesford and the couple set up home at 8, Church Street, Chadsmoor, before moving to live at number 33. The couple's only child died shortly after birth in 1914. On the 23rd March, 1915 George attested for the Army at Cannock, joining the Royal Welsh Fusiliers and was posted to the 9th Battalion on the 27th April. George saw service in the Dardanelles and in Mesopotamia where he was wounded in the arm, but returned to his unit. George met a tragic death on the 1st June, 1916 when he was drowned after falling overboard from a steamer on the River Tigris, aged 25. A Court of Inquiry was set up at Basra on the 14th June, returning a verdict of accidental death, although it was noted that no inquiry was held on the boat and there was no officer on board. George was buried at Amara War Cemetery in Iraq. George's brother Samuel also served in the war.

Private David Downes
25753

David Downes was the third son of John and Ann Downes and was born at Swallow Nest, Yorkshire in 1893. The family were used to moving around the country. John came from Bolton, Ann from Coseley, John their eldest child was born at Livington, Derbyshire, Clara at Oldbury, Ada and Samuel were also born at Swallow Nest and Albert was born at Darnall in Yorkshire. By 1911, the family had moved to live at West Hill, Hednesford where the men of the family, with the exception of Albert who was still at school, were employed in local pits. David volunteered for the Army in early 1916, joining the 6th Battalion, King's Own Yorkshire Light Infantry and was sent to France later that year. In September

1916 he was badly wounded and died from his injuries on the 17th September, 1916 at the age of 23. His body was buried at La Neuville British Cemetery at Corbie, near Albert on the Somme in France.

Corporal William Drury
18450

William Drury was born at Pontypridd in South Wales in 1893 and was the son of William Drury from Cannock who was living and working as a butcher in Pontypridd in 1891. William senior married Bessie Walters at Pontypridd in 1892, with William and his brother Horace being born at Pontypridd before the family moved to Swindon in Wiltshire. William senior, in turn, was the son of William and Sarah Drury from Hednesford who had run a butcher's shop in Cannock and Hednesford for a number of years. In 1901 young William was only eight years of age but was being brought up by his grandparents at Church Villas, Church Hill, in Hednesford. William managed to find employment as a clerk with a large Birmingham manufacturer and he was a member of the Church Hill School Choir. On the 1911 census, William junior was living in Swindon with his family, where Leonard and Jessie had been born. However, on the 20th June, 1911 William decided to leave England and sailed on the P&O ship Commonwealth to Sydney in Australia, where he found work as a stockman on a large fruit and livestock farm. On the 17th November, 1915 William decided to enlist in the Australian Imperial Forces at Casula in New South Wales. Initially he joined the infantry but transferred to the Australian Field Artillery, 25th Battery. He arrived in France on the 29th December, 1916 and was promoted to the rank of Corporal on the 29th September, 1917. On the 8th October, William was badly wounded with multiple gunshot wounds to the head, face, hands, right thigh and legs. He was taken to the 44th Casualty Clearing Station near Poperinghe in Belgium, but died from his injuries on the 9th October, 1917 at the age of 24. William's body was buried at Nine Elms British Cemetery just outside Poperinghe.

Private Edwin Dudfield
6588

Edwin Dudfield has proved to be something of a mystery. According to contemporary newspaper reports, Edwin was involved in the Boer War and re-enlisted in 1914 with the 2nd battalion, South Staffordshire Regiment, being sent to France on the 13th August, 1914. He was badly wounded in November, 1914 and died from these injuries at the 7 Base Hospital in Boulogne on the 14th November, 1914. The CWGC gives information that his widow, Lilian Dudfield lived at Erdington in Birmingham. Again local reports state that when he came out of the Army, Edwin settled down as a miner living at Hill Top, Hednesford and that he had two children, and worked at the Old Hednesford Colliery. However, the only Dudfield living at Hednesford in 1911 is Harry Dudfield who was born at Aston and who was married on the 20th April, 1908 to Lily Ball. The couple lived at Hill Top, Hednesford and had two children who survived childhood, George and Nellie. However, at only 24 in 1911, he would have been too young to have fought in the Boer War. What is clear is that Edwin's body was buried at Boulogne Eastern Cemetery in France.

Private George Dukes
61845

According to the Commonwealth War Graves Commission, George Dukes was born at Bloxwich and was the son of Thomas Dukes. He was sent to France on the 28th November, 1914, which with his then Army number 9583 would suggest he was a Regular soldier or a Territorial. He was very badly wounded in the closing stages of the war. George married Emma Chell at Hednesford early in 1919, but sadly he died on the 21st October, 1919 at Warrington Military Hospital. George was buried in St. Peter's Churchyard, Hednesford.

Private William Dunkley
13603

William Dunkley was born at Kidderminster in 1885 and was the oldest son of William and Annie Dunkley. Annie had three children from her previous marriage and William and Annie raised two more children of their own, William and Daniel. In 1901 the family were living at Rawnsley Road, Hednesford in a house which they were sharing with William's older brother Richard, his wife Annie and their six children. William senior sadly died in 1905 and in 1911, his widow was living at Cooper's Coppice, Rawnsley with Mercy, who was the eldest daughter from her first marriage, William and Daniel, who had both found jobs at Wimblebury Colliery, and two lodgers, William Lycett and Daniel Parkes. The family then moved to live at Chapel Street, Hazel Slade. With the onset of war, William volunteered for service at the end of 1914 and was sent to France with the 10th Battalion, Royal Welsh Fusiliers on the 19th July, 1915. He served for over two years before he was killed in action on the 8th April, 1917 at the age of 22. William's body was buried at Faubourg D'Amiens Cemetery, Arras in France.

Private George Dyke
7894

George Dyke was born at Coseley in 1891 and was the fifth of six children brought up by Isaac and Harriet Dyke. Isaac was a coal miner from Coseley whereas his wife was born at Tividale. The couple had married at Dudley in 1880 and lived in the Coseley area for some eighteen years before moving to live at Cecil Street, Chadsmoor in 1899. By 1911, the family had moved to live at 53, John Street, Chadsmoor, and by this time George had too started work down the pit. However, on the 5th October, 1913 George married Harriet Roden at St. Luke's Parish Church and the couple moved to 42, Glover Street, Wimblebury where George worked as a miner for the Cannock and Rugeley Colliery Company. In 1914, the couple celebrated the birth of their first and only child, named George after his father. In 1914, George volunteered for service with the 1/5th Battalion, South Staffordshire Regiment and was sent to France on the 5th March, 1915. On the 7th July, 1915 George was shot in the head by a German sniper whilst on sentry duty and was killed instantly. The 24 year old's body was not recovered after the war and George is remembered on the Ieper (Menin Gate) Memorial to the Missing in Ieper, Belgium.

John Edwards

John Edwards may well remain just a name on the Hednesford War Memorial. There is no record of a man of that name with any link to the town. The only information about him was that he lived at Green Heath. The only man from that area on the 1911 census was John Henry Edwards, junior, of High Mount Street, but I can find no evidence to confirm that he was killed in the Great War.

Private George Ellis
16184

George Ellis was born at Cannock in 1897 and was the fourth son of Edward and Annie Ellis. Edward was a coal miner from Bromlow in Shropshire, whilst his wife hailed from Roby in Lancashire. The family moved around the country, Edward the eldest child was born at Wigan, John, James, Violet and George were born at Cannock, Annie was born at Penkridge and Henry and Albert born at Stafford. In 1881 the family were lodging with the Beasley family at Huyton in Liverpool, but by 1891, they had moved back to the Midlands and were resident at Hawks Green, Cannock. In 1901, the family were living at 74, Brindley Heath, Hednesford. However, by 1911 the family had separated, Edward senior and junior were lodging with the Jones family at 78, Mill Street, Cannock whilst Annie had taken the other children to 34, Edlington Street, Denaby near Rotherham. George had started work and was employed as a glass hand. By 1914, George had moved back to Hednesford and was living at 24, Ebenezer Street. On the 9th November, 1914 George enlisted with the 2/4th Battalion, Ox and Bucks Light Infantry and was sent to France on the 18th September, 1915. He was then sent to Salonika before returning to the Western Front and serving on the Somme and at Ieper. On the 10th September, 1917 George was killed in action at the age of 20. His body was buried at Dochy Farm New British Cemetery at Zonnebeke in Belgium.

Sapper Charles Douglas Ellisson
43609

Charles Ellisson was born at Birkdale in Lancashire in 1895, being the eldest son of Charles and Mary Hannah Ellisson. Charles senior was a druggist and chemist, born at Barnsley in Yorkshire, with Mary hailing from Hyde in Cheshire. The couple lived shortly after their marriage in Yorkshire and it was here that Muriel and Kathleen were born, before they moved across the Pennines to Lancashire where Charles junior was born. The family then moved to Market Street, Hednesford where George was born in 1898. In 1911, the family were still living and working in Market Street, but Charles had lost his wife. Charles junior was a boarder with the Mason family at Hob Moat Road, Birmingham where he was working as a toolmaker in the motor trade. He did find employment as an engineer mechanic for Petters Ltd, Engineers of Yeovil. However, he joined the Army on the 1st September, 1914, at Yeovil, electing to join the Royal Engineers, 82nd Field Company as a fitter. Charles was sent to France on the 19th July, 1915 and served until he was killed in action on the 29th July, 1916 at the age of 21. Charles was one of nine Royal Engineers who had volunteered to build a strongpoint at Bazentin-le-Petit. A private memorial to these nine brave men was erected in 1917 and survives to this day. His body was buried at Caterpillar Valley Cemetery at Longueval on the Somme in France near to where he fell.

Private Frank Bernard Emery
46843

Frank Emery was born at Hazel Slade in 1894 and was the fourth son of William and Mary Emery. William was a miner from Penkridge and Mary was born at Madeley in Shropshire, the couple having married at Cannock in 1884. They moved to Hazel Slade where they lived at 5, Cross Street. A family soon followed, Walter in 1886, followed by Clara, George, Thomas, Frank, Nellie and Florrie. The family were still living there in 1911, with the exception of Nellie who was a servant at Cannock Wood, Walter who was married but still living in Hazel Slade and Frank who was a 17 year old Private with the 1st Battalion, North Staffordshire Regiment at Shorncliffe Camp in Kent. When the Great War began, Frank was mobilized straight away, being sent to Aden on the 30th November, 1914. He was then transferred to the 8th Battalion, Welsh Regiment and served with them in Mesopotamia, where sadly on the 9th June, 1917 he was drowned at the age of 23. Frank's body was buried at Baghdad (North Gate) War Cemetery in Iraq.

Lance Corporal John Egbert Espin
5661

John Espin was born at Normanton, Derbyshire in 1883, being the second son of John and Sarah Espin, he being a railway signal fitter from Lancashire and she coming from Derby. Their eldest child, William was a signal erector's assistant whilst John junior was a pork butcher's assistant. Prudence and Mabel worked in a stocking making factory, with Eliza, Alice and George at school. John junior moved to Lichfield and became a slaughterman at Tranter's butchers at Hednesford, as well as having served in the Coldstream Guards. In 1910, John married Catherine Clarke at Lichfield and the couple lived at 139, Sandford Street to begin with, before moving to number 37. A son William was born in 1910, but died just after birth, however, in 1911 a daughter Sarah was born and in 1913 a son Jack. With the outbreak of the Great War, John as a Reservist was called up and was sent to France with the 3rd Battalion, Coldstream Guards on the 12th August, 1914. John saw service at Mons, the Marne, the Aisne, Neuve Chappelle and Ieper. He rose to the rank of Lance Corporal, but in 1916 he was badly wounded and died from his injuries on the 26th April, 1916 at the age of 33. Before his death he had sent a German helmet and sword back to Tranters

3. Hednesford

where they had been put on display in the shop window in Market Street. John's body was buried at Lijssenthoek Military Cemetery near Ieper in Belgium.

Private James Evans
25366

James Evans was born at Hednesford in 1880 and was the second son of Henry and Julia Evans. Henry was twenty-five years older than his wife and was a carpenter from Princes' End. His wife Julia came from Wednesbury and the couple had six children, Emily, Henry, James, Alice, Samuel and Ruth. The family had settled in Hednesford, living at Green Heath and Pye Green. However, in 1896 Henry senior died at the age of 72 and this saw the fragmentation of the family, for in 1901 James and Samuel were living together at Pye Green, whereas Julia and Ruth were living at Croydon in Surrey with their niece Mary Addleton and her family. In 1911, Julia was back at Pye Green with James and Samuel, James was a bread deliverer and Samuel a farm waggoner. By the outbreak of the Great War James was living with his mother at 27, Station Road, Hednesford, and on the 10th December, 1915 he enlisted with the Lincolnshire Regiment. He was placed on the Reserve List and was not posted until the 5th March, 1917 and remained in England until the 23rd March. He was sent to France on the 24th March, 1917 and was then transferred to the 43rd Company, Labour Corps. However on the 19th November, 1917 James was badly wounded suffering a compound fracture of the skull from a shell fragment. He was taken to 52 Field Ambulance and then transferred the next day to 46 Casualty Clearing Station where he died at 11p.m. At the time of his death, James was 37 and his body was buried at Mendinghem Military Cemetery in Belgium.

Private John Thomas Evans
13952

John Evans was the eldest son of Henry and Edith Evans and was born at Norton Canes in 1895. His younger brother Oscar Horace was born at Norton Canes in 1898. The family lived at Norton Canes, firstly on Brownhills Road and then on Hednesford Road where they ran a grocery and beer sales business. Just before the Great War, the family moved to Hednesford and lived on Wood Lane. John volunteered for the Army on the 2nd September, 1914, joining the 11th Battalion, Royal Welsh Fusiliers. He was sent to France on the 5th September,

1915 and was then posted to Salonika. He saw action in this theatre of war, before being admitted to hospital in January 1918 with malaria fever. He died from this disease on the 30th March, 1918 at the age of 23. His body was buried at Mikra British Cemetery, Kalamaria, Greece.

Lance Corporal Edgar Roland Foster
17780

Edgar Foster was born at Cannock in 1893, and was the eldest child of Thomas and Eliza Foster nee Dean. Thomas was a coal miner from Great Wyrley and Eliza was born at Hednesford. The couple were married at Cannock in 1890 and lived on the Walsall Road at Cannock before moving to live at Bank Street, Heath Hayes and later at Gorsemoor Road. In 1911, Edgar had found work as a loader at Old Hednesford Colliery, and was living at home with Evelyn, Leyland, Clarice and Kathleen. Edgar was a noted local footballer and kept goal for Chasetown Vics F.C. and for Bloxwich Strollers and indeed played in nets for the Divisional team when in the Army. In 1914, Edgar married Hannah Smith and the couple moved to live at 6, Bradford Street, High Town where their one child, Lilian, was born in 1915. Edgar volunteered for service in the Army in February 1915, joining the 7th Battalion, South Staffordshire Regiment and he was posted to Gallipoli on the 11th November, 1915. He was then sent to Egypt before the Battalion was posted to the Western Front. Edgar saw action on the Somme, Arras, Ieper, Lens and Messines Ridge and was promoted to Lance Corporal. However, on the 21st November, 1917 Edgar was killed by a shell during a bombing raid at the age of 24. His body was buried at Loos British Cemetery in France.

Private Edwin Joseph Foulk
85768

In 1891 at Cannock, Herbert Thomas Foulk, a postman from Hednesford married Sarah Ellen Mason from Wimblebury. The couple lived at 381, Littleworth, Hednesford and their first child, Louisa was born in 1892. She was followed by Eliza, Edwin, Florence, Gladys and Thomas. By 1911, the fourteen year old Edwin had started work as a hairdresser, a trade he was to continue throughout his life. His older sisters had moved into service, Louisa in Bury, Lancashire and Eliza at Stechford, Birmingham. On the 3rd August, 1917, Edwin was called up to serve, being posted to the 81st Training Battalion on the 7th August, before being transferred to the Northern Cyclist Battalion on the 22nd November, 1917. Edwin was sent to France on the 10th August, 1918, posted initially to the Northumberland Fusiliers before being transferred to the 2/6th Battalion, Durham Light Infantry on the 4th September, 1918, although he did not join the Battalion until the 19th September. At the age of 22, Edwin was killed in action on the 6th October, 1918. His body was buried at Ration Farm Military Cemetery at La Chapelle D'Armentieres in France. Edwin had taken his full hairdressing kit with him to France, but his father only received one pair of scissors with his personal effects. Five razors, clippers, combs and an expensive pair of scissors had disappeared.

Lance Corporal Arthur Freeman
35806

Arthur Freeman was born at Gentleshaw in 1888, and was the second son of Henry and Ann Freeman. Henry was a colliery carpenter, and both he and his wife came from Abbots Bromley in Staffordshire. They lived to begin with at Abbots Bromley, then Old Fallow, Cannock, moving briefly to Tamworth, before settling at 51, Brindley Heath, Hednesford. The couple raised eight children and in 1911, six of them were still living at home. William and Arthur were both coal miners, Eliza was a domestic servant and James a colliery labourer above ground, with Nellie and John still being at school. However, before the Great War, Arthur changed trades and became a carpenter, working as a railway wagon builder. On the 6th April, 1915 Arthur enlisted with the Royal Engineers as a carpenter, although his competence test described him as "indifferent". Arthur was fined two days pay on the 29th August, 1915 for overstaying his pass, and this was the last time he was seen by his family. On the 27th September, 1915 Arthur was posted to Salonika, joining the 139th Army Troops Company on the 4th October, 1915. He was remustered as a Sapper in 1916 and his competence pay was increased when he was designated as proficient. On the 16th March, 1918 Arthur was admitted to 25 Casualty Clearing Station with malaria but was sufficiently recovered to rejoin his unit on the 23rd of March. However, on the 22nd November, 1918 he was admitted to a Hospital Ship suffering from influenza, and was transferred to 43 General Hospital where he was treated until his death at 1.15 in the afternoon on the 12th December, 1918 at the age of 30. Arthur's body was buried at Mikra British Cemetery, Kalamaria in Greece. He had served for three and a half years without any leave.

Private Joseph Gardner
13604

In 1883, Joseph Gardner married Eliza Duce at Wolverhampton. He was a millman in an iron works from Dudley Port in Staffordshire and she came from Parkfield. The couple set up a home at 46, Bloomfield Road, Cradley Heath, and their family began with the birth of Sarah Jane, George, William and Polly. By 1901 the family had moved to live at 23 Albert Street, Hazel Slade, Joseph had become a coal miner and it was here that Elizabeth was born in 1892, Joseph in 1894, Elsie in 1901 and Herbert in 1905. In 1911, William had followed his father down the pit as a loader and Joseph junior had started work as a colliery horse keeper at Cannock and Rugeley Colliery. Joseph was also a good footballer and played in goal for Hazel Slade Church Institute and was good enough to have a trial for Hednesford Town Football Club. On the 28th August, 1914, Joseph enlisted with the 9th Battalion, Royal Welsh Fusiliers and was sent to France on the 19th July, 1915. On the 25th September, 1915 at the Battle of Loos, Joseph was killed in action at the age of 21. His body was never identified after the war and Joseph is remembered on the Loos Memorial to the Missing in France.

Private James Henry Gibbon
28298

In 1894, William Gibbon a shoeing and general smith from Southport in Lancashire married Jane Ann Evans from Burntwood in Staffordshire at Ormskirk. The couple set up a home at 40, Mount Street, Marine, Southport where David was born in 1897, James in 1899 and John in 1902. The family then moved to live at Heath Street, Green Heath, Hednesford, where Tom was born in 1904 and by 1911, David had started work as a newsboy, while James, John and Tom were at school. In 1917 at the age of 18, James was called up and joined the 1st Battalion, Hampshire Regiment. At the age of 19, James was killed in action on the 28th March, 1918. His body was not identified after the war and James was remembered on the Arras Memorial to the Missing in France.

2nd Lieutenant Edward Alan Green

Edward Alan Green was born at Houghton in Huntingdonshire on the 1st September, 1895 the second son of John George Green of Virginia Water in Surrey and Florence May Green nee Toussaint born at Madras in India. The couple had married at Brentford in 1881 and their first child John Leslie was born in 1889. A daughter, Dora Margaret Green was born at Houghton in 1893. John, the eldest was sent to St. Catherine's School at Ware in Hertfordshire, whereas Edward attended King's College Choir School and Felsted School in Essex, where he was a member of the Officer's Training School. Edward was commissioned into the 1/5th Battalion, South Staffordshire Regiment in April, 1914, serving with "F" Company at Hednesford, where he had secured a post as an articled pupil mining engineer. He was sent to France at the start of 1915 and was killed in action on the 13th October, 1915 when leading his Company in a failed attack on the Hohenzollern Redoubt during the Battle of Loos. At the time of his death, Edward was only 19 years old and his body was not recovered after the war. Edward is remembered on the Loos Memorial to the Missing in France. Edward's older brother, John Leslie also served as a medical officer with the same Battalion, before joining the 1/5th Sherwood Foresters. He was killed at Gommecourt on the 1st July, 1916 when trying to help an officer caught on the German barbed wire. For his bravery, he was awarded a posthumous Victoria Cross.

Rifleman Enoch Guy
S/9060

In 1875 at Wellington in Shropshire, Moses Guy a coal miner from Horsehay, married Esther Pinches from the same village. The couple had had two children, John Adam and Amos before moving to live at New Street, Cannock. By 1891, the family had moved to 33, Platt Street, High Town, Hednesford, and Jabez, Lily and Enoch had been born, the latter in 1890. In 1901, John and Jabez had followed their father to work in the pit, as a horse driver and a trammer respectively. Ten years later, only Jabez, a surface labourer, Enoch, a horse driver and Sarah who was still at school, were living at home, although John, now married with three children, was only two doors down at 35 Platt Street. On the 17th March, 1915 at Hednesford, Enoch volunteered for service in the Army. He was now a miner and living at 74, Belt Road, High Town and enlisted with 1 Company, 5th

Battalion, Rifle Brigade, being posted to Winchester on the 1st April. On the 20th April, Enoch was sent to France and transferred to the 7th Battalion. On the 30th July, 1915 at the age of 24, Enoch was posted as missing in action, and on the 4th June, 1916 the Army presumed that he had been killed on that date. Enoch's body was not identified after the war and he is remembered on the Ieper (Menin Gate) Memorial to the Missing in Ieper city centre in Belgium.

Sapper Thomas Guy
112611

Thomas Guy was the second son of Thomas and Hannah Guy nee Bailey and was born at Hednesford in 1890. Thomas senior was a coal miner from Dawley Bank in Shropshire whereas Hannah came from Wyrley and the couple were married at Cannock in 1887. In 1891 they were living in Brindley Heath in the West Cannock cottages and had two children, Hannah who had been born in the Cannock Workhouse and Joseph. By 1901, the family had moved to 28, Bradbury Lane, Hednesford and had increased in size with the births of Thomas, Lucy, John and Harriet. In 1911 Joseph and Thomas junior had joined their father down the pit, with both working as horse drivers, whilst John, Harriet and Sarah Ann were at school, and two more children Ernest and Emily had further swelled the family. Thomas junior volunteered for service in the Army in 1915, joining the 170th Tunnelling Company, Royal Engineers and was sent to France on the 26th August, 1915. He served for over two years before he died at the age of 24 on the 20th June, 1917 from an unspecified illness. Thomas was buried at Wimereux Communal Cemetery in France.

Private John Alfred Hallum
46489

In 1892 George Hallum a coal miner from Tipton in Staffordshire married Sarah Elizabeth Hudson, a girl from Penkridge and some ten years younger than her husband. The couple set up a home at Bradford Street, High Town, in Hednesford where Thomas, John and Elsie were born. By 1911, the family had moved to live at 62, Brindley Heath, and five more children had been born, George, Samuel, Elizabeth, Wilfred and Jesse. There was also a lodger staying with them, Thomas Parker, a 32 year old colliery labourer from Tipton. John was a member of High Town Methodist Church Sunday School and worked as a miner at West Cannock Number 5 pit. In view of his age, John would not have been called up until early 1918, and he joined the 7th Battalion, South Staffordshire Regiment. Sadly at the age of just 21, he died from pneumonia at Cannock Chase Military Hospital on the 12th January, 1919. John's body was buried at Cannock Cemetery with full military honours. His family expressed their thanks to the doctors and nurses who had looked after him.

Leading Seaman Frederick Hammond
Bristol Z/3635

In 1879 at Kidderminster in Worcestershire, William Hammond a tailor from Birmingham married Fanny Curtis. The couple lived at 3, Anchor Fields, Kidderminster where William had set up a business and their first child, Frances was born in 1881, but sadly died at the age of five in 1885. By 1891, the family had just moved to 2, Rose Terrace, Laslett Street, Worcester and in the meantime four children had been born, Agnes, Beatrice, Percy and Harold. The family moved to Hednesford after the birth of Frederick on the 25th February, 1894 and found a house in Hall's Buildings, West Hill, where William was now working as a tailor's cutter. By 1911 they had moved to 4, West View, Rugeley Road and the family had set up its own tailor and costumier business. Beatrice was working as a tailoress and Frederick was an assistant in the shop. Frederick later found work with Foster Brothers in the town and was a noted footballer for Hednesford Thursday F.C. and was a good billiards player. Harold in the meantime had chosen to become an agricultural engineer's clerk. On the 11th January, 1916 Frederick enlisted with the Royal Naval Volunteer Reserve, and was placed with HMS Victory, before joining the 7th Reserve Battalion of the Royal Naval Division. In May 1916, he was transferred to the 2nd Anson Battalion and sent to France. He rose from Ordinary Seaman to Able Seaman (Higher Grade) before asking to revert to Able Seaman following a bout of tonsillitis. However, after rejoining his unit he was promoted to Leading Seaman on the 14th January, 1917. However, on the 21st February, 1917 at the age of 22, Frederick was killed in action, dying from multiple gunshot wounds to the arm, shoulder and hip. His body was buried at Dernancourt Communal Cemetery Extension, near Albert on the Somme in France.

Private Charles Harding
263001

Charles Harding was born at Pelsall in 1893 and was the youngest of four sons born to William and Mary Ann Harding. William came from Pershore in Worcestershire and was a railway shunter and later a colliery labourer. His other sons, Harry, William and Thomas all went into the local pits. The family were living on Station Road, Hednesford in 1891 but by 1901 the family had moved, now living at 3, Grant Street, Walsall. However, by 1911, they had moved again to live at 18, Bradbury Lane, Hednesford although by this time only Charles was still living at home, and he too had gone down the pit. When the Great War broke out, Charles was one of the first to join up, enlisting with the 1/6th Battalion, South Staffordshire Regiment and being sent to France on the 5th March, 1915. He served on the Western Front for over two years until at the age of 24 he was killed in action on the 25th May, 1917. Charles' body was buried at Maroc British Cemetery at Bethune in France.

Private Samuel Harley
11959

Samuel Harley was born in 1893 at Hednesford and was the fifth son of John and Sarah Jane Harley. John was a colliery blacksmith from Wednesbury and Sarah Jane came from nearby Walsall. The couple had moved to the Hednesford area by 1881 and in 1901 were living at Arthur Street in Chadsmoor with eight children. John died shortly after the census and in 1911 the widowed Sarah Jane was living at Glover Street, Wimblebury, where John Thomas, Samuel, Alice and George were still at home. John Thomas was a tub emptier down the pit and Samuel was a horse driver. In 1915, Samuel volunteered for the Army and enlisted with the 1st Battalion, South Staffordshire Regiment, being sent to France on the 5th October, 1915. He served with the Battalion for fifteen months until he was killed in action at the age of 23 on the 11th January, 1917. Samuel's body was buried at Lonsdale Cemetery, Authuile, near Albert on the Somme in France.

3. Hednesford

Private Charles Henry Harrison
202953

Charles Harrison was born at Fulford, near Stone in Staffordshire in 1894 and was the second son of Frederick and Jane Harrison, who were also born at Fulford. The couple had eight children, all of whom survived childhood. On the 1891 census the family were still living at Fulford. In 1901 the family were living at Saverley, near Stone where Frederick was a general labourer, but by 1911, the family had moved to Erdingale in Tamworth where Frederick was employed as an estate woodman. Samuel and his older brother Joseph were both working as farm labourers at Hidderley's Farm at Croxall Grange in Lichfield. The family moved to live at 4, Albert Street, Hazel Slade, Hednesford and Charles joined the Army, probably in 1915. Initially he was with the Staffordshire Yeomanry, but later transferred to the South Staffordshire Regiment. He died on the 18th May, 1918 from serious wounds that had meant he had been brought back to England from the frontline. At the time of his death, Charles was 22 years of age and was buried at Colwich (St. Michael's) Churchyard.

Private James Harrison
9938

James Harrison a 23 year old coal miner from Portobello in Staffordshire married Jane Ellen Maiden, a 22 year old from Dawley in Shropshire, at Cannock in 1883. They lived in Hednesford to begin with and their first two children, Beatrice and James were born there in 1886 and 1888 respectively. The family then moved to live at New Street, Shelfield near Walsall, where William was born in 1890. The family stayed at Shelfield, where George was born in 1893 and Jonah in 1894, followed by a move to Chiswick Row, Staincross Common, Darton near Barnsley where Bertha was born in 1900, and Wilfred in 1903. In 1906, Jane died at the age of 46 and this prompted a move back to Staffordshire. In 1910, a 22 year old James junior married Florence Emily Marklew, aged 19 from Roystone in Yorkshire, at Cannock. The couple moved in with the Hadlington family at 140, Cannock Road, Heath Hayes and their first child, William was born in 1911. They were just a few doors from James senior who was living at 134, Cannock Road with Jonah, Bertha and Wilfred. James junior has followed his father and brothers down the pit and was employed as a fireman by the Cannock and Rugeley Colliery Company at Valley Pit, Hednesford. The family moved to live at 122, Church Hill, Hednesford and two more children were born, James in 1913 and Florence in 1914. When the Great War broke out James volunteered at the Drill Hall at Hednesford on the 10th December, 1914, enlisting with the 2nd Battalion, South Staffordshire Regiment and was sent to France on the 25th May, 1915. Just four months later at the age of 27, James was killed in action on the 25th September, 1915, at the Battle of Loos. James' body was buried at Cambrin Military Cemetery near Arras in France.

Lance Corporal Herbert Harvey
47637

Herbert Harvey was born in 1895 at Hednesford and was the youngest son of William and Lucy Harvey. William was a colliery banksman from Hednesford whilst his wife came from Pensnett near Dudley. In 1891 the family were living on the Rugeley Road, Hednesford, and at that time Sarah, Eliza, Clarice and John had been born. However, in 1901, William was living at Mount Street, Hednesford with John, William, Charles Sarah and Clare, whereas Lucy was living at 9, Waterworth Street, Nelson, Lancashire with her married daughter Mary Taylor and her family, with Herbert, who had been born six years earlier. By 1911, the family were back together at 18, Mount Street, Hednesford, although William senior was now out of work. John was a coal miner and William junior and Charles were roadmen down the pit. Herbert was employed as a carter, but later worked as a miner at Cannock and Rugeley. When the Great War broke out, Herbert volunteered for service in the Army with the South Staffordshire Regiment and was sent to Gallipoli on the 15th September, 1915. He was then posted to France and was transferred to the 10th Battalion, Essex Regiment where he rose to the rank of Lance Corporal. However, at the age of 23, Herbert was killed in action on the 21st September, 1918. His body was buried at Unicorn Cemetery, Vend'huile, between St. Quentin and Peronne in France. Herbert's brother, Charles was also killed in action on the 4th July 1916, at the age of 23 whilst serving with the 2nd Battalion, South Staffordshire Regiment.

Private John Henry Hawkins
9485

In 1884 at Cannock Jonah Hawkins married Rosanna Lucy Williams. He was a 25 year old coal miner from Oakengates in Shropshire and she was a 21 year old from Willenhall. They set up a home at McGhie Street in Hednesford and by 1891 had had four children. By 1901 the family had moved to live on the Rawnsley Road and was now made up of seven children, including John Henry who was born at Hednesford in 1893 and who was known by the family as Jack. In 1911, the family had moved to reside at 35, Bradbury Lane, and Jim, Jack and Jonah had all started work down the pit. Jim and Jack were horse drivers and Jonah worked as a labourer on the pit bank, at Cannock and Rugeley Colliery. Jack was also a member of the Hednesford Territorials and as a result when war broke out, he joined up straight away, enlisting in the 8th Battalion, South Staffordshire Regiment and was sent to France on the 17th December, 1914. He served until the 23rd April, 1917 when he was killed in action at the age of 23. After the war Jack's body was not identified and he is remembered on the Arras Memorial to the Missing in France.

Private Charles Cecil Lee Haycock
27012

Charles Lee was born at Hednesford in 1897, and in 1901 appears as the adopted son of William Haycock and his wife Jemima. This couple had married at Cannock in 1889, and in 1891 were living with William's parents at Pritchard's Buildings, Littleworth, Hednesford. In 1911 the family were living at Victoria Cottages, 1, High Mount Street, Hednesford. Clarence Haycock was described as a nephew and was working as an iron moulder in Hednesford. Charles was also described as a nephew and is under the surname of Lee. He is working as a grocer's errand boy, but later worked as a butcher for Ratcliff's on Market Street in Hednesford. Charles was a keen member of the Salvation Army band in Hednesford. On the 10th December, 1915 Charles enlisted with the South Staffordshire Regiment but was placed on the Reserve List and when he was mobilized on the 20th May, 1916 he was posted to the 3rd Battalion, Lincolnshire Regiment, being sent to France on the 5th September, 1916. On the 20th September, 1916 Charles was transferred to the 1st Battalion, King's Own Royal Lancaster Regiment, joining his new unit in the field two days later. Just a month afterwards on the 23rd October, 1916 Charles was killed in action at the age of 19. Charles' body was not recovered after the war and he is remembered on the Thiepval Memorial to the Missing on the Somme in France.

Private Richard Haycock
7356

In 1873, William Haycock a coal miner from Wolverhampton married Elizabeth Catherine Rowley at Penkridge, and the couple set up a home in Bloxwich where their first child Charles was born. The family moved to Brindley Heath in 1875 and by 1881 three more children had been born. By 1891 the family had increased to seven, and Richard had been born at Hednesford in 1886. The family continued to live at 71, West Cannock Cottages, but by 1901 they had moved to live at 76, Brindley Heath, and Richard had followed his father and brothers down the pit. On the 21st October, 1906 Richard married Mary Ellen Bould at St. Luke's Parish Church, Cannock and the couple lived for a time at Moreton Street, Chadsmoor. In 1907, Richard enlisted with the 2nd Battalion, South Staffordshire Regiment, and saw service in India and South Africa. Interestingly, in 1911 he describes himself as single when at Whittington Barracks, while his wife was working as a domestic servant for Mr and Mrs Fielden at Walton-on-Trent. Richard came out of the Army in 1912 and the couple set up a home at George Lane, Lichfield where Richard had found work as a labourer at Bridgeman and Sons. In 1912, their first child Richard was born and a second child, Mary, was born in October, 1914. Sadly Richard never saw his daughter, because he was called up on the 5th August, 1914 and sent to France on the 12th. On the 11th February, 1915 at the age of 29, Richard died from wounds incurred from shrapnel in the chest. His body was buried at Bethune Town Cemetery in France.

Private William Haycock
66076

William Haycock was born at Castleford in Yorkshire in 1897 and was the eldest son of Charles and Elizabeth Haycock. Charles hailed from Tipton in Staffordshire and his wife was a native of Castleford, the couple having married there in 1894. By 1901, the family of four children were living at 18, Castle Street, Castleford where Charles was employed as a coal miner. By 1911, the family had increased to eight children, with only the eldest, Annie Elizabeth, a 16 year old house maid and William, a 14 year old door trapper in a coal mine, earning additional income for the family. In 1916, William enlisted in the 53rd Young Soldier Battalion of the King's Own Yorkshire Light Infantry and found himself at Brindley Heath with other recruits. His physical health was such that he was not considered fit enough for service overseas and was transferred to the Royal Defence Corps. William died on the 20th December, 1917 at the age of 20 and was buried at St. Peter's Churchyard in Hednesford.

Private Arthur Haywood
G/13939

In 1883 at Walsall in Staffordshire, Arthur Haywood married Mary Ann Barker and the couple set up home at Aldridge, where Annie was born, before moving to Walsall Wood, where Lucy came into the world. The family then moved to Glasgow where Arthur was born in 1897 and George in 1899. A further move back to Aldridge followed, and then Hednesford where Joseph was born. The family then made its way to Yorkshire where Alfred and Clara were born. Still unable to remain in one place, the family then moved back to Hednesford, where they lived at 485, Littleworth Road, Rawnsley. Arthur was now a horse minder under ground at a local colliery, but on the 17th February, 1916 he attested into the Army with the 7th Battalion, The Buffs (East Kent Regiment). He was placed on the Reserve List until the 2nd April, 1917 and was sent to Wallsend, from where he was sent to France on the 20th June, 1917, in time for the Third Battle of Ieper. On the 13th October, 1917 the 20 year old Arthur was posted as missing in action, and this date was presumed by the Army to be when he died. Arthur's body was not recovered after the war and he is remembered on the Tyne Cot Memorial to the Missing near Ieper in Belgium.

Private Richard Joseph Hendy
9607

In 1891 at Cannock, William Hendy, a 26 year old coal miner from Tipton in Staffordshire married a 23 year old also from Tipton named Emma Evans. The couple set up a home at Ghost Row, Hednesford and by 1901, William, Samuel, Richard, Alice and Isaac had been born. These were followed by Thomas and Harold, before the family decided to move to Wales in 1907. They set up home at 8, Penlan Street, Pentrebach, in Merthyr Tydfil and by 1911, Richard had joined his father as a coal miner. Samuel had chosen to remain in Hednesford, and was working as a horse driver in a colliery and was living with the Cotterell family, to whom he was related, at George Street, Hednesford. The eldest child William had decided to enlist with the 2nd Battalion, Royal Warwickshire Regiment and was stationed at Whittington Barracks at Lichfield. Richard must have been a member of the Territorials, which would suggest that he had returned to the Hednesford area before the Great War. This is reinforced by the fact that he was called up at the outbreak of war and was sent to France with the 8th Battalion, South Staffordshire Regiment on the 17th December, 1914. He served until the 9th July, 1916 when at the age of 20 he was killed in action. His body was not recovered after the war and Richard is remembered on the Thiepval Memorial to the Missing on the Somme in France.

Sergeant Thomas Higgs DCM
242478

In 1883 at Wolverhampton, Benjamin Higgs a coal miner from Bilston aged 18 married Sarah Hill, aged a year younger, from Coseley. The couple moved to live at 27, Alfred Street, Bloxwich where the first of their children, Samuel, Benjamin, William and Eliza were born. They shared the house with Benjamin's brother, James, and his wife and family. Around 1895 the family moved to live at 42, Bradford Street, High Town, Hednesford where Thomas was born in 1897, followed by Joseph, John and George. All of the boys became coal miners and Eliza in 1911 was described as a servant away from home. It seems that Thomas was conscripted into the Army in early 1917, serving with the 2nd Battalion, South Staffordshire Regiment where he rose to the rank of Sergeant and won the Distinguished Conduct Medal for bravery. However, on the 29th September, 1918 at the age of 21, Thomas was killed in action. His body was buried at Noyelles-sur-L'Escaut Communal Cemetery Extension, near Cambrai in France.

Private Frederick Hill
13706

Henry Hill a 20 year old house painter from Wolverhampton married 18 year old Martha Ann Bradley from Bradford in Yorkshire, at Walsall in 1874. They set up a home at Station Road, Hednesford where by 1881 they had had four children, all daughters and also living with them was a lodger, James Taylor, a 22 year old teacher from Whitchurch in Herefordshire. In 1891, the family had moved to Church Hill, Hednesford, where four more children had been born, the last three all boys. By 1901 Leonard and Frederick had been born, the latter in 1897, and with the rest of the family growing up, Ada was working as a milliner and Henry was a baker's apprentice. James Taylor was still a lodger and remained a teacher. However, there

3. Hednesford

were major changes following the death of Martha in 1909 at the age of 52. The family was split up, for in 1911, Henry was a boarder with the Grant family at 18, Sheep Fair, Rugeley whilst Robert and Frederick were lodging with the Finch family at George Street, Hednesford where Robert was a baker and Frederick a loader down the pit at West Cannock. In October, 1914, Frederick enlisted in the Army, joining the 9th Battalion, Royal Welsh Fusiliers and was sent to France on the 19th July, 1915. He served until the 7th July, 1916 when he was killed in action during the Battle of the Somme at the age of 21. Frederick's body was not recovered after the war and he is remembered on the Thiepval Memorial to the Missing on the Somme in France.

Private James Victor Holmes
23717

Robert Holmes, a 22 year old colliery carpenter from Swinton in Lancashire married Sarah Berry, 19, from Irlam o' th' Height, Lancashire at Salford in 1887. The couple set up home at Swinton where Peter was born in 1888, before they set off for the United States of America where James was born at Boston, Massachusetts in 1889. However the family had returned to England by 1891 and were living at 30, Manchester Road, Pendlebury. By 1901 they had moved to 68, Park Lane West, Pendlebury and the family had increased to five children. In 1911, the family was living at 17, Kersal Avenue, Pendlebury where Peter was a colliery carpenter like his father and Albert was a waggoner in a pit, but James had opted to become a clerk at a brewery, whilst his sister Alice was a fettler. At some point before the Great War, James moved to Hednesford and lived at 103, Mount Street, Green Heath, in Hednesford. He joined the Army in early 1916, enlisting with the 7th Battalion, Duke of Cornwall's Light Infantry and was sent to France for the "Big Push". On the 16th September, 1916 at the age of 27, James was killed in action. His body was not found after the war and James is remembered on the Thiepval Memorial to the Missing on the Somme in France.

Private Francis William Holt
8734

Francis William Holt was born at Walthamstow in Essex in 1887. His father was Francis Holt, from Colton, and a soldier serving with the North Staffordshire Regiment and his mother Margaret, who was a British subject but born in Burma. It is most likely that the couple met and married in India, but in 1887, Francis senior was a

141

Colour Sergeant in charge of recruiting. By 1891, the family were living at 30, Albion Street, Rugeley where Francis was in charge of local recruitment. Tragically, Margaret died at the age of 26 in 1892, but in 1894 Francis senior married Hannah Elizabeth Sutton, from Rugeley, at Lichfield, and in 1901 the family had moved to 32, Market Street, Rugeley, which was the Headquarters of the Volunteer Company. Francis William decided to follow his father's example and he too joined the Army, enlisting with the 1st Battalion, Essex Regiment, and in 1911, he was a 23 year old Private in "B" Company and was in White Barracks, Quetta, near Baluchistan in India. His parents had moved to live at 15, Rugeley Road, Hazel Slade, where Francis senior worked as a clerk for the Cannock and Rugeley Colliery Company and he was a prominent member of the Hazel Slade Mission. When Francis William came out of the Army, he went onto the Reserve List, but found a job on the railway at Great Wyrley. However, when the Great War began, Francis William was called up into the 1st Battalion, Essex Regiment and was sent to France on the 27th August, 1914. Francis was taken ill in December, 1914 and was sent to Boulogne for treatment, but died from pneumonia on the 15th December, 1914 at the age of 27. Francis' body was buried at Wimereux Communal Cemetery in France.

Gunner John Lewis Hornblower
175884

In 1876 at Madeley in Shropshire, William Hornblower, a tile burner from Dawley married Georgina Franks also from Dawley. The couple moved to Manchester in Lancashire where Susannah was born, before they moved back to Dawley where the rest of their nine children were born. By 1881, Ethel and John Edwin had been born and the family were living at Stocking Road, Dawley. By 1891, the family had moved to Little Dawley and William, Harry, John Lewis and Sidney had all been born. In 1901, they had moved to Blist's Hill in Madeley and Percy and Doris made the family number ten in total, and in 1911 they had moved to live at 35, Coalport Road in Madeley. William senior had risen from a tile burner to become the foreman of a tile works, and his son William was an engine driver and John Lewis was a clerk, whilst John Edwin had married and was an engineer's fitter. In 1916, John Lewis married Julia May Lewis at Madeley, with a child Ethel being born in 1917, and shortly afterwards John moved to Hednesford to work, it was while he was living at Hednesford that he was called up in 1918. John served with the 260th Siege Battery of the Royal Garrison Artillery and he was badly wounded in October, 1918 and was sent to a Base Hospital at Rouen for treatment, but sadly died from his injuries on the 14th October at the age of 30. John's body was buried at St. Sever Cemetery Extension at Rouen.

3. Hednesford

Private Ernest William Horton
58917

Ernest Horton was born at Handsworth, Staffordshire in 1876 and was the fourth son of John and Ellen Horton. John was a gardener domestic servant from Coleshill, Warwickshire and his wife a laundress from Birmingham. The couple had seven children born between 1863 and 1879 and lived for most of that time at 1, Havelock Terrace, Handsworth. The children had a range of different jobs; Mary was a domestic servant, Walter a jeweller, Christopher a painter and Ernest a shoemaker's apprentice. In 1897, Ernest married Sarah Ann Collins at Walsall, with William being born at Handsworth in 1899 before the couple set up home at 82, Field House, Goscote, where Ernest Edward and Lilian were born. The family then moved to live at Hednesford in 1907, where Frederick was born. Ernest had given up his trade as a boot maker to work as a loader in a coal mine. Ernest enlisted in the Army in 1915, joining the 8th Field Ambulance, Royal Army Medical Corps and being sent to France on the 3rd October, 1915. He served until the 21st March, 1918 when he was killed in action on the first day of the German Spring Offensive at the age of 42. Ernest's body was never recovered after the war and he is remembered on the Arras Memorial to the Missing in France.

Private Richard Horton
202751

On the 15th April, 1889 at St. Luke's Parish Church, Cannock, George Horton a 23 year old miner originally from Bilston and living at High Town married 16 year old Eliza Blakesley originally from Dudley. The young couple set up a home at Burgoyne Street, Chadsmoor and their first child, George William was born a year later. The family grew with Richard born in 1892, Catherine in 1895, and John in 1900 and by 1901 they had moved to live at Bradford Street, High Town. By 1911, the family had increased further with Annie in 1903, Fillie in 1907, Joe in 1909 and Doris in 1910. William was now working as a coal miner driver and Richard was employed as a coal miner jigger. They had also moved again and were now living at Moss Street, Chadsmoor. On the 24th December, 1912, Richard married Amy Mills at Nuneaton, and a son, Stanley Richard Horton was born on the 7th December, 1913. However, it would appear that the couple did not remain together, for Amy's address was given as 2, Belle Vue, Stockingford, Nuneaton, Warwickshire, whilst Richard continued to live at Moss Street.

Perhaps it was a tattoo on Richard's arm saying "True love for Ida" that was the root of the problem. On the 13th July, 1915, Richard enlisted at Rugeley. He was 22 and now an insurance agent, and joined the 6th Battalion, King's Royal Rifle Corps. Richard was posted to the 5th Battalion on the 23rd October and appointed as a Lance Corporal on the 3rd November, but was deprived of his stripe on the 12th December. This was closely followed by Richard being stopped 7 days pay on the 2nd January, 1916, and he was then posted to France on the 19th April. He was wounded and returned to England on the 13th June, 1916 and posted to the 6th Battalion again on the 8th September, 1916. On the 12th December, Richard was transferred to the 2/4th Battalion, Royal Scots, and six months later he was transferred again to the 2nd Battalion, Royal Scots Fusiliers. Richard died on the 21, November, 1918 at the age of 26 from influenza. His body was buried with full military honours at Cannock Cemetery.

Corporal Harry Houghton
37187

In 1895, James Houghton, a 28 year old miner from Brereton married Mary Ann Wain at Armitage. She was from Rugeley and was also 28 years of age. In 1899, their first child, Harry was born at Brereton and in 1900, Elizabeth was born. Emily followed in 1902, James in 1904 and Nellie in 1905. By this time the family had moved to live at 4, Cross Street, Hazel Slade, in Hednesford. Harry was called up in 1917, initially joining the North Staffordshire Regiment, but being transferred to the 7th Battalion, East Yorkshire Regiment, where he rose to the rank of Corporal. On the 20th October, 1918 Harry was killed in action at the age of 20. His body was buried at Selridge British Cemetery at Montay, near Le Cateau in France.

Private Harold Hughes
43247

Harold Hughes was born at Betley in Staffordshire in 1897 and was the eldest son of David and Jane Hughes. They had married in 1893 at Wolstanton in Staffordshire. David was from Swansea and worked as a foreman in a colliery and his wife came from Silverdale and her maiden name was Rowley. The couple settled in Silverdale where Lily was born, before moving to nearby Betley where Harold and Leonard were born. In 1901, David, Jane, Lily and Leonard were living at 28, Abbey Street, Silverdale, whereas Harold was staying with his father's parents at

Betley. By 1911, the family had moved to live at Littleworth Lane in Hednesford, where David had secured a position as under manager at a local colliery. Lily and Harold, although old enough to work were both at home, whilst Leonard, Margaret and Mary were at school. When the Great War broke out, Harold enlisted at the end of 1914, although only 17 years of age. He joined the Royal Army Medical Corps and was sent to Egypt on the 30th May, 1915, returning to France on the 19th March, 1916 when he was attached to serve on the Hospital Ship Galeka. On the 28th October, the "Galeka" was returning from England and was attempting to enter the harbour at Le Havre when she struck a mine laid by the German submarine U-26. Nineteen RAMC personnel were killed in the explosion and one of these was the 19 year old Harold Hughes. Harold's body was buried at Ste. Marie Cemetery at Le Havre in France.

Private George Humphries
L/17096

In 1883 at Lichfield, George Humphries an 18 year old coal miner from Wolverhampton married Annie Lyons from Colton in Staffordshire. The couple moved to live at 56, McGhie Street, Hednesford and by 1891 they had four children, Edith, William, Bertram and George who was born in 1890. In 1901 the family had increased to eight children with the births of Louisa, Clara, Basil and Joseph and William had started work as a horse driver in a colliery. In 1911, two more children had further swelled the family, with the births of Fred in 1902 and Jessie in 1905. Bert was a collier loader as was George, with Basil working as an errand boy. Nellie was out of work which placed additional pressure on the rest of the family. In the Great War, George initially joined the Royal Army Medical Corps, but at some point transferred to the 4th Battalion, Middlesex Regiment. On the 31st October, 1917 at the age of 27 George was killed in action at the Third Battle of Ieper. His body was never found after the war and George is remembered on the Ieper (Menin Gate) Memorial to the Missing in Ieper city centre.

Sapper Henry Hyden
120903

In early 1889 at Cannock, Henry Hyden a coal miner from Rugeley in Staffordshire married Ann Thomas from Portobello, Willenhall. The couple set up a home at 23, Bradbury Lane, Hednesford where Sarah Jane was born in

1890 and Henry junior in 1891. In 1901 the family was living at 67, Brindley Heath and had grown to number four children with the births of Ernest Edward in 1893 and Lottie in 1897. 1911 had seen another move to 99, New Buildings, Rawnsley, Hednesford and a further increase to the household with the births of Isaac in 1902, Charlie in 1904 and Herbert in 1908. Sarah Jane had married Charles Frederick Lygo and they were also living with the rest of the family. Henry and Ernest were both working for Cannock and Rugeley Colliery as horse drivers, although both later became coal miners, and Lottie was employed as a tailoress. On the 11th December, 1915 Henry attested for the Army, joining the Royal Engineers and was placed on the Reserve List. However, on the 11th January, 1916 he joined up at his own request, being sent to the Base Depot in France on the 5th February, 1916 and being posted to the 179th Tunnelling Company on the 13th. On the 20th April, 1916 Henry was admitted to 6 General Hospital and was transferred back to the Welsh Metropolitan War Hospital at Whitchurch near Cardiff suffering from anaemia. He was hospitalized for three months, not rejoining his unit until the 22nd August. Henry was again admitted to hospital on the 5th December, 1916 and when recovered was transferred to the 258th Tunnelling Company on the 15th December. On the 2nd February, 1917 at the age of 26, Henry was killed in action. A letter to his parents from 2nd Lieutenant R.L. Ward told them that Henry had been hit by a shell and had been killed instantaneously. Ward went on to add that Henry was a brave soldier. His body was buried at the Guard's Cemetery, Lesboeufs between Arras and Bapaume in France.

Private George Illsley MM
18630

John Illsley was a 21 year old coal miner from Newhall in Derbyshire and in 1888 at Ashby-de-la-Zouch in Leicestershire he married Camilia Stubbs, 28, from Oakthorpe in Derbyshire. The couple set up a home at Oakthorpe and it was here in 1889 that George was born. The family then moved to live at New Street, Chadsmoor, but by 1901 they had moved to 3, Church Street, Chadsmoor. The family had grown rapidly with twins Sarah and Agnes born in 1892, Elizabeth in 1894, Joseph in 1898 and John in 1900. By 1911, Elsie May had been born in 1902, Eliza in 1903 and Louisa in 1904. George and Joseph were working as coal miners, even though Joseph was only 13 years of age, at Number 3 West Cannock Colliery. On the 25th December, 1911 George married Ada Pearce at St. Peter's Parish Church, Hednesford. Both bride and groom were 22 years of age and both gave their address as 3, Bradbury Lane, Hednesford. Early in 1912, a daughter, Evelyn was born to the young couple. George enlisted in the Army in December, 1914 joining the 1st Battalion, Royal Welsh Fusiliers and was sent to France on the 25th May, 1915. He was awarded the Military Medal for bravery, but on the 27th August, 1916 in the Battle of the Somme, George was killed in action at the age of 27. George's body was never identified after the war and he is remembered on the Thiepval Memorial to the Missing on the Somme in France.

Captain Harold Alfred Ivatt MC

In 1885 at St. Ives in Cambridgeshire, Thomas Ernest Ivatt a farmer from the Isle of Ely married Florence Ann Battcock, a farmer's daughter from Hemmingford Abbots in Huntingdonshire. In 1891 the Ivatt family were living at Waterbeach in Cambridgeshire and at that time had three children, Alwyn, Frank and Edith. They also had a cook, Annie Everett, a nurse, her sister Lucy Everett and a housemaid, Mary Dring. However, by 1901 Thomas was helping Martin Poole manage his farm at St. Mary's Street on the Isle of Ely and Florence had gone back to live with her elderly parents at Hemmingford Abbots. The children were at private schools, indeed Edith and Harold, who had been born in 1893, were both at the Wych House School at St. Ives. Harold went on from there to attend King's School, Ely and afterwards went to live at 4, Rawnsley Road, Hednesford where he was employed as a mining student with the Cannock and Rugeley Colliery Company. It was here that Harold joined the Hednesford Territorials and he was gazetted as a 2nd Lieutenant with the South Staffordshire Regiment on the 26th March, 1912. When war broke out, Harold was mobilised on the 4th August, 1914 and was sent to France with the 1/5th Battalion in April, 1915 as Transport Officer and being promoted to temporary Captain on the 14th October, 1915 for "heroically leading the Company at the taking of the Hohenzollern Redoubt" and shortly afterwards was awarded the Military Cross for bravery when he rescued men from a burning mine. He was confirmed in the rank of Captain on the 15th August, 1916. On the 21st May, 1918 this brave officer was killed at the age of 25 when a shell exploded in the dug out where he sheltering. Harold's body was buried at Fouquieres Churchyard Extension near Bethune in France.

Private William Jackson

Unfortunately William Jackson will remain just a name. There is very little evidence of him other that he lived at Brindley Heath, Hednesford. Yet there is nothing to link any man of that name who was killed in the Great War to Hednesford either in terms of birth or residence.

Private Joseph Jennings
17531

Edward Jennings married Elizabeth Jennings at Penkridge in 1872. The couple were both from Bloxwich and Edward was a coal miner. They set up home at 2, Rugeley Road, Pool End, Hednesford, and by 1881 had three children, John, Richard and William. In 1891 the family had grown to number seven, with Annie, Fanny, Edward and Joseph having been born, the latter in 1890. By 1901, Prudence, Esther and Sarah Ann had been born. John, Richard and Edward had followed their father down the pit and the family lodger, an Irishman named Thomas Bryan Farran had remained with them all this time. In 1911, Edward and Joseph were still at home and both were coal miners at the West Cannock sinkings, with Prudence and Esther both working as a tailoress. Sarah Ann although fourteen years of age, and having left school, was without employment at this time. When the Great War began Joseph volunteered in August 1914, joining the 4th Battalion, Grenadier Guards, and was sent to France on the 16th March, 1915. He served with nothing more serious than a case of frostbite, until on the 25th September, 1916 at the age of 26, Joseph was killed in action. The information was sent home in a letter by Private J. Piggott. Joseph's body was not identified after the war and he is remembered on the Thiepval Memorial to the Missing on the Somme in France.

Private Arthur James Nourse Johnson
41731

James Nourse Johnson was born at Maids Morton in Buckinghamshire in 1857 and by 1881 he had moved to live and work in Hednesford. He was employed as a signalman for the London and North Western Railway and lodged with Matthias and Mary White, who also came from the Buckinghamshire/

Bedfordshire area, on the Cannock Road in High Town. He was still living with the White family in 1891, but by now romance was in the air, for on the 14th September, 1891 James married Sarah Ann White, the daughter of Matthias and Mary, at St. Luke's Parish Church, Cannock. The couple moved to live at Market Street, Hednesford and their first child, John Ernest was born in 1892, followed by Arthur in 1897 and William in 1902. By 1911, John was a student teacher and Arthur had just left school. Arthur managed to find a job as a clerk for the London and North Western Railway and was also an energetic worker for the Hednesford Weslyan Sunday School. In 1916, Arthur enlisted with the South Staffordshire Regiment but was transferred to the 4th Battalion, Bedfordshire Regiment. Arthur was badly wounded when the hospital where he was being treated at Etaples was bombarded and was sent back to London where he died from his injuries on the 9th August 1918 at the age of 21. Arthur's body was brought back to Hednesford where it was buried with full military honours at St. Peter's Churchyard, Hednesford.

Private Benjamin Jones
13019

Benjamin Jones was born in Hednesford in 1894 and was the fourth son of Joseph and Hannah Jones. Both Joseph and Hannah came from Sedgley and it was here that their first child, John was born in 1887, before the family moved to Brindley Heath, Hednesford in 1888. Reuben and Nancy were born here, followed by Joseph, Benjamin, Mary and Herbert and by 1901 the family had moved to live at Bradbury Lane. William was born in 1905 and the family had moved again, this time to 46, Abbey Street, Green Heath. By now John, Reuben, Joseph and Benjamin had joined their father down the pit. Benjamin was a member of the Hednesford Territorials and when war broke out he enlisted straight away, joining the 1st Battalion, South Staffordshire Regiment and being sent to France on the 26th January, 1915. Benjamin served until the 31st August, 1916 when he was killed in action on the Somme at the age of 21. After the war Benjamin's body was not found and he is remembered on the Thiepval Memorial to the Missing on the Somme in France.

Corporal Herbert Jones
15245

Joseph Jones a miner from Great Wyrley married Elizabeth Tebbett on the 19th February 1893 at St. Luke's Parish Church, Cannock. He was 22 years of age and she was 19 and both gave their address as West Chadsmoor. The couple set up a home on the Belt Road, West Chadsmoor and Herbert was born in 1893, followed by Sarah Ann in 1895, Fanny in 1897, Emily in 1899 and Caroline in 1900. By 1911, George, Mary, Leonard and John had been added to the family and Herbert had started work as a miner roadman like his father, and Fanny was employed as a nurse. In 1913, Herbert married Susannah Bryan, an 18 year old domestic servant from Cheslyn Hay, at Cannock. When the Great War began, Herbert enlisted in early 1915, joining the 1st Battalion, Northumberland Fusiliers and was sent to France on the 28th July, 1915. Herbert rose to the rank of Corporal, but on the 29th March, 1918 he was posted as missing in action, and it was later presumed that he had died on that date at the age of 28. Herbert's body was not recovered after the war and he is remembered on the Arras Memorial to the Missing in France.

Private Isaiah Jones
13717

Isaiah Jones was born at Great Wyrley in 1887 and was the fourth son of Charles and Sarah Jones. Charles was a miner from Wellington in Shropshire and his wife came from Wyrley. In 1881 the family was living at Church Hill, Hednesford, with Joseph the eldest, a coal miner like his father and Moses, a general labourer, whilst Dinah and Charles were at school. However, in 1892, Charles died at the age of 51, and by 1901 Sarah had married William Harvey and only Dinah, Charles and Isaiah were still living at Church Hill. Dinah was now a domestic servant, Charles a labourer in a mine and Isaiah was a horse driver in a pit. Isaiah was a well known footballer at this time and had played for Hednesford Town, Cannock Town and Wolverhampton Wanderers. In 1914, Isaiah volunteered for the Army, joining the 9th Battalion, Royal Welsh Fusiliers and he was sent to France on the 19th April, 1915. On the 25th July, 1916 Isaiah was killed in action on the Somme at the age of 30. His body was not found after the war and he is remembered on the Thiepval Memorial to the Missing on the Somme in France.

Rifleman John Jones
7667

John Jones was born at Cannock in 1895 and was the eldest child of Morris and Selia Jones who lived at Cemetery Road, Broomhill. Morris came from Newtown in Montgomeryshire whilst Selia hailed from Tunstall in the Potteries. In 1901 the Jones' had three children with George and Elizabeth making up the trio. However, by 1911, Selia was a widow, working as a domestic servant and living with the Whitton family at Lovatt's Buildings, West Chadsmoor. Her five children were staying with her parents George and Louisa Abbots in the same building. John, however, was living in Minsterley, Shropshire with the Betton family and was earning his living as a barites miner. On the 10th July, 1911, Selia married George Webb at St. Luke's Parish Church, Cannock and they moved to live at 423, Forster's Buildings, Pye Green Road, Cannock. Meanwhile, John returned to live at Hazel Slade where he was employed as a miner. With the outbreak of the Great War, John decided to enlist with the Royal Field Artillery and was sent to Gallipoli on the 28th August, 1915. He was then transferred to the 2nd Battalion, Royal Irish Rifles where he served in Flanders until he was killed in action on the 11th August, 1917 at the age of 22. His body was not recovered after the war and John is remembered on the Ieper (Menin Gate) Memorial to the Missing in Ieper city centre.

Private Joseph Jones
10800

Joseph Jones was the second son of Isaac and Annie Jones and was born at Hednesford in 1890. His parents were married at Dudley in 1876, and they set up home in Dudley where William Henry was born in 1878, but sadly he died when he was 9. Meanwhile, the family had moved to live at Brindley Heath and then at 40, Bradbury Lane, Hednesford. This was where Alfred, Rebecca, Dora, Rose and Joseph were born. By 1901 the family had moved again, this time to Belt Road, West Chadsmoor, and the family had increased with the births of Lily, Clara and Isaac junior. In 1910, Isaac senior died and his widow moved to live at 2, James Street, West Chadsmoor with Joseph who was now a 19 year old miner hauler, Isaac junior who was a horse driver and Clara who was still at school. Joseph volunteered for the Army in late 1914, joining the 2nd Battalion, South Staffordshire Regiment and he was sent to Gallipoli on the 21st July, 1915 and from there to Egypt and then to France. At the age of 27, Joseph was killed in action on the 26th January, 1917. His body was buried at Courcelette British Cemetery, between Albert and Bapaume on the Somme in France.

Private Robert Jones
201

Robert Jones was born at Walsall in 1893 and was the fifth son of Lewis and Annie Jones. Lewis came from Penegoes in Montgomeryshire, and his wife came from Kinver in Staffordshire. The couple had married at West Bromwich in 1879 and had then moved to live at 2, Brittania Place, Handsworth, where Annie and Edwin were born, with Lewis working as a milkman. Ten years later the family had increased to seven children with the births of Alfred, Edith, Elizabeth, Joseph and Francis and they had moved to live at 36, Francis Street, Walsall. Lewis had changed jobs completely and was now working as a waggoner at a flour mill. The birth of Robert and his sister Alice meant that there were now nine children, and this must have been immensely difficult for Annie when her husband died at the age of 54 in 1898. In 1901, Annie was living at 27, Mill Street, Walsall with six of her children, but at least Annie junior, Alfred and Joseph were bringing in some money. In 1911, Robert was a railway labourer and was living with his married brother Alfred, Alfred's wife Sarah Ann, their daughter Violet and two more brothers, Joseph and Francis. At some point before the Great War, Robert and his mother moved to live at Cross Street, Hazel Slade. Robert joined the Army in 1914, firstly with the Grenadier Guards, but he was transferred to the 1st Battalion, Welsh Guards and was sent to France on the 17th August, 1915. Robert only served on the Western front for two months, when he was killed in action at the age of 22 at the Battle of Loos on the 15th October, 1915. After the war his body was not identified and Robert is remembered on the Loos Memorial to the Missing in France.

Private Robert Elijah Jones
26533

Robert E. Jones was born in 1879 at Hednesford and was the second son of James and Caroline Jones who both came from Wolverhampton. Their first two children, Richard and Jane were born at Heath Town, but by 1879 they had moved to Crab Lane, Chadsmoor. By 1901, a fourth child, Dinah had been born, but Richard had moved out of the household. By 1911, the family had moved to live at Cemetery Road, and Robert was working as a carter for a tobacconist, rather than following in his father's footsteps and work as a miner. Annie and May had been born in 1902 and 1905 respectively, and Dinah who had married Isaac Turner was also living at home with her husband. In 1916, Robert decided to enlist, joining the Yorkshire and Lancashire Regiment, but was soon transferred to the 14th Battalion, Durham Light Infantry and served on the Western Front. On the 9th April, 1917, at the age of 27 Robert was killed in action. His body was buried at Philosophe British Cemetery, Mazingarbe, between Bethune and Lens in France.

Private William Jones
18860

William Jones was born at Wednesbury in Staffordshire in 1878 and was the third son of Thomas and Ellen Jones, who both came from Wednesbury. In 1891, the Jones family had recently moved to live at Ghost Row, Littleworth in Hednesford and at that time consisted of three children, Thomas, Samuel and William. They decided to move to the Potteries and in 1901 were living at 12, Derby Street, Smallthorne, although Clara, Ada, Sylvia and Ellen had been born while the family were still at Hednesford. John, Fanny and Emma were born while the family were at Smallthorne, and Thomas and Samuel had both become coal miners like their father. Yet by 1911, the Jones family had moved back to Hednesford and were living at 74, Burgoyne Street, High Town, and William too had found work as a miner at West Cannock Colliery. In May 1915, William enlisted in the Army, joining the 1st Battalion, South Staffordshire Regiment and was sent to France on the 2nd October, 1915. Incredibly, just ten days later, at the age of 27, William was badly wounded during the Battle of Loos, and died from his injuries on the 13th October. William's body was buried at Bethune Town Cemetery in France.

Sergeant William Daniel Jones
200650

William Daniel Jones was born at Hednesford in 1890 and was the third son of John and Maria Jones, nee Holder, both of whom came from Wolverhampton. The couple had married at Wolverhampton in 1879, but had moved to live and work at

Hednesford. In 1881, the family were living on the Hednesford Road, Cannock, where their first two children, Richard and Sarah were born. At this time they also had Mary Davis, Maria's mother and Daniel Davis, her brother, living with them. By 1891, they had moved to live at Arthur Street, Wimblebury, and John, Rachel and William had been born, and ten years later, further additions to the family, Harry, Lizzie and Isaac had been born. John and Richard were both working down the pit like their father, as a trammer and loader respectively. Things began to change on the 25th December, 1910 when William married Elizabeth Ann Bradley at St. Peter's Parish Church, Hednesford. The couple moved in with the Cooke family at Reservoir Road, Church Hill, whilst the rest of the Jones family had moved to live at Wood Lane, Hednesford. The young couple then moved to live at 46, Bradbury Lane, Hednesford, and they had two children, William Daniel, born in 1912 and Annie born in 1914. Just after the outbreak of the Great War, William enlisted with the 1/5th Battalion, South Staffordshire Regiment and was sent to France on the 5th March, 1915. He was promoted to the rank of Sergeant, but on the 14th March, 1917 at the age of 27, he was killed in action. His platoon officer, Lieutenant Walham, sent a letter to his widow saying that her husband was "the bravest soldier I have ever met". William's body was buried at Shrine Cemetery, Bucquoy, near Arras in France.

Private Job Jukes
19136

Job Jukes was born at Hednesford in 1894 and was the youngest son of Henry and Emma Jukes. The family had moved to the Hednesford area by 1881, and by 1891, they were living at 1, Hall Drive, New Street, Hednesford, with nine children who had been born between 1868 and 1890. In 1901, the Jukes family were living at Blakemore Street, Church Hill and John, Henry, William, Frank and Frederick were all employed down the pit, as indeed was their father. By 1911, the children had moved away from the home, with the exception of William, Alice and a three year old granddaughter Beatrice. Job was living with James Perry and his family at Church Hill. James was a general haulier and Job was working as his assistant. However, he too went into the pits later, working as a miner for West Cannock Colliery. When the war broke out, Job volunteered for service with the 1st Battalion, Royal Welsh Fusiliers, and was sent to France on the on the 26th May, 1915. Sadly just one month later, Job was killed in action, when a shell blew him and two comrades to bits. His body was buried behind the lines by six friends, but after the war had ended, Job's body could not be located and the 22 year old is remembered on the Le Touret Memorial to the Missing in France.

Corporal Hubert Kenney
13555

John Kenney was a tin man, making his living from working with this metal and in 1871 he married Sarah Styche at Lichfield. The couple lived at Chandler's Lane at Rugeley to begin with, but by 1881, they had moved to 7, Upper St. John Street, Lichfield, and in the intervening ten years, five children had been born, Mary, Bernard, John, Eleanor and Anne. In 1891, the family were living at 24, Cross Street, Hazel Slade, Hednesford, and Bernard was now a blacksmith with John working as an errand boy. Four more children had been born, Leonard, Theresa, Francis and lastly Hubert in 1890. By 1901, two more children had been born, Joseph and Wilfred, while John was now a wagon builder, Leonard a blacksmith and Francis a banksman. Hubert decided to join the Army and in 1911, he was at Pirbright Camp as a Private in the Grenadier Guards. This meant that when the Great War began, Hubert was called up immediately and was sent to France on the 13th August, 1914, with the 2nd Battalion. He saw action at Loos in September 1915 and in 1916 was sent to the Somme, and it was here in the Battle of Morval that he was killed. Hubert had been wounded and was being carried back to the British lines by stretcher bearers when they were hit by a shell and blown to pieces. At the time of his death, Hubert was 26, and as his body was not found after the war, Hubert is remembered on the Thiepval Memorial to the Missing on the Somme in France.

Armourers Crew Cyril James Pinion Kent
F40346

James Kent was the son of James and Ann Kent of Rugeley, and in 1882, he married Annie Cope at Lichfield, to give two generations of husband and wife with the same names. James junior, a stationary engine man, and his wife set up home at 47, Arch Street, Rugeley and began a family, Emma, born in 1884, Ethel in 1885, Cyril on the 4th May, 1886, and Charles in 1888. By 1901, the family had moved to live at 237, Station Road, Hednesford, and it was here that Anne was born in 1898. Emma and Ethel were working as tailoresses and Cyril had found employment as a shoe maker. By 1911, Cyril had moved into insurance and on the 29th June 1912, he married Emily Turner at St. Peter's Parish Church, Hednesford. Cyril was a member of the choir at Green Heath Mission and was a Sunday school teacher at St. Peter's. He was appointed as Superintendant for the Smethwick office of the Britannic Assurance Company, and held this position until he was conscripted on the 24th October, 1917. Cyril joined the Royal Navy as an Armourers Crew and was posted to HMS Daedulus, which was part of the Royal Naval Air Service. From here he was transferred to the Royal Air Force in April, 1918 and completed his service until being demobilised due to ill health. Cyril continued his career briefly, but poor health forced the Kents to leave for Colorado Springs in the United States on the 24th March 1921 from Liverpool. Cyril was taken ill on landing in America and died in the house of Mr. R.S. Turner, at Colorado Springs on the 21st May, 1921 at the age of 35. Cyril Kent, noted for his cheery disposition was buried in Colorado Springs.

Private William Owen Kilgallon
7755

John Kilgallon, a coal miner from Wolverhampton, married Mary Ingram at Cannock in 1891. The couple already had three children, John Thomas born at Cannock in 1886 and Sarah born at Bloxwich in 1888, and William born in 1889 at Cannock. The family were living at Cecil Street, in Chadsmoor in 1891, and were still there ten years later, although the size of the family had increased, with the births of Edward, Frank, Bernard, Margaret, Robert and Ann. James, and Winifred followed soon afterwards and by 1911, the family had moved to live at Cannock Road, High Town. John Thomas was now a loader down the pit, William was a haulier in a colliery, Edward and Bernard were horse drivers and Robert was the only son not working in a mine; he was a general haulier. Early in 1914, William married Sarah Bishop at Cannock, and the couple set up home at Anglesey Street, with William now working as a miner at West Cannock. Their one child, named John was born late in 1914. Meanwhile, William had enlisted at Hednesford, joining the 2nd Battalion, Irish Guards. He was sent to France on the 5th October, 1915, and served at Loos and in Ieper, where he was killed in action on the 1st July, 1916 at the age of 25. William's body was buried at Essex Farm Cemetery just outside Ieper in Belgium, and a special service was held at St. Joseph's school in Hednesford where William had served on Sundays. In 2009, a party of students and staff from Kingsmead Technology College laid a wreath on his grave.

3. Hednesford

Private William Henry Kimberley
9276

William Kimberley was born at Portobello, Willenhall in 1891 and was the fourth son of Benjamin and Hannah Kimberley nee Beddow of Bilston. The couple had married at Wolverhampton in 1874, and by 1891 had had five children and the family was living at Court 7, New Street, Portobello, in Willenhall. At this point, Benjamin was a coal miner, whilst the two eldest children, Mary Ann and John were working as a varnisher and a hand filer respectively. Before 1901 the family had moved to live at Arthur Street, Wimblebury, where Ben junior was working down the pit as a labourer, and George was a horse driver, with Mary now employed as a clay pot maker in a brickyard. William worked as a miner and lived at New Buildings, Rawnsley before deciding to join the Army, enlisting with the 2nd Battalion, South Staffordshire Regiment. When the Great War began, the Battalion were at Aldershot, and were sent to France on the 12th August, 1914, arriving the next day. William was severely wounded in the leg and on a separate occasion was gassed and had to be sent back to Rochester Hospital to recover. William served with the Battalion until the 20th April, 1917 when at the age of 26 he was killed in action. William's body was buried at Croisilles Railway Cemetery, near Arras in France.

Lance Corporal Leonard Langley
15250

In 1883 at Cannock, William Ewan Langley a miner from Brownhills in Staffordshire married Sarah Elizabeth Kay from Darlaston. The couple moved to live at 9, Chapel Street, Hazel Slade, Hednesford and by 1891 five children had been born, William, Joseph, Oscar, Miriam and Jethro. The family were still at the same address ten years later, but Grace, Leonard, Hilda, Lance and Baden had been born. By 1911, the family had moved to live at 1, Chapel Street, and as they grew up the children all made their living down the pit in one way or another. Two more children had also been born in the meantime, Sarah Jane and Ellen. When the Great War began, Leonard enlisted in early 1915 with the 8th Battalion, Northumberland Fusiliers and was sent to serve at Gallipoli on the 9th September, 1915. He went from there to Egypt before being sent to France in July 1916. It was in France on the Somme on the 26th July that Leonard was posted as missing in action and was later presumed to have been killed on that date. At the time of his death, Leonard was 20 years of age and his body, later found, was buried at Regina Trench Cemetery, Grandcourt on the Somme in France.

Private John Lanigan
19114

John Lanigan was born at Chadsmoor in 1891, and he lived in Hednesford and enlisted at the Drill Hall in the town. John joined the 2nd Battalion, South Staffordshire Regiment and was sent to Gallipoli on the 29th September, 1915 and he then served in Egypt before being posted to France. John was killed in action on the 30th November, 1917 during the Battle of Cambrai, at the age of 26. John's body was not recovered after the war and he is remembered on the Cambrai Memorial at Louverval in France.

Private Albert Henry Lawton
9601

In 1894 Albert Lawton a coal miner born in Stafford married Nellie Matilda Barratt from Old Fallow, Cannock on the 22nd December at St. Luke's Parish Church. The couple set up their home at Old Fallow Road, and within six years had had four children. Albert Henry was the eldest born in 1895, followed by Annie, Alice and Doris. The family were still to be found on the Old Fallow Road in 1901. By 1911, the family had moved to 11, Glover Street, Wimblebury, and the family had increased to eight children with the births of Thomas, Arthur, Leonard and Harry. Albert had started work down the pit and was employed as a pony driver underground. Albert joined up in 1914, with the 2nd Battalion, South Staffordshire Regiment and was sent to France on the 16th March, 1915. At the age of 20, Albert was killed just two months later on the 18th May. After the war his body was not recovered and Albert is remembered on the Le Touret Memorial to the Missing in France.

Private Aaron Leighton
16790

In 1878 Aaron Leighton a coal miner from Wroxeter in Shropshire married Elizabeth Coope from Tong in Shropshire at Cannock. The young couple moved to live at Queen Street, High Town, where in 1879 a son named Aaron after his father was born. Staying with them was Ellen, Elizabeth's 14 year old sister and Michael Kelly, a 23 year old coal miner who was lodging with them. By 1891, the family had moved to Platt Street, Chadsmoor and the family had increased with the births of John, Hannah, Albert and Jane. The family had another lodger, William Lyons who was a labourer from Colton in Staffordshire. The family were still living at Platt Street ten years later and by this time Aaron had started work as a coal miner at Littleton Colliery, as had his brother John and William Lyons was also still lodging with the family. However, in 1906, Elizabeth died at the age of 54, and John had moved out following his marriage in 1904, although he was living just a few doors away. In 1911, both Aaron senior and junior were now living at Queen Street, whilst Albert had moved in to live with John and his family at 15, Platt Street. In 1914, Aaron senior married Ellen Deakin at St. Luke's Parish Church, Cannock on the 4th August, and after this Aaron Junior moved to live with John and his family. Aaron enlisted in January 1915 with the 1st Battalion, South Staffordshire Regiment and was sent to France on the 18th May. On the 25th September, 1915 at the Battle of Loos, at the age of 35, Aaron was killed in action. After the war Aaron's body was not found and he is remembered on the Loos Memorial to the Missing in France.

Private John Edward Lewis
15122

On the 25th December, 1890 at St. Luke's Parish Church, Cannock, Harry Easton Lewis a miner originally from Donnington Wood, Shropshire but living at Chadsmoor, married Jessie Perry also from Donnington Wood. The couple set up home at John Street, Chadsmoor and within twelve months their first child, a daughter Mary had been born. She was followed by John Edward in 1894, and then William, Albert and George. By 1911, the family had moved to live on the Belt Road, West Chadsmoor, where John had started work as a horse driver at West Cannock Colliery, whilst William was a billiard marker at the club and institute, with Albert a grocer's delivery boy and assistant. Five more children had been born in the meantime, Margaret, Arthur, Nellie, Reginald and Winifred. John enlisted with the 9th Battalion, Northumberland Fusiliers in early 1915 and was sent to France on the 3rd August. John was killed in action on the 1st October, 1915 at Ieper at the age of 21. His body was buried at Larch Wood (Railway Cutting) Cemetery near Ieper in Belgium.

Lance Corporal Reuben Lewis
15553

Reuben Lewis was born at White Heath, Worcestershire in 1886 and was the sixth child of Reuben and Sarah Lewis. Reuben senior was a miner from Pershore in Worcestershire and his wife, whose maiden name was Barley came from White Heath, the couple having married at Dudley in 1876. In 1881, they were living at White Heath with three children, Jane, Rebecca and Susannah and Sarah's parents Joseph and Susannah Barley and two of her sisters, Rebecca and Lucy Alice. Joseph was a carpenter, whilst Sarah, Susannah and Rebecca were nail makers, with Lucy employed as a domestic servant. In 1890 the family moved to live at John Street, Chadsmoor, and by this time Jane had begun work as a tailor's apprentice. The family had also grown with the births of Lucy Alice, Rose Emma, Reuben and Sarah Ann. In 1901, Reuben had started work as a horse driver down the pit and George, Mary, Robert and John had been born. On the 22nd October, 1907 Reuben married Sarah Jane Marsh at Cannock Register Office, with the couple moving to live at High Mount Street, Hednesford. Their first child George Henry was born on the 15th December, 1908 and in 1911 the family had four lodgers staying with them, Florrie Love, a tailoress, Arthur and John Stubbs, coal miners from the Potteries and Archie Phillipps another miner from Rugeley. A second son, Frederick William was born on the 27th July, 1911. Reuben joined the Hednesford Territorials and served for four years in the 2nd Battalion, Volunteer Reserve, South Staffordshire Regiment, and on the 5th September, 1914 he signed up for three years with the 6th Battalion, Leicestershire Regiment at Attercliffe in Sheffield, where the family had moved before the outbreak of the war, being posted on the 25th October, 1914. Reuben was sent to France on the 29th July, 1915 and on the 18th August was admitted to hospital with a gunshot wound to the left arm. This was followed by a second spell in hospital with cellulatis of the scrotum. Reuben was promoted to Lance Corporal on the 26th February, 1916 and was then in hospital for a third time with a problem with his right foot. On the 14th July, 1916 Reuben was posted as wounded and missing in action and it was later presumed that he had died on that date. His identity disc was sent back to his wife at 105, Wixley Road, Darnall, Sheffield, the only personal effect found. After the war, Reuben's body was not found and he is remembered on the Thiepval Memorial to the Missing on the Somme in France. Sarah Lewis, Reuben's widow, married Thomas Moorley at Sheffield in 1918.

Rifleman Thomas Lewis
88578

Thomas Lewis was born at Hednesford in 1894 and was the eldest son of Hiram and Mary Ann Lewis. Hiram was a mine timberer from Ironbridge in Shropshire, and his wife whose maiden name was Greenfield, came from Wednesbury in Staffordshire. The couple married at St. Luke's Parish Church, Cannock on the 27th April, 1890. They set up a home at 39 Platt Street, High Town, Hednesford, and their first child, Eleanor was born there in 1891. Ten years later the family had increased to four, with the births of Thomas, Emma and Caroline. By 1911, Eleanor was working as a char, Thomas was a horse driver down the pit, and Emma was employed as a nurse girl. Thomas joined the Army when he was conscripted in 1917 and he served on the Western Front, firstly with the East Surrey Regiment and then with the 2/6th Battalion, King's (Liverpool Regiment). Thomas was killed in action on the 21st October, 1917 at the age of 25. His body was buried at Tournai Communal Cemetery Allied Extension in Belgium.

Private Albert Henry Lockett
15335

Albert Lockett was born at Armitage in 1885, and was the second son of Herbert and Eliza Lockett. The couple had married at Stone in 1867 when Herbert was 23 and working as a potter's presser whilst Eliza, whose maiden name was Morris, was three years younger than her husband. The couple began married life at Mount Pleasant, Longton, before moving to Stone and then to Armitage, near Rugeley in Staffordshire. The couple raised eleven children in total, all of whom survived childhood, a somewhat unusual occurrence at this time. Albert began his working life as a bricklayer's labourer, but by 1911, he had left home and was recorded as living at 79, Blewitt Street, Green Heath, although on his Army record his address is given as 117, West Hill, Hednesford. Interestingly, in 1911 Albert earned his living as a butler, being part of the household of Henry Armstrong Westmacott, a bell manufacturer living at Benridge Hall, Penteland near Newcastle-upon-Tyne, but he enlisted on the 5th September, 1914 in the 8th Battalion, South Lancashire Regiment, being posted to the Depot on the 4th November and sent to France on the 28th September, 1915. In the meantime, Albert had married Edith Bird at Southampton on the 3rd August, 1915. Albert was badly wounded with a gunshot wound to the left thigh on the 18th November, 1915, being treated at the 63rd Field Ambulance, a Casualty Clearing Station, 14th Ambulance Train and 26 General Hospital at Etaples before being invalided back to Britain on the 28th November, 1915. He was discharged on the 15th February, 1916 and posted to the 3rd Battalion, before being transferred to the 2nd Battalion, Manchester Regiment on the 26th October, 1916. On his return to the Western Front, Albert was transferred again, this time to the 1st Battalion, Cameron Highlanders on the 8th February, 1917, but on the 13th June, 1917 he was transferred yet again, this time rejoining the 8th Battalion, South Lancashire Regiment. A further transfer took place on the 2nd July, 1917 this time to the 2nd Battalion. A month later on the 3rd August, 1917, ironically, on his second wedding anniversary, Albert was killed in action, at the age of 32. His body was not found after the war and Albert is remembered on the Ieper (Menin Gate) Memorial to the Missing in Ieper city centre in Belgium.

Private Henry Longmore
18565

Henry Longmore was born at Cannock in 1889. His parents were John Longmore a coal miner from Wednesbury and Henrietta Longmore from Willenhall. Henrietta was a widow, and had four children from her previous marriage. The family moved to live at 30 Burgoyne Street, High Town. In the household were John and Henrietta Dunning, John Longmore junior, a son from John's first marriage, William Jonas Dunning, Thomas Dunning, James Dunning, John Dunning, Henry Longmore, George Longmore and Charles Longmore, with a 55 year old boarder, George Allen for good measure. By 1901, Eliza, Mary, Joseph, Hannah and Edward Longmore had been born. In 1911, the household was made up of John and Henrietta, George, Henry and Charles, all working as miner's loaders at West Cannock Colliery, Joseph, now a horse driver and Edward who was still at school. However, in 1913, John Longmore died at the age of 59. Henry Longmore volunteered to serve in the Army in early 1915, joining the 7th Battalion, South Staffordshire Regiment and he was sent to Gallipoli on the 6th October, 1915. Henry was killed in action just two months later, on the 10th December, 1915 at the age of 26. Henry's body was buried at Azmak Cemetery, Suvla in Turkey.

3. Hednesford

Rifleman Walter John Lycett
R/14047

In 1886 at Cannock, John Lycett a 29 year old coachman from Bridgford, Staffordshire, married Harriet Sanders, a 31 year old from Cannock. The couple set up a home at Cannock where Clara was born in 1887, Margaret in 1889 and then they had moved to Etching Hill, Rugeley where Walter was born in 1890 and Dorothy in 1893. By 1901, the family had moved to live at 11, Cross Street, Hazel Slade. Clara had left home to become a domestic servant at Edgbaston, but the rest of the family were still living at home, along with John Round, a lodger who worked as a coal miner, from Kingswinford. John Lycett had given up his job as a coachman and was now employed as a haulage rope winding man in a colliery. John died at Cannock in 1909 at the age of 53, and a year later Harriet married John Round on the 3rd September at St. Peter's Parish Church, Hednesford, with Clara one of the witnesses. In 1911, Walter was living with his mother and step father at 11 Cross Street and was working as a colliery boiler minder. Clara married Samuel Lawley from Hazel Slade on the 28th September, 1912 at St. Peter's Parish Church, Hednesford. With the outbreak of the Great War, Walter enlisted on the 8th June, 1915, joining the 8th Battalion, King's Royal Rifle Corps and he was sent to France on the 12th September, 1915. Walter served until the 15th September, 1916 when he died of wounds on the Somme at the age of 26. After the war, Walter's body was not found and he is remembered on the Thiepval Memorial to the Missing on the Somme in France.

Lance Corporal Ralph Marsh
19908

In 1881 the newly married Thomas and Mary Ann Marsh were living at Mount Street, Hednesford. He was a coal miner from Dudley, Worcestershire and she was from Wolverhampton. Within ten years they had had five children, George, Matilda, Thomas, Sarah Jane, and James and the family was living at 28 Bradbury Lane, Hednesford. They were still living there ten years later, but two more children had been born, Elizabeth in 1893 and Ralph in 1895. George and Thomas had both begun work as labourers in a colliery. In 1909, Thomas senior died at the age of 57 and two years later his widow was living at Blewitt Street, with George, now a colliery lamp cleaner, Ralph, a labourer in a tile works and Joseph who was still at school. Mary Ann had also taken in a lodger, William Walloder from Kidderminster who was a colliery boiler stoker. Not a great deal is known of

Ralph's war record, other than he enlisted with the Leicestershire Regiment, before transferring to the 9th Battalion, Sherwood Foresters, where he rose to the rank of Lance Corporal. He was sent to Gallipoli prior to the 31st December, 1915 and went from there to the Western Front in 1916. Ralph was killed in action on the 9th September, 1916 at the age of 21. His body was buried at Ovillers Military Cemetery on the Somme in France.

Private Albert Joseph Marston
24365

In 1883, at Dudley, Joseph Marston, a boot dealer from Willenhall, Staffordshire married Mary Ann Hammond from Tipton. By 1881 the couple had set up a business on Cannock Road, Hednesford, and had started a family with the births of Winifred in 1885, Frank in 1887, Annie in 1888 and Albert in 1890. Staying with them at this time was Sarah Clark, a 13 year old niece and Alice Barratt, who was a 17 year old servant from Gnosall. In 1901, the family had moved to live at 1, Station Road, Hednesford and the business had developed successfully into a boot and shoe dealership. Another two children, Ida in 1893 and Sidney had in 1894 had been born, and the family still employed a servant, Mary Ann Astin from Walsall. By 1911, Winifred had left home and was a French Teacher at a school in Hunslet, whilst Frank and Albert assisted their father in the family business. Annie and Ida were both school teachers, while Sidney was a student, and the family servant was now Martha Turner from Chadsmoor. Winifred married a handicrafts teacher, Edwin Dent from Crook, County Durham at Leeds in 1912. Albert joined the Army in April, 1915, enlisting with the 1st Battalion, South Staffordshire Regiment and he was sent to France after only eleven weeks training. On the 31st August, 1916, Albert was killed in action on the Somme. His family received the news about their 26 year old son from his Platoon Sergeant who had had Albert's death confirmed by a comrade. After the war, Albert's body was not found and he is remembered on the Thiepval Memorial to the Missing on the Somme in France.

Sapper John Martin MM
155855

In 1869, Thomas Martin a gamekeeper from Brockton, Staffordshire, married Hannah Maria Stretton from Chorley, the wedding taking place at Lichfield. Their first child, Florence was born at Brewood the following year, but the family then moved to Acton, near Wrexham. The family continued to travel around the country, as Harry was born at Worfield, Shropshire, and George at Fletching, Sussex. Hannah and Albert were born at Walton, Derbyshire, before they moved back to Cannock Wood in 1881 where Ernest was born. Frederick, Alice and Thomas were all born at Cannock Wood, before Thomas senior became a coal miner and the family moved to live at 2, Cross Street, Hazel Slade where James was born in 1890, and John in 1892. In 1901, Ernest was working as a railway engine stoker, Frederick as a labourer in a colliery yard and Thomas as a blacksmith's striker. In 1907, Thomas left England to set up a new life in Canada and in 1911 John followed his example and also went to settle in Canada. In 1915, John returned to England and enlisted in the South Staffordshire Regiment and was sent to France on the 30th September, 1915. On the 2nd July, 1916 John was awarded his Military Medal for bravery and afterwards he was transferred to the 251st Tunnelling Company, Royal Engineers. On the 10th April, 1918 at the age of 27, John died from wounds. His body was buried at Lillers Communal Cemetery, near Bethune in France.

Lance Corporal Thomas Martin
231121

Thomas Martin was the older brother of John Martin and was born at Cannock Wood on the 8th August, 1885. He had attended Rawnsley School, and at the age of 16, Thomas was working as a blacksmith striker but later became a miner at Cannock and Rugeley Colliery. However, in 1907 he made the decision to seek a new life in Canada. He had married in Canada and he and his wife Eliza were living at 9207, 112th Avenue, Edmonton, Alberta and Thomas was working as a sales manager. On the 5th March, 1916 Thomas enlisted in Alberta with the 202nd Battalion, serving in "D" Company and after nine months training he was sent to England, arriving at Witley Camp on the 30th November, 1916. Thomas was given a short leave and came back to Hazel Slade to visit his family. On his return to Witley camp he was given the rank of acting Sergeant, but asked to be reverted to permanent grade on the 18th May, 1917 in order to proceed overseas. On the 27th May he was transferred to the 50th (Sportsmen's) Battalion, and landed with the Battalion at Etaples being made Lance Corporal (unpaid) on the 3rd August, 1917. On the 20th August, 1917, just after his 32nd birthday, Thomas was killed in action at Lens when he was hit by a shell. His body was not recovered after the war and Thomas is remembered on the Vimy Memorial to the Missing, which forms part of the Canadian National Memorial at Vimy in France.

Private Roland Mason
235018

In 1889 at Cannock, Thomas Mason, a 28 year old sub post master from Sedgley, married 27 year old Mary Ellen Edgley from Birmingham. The couple set up a business at Glover Street, Wimblebury and in 1890, their first child, Thomas William Richard Mason was born. By 1901, the family had moved to 40a John Street, Wimblebury, and the family had increased with the births of Harold in 1892, John in 1894, Roland in 1897 and Millicent in 1901. In 1911, Thomas was working as a horse driver in a colliery, Harold was a postman, John had found employment as a railway porter and Roland was an errand boy, with Millicent still at school. Roland began to help his father run the post office business, but in 1916 he was conscripted into the Army. To begin with Roland joined the South Staffordshire Regiment, but was later transferred to the 1st Battalion, Worcestershire Regiment, and it was with this unit that he was killed near Ieper on the 1st August, 1917 during the push for Passchendaele. After the war, the 20 year old Roland's body was not found and he is remembered on the Ieper (Menin Gate) Memorial to the Missing in Ieper city centre in Belgium.

Lance Corporal Walter Mason
R/14046

In 1888 at Tamworth in Staffordshire, Thomas Mason a 24 year old gamekeeper from Sutton Coldfield, Warwickshire, married 22 year old Alice Cross from Hints in Staffordshire. The couple set up home on the Rugeley Road, Hazel Slade where Thomas was working and in 1889 their first child, Elsie Gertrude was born. By 1901 the family had moved to live at Shakers Lodge, and in the intervening ten years, Walter was born in 1892, followed by Harold in 1895 and Albert in 1898. However, later in 1901, Alice died at the age of 37, and Thomas met Ruth Burton, known as Flossie. The couple had their first child, Percy in 1904, before they decided to marry at Lichfield in 1905. Other children soon followed; Frederick in 1906, Violet in 1908 and Madge in 1909. Walter meanwhile, had started work as a loco engine cleaner, whilst Harold, Albert and Percy were employed as kennel boys. In 1915 Walter volunteered for the Army, joining the 9th Battalion, King's Royal Rifle Corps being sent to France on the 12th September, 1915. He served for over two years but died from wounds on the 19th December, 1917 at the age of 25. Walter's body was buried at Nine Elms British Cemetery, near Poperinghe in Belgium.

3. Hednesford

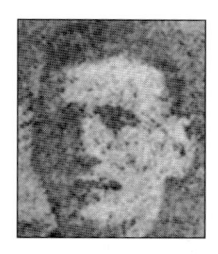

Private John Matthews
203254

John Matthews was born at Hazel Slade, Hednesford in 1894 and was the seventh son of Henry and Eliza Matthews. Henry was a coal miner from Pensnett and Eliza originally came from Walsall. The couple were living at 13, Albert Street, Hazel Slade in 1881 and had two children, Herbert and Mary Ann. By 1891, the family had moved to live at 3, Cross Street, Hazel Slade and the family now consisted of seven children with the births of George, Elizabeth, Florence, William and Henry junior. By 1901 Herbert and George had become coal miners, whilst William was a coal door minder. The family had now increased to total twelve children with Albert, John, Elijah, Phyllis, and Edward, and the family had moved again to 27, Chapel Street, Hazel Slade. In 1911 Henry, Albert and John were still at home and all were working as coal miners, with Phyllis and Edward still at school. In September, 1915, John enlisted in the Army, joining the 1/5th Battalion, South Staffordshire Regiment, and was sent to France in 1916. He was wounded but returned to his unit upon recovery, but on the 8th June, 1917, John was reported missing in action. This was later presumed to have been the date of his death at the age of 23. After the war, John's body was not recovered and he is remembered on the Arras Memorial to the Missing in France.

Private Henry Matthews
6392

Henry Matthews was John's older brother and he too was born at Hazel Slade in 1890. He became a coal miner and was married with two children with his wife residing at Rugeley. Henry enlisted in 1914, joining the 1st Battalion, Irish Guards, and was sent to France on the 17th August, 1915. He was wounded at the Battle of Loos on the 25th November, 1915 and sent back to England to recover, but was then sent back to the Western Front, where he was wounded for a second time. Henry came home on leave in October, 1917 returning to the Front in early November. On the 30th November, 1917, Henry was killed in action at the Battle of Cambrai at the age of 27. After the war Henry's body was not found and he is remembered on the Cambrai Memorial to the Missing in France.

Private John Henry Maund
39587

In 1884 at Cannock, Israel Maund a 21 year old miner from Dudley Port in Staffordshire, married Eliza Rogers, aged 19 from Dawley Bank, Shropshire. The couple set up a home at Huntington Terrace, Chadsmoor, and within the space of 7 years had had four children, William born in 1884, Margaret born in 1886, Israel junior, born in 1888 and John Henry born in 1890. Yet in 1901, Israel was living by himself at Huntington Terrace, William was a 17 year old coal miner lodging on the Green Heath Road in Hednesford and Margaret was a servant living on the Cannock Road at Chadsmoor. There is no trace of Eliza, Israel junior or of John Henry. Yet on the 23rd April, 1910, Israel junior married Sarah Jane Roden at St. Peter's Parish Church, Hednesford, with the couple living with her parents at Hill Top in 1911, with their first child, Ethel. John Henry Maund was working as a miner's loader in 1911 and lodging with John and Sarah Jones, both aged 70 at South View, Green Heath, Hednesford, this being the same address given by Israel on his marriage certificate. Indeed, on the 25th December, 1912, John married Charlotte Bradford, and the couple went on to have three children, William H. Maund, born in 1913 and Dorothy M. Maund and Evelyn Maund, both born at opposite ends of 1914, and were recorded as living at 179, Littleworth Road. John enlisted in 1916, choosing to join the South Staffordshire Regiment, but being transferred to the 2nd Battalion, Worcestershire Regiment. He served in France until the 21st May, 1917, when at the age of 27 he was shot by a sniper and killed. After the war, John's body was not recovered and he is remembered on the Arras Memorial to the Missing in France.

Lance Corporal Frederick Mears
14888

In 1883 at Cannock, William Mears a 20 year old coal miner from Kiddemore Green, Staffordshire, married the 19 year old Sarah Richards from Great Wyrley. 1891 saw the couple living on the Hednesford Road, Cannock and they already had three children, William junior, Ethel and Fred. Ten years later the family had moved to live at Abbey Street, Green Heath, Hednesford and the family had grown with the births of Thomas, Walter, Ernest and Mary Ann, whilst William junior had started work as a labourer underground at a colliery. In 1911, eight children were still living at home in Abbey Street, with Fred, Thomas and Walter earning their living as colliery horse drivers, while Ernest was working as a labourer on the pit bank. Fred later went to work at Stafford Asylum. In 1915, Fred married Lizzie Lloyd at Stafford, and moved into 103, Peel Terrace in the town. In 1916, Fred was conscripted into the Army, serving in the 6th Battalion, Duke of Cornwall's Light Infantry. He was in France until the 23rd August, 1917 when he died from his wounds in Belgium at the age of 27. Fred's body was buried at Menin Road South Military Cemetery, just outside Ieper in Belgium.

Private Thomas Mears
30191

Thomas Mears was the younger brother of Fred and was born at Cannock in 1892. He worked as a coal miner at West Cannock Colliery. Thomas volunteered for the Army in early 1915, joining the 8th Battalion, South Staffordshire Regiment and rose to the rank of Lance Corporal, but later relinquished his stripe. He was sent to France on the 14th July, 1915, but was then transferred to the 9th Battalion, Devonshire Regiment as a Private soldier. Whilst back in England in 1916, he married Amelia Wright at St. Peter's Parish Church, on the 6th May, and a daughter named Ethel was born later that year. Thomas then returned to the Western Front and it was here that he was killed in action on the 7th May, 1917 at the age of 25. After the war, Thomas' body was not recovered and he is remembered on the Arras memorial to the Missing in France.

Private Alfred Merrick
8303

In 1893, at Brownhills, Staffordshire James Merrick a 23 year old coal miner from Austry, Warwickshire, married Sarah Ann Johnson, also aged 23 from Brownhills. The couple set up a home at Friezland Lane, Brownhills and their first child Alfred was born in 1894, followed by Mabel in 1895, James in 1897 and William in 1901. By 1911, two more children had been born, Ada in 1903 and Ethel in 1908. The family had also moved to live at Hednesford Road, Norton Canes. Alfred had started work as a coal miner loader at the Conduit Colliery, and his brother James was working as a colliery labourer on the surface. The family then moved to live at 34, Glover Street, Wimblebury. Alfred had joined the Hednesford Territorials, serving for four years, and so when the Great War began, Alfred joined up straight away. He enlisted in the 1/5th Battalion, South

Staffordshire Regiment and was sent to France on the 5th March, 1915. He served until the 13th October, 1915, when during the Battle of Loos, he was badly wounded whilst charging the Hohenzollern Redoubt. He managed to walk back to the Dressing Station but died of his wounds, aged 21. After the war, Alfred's body was not recovered and he is remembered on the Loos Memorial to the Missing in France.

Private James Merrick
201298

James Merrick was the younger brother of Alfred and was born at Ogley Hay, Staffordshire in 1897. Like his father and brother, he too became a miner and moved with the family to Glover Street, Wimblebury where jobs had been secured at the local pit. James did not join up until 1916, and like his brother, joined the 1/5th Battalion, South Staffordshire Regiment. He served on the Western Front until the 29th September, 1918 when he was killed in action at the age of 21, ironically the same age that his brother had been at his death three years earlier. James' body was also not found after the war, and he is remembered on the Vis-en-Artois Memorial to the Missing in France.

Acting Corporal Albert Edward Millington
R/13293

In 1892 at Wolverhampton, Staffordshire Edward Millington a mechanical blacksmith from Bradley near Bilston, Staffordshire married Alice Jane Corbett from Dawley, Shropshire. He was 27 years of age and his wife was only 19 at the time of the marriage. They settled on the Cannock Road, Chadsmoor, and in 1894 celebrated the birth of their first child, Albert. In 1896 a second child, christened Lois but known as Dolly was born and in 1899, Clara was born. By 1911, the family had moved to live at 174, Church Hill, Hednesford, although only Albert was still living at home. Dolly was living on Market Street and Clara could not be traced. Albert had started work as a wagon builder, presumably for a colliery company. Albert was also well known as a clever footballer for Hednesford Town F.C. and a good cricketer for Littleworth. Albert later became a coal miner, working at West Cannock Colliery. Albert enlisted in the Army at Hednesford on the 20th May, 1915 and was posted to the 15th Battalion, King's Royal Rifle Corps. He had a number of minor breaches of discipline, from being absent without leave to losing a pair of underpants. Albert was posted to the 8th Battalion and then sent to France on the 13th September, 1915, being promoted to Lance Corporal on the 4th August, 1916. Albert was badly wounded on the Somme on the 15th September, 1916 and was sent back to 36 Casualty Clearing Station, but died there from his injuries the next day, aged 22. Shortly before his death, Albert had written home to say that the fighting was the worst he had experienced. Albert's body was buried at Heilly Station Cemetery, Mericourt L'Abbe on the Somme in France. His death affected his parents, for in 1917, Edward was living at Littleworth, whilst his wife and Millicent were living with Alice's sister at Hill Crest, Hednesford.

Private Arthur Moore
20412

In 1889 at Dudley, Samuel Moore a 21 year old coal miner from the same town married Alice Timmins, also 21 and likewise from Dudley. Within a few months of the marriage, their first child Arthur was born, and then the family decided to move to Green Heath, Hednesford, where John was born in 1890. In 1901, the family had moved to live at 14, Bradford Street, High Town, and now consisted of John, Eliza, Benjamin, Daniel, Charles and George, whilst they also had a lodger, Charles Stokes living with them. At this point, Arthur was back in Dudley, living with his grandparents, John and Mary Moore at 4, Lawley Street. Two more children were born in the early years of the new century, Alice in 1903 and Lizzie in 1907. Shortly afterwards though, the father of the family, Samuel died at the age of 40. Alice Moore married Charles Stokes, the ex lodger in 1910 and the family celebrated another wedding on the 25th December, 1910 when Arthur, now a coal miner, married Mary Ann Stokes at St. Luke's Parish Church, Cannock. The couple moved in with the rest of the family at 14, Bradford Street, and in 1911 celebrated the birth of their first child, named Alice. A son named Samuel was born in 1913 and twins, named Arthur and George the following year, although, sadly, Arthur died shortly after birth. In 1917, a third son was born which again was named Arthur. Arthur senior joined up in 1915 and was sent to France on the 9th September, 1915, serving with the 16th Battalion, Northumberland Fusiliers. He served until the 12th July, 1917 when he was killed in action, dying quickly according to contemporary reports. After the war, the body of the 28 year old could not be found and Arthur is remembered on the Nieuport Memorial to the Missing in Belgium.

Private Benjamin Moore
20556

Benjamin Moore was the younger brother of Arthur Moore and was born at Hednesford in 1895. Like his brother, he became a coal miner at West Cannock Colliery, after initially looking after horses down the pit. Benjamin was a well known local character. When the Great War broke out, Benjamin enlisted almost at once, joining the 3rd Battalion, Grenadier Guards in August 1914, and being sent to France on the 26th July, 1915. Benjamin served until the 11th March, 1916, when he was badly wounded in a tragic accident. Twenty four soldiers were practising throwing grenades, when a grenade was dropped, killing five and wounding seventeen. Although every effort was made to save his life, Benjamin succumbed to his injuries in the 11th March, aged 21. Benjamin's body was buried at Calais Southern Cemetery in France.

James Morgan

Sadly at present, James Morgan will remain a half forgotten name. There is a reference to J.C. Morgan of the Machine Gun Corps in the Hednesford Roll of Honour giving his address as Hazel Slade, but there is no record of anyone of that name living there, nor any record of anyone serving with the MGC with a connection to Hednesford. There is also a reference to James Morgan of Blackfords being killed on the 10th July, 1918 but his is not corroborated by either the CWGC site or the SDGW register.

Private William John Morris
156593

In 1879 at Cannock, Benjamin Morris a 19 year old coal miner from Wedges Mills, Staffordshire married Agnes Annie Hawkesworth, also 19 from Hanbury, Staffordshire. The couple found a house at Pye Green, Cannock and their first child William John was born there in 1880. By 1891, they had moved to live at 16, Bradbury Lane, Hednesford, and the family had increased with the births of Laura, George, Ernest, Agnes and Frederick. By 1901, William had started work as a horse driver in a colliery. On the 20th February, 1911 William married Mary Bailey at St. Peter's Parish Church, Hednesford, and the couple moved to live at

80, Brindley Heath, just a few doors away from William's family who had moved to live at 84, Brindley Heath. Interestingly on the 1911 census there are four children, listed as living at the address, Mary Bailey, born in 1904, Violet Bailey born in 1906, Jack Bailey born in 1907 and Agnes Morris Bailey born in 1909. It appears that the couple had two children of their own, Edna born in 1915 and Lilian born in 1917. William volunteered for the Army in 1915, choosing to join the South Staffordshire Regiment and being sent to France on the 29th September, 1915. He later transferred to the 17th Company, Machine Gun Corps (Infantry), and it was with this unit that William was killed in action on the 9th September, 1918 at the age of 38. After the war, William's body was not recovered and he is remembered on the Vis-en-Artois Memorial to the Missing in France.

Sergeant James Mottram
17384

In 1876 at Lichfield, John Mottram a 19 year old labourer from Tutbury in Staffordshire married Caroline Jarvis from Yoxall, ten years his senior and a widow with two children. The couple set up home at Hadley End, Yoxall and began a family of their own, with the births of Florence in 1878, Thomas in 1879 and James in 1881. The family then moved to live at 5, Rawnsley Buildings, Hednesford, where John began work as a coal miner. More children had been born in the meantime, Walter in 1895 at Burntwood, and Alice in 1897 at Longdon. Caroline's children from her first marriage, Charles and Arthur Jarvis were still living with the family and were both coal miners. In 1898, the 17 year old James married Sarah Ann Lycett from Brereton, at Lichfield and in 1901 they were living at 3, The Springs, Longdon where their first child, Florence had been born in 1899. In 1911, the family had moved to live at 13, Simcox Street, Church Hill, Hednesford and Thomas, Alice Mary, Emily and Doris May had been born. Two further children were added to the family later on, Walter in 1912 and Violet in 1915. James enlisted into the Army in February 1915, joining the 4th Battalion, South Staffordshire Regiment but he was not sent to serve on the Western Front until September 1917. He rose to the rank of Sergeant but on the 14th April, 1918 at the age of 37, James was killed in action near Ieper. After the war his body was not recovered and James is remembered on the Ploegsteert Memorial to the Missing in Belgium.

Private James Thomas Neville
19639

James Neville, a coal miner from Longdon, Staffordshire married Emma Moorcroft at Lichfield in 1859. The couple lived at Cannock Wood and began their family in 1860 with the birth of John. They continued to live at Cannock Wood and by 1871 they had had another three children, Martha, Samuel and Caroline. They also shared the house with Emma's widowed mother, Martha Moorcroft. By 1881, the family had moved to live at Green Heath, Hednesford, and Emma and Hannah had been born. James was born in 1894, at a time when most of the family had left home. However, shortly afterwards he was left without parents when both his father and mother died. In 1901, James was being looked after by his grandparents, James and Eliza Neville, at Abbey Street, Green Heath, but he was then, in essence, brought up by John and Sarah Till of Cannock Wood. In 1911, James had become a gamekeeper's assistant and was living at The Stables, Chestall near Rugeley, but he later became an engine driver. On the 7th January, 1915, James presented himself at Hednesford to enlist with the Coldstream Guards. He was sent to Caterham on the 8th January but was discharged on the 21st May, 1915 on medical grounds. The Guards were concerned by an abdominal belt worn to protect an appendix scar, and by a hernia operation which he had had five years before. Not to be denied, James joined the 1st Battalion, South Staffordshire Regiment in July 1915 and was sent to France on the 8th December, 1915. He served until the 28th March, 1917 when he was killed in action at the age of 22. James' body was buried at St. Leger British Cemetery, between Arras and Bapaume in France.

Private Herbert Nicholls
G/63020

In 1893 at Cannock, Thomas Nicholls a 21 year old miner from Dudley married Mary Ann Hawkins, a 19 year old from Rugeley. They moved to live at 4, Kings Street, Hednesford, and in 1897 their first child, William was born. He was followed in 1898 by Herbert and then Joseph, who was born in 1900, with Thomas being born in 1901. By 1911, the family had moved to Barton's Buildings, Littleworth, Hednesford and Walter, John, Hilda and Eliza swelled the number of children to eight. William had started work as a tile picker up with Herbert working as a carrier off, from a tile moulder. Herbert became eligible for military service in late 1916, but he was not conscripted into the North Staffordshire Regiment until the 23rd April, 1918 and was sent to Newcastle to complete his training, but was then transferred to the 7th Battalion, Middlesex Regiment. Herbert served until the 27th August, 1918 when he was killed in action in his first battle at the age of 20. Herbert's body was buried at Suzanne Military Cemetery Number 3, on the right bank of the Somme near Albert in France.

Private Joseph Nicholls
7615

Daniel Nicholls a 21 year old coal miner from Wolverhampton married Prudence Jones, aged 19 at Dudley, her home town in 1873. The couple lived in the Parkfield area of Wolverhampton and it was here that their first child, Isaac was born in 1873. In 1880 the family moved to live at Station Road, Hednesford and it was here that first Alice in 1880 and then Joseph in 1881 were born. By 1891, they had moved again to live at Mount Street, Hednesford and the family had grown to number nine children with the births of Florence, Mary, David, Sarah, Daniel and William. In 1901, the family were now living at 72, Brindley Heath, Hednesford and there were still eight children at home, although Alice, a coat and trouser machiner, Joseph, a horse driver in a colliery, Mary, also a coat and trouser finisher, and David, like his brother a horse driver in a colliery, were all working. On the 21st June, 1901 at the age of 19, Joseph joined the Army, enlisting with the Royal Scots. The family had moved again as his address was now 31, Moreton Street, Chadsmoor. Joseph made his way to Glencorse on the 21st June and was posted to the 1st Battalion on the 7th July, 1902, and receiving his good conduct pay on the 1st April, 1904. He was released to the Army reserve after completing thirteen years, and finally discharged on the 14th August, 1913. Joseph had married Florence Hodgkiss on the 9th October, 1905 and the couple had six children; George in 1907, Arthur in 1908, Dorothy in 1910, Florence in 1911, Nellie in 1912 and Elizabeth in 1914. With the outbreak of war, Joseph was mobilized on the 5th August, 1914, and was posted to the 2nd Battalion two days later, being sent to France on the 20th September, 1914. He was wounded at La Basse, and sent back to Cannock to recover from his wounds before being sent back to his unit in France on the 4th January, 1915. On the 25th September, 1915 at Sanctuary Wood, just outside Ieper, Joseph was buried by a shell explosion. This badly affected his nerves and he was brought back to England for treatment at Cambridge and then at the Convalescent Hospital at Rickmansworth. He was sent back to the Western Front and was gassed and returned to the Military Hospital on Cannock Chase for treatment. Joseph complained that he felt weak and nervous, and on the 24th January, 1919 Captain Smith reported that Joseph had a rapid heart rate, palpitations on exertion, a fine hand tremor, and that his knee jerks were more active than normal. Joseph remained in hospital until the 8th February, 1919 when he was discharged from the Army, but he was readmitted on the 13th August, with a valvular disease of the heart. He had attempted suicide on the 24th August but the razor had been taken away from him. On the 28th August at 10.30 am he was given a cup of tea by Nurse Williams. Five minutes later Joseph was discovered with a gashed throat, the razor still in his hand. Joseph had served in the Army for seventeen and a half years, but died in mental turmoil at the age of 39. A verdict of suicide while temporarily insane was passed.

Private John Noble
12775

John Noble was born at Walsall in 1869 and was the fourth son of George and Selina Noble. George was a coal miner from Ripley, Derbyshire and at the time of his marriage was 25 years of age, whilst Selina, whose maiden name was Harris and who came from Stretton in Warwickshire, was 18. The couple had married at Walsall in 1864, although George had three children from a previous marriage. The family settled in Walsall, where Thomas, David and John were born, before moving to live at Burgoyne Street, High Town, Hednesford, and it was here that Selina, George, Hannah, Martha and James were born. By 1891, David and John were earning their living as coal miners, and Daniel, John senior's son from his first marriage was also living with the family. Whilst the rest of the family remained at Burgoyne Street, John junior left to live at Bulwell, Nottinghamshire, and it was here in 1896 that he married Clara Louise Fletcher. By 1901, they were living at 62, Bancroft Street, Bulwell, and they had three children; Selina born in 1897, Frank born in 1899 and George born in 1900. They continued to live at Bancroft Street, and by 1911 John, Clara Louise and Jane had been born. A seventh child, Alice was born in 1913. John volunteered for the Army in 1915, joining the 8th Battalion, North Staffordshire Regiment, and was sent to France on the 18th July, 1915. John served until the 6th July, 1916 when he died from wounds incurred on the Somme, aged 47. John's body was buried at Heilly Station Cemetery, Mericourt L'Abbe on the Somme in France.

Sergeant John Thomas Noble
R/12380

In 1887 Thomas Noble a 21 year old coal miner from Walsall, Staffordshire married Mary Ann Warrender, a 22 year old dressmaker from Brewood, Staffordshire at Mansfield, Nottinghamshire. The couple moved back to live at Pye Green, Hednesford, where George was born in 1889 and John Thomas in 1890. In 1901, the family had moved to live at 9, Bradbury Lane, Hednesford, and Sydney, Selina and Alice had been born, followed in 1906 by the birth of Mercy Ellen. By 1911, John was working as a coal miner, Sydney was a horse driver in a colliery and Selina was a tailoress machinist. On the 27th May, 1912 John married Fanny Barnett at St. Peter's Parish Church, Hednesford, with the couple moving to live at 152, High Mount Street, Hednesford. They had two children, Thomas David born on the 14th January, 1913 and Mabel Edith born on the 5th November, 1914. On the 22nd April, 1915 John enlisted in the Army, joining the King's Royal Rifle Corps. He was posted to the 15th Battalion at Westcliffe-on-Sea and appointed as a Lance Corporal on the 2nd July, being made up to full Corporal on the 23rd October. John was transferred to the 11th Battalion on being sent to France on the 30th December, 1915, and appointed acting Sergeant on the 24th January, 1916. He was then posted to the 7th Battalion, and had to revert to Corporal before having his third stripe restored on the 7th July, 1916. John was then wounded, suffering a gunshot wound to the buttock on the 15th September, 1916 which meant hospital treatment, and he did not rejoin his unit until the 9th December. On the 25th March, 1917 John was badly wounded in the leg, and taken to 44 Field Ambulance where he died from his injuries aged 27. John's body was buried at Faubourg D'Amiens Cemetery at Arras in France.

Private Samuel Oakley
9313

In 1876 at Dudley, Worcestershire, Samuel Oakley, a 20 year old bricklayer from Upper Gornal, Staffordshire married Phoebe Buckley, aged 17, a nail maker, from the same village. The couple moved to live at 49, Pale Street, Sedgley where their first child Hannah was born in 1880. Samuel was struggling to find work locally and so the decision was made to move to Mount Street, Hednesford and by 1891, the couple had had three more children, Samuel born in 1884, Clara born in

1885, Thomas born in 1890, with a fourth, Arthur born shortly afterwards in 1895. By 1901, Hannah and Clara were both working as dressmakers and Samuel junior was a bricklayer like his father, although Samuel junior worked for the Cannock and Rugeley Colliery Company. By 1911, Samuel junior had married and he and his wife Margaret were living at 33, Mount Street, Hednesford with their first child Florence. Samuel was a member of the Hednesford Territorials and so when the Great War began, he was enlisted into the Army in 1914, joining the 1/5th Battalion, South Staffordshire Regiment, being sent to France on the 5th March, 1915. Samuel served as a machine gun officer's orderly and he was killed in action on the 24th August, 1915 near Ieper in Belgium when he was struck by shrapnel. Samuel was 31 at the time of his death and was a father of three. His body was buried at Perth (China Wall) Cemetery near Ieper in Belgium. His widow received two letters about her husband, one from Major William Burnett, who had organized the Territorials in Hednesford and was fighting with the Battalion, and one from the Platoon Sergeant, E. Martin to say that her husband had been decently buried.

2nd Lieutenant Percy Vincent Oswell

On the 24th November, 1890 at St. Luke's Parish Church, Cannock John Oswell a 21 year old coal miner from Madeley, Shropshire, married Elizabeth Ward, aged 20 from Darlaston, Staffordshire. The couple moved to live at Blewitt Street, Hednesford and their first child, Lilian was born in 1895. She was followed by Percy in 1897 and Laurence in 1900. The family moved to live at 42b, Heath Street, Green Heath and it was here that Allan was born in 1906. By 1911, Lilian had started work as a tailoring finisher and Percy was a printer's apprentice. Percy enlisted with the Army on the 3rd April, 1915, and was initially a gunner with the Royal Field Artillery, but was then transferred to the infantry, serving with the Leinster Regiment, where he became a Corporal. Percy was sent back to England for officer training, and gained his commission on the 3rd May, 1917. He was sent back to France as a 2nd Lieutenant with the 6th Battalion, Royal West Surrey Regiment on the 2nd August, 1918 and was killed in action at Epehy Wood on the 20th September, 1918 at the age of 21. Percy's body was buried at Epehy Wood Farm Cemetery, Epehy, between Peronne and Bapaume in France.

3. Hednesford

Private Arthur Richard Owen
10847

Arthur Owen was born at Hednesford in 1897 and was the sixth son of Charles and Eliza Owen. Charles came from Stonnal, Staffordshire and married Eliza Burton at Walsall in 1881. Charles was a boot and shoe maker by trade and the couple lived at Shire Oak and Walsall Wood before moving to Hednesford in 1890. Prior to this they had had five children, Charles Henry being born at Shire Oak and Alfred, William, Thomas and Alice all born at Walsall Wood. After moving to Hednesford, the family settled down to live at 62, Cannock Road, High Town where George was born in 1894, Arthur in 1897 and Annie in 1901. By 1911, only George, a housepainter, Arthur, a fish seller and Annie, still at school were still living at home. Arthur became a labourer, working at West Cannock Colliery and then helping to build the new military camp on Cannock Chase, before volunteering for the Army on the 10th April, 1915, joining the 7th Battalion, South Staffordshire Regiment. He was sent to Gallipoli on the 6th October, 1915 and was killed in action, just six days after arriving on the 12th October at the age of 18, when hit by a shell. Arthur's body was not recovered after the war and he is remembered on the Helles Memorial to the Missing in Turkey.

Private Charles Parker
15561

Charles Parker was born at Dundalk, Ireland in 1887 and was the son of Thomas and Annie Parker. By 1901, Annie was a widow, living at 21, Spring Hill Passage, Birmingham where her 14 year old son was a mechant's warehouse boy and with her daughter, Ethel, who was only three and who had been born in India. Sometime before 1910, Charles had moved to work as a miner in the Hednesford area and on the 31st July, 1910 he married Alice Maud Gould, at St. Peter's Parish Church, Hednesford. Both gave their address as West Hill, Hednesford, but in 1911, the couple were boarding with John and Mary Farmer and their one year old son, Samuel at 12, Queen Street, High Town, Hednesford. Charles and Alice had two children, Thomas born in 1911 and Ethel born in 1914. Charles enlisted in the Army in early 1915, joining the 13th Battalion, Northumberland Fusiliers and he was sent to France on the 9th September, 1915. On the 26th September, he was posted as missing in action in the Battle of Loos, and it was later presumed that he had been killed on that day at the age of 28. Charles' body was not identified after the war and he is remembered on the Loos Memorial to the Missing in France.

Private Norman Arthur Parton
39869

In 1893 at Cannock, Albert Arthur Parton a 21 year old draper and manager from Wolverhampton, Staffordshire married Susannah Curry Longstaff, aged 23 from Frimdon, Durham. The couple set up a business on Station Road, Hednesford and began a family. Norman was born in 1894, Dudley in 1896 and Millie in 1899. Indeed in 1901 the couple could afford to employ a servant, Emma Benn from Hednesford. However, by 1911 there had been drastic changes to their lifestyle. It would appear that the business had folded and Albert was now employed as a weigh clerk at a colliery. Norman, now 17 was a plasterer's labourer and Dudley an errand boy. The family had moved to live at 39, Cannock Road, Chadsmoor. In early 1916, Norman volunteered for the Army, enlisting initially with the South Staffordshire Regiment but then being transferred to the 10th Battalion, Worcestershire Regiment. He served until the 18th November, 1916 when he was posted missing at the age of 23. It was later presumed that Norman had been killed on this date. After the war, Norman's body could not be found and he is remembered on the Thiepval Memorial to the Missing on the Somme in France. Norman's parents emigrated to Canada at the end of the war.

Guardsman Harold William Peake
16007

In 1885, at Cannock Harry Peake a beer seller born in Cannock married Emma Wallbank, also born at Cannock. The couple had a brief stay in Derby where their first child, John was born before returning to Staffordshire to live at Littleworth Castle, Ford Row, Littleworth, in Hednesford. By 1891, two more children had been born, Nellie in 1888 and Harold in 1890. In 1901 the business appeared to be thriving, and Harry was now a wine and beer merchant. The family were still at the same address, but had increased with the births of Hettie, Charles, Gladys and William. However, by 1911 there had been changes. Harry was now a carpenter, as the business had folded, John was a bricklayer, whilst Harold was a fitter and Charles a butcher, with William employed as a tailor. Indeed, Harold later found employment at Moore's clothing factory in Hednesford. In May, 1915, Harold decided to enlist in the Army, joining the 3rd Battalion, Coldstream Guards and he was sent to France on the 21st December, 1915. Harold served until the 21st June, 1916 when he was killed in action just outside Ieper in Belgium at the age of 26. Harold's body was buried at Essex Farm Cemetery near Ieper. In July 2009 a party of students and staff from Kingsmead Technology College, Hednesford laid a wreath on his grave.

Private William Pearce
5397

In 1882 at Cannock, Aaron Pearce a 26 year old coal miner from Oakengates, Shropshire married Mary Ann Mears, 22, from Kiddemore Green, Staffordshire. The couple moved to Station Road, Hednesford and by 1891, they had had four children. These were Bertha, born in 1882, Florrie, born in 1884, James, born in 1886 and Freddie, born in 1890. By 1901, the family had moved to live on the Rugeley Road, Hednesford, with Fred now a horse driver in a colliery. The family had also grown with the births of William in 1892, Sissy in 1894, Hilda in 1895 and Elsie in 1898. In 1911, the Pearce family had moved to live at Reservoir Road, Church Hill, Hednesford, but William had decided to move to Birmingham where he was employed as a barman by William Morris the licensee of the Eagle and Ball Public House at 28, Sherlock Street, Birmingham. In November, 1915 William enlisted in the Army, joining the 1/5th Battalion, Royal Warwickshire Regiment, and he was sent to France in 1916. On the 3rd July, 1916, William was badly wounded in the abdomen and legs by shrapnel. He was invalided back to England where he was treated at Sheffield, but sadly, William died aged 24 on the 17th July, 1916. His body was brought back to Hednesford, where it was buried with full military honours at St. Peter's Churchyard, Hednesford, with the band of the West Yorkshire Regiment playing the Last Post and firing a volley over the grave.

Sergeant George William Pearson
13601

George Pearson was born at Hazel Slade in 1892, the eldest child of Joseph and Sarah Ann Pearson. Joseph was born in Hampshire, whereas his wife, whose maiden name was Reece, was born at West Bromwich, Staffordshire. Joseph earned his living as a coal miner, and in 1901, the family was living at 6, Cross Street, Hazel Slade. At that point there were three children, George, Lilian and Eliza. By 1911, the family had moved to live at 2, Albert Street, Hazel Slade, and two more children had been born, Selina and Nellie. George was working as a coal miner surveyor. In early 1915, George enlisted in the Army, joining the 13th Battalion, Royal Welsh Fusiliers and he was sent to France on the 9th July, 1915. He served on the Western Front, and rose to the rank of Sergeant before he was killed in action on the 20th October, 1918 at the age of 26. After the war George's body could not be identified and he is remembered on the Vis-en-Artois Memorial to the Missing in France.

Lance Corporal Frederick Porter
R/9964

In 1875, at Dudley, Worcestershire, William Henry Porter a 20 year old coal miner, married Mary Ann Hartill, also aged 20. Both came from Sedgley in Staffordshire, and after they were married moved to live at 25, Moden Hill, Sedgley. Their first child, Sarah Ann was born in 1877, followed by Rebecca in 1879. The couple had one more child at Sedgley, William Henry junior, born in 1882, before moving to Huntington Terrace, Chadsmoor, where Emily was born in 1883, Charlotte in 1886, Frederick in 1890 and Howard in 1895. By this time, Sarah had started work as a tailor's apprentice. In 1911, the family were living at McGhie Street, Hednesford, where William junior and Frederick were working as coal miners, Lottie was a domestic servant and Howard was a pit motor driver. Just after the outbreak of war, all three Porter brothers enlisted in the Army, Frederick joining the 7th Battalion, King's Royal Rifle Corps and he was posted to France on the 4th August, 1915. Frederick was killed in action on the 18th August, 1916 at the age of 26. His Company officer, Captain G.W. Northolomew wrote to his parents to say that Frederick "was one of my best Lance Corporals and marked for promotion. He was always cheerful and ready to do anything. He was universally liked". Frederick's body was buried at Delville Wood Cemetery, Longueval on the Somme in France.

Corporal Joseph Postings
11949

Joseph Postings was born at Hednesford in 1892, and was the second son of John and Hannah Postings. The couple had married at Burntwood in 1879, when John was a 21 year old coal miner from Darlaston, and his wife, Hannah Westwood as she was born, was 16, and came from Burntwood. Their first child, Thomas was born at Burntwood in 1881, followed by Emma in 1885 and Agnes in 1887 before the family moved to live at Station Road, Hednesford. It was here that Joseph was born, followed by his brother, Leonard who was born in 1894. Annie was born in 1903 and finally David in 1910. By 1911, the family had moved to live at 130, Church Hill, Hednesford, although Joseph had moved out to live with his grandmother, Emma Westwood, who was 78 and lived at The Hole, Burntwood, Staffordshire. In September, 1915 Joseph volunteered for the Army, joining the North Staffordshire Regiment and was sent to France in 1916. He then volunteered for service in the Machine Gun Corps and rose to the rank of Corporal before he died from wounds at the age of 26 on the 20th April, 1918. Joseph's body was buried at Doullens Communal Cemetery Extension Number 1, near Amiens in France.

Gunner Leonard Postings
214115

Leonard Postings was the younger brother of Joseph and was born at Hednesford in 1894. He was a coal miner, but this did not stop him joining the Army on the 18th February, 1916 under the Derby Scheme. He was immediately placed on the Reserve List, to be called upon when needed. Leonard was mobilized on the 30th April, 1918, just ten days after his brother's death and was sent to Ripon, to the Number 4 Depot, Royal Garrison Artillery. From here he was sent to the 3rd Reserve Brigade on the 10th June, 1918 and then Leonard was posted to France on the 26th September, 1918. He joined the 238th Siege Battery and he was killed in action on the 16th October, 1918 at the age of 24. Leonard's body was buried at Becquigny Communal Cemetery, between Le Cateau and Cambrai in France. Leonard's father John received his son's personal possessions, 5 pence, 1 farthing, a religious book, a small pocket case and a cigarette lighter.

Private George Potts
17779

In 1877 at Wolverhampton, Staffordshire, Samuel Potts a coal miner from Willenhall, Staffordshire, married Mary Evans, also from the same town. Their first child, John was born at Portobello, Willenhall in 1878, before the family moved to live at Ironstone Road, Burntwood, where the second child, Ellen was born in 1880. Samuel junior was born here in 1891, whence the family moved again to George Street, Hednesford. It was here that Jane was born in 1884, George in 1886, Mary in 1888 and Minnie in 1890. By 1901, the family had moved again to Arthur Street, Wimblebury where Amy, Betsy and Ada were born. John had left home by this time and Samuel junior was now a coal miner and George was a pit lad. On the 28rd March, 1910 George married Elizabeth Earp at St. Peter's Parish Church, Hednesford, with the couple moving to live at 161, Wimblebury Road, Heath Hayes where their first child Jack was born in 1911. A second child, Harriet was born in 1915 but by this time the family had moved to live on Rugeley Road, Hednesford. George joined the Army in early 1915, enlisting with the 7th Battalion, South Staffordshire Regiment and he was posted to Gallipoli on the 5th December, 1915. From here he went to Egypt before returning to the Western Front in 1916. George served here until the 9th June, 1917 when he was killed in action near Ieper at the age of 30. George's body was not identified after the war and he is remembered on the Ieper (Menin Gate) Memorial to the Missing in Ieper city centre in Belgium.

Private George Powell
17618

In 1897, at Cheadle, Staffordshire David Powell, a 20 year old general labourer from Alton, Staffordshire married 21 year old Amy Ann Mountney from Doveridge, Derbyshire. They lived at Threapwood, near Cheadle and in 1898 their first child George was born, followed by Albert in 1901, Percy in 1903, Wilfred in 1905, and Arthur Baden in 1913. Shortly after the birth of Wilfred, the family moved to live at Hednesford, settling in John Street, Wimblebury where David found employment as a domestic coachman. George, like many men from the area found employment as a coal miner, but on the 25th May, 1915 at the age of only 16, he enlisted in the Army. George joined the 7th Battalion, North Staffordshire Regiment, serving in "C" Company, and was sent to the Dardanelles in December 1915 and from there he was posted to Mesopotamia. George served without leave until the 25th January, 1917 when he was killed in action at the age of 18. George's body was buried at Camara War Cemetery in Iraq. The information was sent to his family who were then living at 7, Wimblebury Road, Littleworth, next door to where George had been living when he enlisted.

Private John Henry Poyner
11354

John Poyner was born at Cannock in 1894, and was the second son of William and Ann Poyner. William was a coal miner from Dudley and he married Ann Wood, also from Dudley in 1891. Ann had a son, William, born in 1890, from her first marriage to John Wood, who had died in 1891 at the age of 27. Whilst they were still living at Dudley, the couple had their first child together, Mary Ann born in 1892. Shortly after this the family moved to live at 13, Bradbury Lane, Hednesford. It was here that John was born, along with Matilda in 1897, Thomas in 1899, Alice in 1901, Beatrice in 1905, Robert in 1907 and George in 1909. John had by this time begun work as a horse driver at West Cannock Colliery, a job he was to do for two and a half years. However, on the 4th January, 1912, John joined the 5th Battalion, South Staffordshire Regiment, which was the Territorial Force based at Hednesford and led at that time by William Burnett. He went on the summer camp to Aberystwyth in 1912, and then on the 4th January, 1913, John applied for permission to join the Royal Scots. Permission was granted and he was sent to Glencorse on the 8th January, where he was initially posted to the 3rd Battalion, but on the 20th April, 1913 was sent to the 2nd Battalion. This would appear not to have been to his liking, for over the next year, John was in trouble for minor military offences on no fewer than ten occasions. Following the outbreak of war the 2nd Battalion, Royal Scots was sent to France on the 13th August, 1914. On the 24th August, John was wounded in the left thigh, and was unable to move. His step brother, William Wood who was in the same Battalion tried to get John back on his feet. John was unable to do so, and John told William to get away as he had a wife and children to think of. The two men shook hands, kissed and William went away to try and find his unit. John was taken prisoner and sent to a camp at Doebritz in Germany. Meanwhile, the War Office had sent a telegram to Mrs. Poyner at 72, Bradbury Lane, telling her that John had been killed in action at Vailly. A few days later, she received a postcard from John saying that he was a prisoner of war. Thoroughly confused and distraught, the poor woman asked Mr. Horrocks-Brown of Station Road, Hednesford to contact the War Office on her behalf. This he duly did, and after seeing the postcard, the Army changed its mind, but not before they had managed to confuse Mrs. Poyner with someone in Leicester. In April, 1915 John sent a letter to Albert Stanley M.P. reminding him that his sons used to play football with Poyner and J. Tranter who was also a prisoner at Doebritz. Poyner asked for cocoa, sugar, tea, cake and "fags" to be sent. He made the point that the favour would be returned at the end of the war. At some point, John was moved to Hameln but on the 22nd January, 1918 he was one of some 16,000 British and German prisoners who were sent to neutral Holland for safe internment until the end of the war. John was sent to a camp at The Hague. However, on the 3rd November, 1918 John was admitted to the camp hospital with influenza, and his condition worsened considerably after the 10th November and tragically at the age of 23, John died at 1.30 in the morning on the 13th November, 1918. John's body was buried at The Hague General Cemetery in Holland.

Corporal Joseph Edward Preece
18535

In 1894 at Cannock, Christopher James Preece a 22 year old coal miner from Hednesford married 20 year old Priscilla Garbett, also from Hednesford. The couple set up a home at Rawnsley Road, Hednesford. Their first child, Elsie was born in 1895, followed three years later by Joseph. By 1911, the family had moved to live at 3, Cross Street, Hazel Slade and the family had grown with the births of Daisy, Ada, Violet, Cyril and Nellie. The family had moved to live at 47, Arthur Street, Wimblebury before the war. Joseph joined the Army on the 13th April, 1915, aged only 17, enlisting with the 8th Battalion, South Staffordshire Regiment, training at Sunderland and Backworth. He saw service at Albert, Vermelles and Vimy Ridge, before being wounded on the Somme and sent back to Birmingham to convalesce. When he had recovered he was returned to the Western Front on the 1st April, 1917. He saw action at Arras, Vimy Ridge and at Passchendaele, before he was posted as missing in action on the 12th October, 1917. It was presumed six months later that he had been killed on that date at the age of 19. After the war, Joseph's body was not found and he is remembered on the Tyne Cot Memorial to the Missing, near Ieper in Belgium. Joseph's father Christopher also served in the Great War and survived.

Private Arthur Prince
3198

In 1877 at Walsall, Staffordshire Arthur Prince, a 19 year old engine fireman from Barton-under-Needwood in Staffordshire married 25 year old Mary Johnson Emery from Hopwas near Tamworth. The couple lived briefly at Chase Terrace where their first child John Thomas was born in 1878, before moving to live at 2, Albert

Street, Hazel Slade, where William was born in 1879 and Fanny in 1881. Tragically, Mary died in 1883 at the age of 31, but Arthur married again in 1887. His bride was Jane Anne James, who was 23 and came from Wolverhampton. The family moved to live at Church Hill, Hednesford where Joseph John was born in 1888 and Levinia in 1891. In 1901, the family had moved again to live at 7, Blakemore Street, Church Hill where Arthur junior was born in 1893 and his brother Harry in 1900. Fanny was now a domestic servant and Joseph had found a job on the pit bank. By 1911, Arthur senior was now employed as a boat loader on the canal wharf, while Joseph was a carter. Arthur junior was working as a waggoner on a farm. Arthur senior's father, Thomas Prince was also living with the family. On the 29th January, 1914 Arthur junior left England for a new life in Western Australia. He found a job as a barman and was living at 132, Albany Road, Victoria Park, Perth. However, on the 28th October, 1916 Arthur enlisted in the Australian Imperial Forces. He left Perth on the 23rd December, 1916, arriving at Devonport on the 14th February, 1917. Arthur was sent to France on the 4th June, 1917, joining his unit, the 48th Battalion on the 21st June. Arthur was wounded in action on the 1st October, 1917, receiving shrapnel wounds to the left arm. He was treated at the Australian Field Ambulance, transferred to the 3rd Canadian Casualty Clearing Station, and then to the 18th General Hospital at Camiers. From there he was sent to the 14th Convalescent Depot at Trouville, before rejoining his unit on the 26th November, 1917. On the 8th March, 1918, Arthur was sent back to England on leave and visited his family at 23, Blakemore Street, Church Hill, returning to France on the 21st March, 1918. Just one week later on the 28th March, 1918 Arthur was killed in action at the age of 25. Arthur's body was buried at Ribemont Communal Cemetery Extension, near Albert on the Somme in France.

Private Charles George Pritchard
260026

In 1873, Henry Williams a carpenter from Brewood, Staffordshire married Eliza Jane Allsop, also from Brewood, the marriage taking place at Penkridge. The couple set up a home at North View, Bradbury Lane, Hednesford and their first child, Eliza was born in 1874. Agnes, Clarissa, Frederick and Frances soon followed, with the household completed by Walter Hudson, a lodger from Burton-on-Trent. However, in 1887, Henry died at the age of 35, and within a year, Eliza had married Charles Pritchard, a painter and glazier from Darlaston. The family moved to live at Church Hill, Hednesford and in 1889, their first child Charles was born. By

1901, Agnes was helping her mother with the housework and Fred was a brick loader, whilst Frances worked as a tailoress. Charles senior died in 1910 at the age of 60, and his widow continued to live at Church Hill, with her son, Charles who was now a tailor working at Moore's Clothing Factory at Hednesford. Also living in the house was Fred Goodwill, described as a 6 year old grandson, born at Didsbury, Lancashire, and John Smith, a 22 year old lodger from Hednesford. Charles joined the 1/6th Battalion, South Staffordshire Regiment in 1916, and was sent to serve on the Western Front where he died of wounds on the 25th June, 1917 at the age of 28. Charles' body was buried at Loos British Cemetery in France.

Private Frederick "Fritz" Proverbs 5351

Fritz Proverbs was born at Hednesford in 1884, and whose given name was Frederick, but was known to all as Fritz. His parents were John and Harriet Proverbs who had married at Penkridge in 1876. John was a coal miner from Stone Port, Worcestershire while Harriet, whose maiden name was Evans came from Sedgley. The couple lived at Cannock to begin with and it was here that their first child Amelia was born, but by 1881 the family had moved to Hednesford where Frank was born in 1881. By 1891 the family had moved to live at Green Heath, Hednesford, and the family had increased in size with the births of Mary, Fritz, James, Rachel and Ernest. In 1901, the family was living at Heath Street, Hednesford, and William and Bertram had been born. Frank was working as a mechanical labourer, while Fritz was a coal miner horse driver along with James. John Proverbs died in 1908, and in 1911, the family was living at New Buildings, Rawnsley. Frank was now working on the pit bank, whereas Fritz and James both worked as coal miner loaders, Ernest was employed as a colliery loco stoker and William was an engine man below ground. Fritz joined the Hednesford Territorials and so when war broke out in 1914, he was quickly drafted into the 1/5th Battalion, South Staffordshire Regiment and was sent to France on the 5th March, 1915. Fritz was wounded three times while in France, but on the 13th October, 1915 at the Battle of Loos, he was killed in action aged 32. Fritz was killed during the attack on the Hohenzollern Redoubt, when having got back to the relative safety of the British trenches he went out with a field dressing for Captain William Milner who was lying wounded in No Man's Land. As he was trying to apply the dressing both Fritz and Captain Milner were killed by shrapnel. After the war Fritz's body could not be identified and he is remembered on the Loos Memorial to the Missing in France.

Private George Purcell
8173

In 1882 Richard Purcell a 20 year old farm labourer born at Stafford, married Hannah Wright from Cannock, the marriage taking place at Stafford. The couple moved to Pye Green, Chadsmoor and their first child, Hettie was born in 1884, followed by Mary and Edward. John was born in 1891 and George was born at Hednesford in 1896. In 1900, Hannah died at the age of 38, and the family had moved to live at West Cannock Cottages at Brindley Heath by 1901. Later that same year, Richard married Susannah Frazer at Cannock, and the family moved to 83, Platt Street, High Town, Hednesford. Richard and Susannah started a family of their own with Richard junior born in 1903, Thomas in 1908 and Henry in 1909. Meanwhile Edward was a colliery surface labourer like his father, John was a colliery labourer underground and George worked as a colliery motor driver at Cannock and Rugeley Colliery. George joined the Hednesford Territorials in 1913, and again when war was declared, he joined the 1/5th Battalion, South Staffordshire Regiment and was sent to France on the 5th March, 1915. George was killed in action on the 1st July, 1916 on the unsuccessful diversionary attack at Gommecourt, aged 20. George's body was buried at Foncquevillers Military Cemetery on the Somme in France.

Private John Purcell
19441

John Purcell was the older brother of George and he too was born at Hednesford in 1891. He worked on the pit bank at Mid Cannock Colliery and joined the Army in 1915, enlisting with the 2nd Battalion, South Staffordshire Regiment. He was wounded in the arm on the same day that his younger brother was killed and was sent back to the Military Hospital in Manchester to recover, before being returned to the Western Front. John was wounded on the 27th April, 1917, with a letter being sent to that effect on the same day. Sadly on the following day, John died from his injuries at the age of 26. John's body was buried at Anzin-St. Aubin British Cemetery, on the western outskirts of Arras in France.

Able Seaman Percy Rawlings
Bristol Z/9906

Percy Rawlings was born at Cannock on the 20th November, 1897 and lived at 66, McGhie Street, Hednesford. It is not clear who his parents were, for on the 1901 census he was living with his widowed grandmother Margaret Lester. She had married James Lester at Cannock in 1884 following the death of her first husband Edward Rawlings in 1882. James and Margaret had one child Jemima who was born at Hednesford in 1885, but who died at the tragically young age of 17 in 1902. Margaret had children from her first marriage, Susan, Harriett, Margaretta, Phoebe and William, and in 1911, William was still living with his mother and working as a general labourer, with Percy working as an office boy, although he was later to become a clerk. On the 22nd November, 1916 Percy joined the Royal Naval Volunteer Reserve Division at Bristol, and was posted to HMS Victory as an Ordinary Seaman. He also saw service on HMS Excellent and HMS President, by which time he had risen to Able Seaman. Sadly on the 16th February, 1919 Percy died from Pleuro Pneumonia at the Royal Naval Hospital, Haslar in Gosport at the age of 21. His body was brought home to Hednesford and buried at St. Peter's Churchyard.

Private Albert William Richardson
42406

In 1876 Frederick Richardson a coal miner hailing from Bloxwich, Staffordshire married Bertha Agnes Smith, also from Bloxwich. The couple settled in Pelsall to begin with where Henry their first child was born, before moving to Bloxwich for the birth of their second child James. The family then moved to live at Green Heath, Hednesford and it was here that Albert was born in 1882, quickly followed by Mary Jane, Frank, Edwin and Bertram. 1901 found the family living at Mount Street, Hednesford and the family had been further increased with the births of Alfred and Clara. James was now a coal miner loader, as was Albert, with Frank and Edwin both employed as horse drivers. In 1911, the family had moved to 19, Abbey Street, Green Heath, with James and Albert both working as miners, with Edwin and Bertram working as miner's labourers. Frederick had gone against the family trend and was working as a tailor machinist at Moore's Clothing Factory. Frederick Richardson died in 1913 at the age of 55. On the 29th March, 1916 Albert enlisted in the 8th Battalion, Durham Light

Infantry, and after his training was sent to France on the 10th August, 1916, sailing from Folkestone to Boulogne. He was transferred to the 15th Battalion on the 31st August, joining his unit the following day. Just two weeks later, Albert was killed in action at the age of 34. Neither the gold chain that his sister Clara had given to Albert as a gift, or the watch given to him by his brother Fred was ever found. After the war Albert's body was not identified and he is remembered on the Thiepval Memorial to the Missing on the Somme in France.

Private Walter Joseph Roberts
97927

Thomas Roberts was a 23 year old coal miner born at Mold, Flintshire when he married Dinah Rogers at Holywell in 1893. She was also 23 and came from Bradley, Staffordshire. The couple settled in Mold and it was here that their first three children, Edward, Robert and Sarah were born. The family moved to live at 219b, Littleworth, Hednesford in 1899 and later that year Walter was born, followed by William, Arthur, Roland and George. By 1911, Edward and Robert were both employed as coal miner drivers, with the next four children all at school. Walter found work as a horse driver at Cannock Chase Colliery, but on the 13th March, 1917 at the age of 18, he was conscripted into the Army. He was posted initially to the 11th Training Reserve battalion at Brocton Camp, but was transferred to the 2nd Battalion, Notts and Derbys Regiment on the 1st December, 1917. Walter was sent to France on the 13th February, 1918, joining his Battalion in the field on the 18th. Walter was posted as missing in action on the first day of the German Spring Offensive, 21st March, 1918, it later being confirmed that he had been taken prisoner. On the 22nd July, 1918 in a prisoner of war camp near Berlin, Walter died from influenza, aged 19. Walter's body was buried at Berlin South Western Cemetery in Germany.

Lance Corporal Frederick Robson
18184

Robert Robson came from the farming community of Abbots Bromley, Staffordshire and in 1864 he married Mary Bradbury from Colton, Staffordshire. Robert was an agricultural waggoner and later became an agricultural labourer. The family settled to live in Colton and began a family. By 1871, James, George and Mary had been born, followed by Thomas, Eliza, Robert and Sarah. Frederick, the youngest of their children was born in 1885 at Colton, when the family were living in the nearby hamlet of Hamley. In 1901, Frederick was living with Samuel Norman, a widower of 83 who was still working as a beerhouse and shop keeper at Colton. By this time Frederick was working as a carter, but shortly after this he moved to work in Hednesford. On the 31st May, 1908, Frederick married Florence Jane Caddick at St. Peter's Parish Church, Hednesford. The couple were then living at 16, Mount Street, Hednesford and Frederick was working as a coal miner. They began a family, with the birth of Doris May in 1907, with Leonard following in 1909 and Norman in 1910. Two more children were born, Frederick in 1914 and Colin in 1915. Frederick joined the Army in 1916, enlisting with the 2nd Battalion, South Staffordshire Regiment, and he served with this unit until the 15th March, 1917 when he was killed in action at the age of 32. Frederick's body was buried at Adanac Military Cemetery, Miraumont near Albert on the Somme in France.

Private John William Roden
9609

On the 3rd April, 1899 at St. Peter's Parish Church, Hednesford John Wilkes a 24 year old coal miner from Wednesbury, Staffordshire married Mary Ann Roden, aged 31, from Wolverhampton. She already had a child, a son, John William Roden who had been born at Hednesford in 1896. The family set up a home at 30, Wood Lane, Hednesford, and in 1900 their first child, Harry was born. By 1911, Clara and Hilda had been added to the family and John had started work as a nipper in a colliery, and later became a miner. Shortly after the outbreak of war, John volunteered for the Army, joining the 1st Battalion, South Staffordshire Regiment on the 7th August, 1914 and being sent to France on the 17th December, 1914, even though at 18 he was too young to serve overseas. On the 1st July, 1916 the Battalion was part of the successful attack at Mametz that morning, but sadly John was one of the soldiers killed in action. He was only 20 at the time of his death. After the war his body could not be identified and John is remembered on the Thiepval Memorial to the Missing on the Somme in France.

Gunner Frederick Charles Rogers
116556

William Rogers was a brewer's drayman born at Tibberton, Worcestershire and in 1886 he married Harriet Shelton at Wolverhampton. William was 23 at the time of his wedding and his bride was 24. The couple set up home at Spring Valley

Street, Wolverhampton and by 1891 had had three children, James, William Henry and Frederick Charles. Harriet's 26 year old brother, Joseph Shelton was also staying with them and he was employed as a general labourer. By 1893 the family had moved to live at Station Road, Hednesford and it was here that Frank was born. By 1911, William had left home to join the Royal Navy and Frederick was working as a printer's compositor for Mr. B. Evans at Hednesford. Frank was working as a colliery and estate clerk. The family had also adopted Rose Shelton, who was presumably related to Harriet, and were living at 150, Church Hill, Hednesford. Frederick was a noted organist, and was deputy to Mr. Duffield at Tettenhall Church, Wolverhampton. On the 14th January, 1916 Frederick attested for the Army and under the terms of the Derby Scheme was placed on the Army Reserve List. He was mobilized on the 28th August, 1916 and the 5 feet 11 inch Frederick made his way to the Citadel, Plymouth to join Number 3 Depot, Royal Garrison Artillery. Frederick was posted to 4 Company on the 16th September, 1916 and posted again to the 244th Siege Battery on the 22nd September. On the 25th December, 1916 at St. Peter's Parish Church, Hednesford, Frederick married the 28 year old Sophia Letitia Croft, and their "honeymoon" was spent at 4, Anglesey Street, Hednesford, her parent's house. Frederick was sent to serve at Ieper on the 29th January, 1917 and served in that sector until the 10th July, 1917 when he was killed by a shell. His personal effects were returned to his widow, including a silver watch and a book entitled "Harmony-Its theory and practice". Frederick's body was buried at Duhallow Advanced Dressing Station Cemetery near Ieper in Belgium.

Stoker First Class William Henry Rogers K/4807

William Rogers was the older brother of Frederick and was born at Wolverhampton on the 24th January, 1889. William began his working life as a bricklayer, but on the 16th November, 1909 he decided to join the Royal Navy. He served on a number of vessels but was posted to HMS Doris on the 2nd August, 1914. On the 28th December, 1914 at Port Said, William suffered heart failure due to pneumonia, dying at the age of 25. William's body was buried at Port Said War Memorial Cemetery in Egypt.

Private Bert Roper
48209

In 1882 at Cannock Thomas Roper a 21 year old coal miner from Willenhall, Staffordshire married Margaret Tennant, 19, from Wolverhampton. The couple moved to Bank Street, Heath Hayes, where their first child Thomas junior was born in 1885 and their second child, Florence was born there in 1890. By 1901, the family had moved to live on the Hednesford Road, Heath Hayes and the family had increased in size with the births of Harold in 1892, Annie in 1895, Bert in 1897 and Walter in 1899. Thomas junior had started work and had become a French polisher. In 1911, the family had moved to live at Gorsemoor Lane, Heath Hayes, and two more children had been born, Horace in 1902 and Howard in 1906. Harold had started work as a coal miner's loader and Bert was a nipper down the pit, whilst Thomas continued with his trade as a French polisher. Bert joined the Army on the 23rd March, 1918, being posted to the 7th Battalion, Leicestershire Regiment, and being trained at Leicester, Patringham and Elsham. He was sent to France in July 1918, going into action with the Battalion, and he served until the 23rd October, 1918 when he was killed in action when struck by a dud shell at the age of 21. Bert's body was not found after the war and he is remembered on the Vis-en-Artois Memorial to the Missing in France.

Sergeant Major William Rowley
8780

William Rowley was born at Bridgtown, Staffordshire in 1887 and was the second son of William and Mary Ann Rowley. The couple had married at Aston, Birmingham in 1868, although both of them were natives of Herefordshire. In 1871, they were living at Ledsam Street, Birmingham and it was here that Emily was born. The family then moved to Wales where William found work as a coal miner, and while they were in Wales, Alice and Mary Ann were born, but in 1881 the family returned to the Midlands, settling in Walsall Wood where David was born in 1881. The family then moved on to Bridgtown where William was born and then onto Brownhills where Thomas was born in 1889. In 1901 the family were living at Newland Terrace, Clayhanger Road, Brownhills and by this time William had begun working down the pit as a horse driver. This was clearly not to his liking and in 1903 he joined the Army, enlisting in the 2nd Battalion, Royal Welsh Fusiliers and in 1911 he was serving in India. On returning to England at the end of his service, he was placed on the Reserve List and found a job as a miner at Littleton Colliery, living in Hednesford. On the outbreak of war William was called back to the Colours and was sent to France with the Battalion on the 29th August, 1914. He rose to the rank of Sergeant Major and at some point was transferred to the 10th Battalion, probably after recovering from one of the three times he was wounded. On one of these occasions in 1915, he married Lizzie Butler and the couple set up home at 82, Whitehall Road, Walsall. It was here that their one child, a son named William after his father was born in 1917. Sadly his father never saw his son as he was killed in action at the age of 30 on the 24th September, 1917 during the battle of Passchendaele. William's body was not identified after the war and he is remembered on the Tyne Cot Memorial to the Missing near Ieper in Belgium.

Corporal William Rowley
132535

William Rowley was born at Willenhall, Staffordshire in 1877 and he was the third son of John and Mary Rowley. John was a labourer from Sedgley and his wife was from Tipton, which was where the couple lived for a time, and it was here that Mary and John, their first two children were born. They then moved to live at 7, St. Ann's Terrace, Willenhall where Charles, William, Joseph and Prudence were born. In 1891, William was working as a brass caster in a local foundry, and an additional member of the family had been born, Arthur. William then moved to Cannock and it was here that he married Annie Evans on the 13th November, 1899, with the couple living at John Street, Chadsmoor, before moving to High Croft Terrace, West Chadsmoor, and finally to 7, Holly Street, off Belt Road. They had one child, Hilda who was born on the 2nd January, 1912, although in 1901, John Shepherd was living with them, and was described as a step son. Although in a safe occupation, William enlisted in the Army on the 4th October, 1915, joining the Royal Engineers in a Tunnelling Company. He went to France on the 23rd October and was transferred to the 185th Tunnelling Company where he rose to the rank of Corporal. On the night of 14/15th July, 1917, four rum jars were under the charge of 2nd Lieutenant V.D. Poole and bombs and two rum jars were issued to two companies carrying out a raid. The operation was postponed and the bombs and rum returned to the dump. Meanwhile Poole had gone to tend to some casualties and failed to notice the rum had been returned. Private Wykes of the East Surrey Regiment was told to look after the dump, where he found the rum. At 8.30 am on the 15th July, Major Ewan Tulloch visited the dug out where Corporal Rowley and his section had just finished their night shift. The men were resting, drying out clothing and were all sober. At 2 pm Lance Corporal McAlpine came off shift and had his dinner, then went to the cookhouse where he saw Rowley eating. McAlpine was aware that rum was being passed round the dugout by Private Wykes and Private Gibbard of the East Surreys. He reported this to Lieutenant Forrest who confiscated the rum and told the men to make less noise. Sapper Benton saw Rowley have some rum but said that he did not see Rowley drunk, and that Rowley went to his own part of the dugout at around 2 pm. Private Walker reported that Rowley sat on the edge of the bed and fell on the floor. Walker picked him up and put him to bed as he was helpless. He was certain that Rowley did not leave the bunk between 4 pm and 9.30 pm and that Rowley had no rum with him. Forrest said that Rowley did not appear to be drunk and that half an hour later he was asleep in his bunk. At 9.30 pm Forrest was relieved by Lieutenant Smith. He told Smith that Rowley had had some rum and was sleeping it off. At 10 pm Smith visited Rowley and ordered McAlpine to waken him but he was unable to do so. At 7 am Smith went back to Rowley's bunk and again was unable to wake him. He noticed that his eyes did not respond to light and sent for Captain Wick, the Medical Officer, who insisted that Rowley was taken to the Regimental Aid Post. After an examination, Wick sent Rowley to the Advanced Dressing Station where Captain Pearson tried to revive him using strychnine, dystalone, artificial respiration and heart massage, but William Rowley died at 11.45 am on the 16th October, 1917 at the age of 40. An inquiry heard the evidence and decided that Lieutenant Poole would be censured as he was responsible and that Wykes and Gibbard would face a Field General Court Martial. William's body was buried at Roclincourt Military Cemetery, near Arras in France.

Lance Corporal Frederick Rushton
R/10975

In 1882 at West Bromwich, Staffordshire Thomas Rushton a coal miner from West Bromwich married Annie Leadbeater from Leamington Spa, Warwickshire. They lived at West Bromwich to begin with and it was here that Frederick was born in 1885, followed by his brother Samuel in 1888, Violet in 1891 and Mabel in 1897. The family then moved to Arthur Street, Wimblebury where Francis was born in 1899 and Hilda in 1906. Frederick began work as a horse driver but then became a coal miner, and on the 25th December, 1905 he married Sarah Dainty at St. Peter's Parish Church, Hednesford. The young couple set up home at 21, Arthur Street just a few doors from Frederick's family. Their first child, Frederick was born in 1907, followed by Sarah in 1911 and Evelyn in 1914. Frederick enlisted in March 1915, joining the 7th Battalion, King's Royal Rifle Corps. He was trained at Sheerness

3. Hednesford

and was then sent to France on the 16th July, 1915 where he saw service in Belgium and France before being wounded in the Battle of Hooge, being treated in the hospital at Etaples. On his return to action, Fred was attached to the Machine Gun Corps as a Lewis gunner. He served until the 13th May, 1917 when he was killed in action by a grenade at the age of 33. Fred's body was buried at Beaurains Road Cemetery, Beaurains, near Arras in France.

Private Charles Russell
G/64180

Charles Russell was born at Stafford in 1883, and was the third son of John Henry Russell and his wife Caroline. The couple had married at Cannock in 1877, and Caroline's maiden name was Cope. John was a butcher by trade and in 1881 they had moved to Stafford and were living at 73, Backwalls, North Stafford. In 1879, their first child Frank was born and in 1890 Edward was born. Their world was turned upside down when Caroline died at Cannock in 1884 at the age of 27. By 1891, John was working as a gardener servant and was living at 27, Brook Street, Stafford, whilst Charles was living with his aunt and uncle, Sarah and George Tildesley. By 1901, Charles was working as a grocer's porter, and was living on the Stafford Road, Huntington, with his brother Frank who was a colliery engine stoker, while George and Sarah Tildesley were also lodging at the house which was rented by Henry and Elizabeth Talbot. In 1911, Charles was now a colliery labourer and was living at Paddy's Lane, Cannock with his brother Frank who was now married to Sarah. Charles was an active member of High Town Sunday School and High Town Bowling Club and he moved to live at McGhie Street, Hednesford and found employment as a miner at Wimblebury Colliery. Charles was conscripted in 1917 and was sent to France in July of that year with the 4th Battalion, Royal Fusiliers. He served on the Western Front until the 31st August, 1918 when he was killed in action at the age of 36. Charles' body was buried at the Honourable Artillery Company Cemetery, Ecoust-St. Mein, between Arras, Cambrai and Bapaume.

Private Joseph Sanders
16635

Joseph Sanders was born at Bloxwich, Staffordshire in 1889, and was the second son of Joseph and Mary Sanders. Joseph was a green grocer from Bloxwich whereas his wife came from Walsall. In 1891, the family were living at 13, Elmore Row,

Bloxwich and had five children, the eldest of which, William was described as an imbecile on the census. There were five daughters, Sarah Ann, Minnie, Ellen, Lily and Rose. However, Joseph senior died in 1896 at the age of 49, and this meant that his widow had the task of looking after a disabled son and six other children as well as running the green grocer's business. In 1910, Joseph junior married Maud Worrall at Walsall, and took up residence at 2 House, 1 Court, Alfred Street, Bloxwich, with their first child Lilian Maud born in 1910. Two other children, Gladys and Leonard were born in 1912 and 1914 respectively. There is no clear evidence to link Joseph Sanders to Hednesford, although the Roll of Honour has a Joseph Sanders who was serving with the South Staffordshire Regiment. This is the only Joseph Sanders who fits that requirement, and so is the most likely man. Joseph joined the 2nd Battalion, South Staffordshire Regiment in 1914 and was sent to France on the 17th March, 1915. Joseph died of wounds on the 29th July, 1916 during the Battle of the Somme at the age of 27. His body was not found after the war and Joseph is remembered on the Thiepval Memorial to the Missing on the Somme in France.

Private Edward Saunders
116573

Edward Saunders was born at Gentleshaw, Staffordshire in 1897 and was the second son of Edward and Eliza Saunders, both of whom came from King's Bromley, Staffordshire. Edward worked as a miner and in 1891 the family were living at Coldwell, Longdon, in Staffordshire. They were still living there in 1901, although William, the eldest, was now working as a coal loader. However, in 1911 Eliza was living at 6, Rugeley Road, Hazel Slade with Emma, Edward, who was now a painter, Albert and Robert Hutton Lightfoot, a 24 year old jockey from Carlisle. Edward senior was living with his now married son William, and his wife and family at Nuneaton, where they were both working as coal miners. Before the Great War, Edward also became a coal miner, but on the 11th October, 1915 he enlisted with the 19th Battalion, Sherwood Foresters. He was transferred to the 15th Battalion when he was sent to France on the 18th December, 1915. Edward served in this Battalion until the 7th May, 1917 when he was transferred again to the 195th Labour Corps. He was told in a letter from home that his mother had died on the 6th June, 1917 and just two months later, on the 7th August, 1917 Edward died from wounds at the age of 20. Edward's body was buried at Brandhoek New Military Cemetery near Ieper in Belgium.

3. Hednesford

Private Albert Edward Sanderson
28466

On the 31st August, 1889 Frederick George Sanderson, an 18 year old banksman from Hednesford, married 19 year old Mary Ann Hayward at St. Luke's Parish Church, Cannock. The couple lived in Hednesford where Emma was born in 1892, before moving to Widnes, Lancashire where Albert was born in 1894. The family then moved back to Queen Street, High Town where Arthur was born in 1897 and Alfred in 1899. In 1911, the family had moved to live at Cannock Road, High Town, and Ada was born here in 1906. Mary Ann had set up a business as a coffee dealer, but by 1911, she was an assistant in the fish trade, helped by Emma, with Albert and Arthur both selling fish. Frederick was working at a colliery as a pit bank foreman. It appears that Albert joined the Army in 1916, enlisting with the 8th Battalion, South Staffordshire Regiment, a unit he served with until the 23rd April, 1917 when he was killed in action at the age of 23. After the war Albert's body could not be identified and he is remembered on the Arras Memorial to the Missing in France.

Private Wallace Sargent
G/23129

In 1874 at Hailsham, Sussex William Wenham Sargent, a 27 year old agricultural labourer from Bexhill married Charlotte Ann Head, 23, also from Bexhill. They lived at Ninfield, Sussex and their first child, Charlotte was born in 1875, followed by William in 1878 and Wallace in 1880. In 1891, the family were living and working at Moor Hall Farm, Ninfield, with William having joined his father as an agricultural labourer, and in 1901, the family were still living there, with Wallace working as a general labourer. Charlotte died in 1909 at Hailsham at the age of 58, and in 1911, William was still working as an agricultural labourer at the age of 61, with Wallace also working on the same farm, as was Ernest, the youngest of the children, while Florence was acting as a housekeeper. For an unknown reason, Wallace decided to move to Hednesford, probably around the time of the Great War and on the 27th June, 1916, he joined the Army, giving his job as a general foreman. Interestingly, he enlisted at Kingston-upon-Thames and this may have been because on the 20th February, 1915 he had married Clara Manning at Poole, Dorset with the couple moving to live at 28, Chapel Street, Hazel Slade. The couple had two children, Edith May, born on the 22nd July,

1916 after Wallace had enlisted and Wallace John born on the 2nd July, 1917 after his father had died. Wallace joined the 24th Reserve Battalion, Middlesex Regiment for training and was then transferred to the 1st Battalion, Royal West Kent Regiment, after he had been sent to France on the 23rd October, 1916. On the 10th February, 1917 Wallace was badly wounded in the left arm with shrapnel. He was taken to the 13th Field Ambulance and then to a Casualty Clearing Station, before being sent to the 3rd Canadian General Hospital at Boulogne. Here an operation was carried out to remove some of the shrapnel splinters from his arm. Wallace was then sent back to England, to the Metropolitan Hospital in London for further treatment. Unfortunately, severe sepsis had set in and the hospital did all it could with irrigation and a further incision to drain pus from the wound. On the 21st February, 1917 Wallace was visited in hospital by his family but at 5.25 am on the 22nd February, 1917, he died from heart failure caused by acute septicaemia. At the time of his death, Wallace was 38 years old and his body was returned to Hednesford where it was buried with full military honours at St. Peter's Churchyard.

Private Daniel Charles Seabury
7749

Daniel Seabury was born at Harley, Shropshire in 1880 and was the eldest son of Edwin and Catherine Seabury. Edwin was a labourer and had married Catherine Meara at Bridgnorth in 1875. They lived at Pensnett to begin with where Jane was born in 1876, before moving to Shropshire. Catherine was born at Church Stretton in 1883, before the family moved to live at Rugeley Road, Hednesford where Edwin worked as a labourer in a corn store. At the age of 18, Daniel joined the Army, enlisting with the South Staffordshire Regiment and he served during the Boer War, before coming out of the Army in 1902. Later that year, Daniel married Alice Follows at Stafford and the couple lived at Green Heath, Hednesford, where James was born in 1904, George in 1906 and Anne in 1910, before they moved to the Rawnsley Road. Sadly in 1913, at the age of 31 Alice died. In 1914, as he had been serving with the Hednesford Territorials, Daniel enlisted in the Army, Joining the 1/5th Battalion, South Staffordshire Regiment and he was sent to France on the 5th March, 1915. He served until the 7th June, 1915 when he was killed in action at the age of 35. Daniel became the first member of the Hednesford Territorials to be killed. His body was buried at St. Quentin-Cabaret Military Cemetery, near Wijschate in Belgium.

3. Hednesford

Guardsman John Thomas Scott
24217

In 1891 Thomas and Rosia Scott were living at Watling Street, Bridgtown where he was employed as a miner. Thomas was from Norton Canes and his wife came from Great Wyrley, both villages in Staffordshire. In 1901, John Scott who had been born at Bridgtown in 1892 was living with his grandparents John and Amy Stokes at Bridgtown, whereas the rest of the family were living on the Brownhills Road, Norton Canes. However, by 1911 the family were again reunited and living at the same address in Norton Canes. John was now a road repairer at the Conduit Colliery, Albert was a haulier in the same pit, and Cyril attended the pumps and their father was still a coal miner. Out of the five other children, four of them were still at school. John was conscripted into the Army in 1918, joining the 1st Battalion, Grenadier Guards. He was sent to the Western Front in 1918 and served until the 13th September, 1918 when he was killed in action at the age of 26. John's body was buried at Vaulx Hill Cemetery, near Bapaume in France.

Private William Henry Shemwell
19010

In 1860 at Chesterfield, Derbyshire William Shemwell a coal miner born in the Derbyshire town, married Anna Maria Dutton, also from Chesterfield. The newly weds set up home at Locksford Lane, Tapton, Derbyshire. In 1871, they were living at Newbridge Lane, Whittington and in the intervening ten years they had had five children, Sarah, Lancelot, Richard, Mary and George. The family continued to grow with John born in 1873, and Maria in 1875 before the family moved to live at Fair Oaks, Rugeley where William was born in 1879 and Alice in 1880. The family also had a lodger staying with them, David Shepherd, a 41 year old labourer from Norfolk. By 1891, the family was starting to thin out slightly as the older children left home, but George was now a coal miner as was John, with William, Alice, Albert and Selina all at school. A lodger was still living with the family, this time it was George James a 72 year old agricultural labourer from London. They had once again changed address and were now living at 81, West Cannock Colliery Buildings at Brindley Heath, Hednesford. In 1901, only George, John, William, Albert and Selina remained at home. William and Albert were both coal miner labourers, whilst John had become a railway porter. By 1911, William was living with his brother Lancelot at 46, Mount Street,

Hednesford, with both men working as coal miners at Cannock and Rugeley Colliery. Also living with them was Selina who had married George Morris, an engine road man from Hednesford, and they had a son, named George William. In May 1915 William enlisted in the Army, joining the 7th Battalion, South Staffordshire Regiment and he was sent to Gallipoli on the 25th November, 1915. From there, William was sent to Egypt and it was here on the 18th May, 1916 that he was drowned. He was bathing in the Suez Canal with the Lance Corporal from his section, when he disappeared from view. William could not swim and despite frantic efforts to save him, he was dead when found. At the time of his death, William was 37 and the information was sent to his sister Selina by Private Partridge. William's body was buried at Ismalia War Cemetery, Egypt.

Rifleman Arthur Simister
R/12382

The Simisters were a Wolverhampton family in essence, although George Simister actually came from Grindle, Shropshire and worked as a locomotive driver. He married Mary Bennett at Cannock in 1878, but they moved to Wolverhampton, which was his wife's hometown. By 1891, they were living on Stafford Road, Bushbury with five children, Joseph, George, Thomas, Frank and Rose. In 1901, the family had moved to 20, Sherwood Terrace, Bushbury and it was here that Alfred was born in 1893, Elsie in 1897 and Arthur in 1898. In 1911, the Simisters had moved to live at 8, Mount Side Street, Hednesford, where Alfred was working as a horse driver down the pit, with Arthur and Herbert, born in 1901, still at school. Arthur enlisted in the Army on the 23rd April, 1915, when he was only 16, although he gave his age as 19 on the attestation form. He was posted to the 15th Battalion, King's Royal Rifle Corps and was sent to France on the 30th December, 1915. On the 2nd January, 1917 Arthur was invalided home suffering from trench foot, and did not return to France until the 13th July, 1917. He was then wounded in action, when a bullet went into his left ankle, and was sent back to Bexhill and Barnstaple for treatment and convalescence, including an operation on a hernia. During this time, Arthur was given three periods of leave which he spent at home. On the 18th March, Arthur was posted back to France, joining the 8th Battalion, and was then transferred to the 1/15th Battalion, London Regiment on the 19th August, 1918. Just two weeks later on the 2nd October, 1918 Arthur was killed in action at the age of 19. His body could not be identified after the war and Arthur is remembered on the Vis-en-Artois Memorial to the Missing in France.

Private William Joseph Simmons
7900

William Ducal Simmons was a coal miner who was born in London and in 1891 was living at Rugeley with his widowed mother. He met Selina Rogers who came from Landywood, Staffordshire and the couple had a child, Austin born at Landywood in 1890. In 1892, William and Selina married at Cannock and in 1901 were living at The Springs, Longdon near Rugeley and it was here that William Junior was born in 1894, followed by Lizzie, Minnie, Florence, Herbert and Gladys. After the birth of Gladys in 1907, the family moved to live at 90, McGhie Street, Hednesford. Austin was now working as a mine timberer and William junior was a horse driver at the Fair Lady Colliery, Heath Hayes. William joined the Hednesford Territorials and so when the Great War began, he was enlisted in the 1/5th Battalion, South Staffordshire Regiment and sent to France on the 5th March, 1915. He was a well liked soldier, but on the 29th August, 1915, William was shot in the head by a sniper when on sentry duty, dying at the age of 21. Letters of condolence were sent by Private Lane and by Lieutenant Colonel William Burnett. William's body was buried at Blauwepoort Farm Cemetery, near Ieper in Belgium.

Private George Thomas Sishton
11374

On the 1st August, 1893 at St. Luke's Parish Church, Cannock Thomas Sishton, a blacksmith from Cannock and the son of a blacksmith, married Elizabeth Ann Bullock from Wolverhampton. The couple lived in Cannock and their first child, George was born in 1895, followed by Fanny in 1896. Thomas died at the early age of 26 in 1899. In 1901, George and Fanny were staying with George and Hannah Evans. Elizabeth Sishton married Henry Astell at Wolverhampton in 1908 and the couple moved to live at 37, Queen Street, High Town, Hednesford and in 1911, George was earning a living as a grocer's shop assistant. Fanny had left school but had yet to find a job, and the newly weds had had their first child, Charles Henry Astell who was born at Hednesford in 1910. George later decided to train as an electrician and secured a job at Littleworth Colliery. George joined the Hednesford Territorials and after the outbreak of war in August, 1914 was one of the first to volunteer, joining the 1st Battalion, South Staffordshire Regiment, and he was sent to France on the 17th December, 1914. At Armentieres in May, 1915, George was badly wounded in the spine and was invalided home to the Whitechapel Hospital in

London where he remained bed-redden for twelve months, dying there on the 18th May, 1916 aged 20. His body was brought back to Cannock, where the funeral took place on the 24th May. The coffin was carried shoulder high by eight wounded soldiers, and on the way the boys of Chadsmoor School stood in silent salute. At the grave in Cannock Cemetery, buglers played the Last Post and a volley of rifle fire was fired by a party from the camp at Cannock Chase. The Reverend O.H. Thomas conducted the service at St. Chad's and at the United Methodist Church.

Private Leonard Slade
17418

In 1886 at Cannock, John Slade a coal miner from Wednesbury, Staffordshire married Charlotte Annie Rollings from Tettenhall, Wolverhampton. The couple lived at 11, Cannock Wood Street, Hazel Slade and in 1891 they had had three children, Noah, John and Florence. Charlotte's father John Rollings and her brother George were also staying with them. In 1901, the family had moved to live at 6, Chapel Street, Hazel Slade, and by this time Horace had been born in 1892, Leonard in 1893, Violet in 1897, Elsie in 1898 and Bertie in 1900. In 1911, they were living at Albert Street, Church Hill, Hednesford, with Noah, John, Leonard and Horace all working as coal miners. In Leonard's case he had found employment at Cannock and Rugeley Colliery. On the 6th August, 1914 Leonard enlisted at Lichfield in the 2nd Battalion, Grenadiers Guards, at the same time as John and Horace. Leonard was sent to France on the 23rd November, 1914 and served in 4 Company. On the 19th February, 1915 Leonard was killed in action when a shell killed him and another soldier from the Battalion. Leonard was 21 at the time of his death and his body was buried with a service from Captain G.W. Ridling the Chaplain of the 2nd Guard's Brigade. A letter was sent back to his parents by Private Harry Kenney of Hazel Slade who was serving in the same Battalion. He described Leonard as a "good soldier and a reliable man". Leonard's body was buried at Cuinchy Communal Cemetery, near Bethune in France.

Corporal Cyril Henry Arthur Smart
242240

Cyril Smart was born at Kings Lynn, Norfolk in 1894. He was the eldest child of Henry and Catherine Smart, both of King's Lynn. The couple had married in 1886, when a 20 year old Henry had married Catherine Wright who was aged 18.

Henry was a grocer's assistant when he married but was ambitious to improve his prospects. In 1901, the family were living at Diamond Terrace, South Lynn, with Cyril and his sister Pansy who had been born in 1897. In 1911, they were living at 20, Carlton Street, Leeds where Henry was a provisions manager and Cyril was his assistant butterman. Soon afterwards, the Smarts moved to live at Eskrett Street, Hednesford where Henry was again employed as a grocery manager, although Cyril moved away for a time to work in Cardiff. Cyril came back to Hednesford to enlist in the Army in 1916, joining the 2/6th Battalion, South Staffordshire Regiment and he was sent to fight on the Western Front. He served here until the 2nd December, 1917 when he died of wounds at Etaples Military Hospital at the age of 24. Cyril's body was buried at the nearby Etaples Military Cemetery in France.

Private George Henry Smith
33011

George Smith was born at Hednesford in 1895 and appears to have been the child of John and Blanche Smith, according to the 1901 census. John was a jockey from Hednesford and his wife came from Germany but was a British Subject. They had four children, George, Annie and Arthur who were born in Hednesford and Clara who was born in Russia but again was a British Subject. They were staying with John and Ann Shortland at 3, Mill Street, Cannock. Also living there were Christopher and Hannah Brown and their 10 month old son, Christopher. Intriguingly, the CWGC gives Hannah Brown of 52, George Street, Hednesford as George's mother on their database, and this is confirmed by contemporary reports at the time of George's death. In 1911, George was working as a shop assistant for Roland Summers at Bilston. He enlisted under the Derby Scheme in 1916 and was originally placed with the North Staffordshire Regiment, but he later transferred to the 2nd Battalion, Lincolnshire Regiment, being sent to France in March 1917. On the 31st July, 1917 George was reported as missing in action, during the first day of the Battle of Passchendaele, and it was later assumed that he had been killed on this day at the age of 22. After the war, George's body was not found and he is remembered on the Ieper (Menin Gate) memorial to the Missing in Ieper city centre in Belgium.

Private John Smith
16380

John Smith was the son of Samuel and Ann Smith and was born at Hednesford in 1899, the family living at West Hill. In 1901, he was lodging with his widowed father at Hall Buildings off McGhie Street, Hednesford, with the Stokes family. In 1911, John was working as a tailor and boarding with Eliza Pritchard and her son Charles, who was also a tailor, at Church Hill, Hednesford. John enlisted with the Royal Welsh Fusiliers in late 1914 and was sent to France on the 19th July, 1915. He died from wounds on the 24th July, 1917 at the age of 18. He had resided at West Hill Avenue in Hednesford. John's body was buried at Locre Hospice Cemetery, near Ieper in Belgium.

Private William Henry Sockett
14319

On the 25th December, 1897 William Henry Sockett, a coal miner from Darlaston, Staffordshire married Sarah Ada Fisher from Tipton at St. Luke's Parish Church, Cannock. The groom was 21 and his bride two years older, and they moved to live at Chadsmoor and by 1911, the couple had had five children, Alice born in 1899, William born in 1901, Ethel born in 1904, Ada born in 1907 and Bertha born in 1910. They resided at Cecil Street, Chadsmoor and William was still earning his living as a coal miner. However, in early 1915, William Henry enlisted in the Army, joining the 9th Battalion, South Staffordshire Regiment and he was sent to France on the 24th August, 1915. He served until the 11th November, 1915 when he died from wounds incurred from shellfire when he was trying to assist wounded comrades. At the time of his death, William was 38 and his body was buried at Erquinghem-Lys Churchyard Extension, near Armentieres in France.

Lance Corporal Arthur Spencer
7663

Arthur Spencer was born in 1899 at High Town, Hednesford and was the second son of George and Margaret Spencer. The couple had married at Walsall in 1897, although they had already had a child, Edith born in 1895. William was born in 1897, Arthur in 1899, and Hannah in 1900. The family lived on the Cannock

Road, High Town and by 1911 the family had increased further, with the birth of Ellen in 1903, George in 1905, Theresa in 1908 and Leonard in 1910. William, now aged 14 was a horse driver in a colliery, whilst the other children aged between 12 and 6 were at school. In 1915 at the age of only 16, Arthur volunteered for the Army, joining the 2nd Battalion, Royal Irish Rifles and he was sent to France on the 31st December, 1915. Arthur rose to the rank of Lance Corporal and served on the Western Front until the 10th June, 1918 when he died from wounds at the age of 19. Arthur's body was buried at Avesnes-sur-Helpe Communal Cemetery, near Landrecies in France.

Private Fred Spinks
50010

On the 22nd April, 1889 at St. Luke's Parish Church, Cannock the gloriously named Zorababel Spinks from Sedgley, Staffordshire, a 39 year old widower and coal miner, married Sarah James, from Wellington, Shropshire. Sarah was a 26 year old widow and the couple moved to live at 17, Bradbury Lane, Hednesford. Zorababel had five children from his first marriage and Sarah had two from hers, but in 1890 they had their first child together, Mary Ann. By 1901, James, born in 1892, Arthur, born in 1894 and Fred born in 1897 had arrived. However, in 1906 at the age of 56, Zorababel died at Cannock, although in 1911, the family were still living at the same address and Arthur and James were colliery horse drivers, while Fred was working as a labourer in a factory. Fred joined the Army in 1916, enlisting with the 10th Battalion, Lincolnshire Regiment, and he was sent to serve on the Western Front. However, on the 22nd March, 1918 during the German Spring Offensive, Fred was killed in action at the age of 22. After the war his body could not be identified and Fred is remembered on the Arras Memorial to the Missing in France.

Private Albert John Spruce
7800

Albert Spruce was born at Warrington, Lancashire in 1880 and was the eldest son of Thomas and Elizabeth Spruce from Shropshire. Thomas was a general labourer from Horsehay and his wife came from nearby Hadley. In 1891 the couple had moved to live at Church Hill, Hednesford after a brief stay in the North West where Albert and Mary were born. In 1901, the family had moved to live in

Walsall and Elizabeth had opened a grocer's shop with Albert helping his mother run the business. Albert married Ruth Ellen Davies at Walsall in 1902, but tragically, she died in Walsall just a year later. In 1911, Albert was working as a night porter and was living on Birmingham High Street, although Thomas and Elizabeth were living back in Hednesford in Station Road. In 1915 Albert enlisted in the Army, joining the 8th Battalion, Royal Fusiliers and he was sent to France on the 14th November, 1915. He fought on the Western Front until the 7th October, 1916 when he was posted as missing in action at the age of 36. It was later presumed that Albert had died on this date. After the war, Albert's Body could not be found and he is remembered on the Thiepval Memorial to the Missing on the Somme in France.

Private George Stanier
13020

George Stanier was born at Cheadle, Staffordshire in 1887 and was the eldest child of George and Sarah Stanier. In 1901 the family were living at Meir Lane, Caverswall where George had started work as a brick presser. However, by 1911, George had moved to Hednesford where he was living at 57, Platt Street, High Town and working as a coal miner hewer loader at West Cannock Colliery and sharing the house with William Weetman. On the 16th March, 1913 George married Fanny Stanley at St. Luke's Parish Church, Cannock and the couple moved to live at 131, Clifton Terrace, Littleworth where they had two children, Thomas born in 1914 and James in 1915. In September 1914, George joined the Army, enlisting with the 8th Battalion, South Staffordshire Regiment and he was sent to France on the 14th July, 1915. He served until the 10th July, 1916 when he was killed in action at the age of 29 during the Battle of the Somme. After the war George's body could not be found and he is remembered on the Thiepval Memorial to the Missing on the Somme in France.

Private Dennis Hayward Stanley
300984

In 1878 at Shifnal, Shropshire Alfred Stanley a coal miner married Sarah Hayward. Both groom and bride were born at Dark Lane, Shropshire, and in 1881 they were living at Shifnal, although their first child, William had been born at Hednesford in 1880. It may have been that they had to look after 70 year old

Joseph Bennett who was a relative. In 1881, the family had moved back to Hednesford and were living at West Hill, and by this time Alfred, Enoch, Miriam and Alice had been born. In 1901, Alfred senior had become a Deputy Manager of a pit at Church Gresley, Derbyshire and the family were living at 3, Regent Street in that town. Percy had been born in 1893 and the twins, Winifred and Dennis had been born in 1898, just before the family moved to Derbyshire. However, in 1911, they had moved back to West Hill, Hednesford where Arthur was a colliery fireman and Sarah had opened a shop. Enoch was working as an engine plain man and Percy was a station minder in a colliery. Dennis was still at school. Dennis joined the Staffordshire Yeomanry and in 1917 was conscripted into the Corps of Hussars and was sent to fight in the Middle East. On the 18th October, 1918 Dennis was killed in action at the age of 20. His body was buried at Damascus Commonwealth War Cemetery in Syria.

Private Frank Stanton
45223

In 1889 at St. Peter's Parish Church, Hednesford Samuel Joseph Stanton a 24 year old baker and confectioner married the 25 year old Eliza Jemima Hindley. The groom hailed from Coseley, Staffordshire and his bride came from Brownhills, Staffordshire. The bakery set up by Samuel Stanton became a major employer in the town. Their first child, Samuel Harold Stanton was born in 1890 and in 1891 the family were living at the Bread Shop on Market Street, Hednesford. Living with them were Joseph and Alice Hindley, Eliza's brother and his wife. Alice worked in the shop and Joseph was an apprentice baker. They also had a servant, Elizabeth Partridge from Bridgtown. In 1901, the family were still living in Market Street, but by this time Roland had been born in 1893 and Frank in 1895. Alice and Joseph Hindley were still living and working with them, and again the family employed a servant, Lucy Bailey from Kidsgrove, Staffordshire. By 1911, Samuel junior and Roland were both helping in the business, while Frank, although 16, was still at school. They were also looking after Clara Gilbert Hindley their 7 year old niece and Lucy Bailey was still with the family. Shortly after this the family moved to live at Weston House on Western Avenue, Hednesford. On the 11th December, 1915 to pre-empt the Derby Scheme, Frank volunteered for service in the Army Service Corps. He was placed in the Army Reserve and was not mobilized until the 28th June, 1916, being posted to the ASC on the 30th June, and joining the bakery section on the 2nd July, 1916 where he was assessed as a "fair baker". He was posted to France on the 1st November, 1916. On the 11th July, 1917 Frank was transferred to the 3rd Battalion, West Riding Regiment a front line infantry unit and from here to the 14th Battalion, Durham Light Infantry on the 3rd November. One month later during the Battle of Cambrai Frank was posted as missing in action on the 3rd December, 1917. Despite requests for information from his parents, none was forthcoming and it was later assumed that Frank had died on that date at the age of 22. Frank's body was not recovered after the war and he is remembered on the Cambrai Memorial to the Missing at Louverval in France.

Private Richard Stephens
9302

In 1888 at Cannock, Richard Stephens a 22 year old coal miner from Dawley, Shropshire married the 22 year old Hannah Darral from Bilston, Staffordshire. The couple moved to live at Arthur Street, Wimblebury and their first child, James was born in 1889. In 1901, the family were still living at Arthur Street, but more children had been born, with John in 1892, Richard in 1895, Harry in 1897 and Thomas in 1900. By 1911, the family had moved to live at 27, Piggott Street, Wimblebury and John was working as a coal miner's loader at the Coppice Colliery, Heath Hayes, while Richard was a horse driver at 8's Pit, Cannock Chase Colliery. Harry was also working down the pit, as was James who although married was living at home. The family had also had a daughter, Lily, born in 1903. With the outbreak of the Great War, Richard and his brother John volunteered for service with the 1/5th Battalion, South Staffordshire Regiment on the same day in September, 1914. They were sent to France on the 5th March, 1915, and on the 13th October, 1915 during the Battle of Loos, both were killed in action. Richard was 20 at the time of his death and as his body was not found after the war, he is remembered on the Loos Memorial to the Missing.

Private John Stephens
9303

John enlisted on the same day as his younger brother Richard and was sent to France on the same day, the 5th March, 1915. John was killed in action on the same day as his brother the 13th October, 1915 during the Staffords' gallant attack on the Hohenzollern Redoubt. Sadly like his brother, the 22 year old John's body was not found after the war and he too is remembered on the Loos Memorial to the Missing in France.

Private Edward Stevens
9308

Edward Stevens was the eldest son of William and Elizabeth Stevens and was born at Quarry Bank in 1881. In 1891, the family were living on the High Street, Kingswinford, where William was employed as a galvaniser. Edward had moved to the Hednesford area and married Florence Mabley at Cannock Register Office in 1898. In 1901 the young couple were living at Littleworth Lane, Hednesford with their two children, William and Sarah Ann and Edward's mother, Elizabeth. Two more children were born to the couple, Edward in 1903 and Leonard in 1915. In 1911, the family had moved to live at 41, Piggott Street, Wimblebury and Elizabeth Stevens was living with them along with her second husband, Edward Stevens, senior. In 1914, Edward enlisted with the 1/5th Battalion, South Staffordshire Regiment, and he too was sent to France on the 5th March, 1915. Edward was killed in action on the 12th November, 1915 at the age of 34, when a shell splinter went straight through his head. Edward was buried at Rue-des-Berceaux Military Cemetery, Richebourg L'Avoue, near Bethune in France.

Company Sergeant Major Alfred Edward Stokes
8550

Alfred Stokes was the only son of Edward and Mary Stokes. Edward was a soldier who had been pensioned out of the Army and was acting as a Recruiting Sergeant when he met Mary Ann Whitehouse at Hanley, Staffordshire. The couple married in 1893 and two children were born, Alfred in 1895 and Florence in 1898. In 1901, the family was living at 15, Hart Street, Walsall where once again Edward was in charge of the Recruiting Office. By 1911, they had moved to 118, Station Road, Hednesford where Edward was working as a clerk and Alfred was in the Army. They had two boarders staying with them, Robert McMahon who was born in South Africa and was also an army pensioner and Geoffrey Fowell, a medical dispenser from County Durham. It would appear that Alfred came out of the Army, as he did not enlist until 1916, when he joined the 3rd Battalion, South Staffordshire Regiment, and was sent to France primarily as a physical training instructor. He rose to the rank of Company Sergeant Major, but on the 28th October, 1918 at the age of 24 he was posted as killed in action. His body was buried at Bronfay Farm Military Cemetery, Bray-sur Somme in France.

Corporal Harold Benson Stokes
1623

James Stokes, an engine fitter from Walsall Wood, Staffordshire married Mary Jane Fox at Walsall in 1891. The couple moved to live at Hednesford on the Cannock Road, and it was here that Harold was born in 1897 and his sister Eveline in 1899. A third child, Hilda was born in 1900 but died at the age of 5 in 1906. Mary was running a tobacconist and newspaper shop in order to improve the family lifestyle. Harold proved to have a gifted singing voice and sang in the choir at St. Peter's Church and was then taken to the Cathedral Choir at Lichfield, and was living at the Chorister's house at Dam Street, Lichfield in 1911. Afterwards Harold went into the banking profession, and worked at Bristol and Swansea before moving back to Hednesford to enlist in 1914 shortly after the outbreak of war. Harold joined the 13th Battalion, Royal Fusiliers and was sent to France on the 30th July, 1916. On the 20th November, 1916 Harold was hit by shrapnel and died the following day from his injuries aged 19. Harold's body was buried at St. Sever Cemetery Extension at Rouen in France.

Private Oliver William Suffolk
10221

Abraham Suffolk a coal loader from Stockingford, Warwickshire married Lucy Louise Bealey at Penkridge in 1873. The couple lived at Hednesford to begin with and it was here that their first two children, Oliver William and Josiah were born, in 1873 and 1876 respectively. The family then moved to live at 27, Johnson Street, Leicester where a third son, Thomas was born in 1878. In 1891, Abraham was working and living at Nuneaton, so Lucy had the job of looking after the family at 282, Syston Street, Leicester. Oliver was working as a shoe finisher, Josiah as a saddler's apprentice and Thomas as a rope winder. In 1893, Oliver married Emma Elizabeth Kent at Leicester and in 1901 the family were living at 112, Birstall Street, Leicester where Oliver was working as a head railway drayman, and Emma as an elastic binder and card wrapper. Their first child, Oliver Roland had been born in 1899. By 1911 the family had moved to live at 31, Piggott Street, Wimblebury where Oliver senior was a coal miner. Oliver junior was at school, as were Elsie and Louisa, and the two remaining children, Ellen and Leslie were at home, both of whom had been born since the move to Wimblebury. On the 6th August, 1914 Oliver senior decided to enlist in the

Army, joining the 7th Battalion, South Staffordshire Regiment. He was sent to Gallipoli on the 21st July, 1915 and from there he was sent to serve in Egypt before being posted to the Western Front. He was badly wounded in 1917 and was sent back to England where he died from his injuries on the 9th April, 1917. Oliver's body was buried at St. Peter's Churchyard, Hednesford with full military honours. Oliver was 43 at the time of his death. His son, Oliver also served in the Great War.

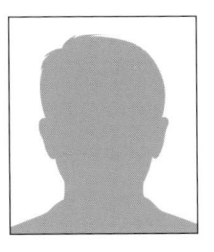

Ships Steward's Assistant Frank Suthard
M/26371

Peter Suthard came from Chester, Cheshire and in 1887 at Wolverhampton where he was working as a steam engine maker he married Catherine Bateman who was born in the town. In 1891, the family was living at 111, Chester Street, Wolverhampton where Samuel had been born in 1889 and Nellie in 1890. In 1901, the family had moved to live at Little Brick Kiln Street, Wolverhampton and Peter had changed careers to become a public house manager. The family had grown with the births of Ethel in 1897 and Frank on the 5th June, 1899. They also had a domestic servant, Elizabeth Thomas living with them. Tragically, Catherine died at the age of 39 in 1903, but in 1907 Peter married Lily Painter again at Wolverhampton. In 1911, the family had moved to Market Street, Hednesford to run a Club there. Peter was the Club steward and was helped by both Lily and Nellie. Ethel and Frank were still at school. However on the 13th June, 1917 Frank enlisted for twelve years in the Royal Navy, serving first of all on HMS Pembroke and then on the 23rd October, 1917 being posted to HMS Raglan. He served on the Raglan until the 20th January, 1918 when she was sunk in an action against the German ships Breslau and Goeben which were serving with the Turkish Navy, at Kusu Bay, Pyrgos. The Raglan went down with the loss of 157 crew members. Frank was only 17 at the time of his death and his body was buried at Lancashire Landing Cemetery in Turkey.

Private Uriah Talbot
18348

Uriah Talbot was born at Hednesford in 1896 and was the second son of Henry Charles and Emily Ann Talbot. Henry came from Congreve, Staffordshire and was a coal miner and his wife came from Brewood, Staffordshire. The couple had married at Cannock in 1889, and Emily's maiden name was Bailey. Their first child was born in 1890 and named Abner William, but in 1891 he was living with his grandparents in Pillaton near Penkridge. His parents were living at Platt Street, Chadsmoor where a second baby Henry Charles had just been born, but this second child died shortly afterwards. In 1901, the family had moved to live at Bradbury Lane, Hednesford, and in the meantime Mary Ann, Elizabeth, Uriah and Kate had been born. In 1911, the family had moved to live at 72, Brindley Heath. Abner had married and left home and Uriah was working as a coal miner engine road man. Two more children had been born into the family, Arthur and George. On the 3rd April, 1915 Uriah enlisted in the 2nd Battalion, South Staffordshire Regiment and he was sent to Gallipoli on the 6th October, 1915. From there he served in Egypt before being sent to France in time for the Big Push. Uriah was killed in action at Delville Wood on the 27th July, 1916 at the age of 19. His body was not found after the war and Uriah is remembered on the Thiepval Memorial to the Missing in France. Uriah's sister, Elizabeth married Henry Thomas Gaskin and was murdered by him at Hednesford in 1919.

Corporal Thomas Charles Thacker MM
R/10974

Thomas Thacker was born at Hednesford in 1891 and he was the eldest child of Thomas and Sarah Thacker. Thomas had married Sarah Matilda Chapman the year before at Cannock and in 1891 the young family was living with Sarah's parents and their six other children at John Street, Wimblebury. In 1901, the family had moved into their own house at John Street and now had six children of their own, Thomas, Wilfred, George, John, Edward and Percy. By 1911, the family had moved to live at 39, Piggott Street, Wimblebury and in that ten years another five children had been born, Walter, Lizzie, Minnie, Lily and Isaiah. Thomas was now a coal miner driver, as were Wilfred and George. John was a coal miner gripper and Edward was a nipper down a colliery. On the 25th December, 1913 Thomas married Florence May Worrall at St. Peter's Parish Church, Hednesford. The couple had one child, Violet who was born in 1915. Indeed it was in early 1915 that Thomas enlisted in the Army, joining the 4th Battalion, King's Royal Rifle Corps and he was sent to France on the 28th July, 1915. He rose to the rank of Corporal and was awarded the Military Medal for bravery, but on the 7th November, 1918, just four days before the Armistice, Thomas was killed in action at the age of 27. His body was buried at St. Remy-Chaussee Communal Cemetery in France.

3. Hednesford

Private John Thomas
36691

John Thomas was the third child of George and Catherine Thomas. George was a general dealer from Stourport, Worcestershire and his wife came from New Cross, London although they were living at Littleworth Road, Hednesford in 1881 where Sarah was born. By 1891, the family had moved to The Crossings, Hill Street, Hednesford and their four other children, Mary born in 1879, John born in 1881, Eveline born in 1883 and Catherine born in 1887; all were at school. 1901 saw the family again living on the Littleworth Road where John was working as a boat loader on the canal and Eveline had become a day school teacher. Joseph had been born in 1893. However, George died at the age of 62 in 1906 and this meant that Catherine had to take over the running of the shop. Catherine joined her sister as a school teacher and Joseph was now a mechanic. John was probably conscripted into the Army in 1917, and after training was posted to the 23rd Battalion, Northumberland Fusiliers (Tyneside Scottish). He was sent to France but was posted as missing in action on the 4th August, 1918 at Ieper. It was later presumed that John had died on this date at the age of 37. After the war John's body was never found and he is remembered on the Ploegsteert Memorial to the Missing near Ieper in Belgium.

Private Joshua Thomas
16569

In 1882 at Cannock a Welsh miner Thomas Thomas married Charlotte Rowley. They moved to live at Mount Street, Hednesford and it was here that Lydia was born in 1884, Thomas Roland in 1885, Paul in 1886 and Joshua in 1891, indeed on the day of the census he was only 18 days old. Charlotte died at the age of 32 in 1896, and this seems to have triggered the break up of the family for in 1901, all of the children with the exception of Paul were living with the Hodgkiss family at Plantation Road, Cannock. The whereabouts of Thomas and Paul are not known. On the 13th April, 1903 Lydia married Edward Thomas, a miner at St. Peter's Parish Church, Hednesford. They set up a home at Glover Street, Wimblebury and by 1911 they had had three children, William, John and Horace. Living with them were her three brothers, all of whom were coal miners, Thomas, John and Joshua. When the Great War broke Joshua enlisted in late 1914, joining the 5th Battalion, Oxfordshire and Buckinghamshire Light Infantry and he was sent to France on the 20th May, 1915. Joshua was wounded twice but each time returned to the Western Front on recovery. However, on the 9th April, 1917 he was killed in action at the age of 26. Joshua's body was buried at Tilloy British Cemetery, Tilloy-les-Mofflaires near Arras in France.

Corporal Edmund Thurstance 18551

Edmund Thurstance was born at Penkridge, Staffordshire in 1889. His father was Edwin Thurstance, who was a former stone quarryman, but he later became a railway labourer, and his mother was Emily Butler before she married Edwin at Penkridge in 1869. Edmund came from a large family as he had seven brothers and two sisters and in 1891 the family was living at Market Place, Penkridge. By 1901, they had moved to live at Cotton's Buildings, Penkridge, and two of his brothers, John and Fred had joined their father as railway labourers. On the 20th April, 1908 Edmund married Elizabeth Conn at St. Luke's Parish Church, Cannock, and the couple moved to Cecil Street, Chadsmoor where Edith Ann was born in 1909. The family then moved to live at 271, Main Street, Danesmoor, near Clay Cross where Elizabeth was born in 1910. In 1911, tragedy struck with the deaths of both Edith and Elizabeth and this double tragedy prompted Edmund and Elizabeth to return to Hednesford where they moved into 143, Station Road. Here a son, named Edmund after his father was born on the 20th July, 1913. On the 19th January, 1915 Edmund presented himself at the Recruiting Hall at Cannock and joined the Royal Scots. He was sent to Glencorse, where he was posted to the 14th Battalion on the 23rd January. On the 10th April, 1915 his son Edmund died from measles and broncho-pneumonia. This badly affected Edmund and he was charged for refusing to obey an order and for being absent without leave, as the distraught father probably tried to get home to comfort his wife. On the 1st January, 1916 he was posted to the 11th Battalion and was sent to France on the 23rd of that month. On the 1st May, 1917 Edmund was wounded in action with a bullet wound to his right arm. He was sent to the 28th Field Ambulance and from there to the 7th Canadian General Hospital at Etaples. Next was a trip to England on the Hospital Ship Stad Antwerpen for further treatment and convalescence. Edmund was sent back to France on the 31st July, 1917 and was posted to the 17th Battalion where he received a further punishment for absence. However, on the 13th April, 1918 he was promoted to unpaid Lance Corporal, the promotion being confirmed with pay on the 19th May. Just a month later he was promoted to full Corporal, but on the 17th July, 1918 Edmund was killed in action at the age of 29. Captain A. D. Loch wrote to his widow to tell her that Edmund was "one of the best NCO's I have ever had. He was fearless and good and was loved by the Company". Edmund's body was not identified after the war and he is remembered on the Tyne Cot Memorial to the Missing near Ieper in Belgium.

Lance Corporal George Thomas Tolley
325043

The Tolleys were originally a Bromsgrove family. George Tolley a 21 year old wagon builder from the town married Ann Davenport there in 1883. In 1891 they were living at 42, Strand, Bromsgrove and at that time had five children, Ellen, Alice, Edwin, Harry and William. By 1901, they had moved to Hednesford and were living at 3, Cross Street, Hazel Slade where George Thomas, James and Samuel were born. In 1911, the family had moved to live at 2, Ford Row, Littleworth. George senior was now working as a carpenter, whereas Edwin and William were coal miners. Harry was employed as a labourer and George Thomas was a truck painter at Cannock and Rugeley Colliery. George Thomas volunteered for the Army in 1916 and served, to begin with, with the Army Ordnance Corps but was later transferred to the Notts and Derbys Regiment where he was wounded. After recovery he was posted to the 8th Battalion of the Regiment and he was serving with this Battalion when he was posted as missing in action on the 3rd October, 1918. It was later confirmed that he had been killed on this date at the age of 23. George's body was buried at Bellicourt British Cemetery, between St. Quentin and Cambrai.

Private Samuel Tolley
13629

Samuel Tolley was born at Hazel Slade, Hednesford in 1893, although who his parents were has been too difficult to fathom. The 1891 census records Walter and Mary Ann Tolley residing at 1, Chapel Street, Hazel Slade, with their 25 year old daughter Caroline, her 21 year old brother Walter, William who was 19 and another Walter, aged 2 who is recorded as a grandson. In 1901 Samuel was living at 77, Brindley Heath, Hednesford with his grandparents Walter and Mary Ann Tolley and also Walter. In 1911, he was living with another Walter and Mary Ann Tolley, Walter being the son of Samuel's grandparents and his relationship to them is a nephew. Also living at 22, Chapel Street, Hazel Slade are William and Walter Tolley, also nephews, together with William Childey and Elizabeth and Annie Harris who are also described as a nephew and two nieces. What is more certain is that Samuel enlisted in the Army in 1914, joining the Royal Welsh Fusiliers and being sent to France on the 19th July, 1915. He served until the 21st November, 1918 when he died in England, most probably from influenza at the age of 27. Samuel's body was buried with full military honours at St. Peter's Churchyard, Hednesford.

Private Edmund Tomkinson
16107

In 1885 at Cannock, Staffordshire, Edmund Tomkinson, a 20 year old coal miner from Rugby, Warwickshire married Ellen Tilsley from Aston, Warwickshire. They set up home at Hazel Slade, Hednesford where their first child Edmund was born in 1886. The family then moved to live at Quarry Cottages, Colliery Yard, Handsworth where Rose, Nellie, Joseph, Sarah, Alice and Ernest were born, before they moved back to live on the Stafford Road, Cannock where Tilly was born. On the 26th May, 1908 at St. Peter's Parish Church, Hednesford Edmund married Nellie Millward and the couple moved to live at 29, Piggott Street, Wimblebury where Edmund junior was born in 1909, followed by Joseph in 1911, Rose in 1912 and Nellie in 1914. Edmund worked as a miner at Number 4 pit, West Cannock Colliery. Just after the outbreak of war, Edmund enlisted with his brother Joseph. Both men joined the 2nd Battalion, South Staffordshire Regiment and Edmund was sent to France on the 17th March, 1915. On the 18th May, 1915 Edmund was posted as missing in action. Joseph was summoned to the Battalion Headquarters where he was told that his brother was one of 19 men killed in a trench but that his body could not be identified. Edmund died at the age of 29 and as his body could not be identified, he is remembered on the Le Touret Memorial to the Missing in France.

Private Joseph Tomkinson
16933

Joseph Tomkinson was born at Great Barr, Staffordshire in 1893 and he was the younger brother of Edmund. He too was a coal miner and was employed at the East Cannock Colliery. On the 9th March, 1913 Joseph married Fanny Millward the sister of Edmund's wife Nellie, at St. Peter's Parish Church, Hednesford. They had two children, the second of which, Joseph was born in 1917. In 1914, Joseph enlisted with the 2nd Battalion, South Staffordshire Regiment, but he was not sent to France until the 25th May, 1915, a week after his brother's death. He was told that his brother's body could not be identified. Joseph served on the Western Front until the 14th February, 1918 when he was killed in action at the age of 25. The news of his death was conveyed to his widow and children at 35, Piggott Street, Wimblebury. Joseph's body was buried at Metz-en-Couture Communal Cemetery British Extension in France.

Private Albert Tortoishell
9466

Albert Tortoishell was the eldest son of Samuel and Sarah Tortoishell and was born at Lichfield in 1886. Samuel came from Rocester, Staffordshire and was originally an agricultural farmer with a holding at Abbots Bromley, but by 1901 Samuel was a brewer's drayman and the family had moved to live at 39, Beacon Street, Walsall. Albert was an errand boy for an electric light works. By 1911, they had moved to 81, Beacon Street where Albert was a polisher, working for Sydenham and McOudra's foundry. Albert was probably a member of the Hednesford Territorials and was an early volunteer for the Army, enlisting with the 1/5th Battalion, South Staffordshire Regiment and being sent to France on the 5th March, 1915. He was wounded in action in the summer of 1915, but recovered and was sent back to his Regiment. However, in late October, 1915 Albert was seriously wounded and was sent back to Le Treport Military Hospital for treatment. He had suffered severe head wounds following a charge at the enemy and as a result of these injuries, Albert died on the 1st November, 1915 at the age of 29. Albert was buried at Le Treport Military Cemetery, near Dieppe in France.

Driver Ernest Tranter
M/316411

In 1872 at Penkridge, Staffordshire Mark Tranter a butcher from Bicknell, Warwickshire married Elizabeth Tye from Birmingham. The couple set up a butcher's shop at John Street, Wimblebury and they began a family with the births of William, Mark, George and Alfred and they also employed a domestic servant, 12 year old Emma Jennings from Fazeley, Warwickshire. In 1901, the family were living at Anglesey Street, Hednesford where Joseph was working as a carter and Ernest, Rosy, Harry and Fanny had been born. The family was still living at the same address in 1911, but Ernest was now a pork butcher, Harry was a grocer's assistant and Fanny helped her mother at home. On the 12th January, 1913 Ernest married Alice Gwilt at St. Peter's Parish Church, Hednesford, and the couple set up home at 8b, Mellor's Buildings, West Hill, Hednesford, where Ernest was now a slaughterman for George Tranter his older brother. The couple had three children, Hilda born on the 20th July, 1913, Stanley born on the 20th October 1914, and Ernest born on the 15th June, 1917. On the 6th June, 1916 Ernest attested at Hednesford under the Derby Scheme and was immediately placed on the Reserve List and was mobilized on the 28th April, 1917, joining the Army Service Corps. He passed his Ford Learner's Test on the 11th June, 1917 and was sent to Grove Park, the base of the ASC Motor Transport Reserve Depot. On the 22nd July, 1917 Ernest was posted to Mesopotamia, and on the 7th October, 1917 he was admitted to the 40th British General Hospital suffering from malaria, being discharged on the 24th October. On the 2nd November, Ernest was readmitted to the same hospital, this time suffering from dysentery. He was placed on the seriously ill list on the 6th November, and despite treatment his condition worsened and he died at 3.45 pm on the 10th December, 1917 at the age of 28. He was described as being conscious and cheerful right up to his death. Ernest's body was buried at Basra War Cemetery in Iraq.

Private William Tranter
18524

William Tranter was born at Donnington Wood, Shropshire in 1882. He was the fourth son of Enoch and Mary Ann Tranter who had married at Wellington, Shropshire in 1866. Enoch was a coal miner and the newly weds set up home at 9, Donnington Barracks, Lilleshall, Shropshire. In 1870 their first child, a daughter named Jane Ellen was born, and by 1881 she had been joined by John, Lucy, Enoch and Alick. The family continued to live at the same address and by 1891 the family had increased further with the births of William, Linda, Florence and Amy. John by this time was an 18 year old iron labourer. By 1901, the family had moved to live at 74, Queen Street Row, Lilleshall where Enoch junior and William had joined their father as coal miners. Amy was also still living at home and the family was completed by Jennie who was 2 years of age and described as a granddaughter. On the 28th March, 1910 at Wellington Register Office,

William married Hannah Pagett and the young couple moved into a house at 106, School Road, Donnington Wood, Shropshire. It was here that their first child Evelyn was born on the 17th May, 1911. Shortly after this the family moved to Hednesford where they lived at 50, George Street. It was here that their second child, Maud Florence was born on the 11th March, 1914. On the 19th January, 1915 William enlisted with the Royal Scots and was sent to Glencorse the following day. He was posted to the 14th Battalion on the 22nd, and was sent to France on the 28th July, 1915 when he was transferred to the 13th Battalion. On the 26th September, 1915 William was posted as missing in action. On the 10th December, 1915 Hannah wrote to the Army saying that she had had a letter from Sergeant Major McFarlane saying that he had seen William in hospital at Noeux-Les-Mines on the 1st November. She had written to the Matron and to her husband but received no reply. Hannah sent a second anguished letter on the 25th February, 1916, but on the 2nd October, 1916, she received a letter from the Army to state that for its records they had assumed that William had been killed on the 26th September, 1915. At the time of his death, William was 32. As his body was not found after the war, William is remembered on the Loos Memorial to the Missing in France. On the 1st March, 1916, Evelyn Tranter died from diphtheria, and on the 19th June, 1916 Hannah found out that she was to receive 15 shillings per week in pension payments for her husband.

Sergeant Ernest Benjamin Wadeley
52413

In 1878 at Cannock Ernest James Wadeley a 23 year old coal miner from Dudley, Worcestershire married Sarah Ann Mansell from Dudley Port, Staffordshire. The young couple set up home at Church Hill, Hednesford but their first child, a son named John William was born at Dudley Port as Sarah had gone back to her mother's to give birth. Ten years later, the family had grown with the births of Sarah Jane, Arthur, Polly and Sarah Ann. Ernest Benjamin was born at Hednesford in 1892 and the family continued to live at Church Hill with John now a coal miner. By 1911 Arthur was a coal miner fireman and Polly was a tailoring machinist while Ernest was a tailor fitter. Ernest probably enlisted in 1916, joining the Royal Warwickshire Regiment where he rose to the rank of Corporal. He was then transferred to the 15th Battalion, Royal Irish Rifles and rose to the rank of Sergeant before he was killed in action at the age of 26 on the 22nd October, 1918. Ernest's body was buried at Harlebeke New British Cemetery, near Kortrijk in Belgium.

Private Harold Walters
13147

Charles Walters a 22 year old coal miner from Portobello, Staffordshire married Joanna Fletcher also 22 from St. George's, Shropshire at Cannock in 1880. They moved to live at Station Road, Hednesford and in 1881 their first child Agnes was born. In 1891 the family had moved to live at Abbey Street, Green Heath, and the family had grown with the births of Harry, Sarah, Charles and Ernest. In 1901 they were living at Blewitt Street, Hednesford and Percy had been born in 1893, Harold born in 1894 and May born in 1896. Harry was now working as a coal miner and Charles was a horse driver in a colliery. In 1903, Joanna died at Cannock at the age of 45 and by 1911, Charles had moved back to Green Heath to live at Cross Street. Ernest and Harold were both coal miner horse drivers and Percy was a coal miner's loader. Following the outbreak of war, Harold enlisted in September 1914, joining the 2nd Battalion, South Staffordshire Regiment and he was sent to France on the 14th July, 1915. He saw action at the Battles of Arras and the Somme and served on the Western Front for almost three years when he died from wounds on the 25th March, 1918 at the age of 23. Harold's body was buried at Bac-du-Sud British Cemetery, Bailleulval, near Arras in France.

Private George Ward
51522

Jacob Ward a 24 year old coal miner from Cannock, married his wife Mary Ann, 22 from Walsall at Cannock in 1886. Their first child, a son named George was born later that year. The family were living at Piggott Street, Wimblebury and their second child, a daughter, Ethel, was born in 1889. The family then moved to live at Littleworth, Hednesford and here Edwin and Harriett Anne were born, followed by Gladys in 1902. By 1911, the family had moved to live at Church Street, Chasetown where Jacob had started a new career as a licensed victualler. George had become a butcher, working for Etherington of Cannock, whilst Edwin was a nipper in a colliery. Living with them was a 20 year old servant, Sabrana Read from Norton Canes and two actors, Ernest Eykyn from London and his wife Eva from Somerset. Sadly Jacob's new venture was short lived for in 1912 he died at the age of 49. On the 12th April, 1913 George married Sabrana Read at St. James's Parish Church, Norton Canes and the couple moved to live at 52, Wood Lane, Hednesford where their first child, Bertha was born on the 4th

August, 1913. A second child, Dorothy was born in 1916. On the 1st September, 1914 George enlisted in the Army, joining the Army Service Corps as a butcher, before he was transferred to the K Supply Company on the 22nd March, 1915, and was then posted to the 123rd Company on the 4th April, 1915. George was posted to Mesopotamia on the 29th June, 1915 and served there until he was posted back to England on the 11th November, 1915. He stayed in England until the 1st August, 1917 when he was posted to France. On the 17th August George was posted to the 21st Battalion, Manchester Regiment and on the 4th October, 1917 he was posted as missing in action, it later being presumed that he had died on this date at the age of 30. George's body was never found and he is remembered on the Tyne Cot Memorial to the Missing near Ieper in Belgium.

Private James Ward
17818

On the 19th April, 1897 at St. Peter's Parish Church, Hednesford John Ward a 22 year old winding engine driver at a colliery married Fanny Muriel Moss. John was from Slitting Mill near Rugeley and Fanny hailed from Polesworth, Warwickshire. They set up home on the Rawnsley Road, Hednesford and it was here that James was born in 1898, followed by his sister Gladys in 1900. Florence was born in 1903, Rose in 1904, Frank in 1906 and finally Mary Ellen in 1908. By 1911, the family were living at Harvey's Buildings, Littleworth and James had started work as a colliery bank labourer. Despite being under age, James volunteered for the Army in early 1915, joining the 2/6th Battalion, South Staffordshire Regiment and was sent to Gallipoli on the 5th December, 1915 and from there to Egypt before being sent to the Western Front. He served in France until the 20th November, 1918 when he died of influenza at the age of 21. James' body was buried at the St. Symphorien Military Cemetery near Mons in Belgium.

Private John Thomas Wassell
36304

In 1889 at Cannock, George Wassell a 24 year old coal miner born in the United States of America, but a British Subject, married 23 year old Mary Jane Matthews from Brockton, Shropshire. The couple moved to live on the Huntington Terrace Road, Chadsmoor and it was here that their first child, Joseph was born in 1890. By 1901, the family had moved to live at 26, Queen Street, High Town,

Hednesford and it was here that Sarah, Isaac, John (in 1898) and Richard were born. By 1911, Margrett and Gertrude had been born and Joseph and Isaac were both horse drivers in a colliery. John most probably joined up in 1917 and was posted to the 6th Battalion, King's Own Yorkshire Light Infantry, although he was later attached to the 2/4th Battalion, Royal Fusiliers. On the 25th April, 1918 John was posted as missing in action and it was later presumed that he had been killed on that date at the age of 20. After the war John's body was identified and he was buried at Villers-Bretonneux Military Cemetery in France.

Corporal John Henry Webster
7867

Henry Webster was a brickyard labourer from Lichfield, Staffordshire and his wife Sarah Jane came from Islington, London. In 1881 they were living at John Street, Wimblebury and ten years later had moved to live at Green Heath, Hednesford. By this time they had had three children, Elizabeth, George and Sarah Ellen. John was born in 1894 and in 1901 George had started work as a colliery engine driver. By 1911, only Elizabeth, John who was a motor engine driver, and Hilda, who was born in 1906, were still at home at South View, Green Heath Hednesford. John volunteered for the Army in 1914, joining the 1/5th Battalion, South Staffordshire Regiment and he was sent to France on the 5th March, 1915. At the age of 22, John was killed in action on the 8th June, 1915 and his body was buried at St. Quentin-Cabaret Military Cemetery, near Wulvergem in Belgium.

Private Frank Herbert Wells
20723

In 1874 at Penkridge, Staffordshire William Wells a local board road man married Catharine Jenkinson. The couple moved to live at Forge Street, Hednesford and their first child Sarah Ann was born in 1877, followed by Mary Ann in 1879. The following year Catharine died at the age of only 26 and William married Caroline Green at Cannock in 1881. By 1891, the family was living at Station Road, Hednesford, where Lizzie had been born in 1883, Frank in 1884, Henry in 1886, Caroline in 1888 and Thomas in 1891. In 1901 the 17 year old Frank had left home and was working as a grocer's assistant and living at 71, Dartmouth Street, Wolverhampton. In 1911, he had moved to Coventry where he was again working as a grocer's assistant and was living at 10, Croft Road. At around the outbreak of the Great War, Frank moved back to Hednesford to become manager of Neale's Tea Stores on Market Street, Hednesford. In January, 1916 Frank enlisted in the Army, joining the 1/8th Battalion, Royal Warwickshire Regiment and was sent to the Western Front later in 1916. On the 4th February, 1917 at the age of 32, Frank was killed in action. His body was buried at Assevillers New British Cemetery, near Peronne in France.

Private John Richard Wilde
7389

Richard Wilde a coal miner from Kingswinford, Staffordshire married Edith Matthews from Worthen, Shropshire at Cannock in 1887. They moved to live at Stafford Lane, Hednesford and their first child, a son named James was born in 1890. He was followed by John in 1891, Eliza in 1893, Richard in 1896 and Ethel in 1900. At the age of 17, John decided to join the Army and served for three years with the 1st Battalion, North Staffordshire Regiment before being placed on the Reserve List. He came back to Chadsmoor, getting a job as a horse driver in a colliery and living with the Hodgkiss family on Plantation Road. On the 26th February, 1912, John married the eldest daughter of his landlady, Ethel Hodgkiss and the couple moved to live at Huntington Terrace, Chadsmoor where their child Phyllis was born in 1913. When the Great War broke out, John was called to the Colours and was sent to France with the 1st Battalion, North Staffordshire Regiment on the 4th December, 1914, going into the trenches for the first time on Christmas Day, 1914. On the 14th March, 1915 this strapping, fearless soldier died from wounds at the age of 24. John was buried at Cite Bonjean Military Cemetery, Armentieres in France.

Aircraftsman 2nd Class Ernest Robert Whilton
142412

Ernest Whilton was the second youngest of fourteen children born and raised by Frank and Sarah Whilton. Frank was a butcher from Shenstone, Staffordshire and he had married Sarah Davis at Penkridge in 1874. They lived at McGhie Street, Hednesford and by 1881 had had four children, Henry, Mary, Frank and Herbert. By 1891 the family had moved to live at Cannock Road, Hednesford and by this time Frederick, Arthur, Emily, Sarah, Fanny and Florence had been born. Henry was helping his father as an assistant butcher, Mary was a draper's assistant and Frank was helping a grocer. By 1901, Miriam, Samuel, Ernest (born in 1896) and Ada had been born, with Herbert and Arthur now helping in the butcher's business. In 1911, only Florence, Miriam, who was an assistant milliner, Samuel, who was now helping his father, Ernest, who was a blacksmith's striker, and Ada, who was at school, were still living at home. Ernest enlisted in the Royal Flying Corps as an aircraftsman and was transferred to the newly formed Royal Air Force on the 1st April, 1918. At the end of the war he went with the occupation forces into Germany and it was here that he contracted pneumonia and died in Cologne at the age of 23. Ernest's body was buried at Cologne Southern Cemetery in Germany.

Private Frederick George Wray
39894

In 1894 at West Bromwich, Staffordshire Francis Wray a 25 year old house painter from Dawley, Shropshire married Josephine Louisa Phipps, aged 21 and who was born at Philadelphia, United States of America, although her family originated in Dudley. The couple set up a home at Hall's Buildings, West Hill, Hednesford and Frederick was born in 1897, followed by his sister Florence Ethel in 1901. By 1911, Frederick had started work as a butcher's boy, employed by Mr. Goodwin on the Cannock Road, Hednesford. In January 1916 Frederick enlisted in the Army, joining the South Staffordshire Regiment and he was posted to Ireland at the time of the Easter Rising. After returning to England, Frederick was transferred to the 10th Battalion, Worcestershire Regiment, and was sent to France. On the 18th November, 1916 Frederick was badly wounded in the right leg by a shell fragment during a British attack. He was left in No Man's Land for two days before he was discovered and sent to a Base Hospital, then being sent back to England where at Huddersfield Military Hospital, Frederick's right leg was amputated. His Army career ended, Frederick returned to Hednesford and once again worked as a butcher before he became the manager of Eastman's Stores in Hednesford. On the 1st April, 1918 Frederick married Catherine Beddow at St. Peter's Parish Church, Hednesford. The couple moved to live at Huntington and they had two children, Dorothy, born in 1919 and Francis born in January 1922. Sadly, on the 14th February, 1922, Frederick died after a short illness, his life having been cut short by the injuries sustained in 1916. The funeral took place at St. Peter's, Hednesford, and was attended by 100 members of the John Wesley Lodge of the Royal Ancient Order of Buffaloes in full regalia, as Frederick had been a fellow member.

Chapter 4

CHADSMOOR

METHODIST CHURCH

Private James Bailey
117890

Benjamin Bailey was a 24 year old coal miner born at Dawley, Shropshire when he married Lois Baugh, aged 19 at Shifnal in 1872. Lois also came from Dawley and the young couple settled there and it was here that John and Elijah were born in 1873 and 1875. The family then moved to live on the Hednesford Road, Cannock and by 1881 Margaret and Fanny had been born at Cannock. By 1891, they had moved again to live at Moreton Street, Chadsmoor and here Esther, Lois, James (in 1888), and Ann were born. John had started his working life down the pit as a coal miner. Between 1891 and 1901 there were two more additions to the family, Lilly born in 1892 and Jessie born in 1894. In 1911, Esther was a domestic servant, Lois a shop assistant and James was loading for his father down the pit, while both Lilly and Jessie were tailor's machinists. On the 25th December, 1912 James married Edith Annie Ward at St. Peter's Parish Church, Hednesford. The couple moved to live at 241, Cannock Road, Chadsmoor and they had one child, a boy named James born in 1915. James continued to work as a miner until the 29th May, 1918 when he joined the Army, enlisting with the 5th Battalion, Notts and Derbys Regiment, being granted 1st Class proficiency pay. James was then transferred to the 1/6th Battalion and then on reaching France on the 29th September, 1918, the 1/5th Battalion. On the 17th October, 1918 at the age of 30, James was killed in action. His body was buried at Busigny Communal Cemetery Extension, between Le Cateau and St. Quentin in France. His widow was paid 20 shillings and 5 pence in pension each week from the 5th May, 1919.

Private Joseph Devney
16731

In 1882 at Cannock, Staffordshire William Devney a 22 year old coal miner from Wolverhampton married 20 year old Ellen Hudson from Wyrley, Staffordshire. The couple set up a home at New Street, Chadsmoor and it was here that their three children were born, Joseph in 1885, Mary in 1887 and George in 1890. By 1901, Joseph was working as a bricklayer's labourer, but he later became a coal miner and on the 2nd August, 1908 at St. Luke's Parish Church, Cannock he married Annie Mallen. In 1909 their first and only child, a son named George was born, but shortly afterwards the family left Hednesford and settled in Clowne, near Worksop, Nottinghamshire, living at 55, North Road. It was at Worksop that Joseph enlisted in the 7th Battalion, South Staffordshire Regiment in 1915 and he saw service at Gallipoli and Egypt and on the Western Front. In July 1917 Joseph was on leave when he deserted and his father, who had helped conceal his son, was sent to prison for one day due to compassion being shown by the magistrates. Joseph was sent back to the Western Front and was killed in action on the 24th October, 1917 at the age of 32. Joseph's body was buried at St. Patrick's Cemetery, Loos in France.

Rifleman George Devney
R/8548

George Devney was the younger brother of Joseph and was born at Hednesford in 1890. He worked as a coal miner's loader at East Cannock Colliery and on the 13th April, 1914 he married Mary Jane Rogers at St. Luke's Parish Church, Cannock. The couple moved to John Street, Chadsmoor and they had two children. In 1915, George enlisted with the 16th Battalion, King's Royal Rifle Corps and he was sent to France on the 21st July, 1915. In 1916, George was badly wounded and spent some time in England recuperating before he was sent back to his unit in October, 1916. On the 1st February, 1917 George was killed in action at the age of 27. After the war George's body could not be identified and he is remembered on the Thiepval Memorial to the Missing on the Somme in France.

Corporal William Garbett
R/12254

For details about William Garbett, see the entry on the same soldier under Cannock.

Private Isaiah Jones
13717

For details about Isaiah Jones see the entry on the same soldier under Hednesford.

Private James Ward Onions
28668

For details about James Ward Onions see the entry on the same soldier under Cannock.

Guardsman William Gallear
22537

For details about William Gallear see entry on the same soldier under Cannock.

Private Arthur Saunders
G/63041

On the 22nd December, 1889 at St. Luke's Parish Church, Cannock, John Saunders a 20 year old coal miner from Rawnsley married Jane Goring a 19 year old from Hamstall Ridware, Staffordshire. The couple moved to live at Huntington Terrace, Chadsmoor and in 1890 their first child, John Thomas was born. By 1901 the family had grown to number four children with the birth of Mary in 1893, James in 1895 and Arthur in 1897. Between 1901 and 1911 a further four children were born, Oliver, Edith, Ann and Leslie. John Thomas, James and Arthur were all employed as colliery horse drivers at Littleton Colliery, with Mary working as a tailoress. Arthur was also a member of Chadsmoor Primitive Methodist Church. Arthur joined the Army on the 22nd April, 1918 and was first posted to the North Staffordshire Regiment, but when he was sent to France, he was transferred to the 7th Battalion, Middlesex Regiment. On the

27th August, 1918, Arthur was killed in action at the age of 21. After the war Arthur's body could not be found and he is remembered on the Vis-en-Artois Memorial to the Missing in France.

Lance Corporal Ernest Leach
R/12249

Charles and Hannah Leach both came from Shropshire, and at the start of their marriage lived at Little Eyton Fold, Dawley where Samuel, William and Ernest were born. The family then moved to live at 98, John Street, Chadsmoor where by 1891 Edith, Bertie, Jonas and Rhoda had been added to the brood. Indeed by this time, Samuel the eldest had started work as a horse driver down the pit, probably the same one where his father worked. By 1901, Ernest was a miner's labourer, while Aaron and William Edge, a step son were both working as horse drivers. In December 1903 Ernest married Elizabeth Smart at Cannock Register Office and they moved in with Ernest's family. However, in 1906 Hannah Leach died at the age of 48 and Charles and the rest of the family moved to live at Churchbridge with the newly weds staying at 98, John Street. Their first child, Nellie was born on the 30th December, 1905, their second child Horace, born on the 27th April, 1908, followed by Ernest Leslie on the 5th November, 1910 and finally Eric on the 27th March, 1913. On the 19th April, 1915 Ernest enlisted in the Army, joining the 15th Battalion, King's Royal Rifle Corps, where he was promoted to Lance Corporal on the 30th July. When he was posted to France on the 12th September, 1915 he was transferred to the 8th Battalion. On the 15th September, 1916 Ernest was seriously wounded in the back with shrapnel. He was taken to the 15th Advanced Dressing Station and from there to the 63rd Field Ambulance where he died on the 16th September at the age of 33. Ernest's body was buried at Dartmoor Cemetery, Becordel-Becourt in France. His widow sent a touching letter to the War Office thanking them for telling her where her husband was buried as this was "some consolation".

Private Elijah Williams
14839

In 1886, Elijah Williams, a brick burner from Broseley, Shropshire married Sarah Ann Howarth from Great Wyrley at Cannock. In 1891, they were living at Cross Street, Bridgtown and Miriam and William had been born. By 1901, Elijah was a foreman at the roofing tile works, and in the meantime, Elijah junior, Frederick, Ernest, Florence and Catherine had been added to the family. In 1911, Mary, Thomas, and James had also been born and the family was living on the Watling Street, Bridgtown. Elijah junior enlisted in early 1915 and was sent to France on the 26th August, 1915, and was killed in action on the 8th June, 1917. Elijah's body was not found after the war and he is remembered on the Ieper (Menin Gate) Memorial to the Missing in Ieper city centre.

Private John Williams
13841

In 1882 at Walsall, Staffordshire Peter Williams a coal miner from Bilston married Charlotte Nickless from Willenhall. The couple moved to live at 34, Cross Street, Hazel Slade and their first child, Sarah was born in 1883, followed by John in 1884, Ellen in 1886 and Charlotte in 1890. Charlotte's mother Sarah Nickless was also living with them as were two boarders, Samuel Clarke who was born at Pennsylvania, USA and James Evans from Bilston. By 1901 the family had grown somewhat with the additions of William, Violet, Thomas, Doris and Peter, and John was already working down the pit as a horse driver. On the 21st May, 1905 John married Elizabeth Ann Massey at St. Peter's Parish Church, Hednesford and the couples' first child Frances Lorraine was born at Hednesford in 1906. Shortly afterwards the family decided to move to Ashton-under-Lyne in Lancashire and here Lucy Maud and Peter were born. A third move saw the family living in Mansfield where Doris was born in 1910 and then the family moved again to live at 48, Frederick Street, Catcliffe, Rotherham. Lucy died at the tragically young age of 4 in 1913. In September, 1914 John returned to Hednesford to enlist in the 2nd Battalion, South Staffordshire Regiment and he was sent to France on the 17th March, 1915. Just two months later on the 17th May, 1915 John was killed in action at the age of 31. After the war John's body could not be identified and he is remembered on the Le Touret Memorial to the Missing in France.

Lance Corporal Ernest Titley
28439

John Titley was a coal miner from Shropshire and he married Martha Elks at Madeley, Shropshire in 1876, with their first child Arthur John being born the following year, and their second child Mary Ann in 1879. Shortly after this, Martha died, and in 1885, he married Jane Ellen Pritchard at Madeley, before the family moved to live and work in Chadsmoor. Whilst at Sandbed Terrace, Chadsmoor, their first child Jane was born, followed by John and Edith.

In 1901 the family had grown considerably with the births of Walter in 1894, Ernest in 1895, and Horace in 1898. Arthur was working as a coal miner's loader. By 1911, Ada and Cyril had been born, while Arthur was now a coal miner. Jane was helping at home and Edith worked as a dressmaker. Walter and Ernest were both butchers' assistants for Walter Webster of Eskrett Street, Hednesford, and Horace was a surface boy at a colliery. Ernest was a keen and excellent cyclist known around the region. On the 28th June, 1916 Ernest enlisted in the Army joining the 1st Battalion, South Staffordshire Regiment, and he was sent to France on the 24th November, 1916. Ernest was awarded a silver medal by the Division for bayonet fighting. He rose to the rank of Lance Corporal and was part of a Lewis gun team. On the 26th October, 1917 the Staffords went over the top at 5.30 am. Ernest was shot and fell back with the words "carry on boys". He was left in No Man's Land which was being heavily shelled. Ernest's body was buried at Hooge Crater Cemetery just outside Ieper in Belgium. He was 22 at the time of his death.

Private William Young
15246

For details about William Young see entry on the same soldier under Cannock.

Private Arthur William Spencer
15436

In 1873 at Whitchurch, Shropshire, Thomas Spencer married Emily Jennings. By 1881, the couple had had three children, John Joseph, Martha and Phylis and were living at New Street, Wrockwardine where Thomas worked as an ironstone miner. The 1891 census records that the family had moved to New Street, Chadsmoor, and that Arthur William, Frances and Jane had been born, whilst Thomas was now a coal miner. By 1901, the family had moved to Church Street, Chadsmoor, where Arthur William was a coal miner horse driver, and a lodger, Francis B. Watkiss, an assistant schoolmaster was staying with the family. In 1911, Arthur William was living at 104, Market Street, Atherton, in Lancashire and was earning his living as a coal miner and boarding with the Hodkinson family. Early in 1915, Arthur William married Ethel Mary

Broomfield at Cannock, shortly before he enlisted with the 1st Battalion, Northumberland Fusiliers, and he was sent to France on the 4th September, 1915. He served until the 26th January, 1916 when he died of wounds at the age of 33. William's body was buried at Reninghelst New Military Cemetery, near Poperinghe in Belgium.

BETHANY BAPTIST CHAPEL

Private Harold Dyke
10327

For details about Harold Dyke see the entry on the same soldier under Cannock.

Private Harold Kelsey
8049

In 1877 at Wolverhampton, Staffordshire James Kelsey married Sarah Rebecca Steward. The groom was a coal miner from Tunstall, Staffordshire and the bride was born in Birmingham, Warwickshire. By 1881 the couple had set up a home at John Street, Chadsmoor where Sarah's brother Joseph was living with them. In 1891 the couple had started a family with the birth of Edith Ann in 1888 and Harold James in 1890. Sarah's sister Ann was staying with them at this point. However, in 1893 James died at the age of 37 and Sarah Rebecca married John James Degg a butcher at Cannock on the 17th May 1896 at St. Luke's Parish Church. In 1901 the family were living at 7, Church Street, Chadsmoor where they had been joined by Ernest Degg, John's son from his first marriage. In 1908, Harold joined the Army, enlisting with the 1st Battalion, South Staffordshire Regiment and in 1911 he was stationed in Gibraltar before going on to Pietermaritzburg in South Africa where the Battalion was stationed when the Great War broke out. They sailed back to England, arriving in Southampton on the 19th September, 1914 and then to France on the 4th October, 1914. On the 29th October, 1914 Harold was posted as missing in action. His body was never found and Harold is remembered on the Ieper (Menin Gate) Memorial to the Missing in Ieper city centre. At the time of his death, Harold was 24 years of age.

Private Ernest Arthur Riley
16169

Ernest Riley was the third eldest son of George and Catherine Riley and he was born at Chadsmoor in 1893. His father was at the time of Ernest's birth a baker and he was born at Bloxwich, Staffordshire. His mother, Catherine also came from Bloxwich. In 1881, the Riley family was living at Moss Street, Chadsmoor with George junior having been born in 1889 and William having been born in 1891. By 1901 they had moved to live on the Cannock Road, Chadsmoor, and during this ten year period, Ernest was born along with Frederick in 1895 and Doris in 1900. 1911 still saw the family at 154, Cannock Road but by this time the boys had all started work. George senior had become a bat picker at a colliery while George junior and William were both edge tool grinders. Ernest and Frederick worked as coal boat loaders at the Cannock and Rugeley Wharf. Ernest enlisted in the Army in November 1914, joining the 11th Battalion, Northumberland Fusiliers, and being sent to France on the 25th August, 1915. Ernest was then attached to the 68th Trench Mortar Battery and it was while he was this unit that he was killed in action on the 26th February, 1917 at the age of 24. A letter from Captain A.W. Hetherington described Ernest as an "excellent example to other men". Ernest's body was buried at the Railway Dugouts Burial Ground near Ieper in Belgium.

Guardsman William Abraham Shaw
20877

In 1890 at Lichfield, Staffordshire William Shaw a steam boiler stoker married Emma Jones. To begin with the couple moved in with the groom's family at Smart's Buildings, Forge Row in Rugeley. By 1901 they had moved to live at Burgoyne Street, Hednesford and they had had five children, William Abraham, the eldest was born in 1891, followed by Sarah in 1893, Joseph in 1899, Minnie in 1900 and Alice in 1901. In 1911, the family had moved to live on Belt Road and two more children had been born, Fanny in 1906 and Albert in 1911. William senior was now a colliery fireman and his eldest son was employed as a coal miner horse driver. William Abraham enlisted in the Army in 1915, joining the 4th Battalion, Grenadier Guards and he was sent to France on the 15th August, 1915. William served until the 28th November, 1917 when he was killed in action at the age of 26. His body was buried at Anneux British Cemetery between Cambrai and Bapaume.

4. Chadsmoor

Private Frank Hayward
20876

In 1885 at Shifnal, Shropshire Richard Hayward a coal miner born at Wellington married Annie Eliza Gitton. The groom was aged 20 and his bride was only 16. The couple moved to live at Bloors Buildings, Gower Street, Wrockwardine and it was here in 1895 that their only child, Frank was born. By 1911, the family had moved to live at 54, Church Street, Chadsmoor and by this time Frank was also working down the pit as a coal miner horse driver at West Cannock Colliery. He was also a noted local footballer. Frank enlisted shortly after the outbreak of war in August, 1914, joining the 3rd Battalion, Grenadier Guards and he was sent to France on the 27th July, 1915. Frank served until the 14th September, 1916 when he was killed in action at the age of 22. After the war Frank's body was not identified and he is remembered on the Thiepval Memorial to the Missing on the Somme in France.

Sapper John Beach
141162

John Beach was born at Chadsmoor on the 29th January, 1888 and was the second son of John and Fanny Beach. His parents were married at Cannock in 1881, John being a coal miner from Pensnett and his wife, whose maiden name was White, came from Gornal. Their first child Geoffrey was born in 1883 and the couple had set up home on the Cannock Road, Chadsmoor. By 1901, more children had been born; William in 1893, Frederick in 1899 and Gladys in 1900, although Alfred who had been born in 1890 had sadly died. In 1911 the family had moved to live at 12, Burns Street, Chadsmoor, with Daisy having been born in 1903 and Alice in 1906 and Fanny's 76 year old father was also living with them. By this time Geoffrey and John were both coal miners at Littleton Colliery and William was a horse driver at East Cannock pit. On the 29th March, 1912, John decided to leave England and sailed from Liverpool to Halifax, Nova Scotia in Canada. Here he established himself as a carpenter, but on the 27th July, 1915 he joined the Canadian Army at Hamilton, enlisting firstly with the 39th Battalion, Canadian Expeditionary Force and then transferring to the 7th Field Company, Canadian Engineers. John embarked for France on the 2nd April, 1916 and served until he was badly wounded on the 26th September, 1916. He was taken to the 2/1st South Midland Casualty Clearing Station at Warloy where he died in the Special Hospital on the 28th September, 1916 aged 28. John's body was buried at Warloy-Baillon Communal Cemetery Extension, near Amiens on the Somme in France.

Sapper William Beach
406033

William Beach was the younger brother of John Beach and was born at Chadsmoor on the 1st April, 1893. Like his brother he began working life down the pit at East Cannock Colliery and he followed his brother to Canada on the 5th October, 1912 sailing from Liverpool to Montreal. He worked in Canada as a labourer and William decided to enlist on the 16th April, 1915 at Hamilton, joining the 18th Battalion, Canadian Expeditionary Force. Whilst John's service record had been exemplary, William's was less impressive. In Canada he was docked two day's pay for absence and on arriving in England he was awarded 14 days field punishment number two for being drunk and disorderly. This continued in France where he received three punishments for absence and refusing to follow orders which resulted in 120 days imprisonment and a transfer to the 36th Battalion. Further misdemeanors ended with a second transfer, this time to the 7th Company, Canadian Engineers the same Company as his brother. On the 20th May, 1916 William was admitted to Number 5 Canadian Field Ambulance with bruised feet, being returned to duty three days later. On the 27th July he was admitted again with a gunshot wound to the left hand, rejoining his unit on the 6th August. However, on the 26th September, 1916 William was killed by a high explosive shell, dying on the same day that his brother was fatally wounded. At the time of his death, William was 23 years of age, but his body was not found after the war and he is remembered on the Canadian National Memorial at Vimy Ridge in France.

Private George Dyke
7894

For details about George Dyke see the entry on the same soldier under Hednesford.

Private Warren Keeling
331308

Warren Keeling was born at Hednesford, Staffordshire in 1887 and was the fourth son of Charles and Mary Ann Keeling. Charles was a colliery stoker from Brocton and his wife came from Middlesex. The couple had married at Holbourn, London in 1876 and Mary Ann's maiden name was Sapsford. In 1871 they were living at Old Sandford Street in Lichfield and they had had three children by that time, Thomas, Emma and Charles. The next time the family surfaced was in 1891, when they had moved to live at New Street, Chadsmoor and the family had grown with the births of Ann, Mary Ann, William, Hannah and Warren. Strangely, the family appear to have disappeared again in 1901, but in 1911, Warren was living with Thomas and Mary Jane Marriott at Town Street, Holbrook, Derby and he was working as a colliery labourer. He must have enlisted in late 1914, joining the 15th Battalion, Notts and Derbys Regiment and being sent to France on the 25th June, 1915. Warren served in France and Belgium until the 20th October, 1917 when he was killed in action at the age of 31 during the Battle of Passchendaele. After the war, Warren's body was not found and he is remembered on the Tyne Cot memorial to the Missing near Ieper in Belgium.

Private William Powell
61159

William Powell was born at Chadsmoor in 1899 and was the eldest child of John and Emily Powell. The couple had married at St. Luke's Parish Church, Cannock on the 16th August, 1896 and lived at 241, Cannock Road, Chadsmoor. Emily's maiden name was Walters. By 1901, William and his brother Arthur had been born, and by 1911, Elsie May and Daisy Muriel had also been born. John's brother Samuel was also living with them. In view of his age, it is unlikely that William would have been called up until 1918, when he joined the 1/6th Battalion, North Staffordshire Regiment, and was sent to France. William died on the 31st October, 1918 at the age of 18. His body was buried at Vadencourt British Cemetery, Maissemy near St. Quentin in France.

Private Ernest Hooper
22761

On the 24th December, 1894 at St. Luke's Parish Church, Cannock, John Thomas Hooper an illiterate 22 year old coal miner from Bilston, Staffordshire married 19 year old Sarah Annie Gough from Cannock. The couple moved to John Street, Chadsmoor and began a family. Ernest was the eldest child born at Chadsmoor in 1895, followed by Ethel May in 1899, Percy in 1900, Winifred in 1903, Horace in 1906 and finally Dorothy Rachel in 1910. Ernest began work as a coal miner hooker on, and then became a coal miner before he enlisted with the Royal Scots on the 10th May, 1915. He was sent to Glencorse on the 11th May and posted to the 3rd Battalion on the 14th. On the 11th August, 1915 Ernest was posted to the 12th Battalion and sent to France on the 12th, landing at Boulogne. On the 25th September, 1915 at the age of 20 Ernest was posted missing in action at the Battle of Loos. It was later presumed that he had been killed on that date. His possessions were sent back to his mother and his medals to his father. After the war, Ernest's body was not recovered and he is remembered on the Loos Memorial to the Missing in France.

Private George Illsley MM
18630

For details about George Illsley see the entry on the same soldier under Hednesford.

UNCOMMEMORATED

Private George Bates
12906

George Bates was born at Chadsmoor in 1898 and was the second son of Levi and Emma Bates. Levi was a coal miner originally from Wolverhampton, as was his wife whose maiden name was Cross. By 1891 the couple had moved to live at Burgoyne Street, Chadsmoor, although their first child, John Thomas had been born at Wolverhampton. The rest of the family, Emma, Mary Ellen, Sarah, George, Edith, Levi, May and James were all born at Chadsmoor. By 1901 the family had moved to live at Moreton Street, and in 1911, they were living at 132, Cannock Road. By this time, John Thomas and George were both working as edge tool grinders at Whitehouse Brothers at Bridgtown. Despite being only 16 years of age, George volunteered for the Army in 1914, joining the 7th Battalion, South Staffordshire Regiment and he was sent to Gallipoli on the 21st July, 1915. On the 22nd August, 1915 George was posted as missing in action, and despite a report that he had been captured by the Turks reaching his parents, a letter from Private Isaac Galley confirmed that he had been shot and killed. At the time of his death, George was only 17 and his body was not identified after the war. George is remembered on the Helles Memorial to the Missing in Turkey.

Lance Corporal John Thomas Bates
15238

John Bates was the older brother of George and was born at Wolverhampton in 1888. He became an edge tool grinder at Whitehouse Brothers at Bridgtown and was also a noted local footballer, turning out for Chadsmoor F.C. In 1912, John married Harriet Pritchards at Cannock Register Office, with the couple setting up home at Huntington Terrace, Chadsmoor. In 1913 they had their first and only child, a daughter named Mary. In late 1914, John enlisted with the 20th Battalion, Northumberland Fusiliers, popularly known as the Tyneside Scottish, and he was sent to Gallipoli on the 21st September, 1915. John was wounded whilst serving in the Dardanelles and was sent to Greece to recover, before he was returned to his Battalion in France. John served until the 9th September, 1917 when he was badly wounded by a shell. He was taken to a Casualty Clearing Station for treatment, but died from his injuries on the following day at the age of 29. John's body was not identified at the end of the war and he is remembered on the Thiepval Memorial to the Missing on the Somme in France.

Private Samuel Ernest Benton
11422

In 1882 at Cannock, Samuel Benton a 24 year old coal miner from Great Wyrley married Esther Tuffy, aged 23 from Cannock. The couple set up home at New Street, Chadsmoor where they began their family in 1883 with the birth of Myra, followed by the birth of Esther in 1885. Ellen was born in 1890 and Samuel Ernest in 1892. By 1901 the family had moved to live at Church Street, Chadsmoor and both Myra and Esther had left home to enter service, Myra working for the Lowe family at Shrewsbury and Esther, closer to home, working for the Harrison family at Cannock. In 1910, Samuel senior died at the age of 52, leaving his widow and son, still living at Rose Cottage, Church Street. Samuel Ernest was now earning his living as a coal miner stallman at West Cannock Colliery. With the outbreak of the Great War, Samuel was in the first rush to enlist, joining the 8th Battalion, North Staffordshire Regiment, and he was sent to France on the 18th July, 1915. Just two months later, Samuel was badly wounded and died from these injuries on the 13th September, 1915 at the age of 23. Samuel's body was buried at Le Touret Military Cemetery, Richebourg-L'Avoue, near Armentieres in France.

Sergeant Albert Bradshaw
10438

Albert Bradshaw appears on the 1891 census as Albert Inskip, having been born three years before at Hanley, Stoke-on-Trent. His mother, Martha Bradshaw was working as a domestic servant to John Inskip a 64 year old widower born at Wolstanton, and living at 78, Newcastle Road, Hanley. In 1895, his mother married Thomas Bettany at Stoke and on the 1901 census she was still living at the same address as before with Albert, now aged 13 and his four year old half sister Lilian Hilda Bettany. In 1908, Albert married Lily Powney at Stoke and their first child, Ethel Florence was born in 1909 at Shelton, before the family moved to live at Heath Hayes. On the 1911 census, they are lodging with the Hathaway family at 28, Bank Street, Heath Hayes with Albert now working as a Trammer in the coal industry. A second daughter, Lilian was born at Cannock in 1912 and by this time the family had moved to live in Chadsmoor. Albert must have enlisted in late 1914, joining the 7th Battalion of the South Staffordshire Regiment and he was sent to serve in Gallipoli on the 21st July, 1915. He rose to the rank of Sergeant before he was killed in action on the 9th August, 1915. Albert's body was not recovered after the war and he is remembered on the Helles Memorial in Turkey.

Private Thomas Briggs
15968

In 1882 at Cannock, Staffordshire, William Briggs a coal miner from Ivetsey Bank, Shropshire married Jane Pickering from Evesham, Worcestershire. The couple settled in Chadsmoor, living on the Huntington Terrace Road and in 1884, their first child, Rose Hannah was born. In 1886, the first son, William Henry was born and he was followed in 1887 by Eliza and in 1890, George was born. Thomas was born in 1892 and by 1901 the family had moved to live at Moreton Street, Chadsmoor. In 1911, the family was again living on the Huntington Terrace Road, where Thomas was now a horse driver at Number 4 Pit, West Cannock Colliery. William Henry was living at home with his wife and child, having married in 1903. Rose Hannah was also at home with her child John Carter, from her marriage to a man of the same name at Shifnal in 1903. There was also William Baker and his wife and child lodging with the Briggs family. On the 4th September, 1914 Thomas and William Henry volunteered for the Army. Thomas enlisted with the 11th Battalion, Northumberland Fusiliers, being placed in "C" Company. He was sent to France on the 25th August, 1915, seeing action at Loos in 1915, before being sent to the Somme. After coming out of the line for a period of rest, Thomas was killed in action by a shell on the 1st August, 1916 on his return to the Front Line. At the time of his death, Thomas was 24 years of age and was buried near where he had fallen at Delville Wood. After the war his body was exhumed and reburied at Flatiron Copse Cemetery, Mametz on the Somme. His gold ring was returned to his parents by four Hednesford men who were serving with him, J.T. Ward, W. Wallace, W. Hamplett and G. Woodhead.

Private Arthur John Brookes
15123

Arthur Brookes was born at Penkridge, Staffordshire in 1890 and was the third son of William and Mary Ellen Brookes. William was born in 1836 and came from Brewood, Staffordshire whilst Mary Ellen came from Penkridge. In 1891 the family were living at the Flax Oven, Penkridge and there were three boys, William Henry born in 1881, Alfred born in 1888 and Arthur in 1890. William was working as an agricultural labourer, and by 1901 he had retired and the family had moved to live at Town End, Penkridge. Alfred had started work as an agricultural labourer, whilst William Henry had gone down the pit at Littleton Colliery. In 1909, William Henry married Florence Mary Larner at Cannock Register Office and the couple set up home on the Huntington Terrace Road and began a family. In 1911, the rest of the family were still living at the same address in Penkridge, but Alfred and Arthur were working as pony drivers at Littleton. William senior, despite having an old age pension and being 75 years of age had had to find work as an engine fitter. William died in 1913 at the age of 77 and his widow and Arthur moved in with William Henry and his family in Chadsmoor.

In early 1915, Arthur enlisted with the 1st Battalion, Northumberland Fusiliers and was sent to Gallipoli on the 10th September, 1915, and from there to Egypt and finally the Western Front in time for the Battle of the Somme. On the 1st July, 1916 Arthur was seriously wounded on the first day of the battle. He was invalided out and finally returned to England where he died from his injuries in the 1st Eastern Hospital, Cambridge on the 27th July at the age of 25. Arthur's body was returned to Cannock where he was buried with full military honours on Wednesday 2nd August, 1916. The pall bearers were from his Regiment as was the firing party. His cap, belt and bayonet were placed on top of the coffin which was carried on a gun carriage, and the service, conducted by the Reverend O.H. Thomas took place at St. Chad's Church, Chadsmoor. An appeal to defray the funeral expenses raised £8 3s.

Sapper Thomas Brough
112557

For details about Thomas Brough see the entry on the same soldier under Cannock.

Private George Albert Dowding
24822

For details about George Albert Dowding see the entry on the same soldier under Hednesford.

Private Benjamin Edge
10748

On the 3rd August, 1891 at St. Luke's Parish Church, Cannock, George Edge a 24 year old coal miner born at Madeley, Shropshire married Mary Ann Reynolds, also 24 but who was born at Walsall, Staffordshire. The couple set up home at Plantation Road, Chadsmoor and began a family. The first child was Alfred Victor, born at Chadsmoor in 1892, followed in quick succession by Charles in 1894, Benjamin in 1895, Dorothy in 1896, Eliza in 1898, Emily in 1899 and George in 1900. By 1911, the family had increased further with the births of Cyril in 1902, Richard in 1906 and Rose in 1909. They had also moved to live at 96, John Street, Chadsmoor. The older children had all started work, Alfred as a coal miner trammer, Charles as a coal miner horse driver and Benjamin as a motor driver below ground. In August 1914, Benjamin volunteered for the Army, enlisting with the 7th Battalion, South Staffordshire Regiment. He was sent to Grantham, Lincolnshire for his basic training and it was here on the 16th December, 1914 that he died from heart failure at the age of 19. Benjamin's body was brought back to Chadsmoor and he was buried at Cannock Cemetery.

Lance Corporal James William Edge
20515

James Edge was born at Chadsmoor in 1887. His father was Matthew Edge, a joiner and his mother was Elizabeth Hannah Edge. There is no record of a marriage between the two, nor is there a death record for Matthew Edge with any connection to Cannock. However, in 1887 at Cannock, Elizabeth Edge married Charles Leech and the family set up a home at John Street, Chadsmoor. Both bride and groom came from Shropshire originally and three of Charles' children from his first marriage to Martha Elizabeth Haycock were born in the county. On the 1891 census, James is noted as Jonas Leech, and on the 1901 census he is referred to as William Edge, indeed, his birth was registered as William James Edge. At this point James had started work as a horse driver down the pit. On the 16th May, 1910 James married Frances Lilian Smith at St. Luke's Parish Church, Cannock, both groom and bride living a few doors apart on John Street, setting up their home at number 52. Their first child, Kathleen was born in 1910, with their second James born in 1913 and their third child John born in 1914. At the start of 1915, James volunteered for the Army, joining the 8th Battalion, Northumberland Fusiliers, and he was sent to Gallipoli on the 30th November, 1915. From there his Regiment was sent to Egypt and then to the Western Front in July 1916 for the Battle of the Somme. On the 26th September, 1916 James was killed in action at the age of 29. After the war his body was not found and James is remembered on the Thiepval Memorial to the Missing on the Somme in France.

Lance Corporal Wallace Flint
13063

In 1884, William Flint a coal miner from Basford, Nottinghamshire married Sarah Perry from Walsall, Staffordshire at Cannock. The couple moved to live at Burgoyne Street, Chadsmoor and their first child, Mary was born in 1885. She was followed by Nelly in 1887, William in 1889 and George in 1891. Living with them at this time were two lodgers, John Ward and John Dale who were both coal miners. In 1901 the family had moved to live on the Cannock Road, Chadsmoor and four more children had been born, John in 1893, Samuel in 1895, Wallace in 1896 and Violet in 1899. The family was completed in 1903 with the birth of Doris. By 1911, the oldest children had started work, George and John were both colliery haulers as was their father; Samuel was a colliery horse driver and Wallace was a nipper at West Cannock Colliery. In August, 1914 Wallace enlisted with the 7th Battalion, South Staffordshire Regiment and he was sent to Gallipoli on the 21st July, 1915. Wallace was badly wounded in November 1915 and was taken to the Hospital Ship Longfranc for treatment but died from his wounds on the 3rd November, 1915 at the age of 19. After the war Wallace's body was not identified and he is remembered on the Helles Memorial to the Missing in Turkey.

Private John Edward Hamplett
16549

In 1878 at Shifnal, Shropshire Walter Hamplett, a coal miner from Madeley married Margaret Elizabeth Britland from Wolverhampton. The couple settled in a house at Church Street, Cross Hill in Madeley. It was here that their family was started in 1878 with the birth of Sarah, followed by Alice in 1880, Thomas in 1882, Harry in 1885, James in 1887 and Walter junior in 1889. Shortly after the birth of Walter, the family moved to live at Cross Row, John Street in Chadsmoor. It was here that John was born in 1892, with William being born in 1894, Edith in 1895 and Harold in 1900. By this time, Thomas, Alfred and James had all begun work down the pit. In 1909 a double tragedy struck the family when Alfred and James were both killed in an accident at Littleton Colliery. In 1911, the remaining family was living at 7, John Street, Chadsmoor where John was now a 20 year old coal miner loader, along with his brother William at Cannock and Rugeley Colliery. Harold on the other hand was aged 14 and was unemployed. On the 18th August, 1914 John presented himself at the Drill Hall at Hednesford to enlist. He passed the medical examination given by Dr. R. Holton and was accepted for service with the 6th Battalion, Leicestershire Regiment and sent to Aldershot. Here he was examined again and was declared to be unfit for service. Not to be deterred, John enlisted again, this time joining the 2nd Battalion, Northumberland Fusiliers. This time he was accepted without question and was sent to France on the 18th May, 1915. Just six days later, John was posted as wounded and missing in action, and it was later accepted that he had died on this date at the age of 23. After the war John's body was not found and he is remembered on the Ieper (Menin Gate) Memorial to the Missing in Ieper city centre in Belgium.

Private Russell John Haycock
325498

For details about Russell John Haycock see the entry on the same soldier under Cannock.

Corporal John Henry Henshaw
12415

William Henshaw an iron worker from Moxley, Staffordshire married Emma Downes from Bilston at Dudley in 1871. William worked as an iron puddler, and to begin with the couple lived at Sedgley where William junior was born in 1872, Mary in 1873, and Elizabeth in 1875, before the family moved to live at Manchester and it was here that Madeline was born in 1878 and Emma in 1880. In 1881 the family were boarding at 72, Farrar Street, Linthorpe near Middlesboro with Emma's married brother William Downes and his family. By 1891 they had moved back to Sedgley and were living at 51, Darkhouse Lane. William was still working in an iron works and both Mary and Elizabeth were employed as brick tamperers, whilst Madeline was in domestic service. John Henry had been born at Sedgley in 1886 and was at school. However, William senior died at the age of 41 in 1892 and in 1901 the widowed Emma was living at 10, Daisy Street, Sedgley with John who was a coal miner and Nellie Evans, her 8 year old grandchild. In 1909, Emma died at the age of 59 and John and Nellie moved in with the now married Madeline and her husband and family at 19, Daisy Street. Shortly after this, John decided to move to Cannock and found a job as a miner at Littleton Colliery. In August, 1914 John volunteered for the Army, joining the 7th Battalion, South Staffordshire Regiment and on the 1st February, 1915 he married Elizabeth Burrows at St. Luke's Parish Church, Cannock. The couple set up home at Church Street, Chadsmoor before John was sent to Gallipoli on the 6th October, 1915. He then served in Egypt before arriving on the Western Front in 1916. John served in Flanders until the 1st August, 1917 when he died from wounds at the age of 31. John's body was buried at Lijssenthoek Military Cemetery in Belgium.

Rifleman William Hill
R/10203

William Hill was born in Australia in 1896, and in 1901 he was living with his brother Thomas Hill at Huntington Terrace Road, Chadsmoor. His parents were given as Isaiah Haddaway and his wife Jane. This couple had married at St. Luke's Parish Church, Cannock on the 3rd April, 1899, with Jane's surname being Hill. Jane died in 1908 at the age of 48 and within a year Isaiah had married Emma Dawson. In 1911, William and Thomas Hill were living with George and Elizabeth Hill and their family of four at Moreton Street, Chadsmoor, and both of them were working as colliery roadmen. In 1914, William enlisted for the Army, joining the 4th Battalion, King's Royal Rifle Corps and he was sent to France on the 2nd April, 1915. Just a month later on the 8th May, 1915 William was killed in action at the age of 19. His body was not found after the war and William is remembered on the Ieper (Menin Gate) Memorial to the Missing in Ieper city centre in Belgium.

Sapper Daniel Holingmode
112623

Daniel Holingmode was born at Dudley, Worcestershire in 1877. In 1897, he married Mary Ann Hickman at Dudley and in 1901 the couple were living at 29, Low Town, Dudley with their first child, a son named Daniel after his father. In 1911, the family were living as boarders with the Hopley family at Old Fallow Road, Cannock. The family had grown, with Florence having been born in 1902 at Dudley before they left for Cannock and it was there that Alice and Maud had been born in 1906 and 1910 respectively. The family was completed by James, born in 1913 and Edward born in 1915. By that time the family had moved to live at Huntington Terrace, Chadsmoor. Daniel was a coal miner working at Littleton Colliery, but when recruitment began for a Company of Tunnellers and Headers in 1915, he volunteered, joining the 175th Tunnelling Company, Royal Engineers at Chelsea on the 16th August, 1915 and being sent to France on the 26th August. Daniel served until the 2nd March, 1916 when he was badly wounded and taken to a Casualty Clearing Station where he died the next day at the age of 39. Daniel's body was buried at Lijssenthoek Military Cemetery in Belgium.

4. Chadsmoor

Private John Thomas Hollinshead
18045

John Hollinshead was born at Hednesford, Staffordshire in 1892. He was the eldest son of Thomas and Emily Hollinshead. Thomas was a coal miner from Hednesford and his wife hailed from Bradley, near Penkridge. Their first child, Ann was born at Hednesford in 1889, but the family then moved to live at Quarry Heath, Penkridge and it was here that Beatrice Lily was born in 1890. In 1901, the family had moved to Stone Cross, Penkridge and here Dorothy or Dolly and Eric were born in 1899 and 1900. In 1911, the family had moved to live at 49, Cannock Road, Chadsmoor, with John having become a coal miner at Littleton Colliery. On the 3rd September, 1914 John enlisted for service in the 1st Battalion, Grenadier Guards and on the 25th December, 1914 at St. Luke's Parish Church, Cannock he married Mary Jane Haddaway, becoming only the second soldier to marry at the Church since the outbreak of the war. On the 16th March, 1915, John was sent to serve on the Western Front, although he came home on leave in August 1916. Some seven weeks after rejoining his unit he was killed in action on the 26th September, 1916 at the age of 24. John's body was not found after the war and he is remembered on the Thiepval Memorial to the Missing on the Somme in France.

Private James Horton
11421

Charles Horton, a 26 year old labourer in an iron works from Wem, Shropshire married 17 year old Caroline Howard from Macclesfield, Cheshire at Wolstanton, in Staffordshire in 1867. In 1871 they were lodging with the Tyrren family at Harrison's House, Warrington Road, in Ince in Makerfield with their 2 year old son Leonard who had been born in Hanley, Staffordshire in 1869. Mary and Jane were born at Warrington in 1872 and 1876 before the family moved back to Wolstanton where Charles junior was born in 1879. In 1891 the family had moved again to live at 7, Lyme Street, Newcastle-under-Lyme and it was here that Ann was born in 1881, Susan in 1884 and James in 1889. In 1897 Charles senior died at the age of 57 and in 1899 Caroline Horton married William Gilford who lived in the house next door. This is where the family were living in 1901, although John Charles who was born in 1901 has the surname Horton. On the 17th April, 1910 James married Annie Rogers, a 27 year old widow, at St. Luke's

Parish Church, Cannock. The couple moved to live at 34, Church Street, Chadsmoor and the first of their two children, Caroline was born in 1910. James was a coal miner at Cannock and Leacroft Colliery, but in August, 1914 he decided to enlist, joining the 8th Battalion, North Staffordshire Regiment, and being sent to France on the 18th July, 1915. James served until the 12th April, 1918 when he was badly wounded and died a few hours later from his injuries at the age of 30. James's body was buried at Lijssenthoek Military Cemetery in Belgium.

Rifleman John Jones
7667

For details about John Jones see the entry on the same soldier under Hednesford.

Sergeant William Lacey
10000

William Lacey was born at Brooklyn, New York in 1888 and was the son of Mr and Mrs John Lacey, who were originally from Scotland. Not a great deal is known about William until 1907 when the 19 year old message boy decided to join the Royal Scots, doing so at Glencorse on the 14th March, 1907. He remained in Britain until the 19th January, 1909 when he was posted with the 1st Battalion to Allahabad in India. William was promoted to Lance Corporal on the 31st July, 1911 and due to exemplary conduct was permitted to extend his service to complete 12 years on the 25th May, 1914. He was promoted to Corporal on the 29th August, 1914. The Battalion returned to Britain on the 16th October, 1914 and William received leave until the 18th December, 1914 when he was posted to France. He served in France until the 17th January, 1915 when he was sent to the 1st East General Hospital in Cambridge, suffering from influenza. When he had recovered, William married Sarah Jane Bradley at Cannock Roman Catholic Church on the 6th July, 1915, the service conducted by Father William Rowley O' Keefe. A son was born on the 26th January, 1916 named William Howard Lacey. Meanwhile, William had returned to France with the 2nd Battalion on the 1st October, 1915, where he went through the stages of promotion again, reaching the rank of Sergeant on the 19th January, 1916. On the 14th July, 1916 William was badly wounded in the abdomen and was brought back to 21 Casualty Clearing Station for treatment. At first he appeared to be doing well, but then William had a relapse and died from his injuries, aged 28, on the 25th July, 1916.

William's body was buried at La Neuville British Cemetery, Corbie, between Albert and Amiens on the Somme in France.

Rifleman Enoch Lane
R/12419

In 1870 John Henry Lane, a 21 year old Shropshire miner from Dawley married the 21 year old Emily Churm at Wellington in Shropshire. The couple chose to live in Dawley and by 1881 they had had five children, Thomas born in 1872, Ann born in 1874, Jane Ellen born in 1876 who was both deaf and dumb, Alice born in 1877 and Enoch born in 1881. The family moved to live at McGhie Street, Hednesford, just before Enoch was born. In 1891, they had moved again to live at Mount Street, Hednesford. Two more children had been born, Alexander in 1883 and Edith in 1888, and Thomas had joined his father as a coal miner. By 1901, only Jane, now a dressmaker, Enoch, working as a horse driver down the pit, Alexander, working with Enoch and Edith remained at home. In 1904, Enoch married Hannah Davies at Madeley in Shropshire, although the couple moved to live at 103, John Street, Chadsmoor, and it was here that Alice was born in 1905. Enoch enlisted with the King's Royal Rifle Corps in 1914 and he was sent to France on the 12th September, 1915. He served until the 3rd May, 1917 when he was posted as missing in action, it later being presumed that he had died on that date. At the time of his death, Enoch was 36 and his body was not found at the end of the war. Enoch is remembered on the Arras Memorial to the Missing in France.

Lance Corporal Samuel Lane
11453

In 1888 at Cannock, Staffordshire, William Lane a coal miner from Wolverhampton married Sarah Jane Bould. The groom was 25 and his bride, who came from Brownhills, Staffordshire, was 18. The couple set up home at Burgoyne Street, Chadsmoor and their first child, Mary was born in the same year. In 1889 Samuel was born and he was followed by Thomas in 1890. By 1901 there had been a significant increase in the size of the family with the births of Annie in 1892, Betsy in 1894, Jane in 1896, William born in 1898 and Lily in 1900. In 1911, the Lane family had moved to live at Church Street, Chadsmoor, where Thomas was a coal loader at Cannock and Leacroft Colliery and William was working on the pit bank. There had been four additions to the family with the births of Nellie in 1902, Clara in 1905, Loris born in 1907 and Irene in 1909. Samuel had left home and in 1911 was working as a coal miner in Darfield, Yorkshire. He was living with Jesse Hodgson and his wife Lily at 16, Queen Street, Darfield along with Trilby Macefield, Jesse's niece, and two other lodgers, Tom Sutton and Frank Woodyatt. On the 27th August, 1914 Samuel enlisted in the Army at Pontefract, joining the 6th Battalion, Yorks and Lancaster Regiment. He was transferred to the 11th Battalion on the 1st March, 1915 and was promoted to Lance Corporal on the 16th May. The Battalion were sent to serve in the Balkans on the 2nd July, 1915 and on the 27th October, 1915 Samuel was badly wounded, suffering a gunshot wound to his left foot. He was invalided back to England and on the 9th February, 1916 he was discharged from the Army as he was no longer physically fit to serve. Samuel died in Kinver Sanitorium from pulmonary pneumonia in April 1921 at the age of 32. His family requested a grant from his regiment to help with funeral expenses as they were in "straightened circumstances". Samuel was buried at St. Peter's Churchyard, Hednesford.

Lance Corporal Thomas Lane
13067

Thomas Lane was the younger brother of Samuel Lane. He was born at Chadsmoor in 1891 and like most young men of working age in the district became a coal miner, in Thomas's case at Cannock and Leacroft Colliery. In September, 1914 following the outbreak of war, Thomas enlisted with the 8th Battalion, South Staffordshire Regiment and he was sent to France on the 14th July, 1915. He was wounded on the 14th August and sent back to England to recuperate, before returning to France where he trained as a specialist bomber. On the 23rd April, 1917 Thomas was killed in action at the age of 26. His body was not identified after the war and Thomas is remembered on the Arras Memorial to the Missing in France.

Private Albert Henry Lawton
9601

For details about Albert Henry Lawton see the entry on the same soldier under Hednesford.

Private Fred Leach
13938

Fred Leach was the brother of Ernest Leach, whose name appears on the Methodist Church memorial in Chadsmoor. Fred was also a miner and attested on the 1st September, 1914, joining the Yorks and Lancs Regiment. He was posted to the depot at Frensham on the 4th October, 1914 and was then posted to the 8th Battalion, where he became an unpaid Lance Corporal. On the 1st February, 1916 he was posted to the 11th Battalion as a Lance Corporal before losing his stripe and being posted to the 10th Battalion. Fred appears to have had some problems with punctuality having been absent or overstaying a pass on no fewer than five occasions and it was this that finally cost him his stripe. He was in England from the 1st September, 1914 until the 26th August, 1915 before being sent to France. He served in France until the 27th December, 1915 when he was sent home suffering from neurasthenia. His convalescence lasted until the 2nd May, 1916 when he was once again sent to serve in France. Fred was killed in action on the 3rd July, 1916 during the Battle of the Somme and after the war, his body was not recovered and Fred is remembered on the Thiepval Memorial to the Missing on the Somme in France. On the 12th January, 1915, Fred had married Emily Westwood at Denaby Main in Yorkshire, with her address given as 122, Doncaster Road, Denaby Main, in Rotherham. A daughter named Freda was born early in 1917. Her mother received 15 shillings per week as a pension for her and her daughter.

Private Bert Leach
11620

Bert Leach was the third brother to be killed during the Great War. In 1911, he was boarding with Eliza Alcott and her granddaughter Jane Priest at 15, Newtown Road, Bedworth in Warwickshire. Also lodging there were Noah and Hebra Pool and James Alcott, the grandson of Eliza. Bert worked as a coal tub filler in a local colliery. When war broke out, Bert enlisted at Nuneaton in 1914 and elected to join the 2nd Battalion of the Ox and Bucks Light Infantry, being sent to France on the 26th May, 1915. He was killed in action on the 20th October, 1915 during the Battle of Loos and his body is buried at Chocques Military Cemetery in France.

Sapper William Henry Newell
155850

On the 23rd October, 1895 at St. Luke's Parish Church, Cannock William Henry Newell a 31 coal miner from Shropshire, married Jane Broom a 29 year old from Pelsall, Staffordshire. The couple set up home on Huntington Terrace Road, Chadsmoor, and living with them were Ellen and Charlotte Broom, who were Jane's children. Their first child as a couple was William Henry junior who was born at Chadsmoor in 1895 and he was followed in 1897 by Annie. However, in 1903 Jane Newell died at the age of 37, and the family moved to live at 147, John Street, Chadsmoor. In 1911, Charlotte was working as a domestic servant and William Henry junior was employed as a road boy down the pit. At Easter 1915, William Henry junior enlisted with the South Staffordshire Regiment and was sent to France on the 1st October, 1915. He then transferred to the 251st Tunnelling Company, Royal Engineers and served until the 15th November, 1916 when he was killed in action at the age of 21. After the war William's body was not found and he is remembered on the Loos Memorial to the Missing in France.

Private Joseph Nicholls
7615

For details about Joseph Nicholls see the entry on the same soldier under Hednesford.

Private James Platt
18202

Henry Platt a coal miner from Leicestershire married Elizabeth Smart from Ettinshall, Staffordshire at Dudley in 1864. They moved to Back, Frost Street in Bilston and it was here that Joseph was born in 1865 and Sarah in 1868. John followed in 1872 and George in 1874 before the family moved to live at Green Heath, Hednesford. Here Elizabeth was born in 1875, William in 1875 and James in 1879. By 1891 they had moved again, this time to New Street, Chadsmoor and in the meantime Charlotte had been born in 1882. They also had two lodgers with them, William Hinton and William Jakes. In 1901 James was living at Church Street, Bridgtown where he was lodging with the Moreton family and working as a coal miner's loader. On the 27th July, 1902 James married Sarah Jane Ward at St. Luke's Parish Church, Cannock. The couple moved to live at Church Street, Chadsmoor and in 1903 a son, James Henry junior was born. In 1905 Hilda was born followed by George in 1908, Percy in 1912 and Cyril in 1915. In early 1915, James enlisted with the 7th Battalion, South Staffordshire Regiment and he was sent to Gallipoli on the 11th September, 1915. From there he went to Egypt and then to the Western Front in July 1916. James served until the 13th October, 1917 when he was killed in action at the age of 38. His body was not found after the war and James is remembered on the Tyne Cot Memorial to the Missing, near Ieper in Belgium.

Private Frank Reynolds
22778

In 1881 at Dudley, Worcestershire William Reynolds a 24 year old Police Constable from Dawley, Shropshire married Mary Jane Keay, a 20 year old from West Bromwich, Staffordshire. The couple moved into 12, Church Terrace, Smethwick. Ten years later they were living at 190, Rolfe Street, Smethwick and they had started a family, with the births of Samuel in 1882, William in 1885, Frank in 1887 and Gertrude in 1889. Yet in 1901, William had given up policing and was working as a stationary engine driver. The family had increased with the births of Robert in 1892, Thomas in 1894, Marianne in 1896, Elizabeth in 1898 and Arthur in 1900. They had moved around the area, from Smethwick to Cannock, to West Bromwich and back to Smethwick. They were at that time living at Britannia Place, 12, Oldbury Road, Smethwick. In 1907, Frank married Minnie Elizabeth Wright at Foleshill, Warwickshire. She like her husband was aged 20, and Minnie came from Stoke Golding in Leicestershire. Initially the couple lived at Bedworth, Warwickshire and it was here that Frank Edgar was born in 1908 and Minnie Elizabeth in 1910. The family then moved to live at 49, Alfred Street, Bloxwich, but by 1912 they had moved to live at 113, Pye Green Road, Chadsmoor. It was here that Norman was born in 1912 and Marian was born in 1914. Frank worked at Harrison's Colliery at Great Wyrley. Frank enlisted in the Army in November, 1914 joining the 2nd Battalion, Grenadier Guards and served on the Western Front. He was gassed and spent some time recovering before returning to his Battalion, and only received one short period of leave during his service. On the 27th August, 1918 at the age of 31, Frank was killed in action. His body was buried at Mory Abbey Military Cemetery, Mory between Arras and Bapaume in France. Frank's father William served in the ambulance service for 31 years as a volunteer and he had also tried to enlist in the Army but was turned down due to his age.

Private William Henry Sockett
14319

For details about William Henry Sockett see the entry on the same soldier under Hednesford.

Private William Southwick
18316

Early in 1892, Stephen Southwick a furnace stoker from Hanley in Staffordshire married Matilda Marden at Dudley, although she came from London. In 1901, they were living at 17, Foundry Street, Moxley near Wednesbury, along with their four children, William, Stephen, David and Arthur. By 1911, the family had grown with the births of Eva Florence, Ethel and Samuel and they were now living at 1, Bull Lane, Moxley. Stephen senior was still engaged as a boiler stoker whilst William and Stephen junior were also working in the iron works. David however was making nuts and bolts. In 1913, William married Sarah Hartshorn at West Bromwich, but the young couple then moved to Chadsmoor and their only child, named William after his father was born at Cannock in 1913. When the Great War broke out, William answered the call of Lord Kitchener and enlisted with the 1st Battalion, the South Staffordshire Regiment. He was sent to France and was killed in action on the first day of the Battle of the Somme, the 1st July, 1916 during the attack on Mametz. William was 23 at the time of his death. His body is buried at Dantzig Alley British Cemetery at Mametz in France.

Private Fred Spinks
50010

For details about Fred Spinks see the entry on the same soldier under Hednesford.

Private Arthur Stanton
15545

Reuben Stanton, a coal miner from West Bromwich married Sarah Ann Hill from Hill Top, Staffordshire at West Bromwich in late 1885. In 1891 the couple were living in Burgoyne Street, Chadsmoor in Cannock with Arthur who was four and Walter who was two along with Harriet Stanton, the widowed mother of Reuben. The two boys had both been born at Hill Top. Ten years later the family was now living in Cecil Street, Chadsmoor, and had grown with the births of Frank, Mary, Alice and Selina. Reuben was still working as a coal miner, whilst Arthur was also working down the pit as a horse driver. In early 1908, Reuben died at the age of only 49 and three years later, his widow was living at Moreton Street, Chadsmoor. Arthur was now a coal miner hewer, whilst his brother Walter was his loader. Frank was working as a colliery ropeman. Living with them were two more children, Nellie and Reuben junior, along with Sarah Ann's widowed brother Thomas Hill. On the 12th May, 1913 at St. Luke's Parish Church in Cannock, Arthur married Sophia E. Leach. Their first child, Kathleen was born at Cannock in 1915 and their second child, Raymond was born in the town in 1916. Meanwhile, their father had joined the army, electing to join the 8th Battalion, the South Staffordshire Regiment and he was sent to France on the 14th July, 1915. He served in France until the 16th May, 1917 when he was killed in action at the age of 29. His body was not identified after the war and Arthur is remembered on the Arras Memorial to the Missing in France.

Rifleman Alfred Swann
7244

Alfred Swann was born in 1885 at Ashton-under-Lyme, Lancashire. He was the eldest son of Joseph and Emma Swann. Joseph who was a hatter had married Emma Wardle at Ashton in 1883 and in 1891 they were living at 3, Rochfort Street, Hyde and it was here that Alfred was born along with his brother Joseph who was born in 1887. The family also had three lodgers staying with them, Mary Cash and her two children Abraham and Esther. Emma Swann took in washing in order to help ends meet. In 1911, Alfred had moved to live and work in Chadsmoor. He was now 26 and was a coal miner, lodging with George Price, a 68 year old jobbing gardener, at 63 Cannock Road, Chadsmoor. Also living in the house were George's son Edward, his wife Emma and their three children, Fanny, Sarah and William. Alfred in all probability was a member of the Hednesford Territorials, and it would seem likely that he joined the Army before the outbreak of war in August, 1914. He enlisted with the 2nd Battalion, Royal Irish Rifles and was sent to France on the 15th August, 1914. On the 26th October, 1914 Alfred was killed in action at the age of 29. Alfred's body was not identified after the war and he is remembered on the Le Touret Memorial to the Missing in France.

Corporal Edmund Thurstance
18551

For details about Edmund Thurstance see the entry on the same soldier under Hednesford.

Private George Turner
16887

John Turner a platelayer from Outwood, Staffordshire married his wife Sarah around 1870. In 1881, the family were living at Derrington, near Seighford in Staffordshire and at that time they had four children, Thomas, John, Sarah and George. George was born at Outwoods in 1880. However, in 1888 Sarah died at the age of 37 and in 1891 John Turner was living at 12, Broad Eye, Stafford and he was working as a railway servant. Only George and his sister Mary were living at home and both were still at school. On the 11th January, 1898 George enlisted in the Army, joining the North Staffordshire Regiment, firstly with the 1st Battalion and then transferring to the 2nd Battalion. He was a good soldier and was awarded 3 good conduct badges. His medical history shows a mixture of ailments from herpes to sore throats and scabies. On the 27th October, 1899 George landed in India, where medical problems continued, such as ague, jaundice, bronchial catarrh and sore throats. He returned to England on the 26th January, 1906 and was placed on the Army Reserve List. On the 6th May, 1906 George married Jessie Green at St. Peter's Parish Church, Hednesford. George began work as a coal miner and the couple set up home at Moss Street, Chadsmoor. In 1907 Daisy Ellen was born, followed by Frances Lily in 1909, Agnes Jessie in 1910 and George William in 1913. Following the outbreak of war in August, 1914 George enlisted again, but chose to join the 2nd Battalion, Lincolnshire Regiment and he was sent to France on the 4th May, 1915. He served until the 4th March, 1917 when at the age of 36, George was killed in action. After the war George's body was not identified and he is remembered on the Thiepval Memorial to the Missing on the Somme in France.

Private William Henry Vale
40461

In 1888 at Cannock, David Vale, a 35 year old farm labourer from Tewkesbury, Gloucestershire, married Emma Broom, an 18 year old from Pelsall, Staffordshire. The couple set up home at Huntington Terrace, Chadsmoor. However, by 1901 David was described as a pauper, and William had been born just two years before in 1899. In 1901 Lizzie was born and in 1902, at the age of 50 David died, leaving a pregnant widow and two children. Emma duly gave birth in 1903 to David. In 1911, the family was living at 147, John Street, Chadsmoor, with Emma working as a housekeeper as well as bringing up three children who were all at school. In 1912, William left school and started work as a miner at West Cannock Colliery. However, in 1916 William enlisted under the Derby Scheme, but was not called up until 1917, when he joined the 6th Battalion, Leicestershire Regiment, and he was sent to France in May, 1917. He served until the 14th November, 1917 when he was killed in action during the Battle of Passchendaele. At the time of his death, William was 18 years old and his body was buried at Tyne Cot Cemetery near Ieper in Belgium.

Private Joseph Waldron
20513

Thomas Waldron, a coal miner from Worcester, married Elizabeth Wilkes, also from Worcester at Bromsgrove in 1868. Their first two children, Thomas and Charles were born at Worcester, before the family decided to move to Huntington Terrace, Chadsmoor, around 1878. In the census of 1891, the family now stood at eight children, with William, Martha, Elizabeth, Reuben, Joseph and Arthur having been born at Chadsmoor. Thomas and Charles were now both coal miners along with their father. By 1901, two more children had been born, James and Jane, but only six children now remained at home. William was working as a hauling engine driver and Reuben was an edge tool striker. On the 24th December, 1910, Joseph, now a 22 year old miner married Fanny Oakley, aged 24, from Walsall at St. Luke's Parish Church, Cannock. The couple moved to live at Church Street, Chadsmoor and two children were born, Gladys in 1912 and Gwendoline in 1914. Joseph joined the Army in January 1916, enlisting with the 14th Battalion, Northumberland Fusiliers and he was sent to France in anticipation of the Big Push. On the 14th August, 1916 Joseph was killed in action at the age of 27. His body was not recovered after the war and Joseph is remembered on the Arras Memorial to the Missing in France.

2nd Lieutenant James Henry Westwood

On the 7th June, 1897 at St. Luke's Parish Church, Cannock, James Westwood, a 23 year old coal miner from Bilston, Staffordshire married Sarah Ann Edge, aged 21, from St. George's, Shropshire. The couple settled down at Upper Landywood, Great Wyrley, with James Henry being born in 1899, and his sister Elsie in 1900. By 1911, the family had moved to live at 245, Cannock Road, Chadsmoor, but before they left Wyrley, three more children had been born, Ruby, Annie and William. With the exception of William who was born in 1907, the other children were still at school. James Henry clearly excelled at school, and he joined the Hednesford Territorials as an officer in the South Staffordshire Regiment. Although serving with the 3rd Battalion, James was attached to the 62nd Brigade Mortar Company and was sent to France in 1916. On the 12th July, 1916 James was posted as missing in action, the hope being expressed that he had been taken prisoner. Prayers were said by Father O'Keefe at the Church of the Sacred Heart in Cannock, but after twelve months it was assumed that James had died on that date. At the time of his death, James was only 17 years of age and as his body was not found after the war, he is remembered on the Thiepval Memorial to the Missing on the Somme in France.

Private William Wright
17009

In 1873 at Stafford, John Wright married Matilda Proynold. He was a drayman for a brewer and was born at Hopton, Staffordshire and she was from Ranton in Staffordshire. The couple lived at 51, Eastgate Street, Stafford and it was here that their children were born. The first was Mary born in 1874, followed by John in 1877 and William in 1881. Matilda was born in 1886 and Alice in 1890. Shortly after Alice's birth, the family moved to live at Huntington Terrace, Chadsmoor, where John began work as a colliery fireman. John junior worked as a labourer in a brickyard and Mary was employed in cutting off the bricks in the same yard. On the 8th April, 1901, William married Martha Cork at St. Luke's Parish Church, Cannock. The couple moved to live at 216, Cannock Road, Chadsmoor. William senior was working as a stallman at Littleton Collier. William junior was born in

4. Chadsmoor

1901 at Hednesford, followed by Martha and Olive. John, Lucy and Lizzie were born at Chadsmoor and Martha's two brothers, Joseph and George Cork, were also lodging with them. In September 1914, William volunteered to serve in the 9th Battalion, South Staffordshire Regiment. The Battalion went to Aldershot, then to Shorncliffe and finally to Oxney Park at Borden, Wiltshire. It was here that William was taken ill and he died in the hospital at Freshnam Borden on Saturday 5th June, 1915. His body was buried with full military honours. The service was held at the United Methodist Church, and conducted by the Reverend F.A. Steele and the Reverend G.J. Johnson. The procession then made its way to Cannock Cemetery where the firing party of the East Lancashire Regiment was led by Sergeant G.H. Wood. At the time of his death, William was 34 years of age.

Chapter 5

WIMBLEBURY

Private Stephen Barratt
37133

On the 10th July, 1891 at St. Luke's Parish Church, Cannock, Stephen Harry Barratt, a 21 year old coal miner from Bromstead Heath, Shropshire married the 18 year old Julia Hill from Bridgtown. The couple found a home at New Street, Bridgtown and they soon began a family with the birth of Rhoda in 1894. Leonard followed in 1896 and Harry Stephen in 1898, with Leah being born in 1900. Sadly Leah died in 1903, a year after the birth of Harold in 1902. By 1911, the family had moved to live at John Street, Wimblebury, and Leonard had started work as a coal miner trammer, while Stephen and Harold were still at school. Stephen was conscripted into the Army in 1917 and was sent to France in 1918, serving with the 9th Battalion, King's Own Yorkshire Light Infantry. He was killed in action on the 27th May, 1918 at the age of 19. After the war Stephen's body was not recovered and he is remembered on the Soissons Memorial to the Missing in France.

Lance Corporal Frederick Rushton
R/10975

For details about Frederick Rushton see the entry on the same soldier under Hednesford.

Private Edward Stevens
9308

For details about Edward Stevens see the entry on the same soldier under Hednesford.

Private Thomas Charles Thacker
R/10974

For details about Thomas Charles Thacker see the entry on the same soldier under Hednesford.

Private William Henry Kimberley
9276

For details about William Henry Kimberley see the entry on the same soldier under Hednesford.

Private James Merrick
201298

For details about James Merrick see the entry on the same soldier under Hednesford.

Private Alfred Merrick
8303

For details about Alfred Merrick see the entry on the same soldier under Hednesford.

Private Richard Stephens
9302

For details about Richard Stephens see the entry on the same soldier under Hednesford.

Private John Stephens
9303

For details about John Stephens see the entry on the same soldier under Hednesford.

Private Edmund Tomkinson
16107

For details about Edmund Tomkinson see the entry on the same soldier under Hednesford.

Private Joseph Tomkinson
16933

For details about Joseph Tomkinson see the entry on the same soldier under Hednesford.

Private George Dyke
7894

For details about George Dyke see the entry on the same soldier under Hednesford.

Private Roland Mason
235018

For details about Roland Mason see the entry on the same soldier under Hednesford.

Corporal Joseph Edward Preece
18535

For details about Joseph Edward Preece see the entry on the same soldier under Hednesford.

Private Hyla Witton
18983

In 1894 at Lichfield, Staffordshire, James Witton a 21 year old coal miner from Sedgley, Staffordshire married the 23 year old Mary Hanslow from Ogley Hay, Staffordshire. The couple set up a home at The Spinney, Burntwood and it was here that their first child Eunice was born in 1896. She was followed in 1897 by twins, Hyla and Harold and then in 1900, John was born. Samuel was next in 1904 and Edith completed the family in 1909. By this time, Hyla was working as a nipper down the pit and his twin brother was employed as a rock picker on the pit bank. Shortly after this, Hyla left Burntwood and settled in Wimblebury where he worked as a miner. However in early 1915, he volunteered for the Army, joining the 1st Battalion, South Staffordshire Regiment, being sent to France on the 8th December, 1915. Hyla served until the 13th May, 1917 when he died from wounds at the age of 20. Hyla's body was not found after the war and he is remembered on the Arras Memorial to the Missing in France.

Private Samuel Harley
11959

For details about Samuel Harley see the entry on the same soldier under Hednesford.

Private Albert Henry Lawton
9601

For details about Albert Henry Lawton see the entry on the same soldier under Hednesford.

Private Joshua Thomas
16569

For details about Joshua Thomas see the entry on the same soldier under Hednesford.

Private George Ward
51522

For details about George Ward see the entry on the same soldier under Hednesford.

Chapter 6

HEATH HAYES

Private William Thomas Archer
19300

In 1877, at Cannock, Staffordshire, Edward Archer a 19 year old colliery stoker from Birmingham, Warwickshire, married the 16 year old Eliza Ann Caroline Raybould from Gentleshaw, Staffordshire. The couple moved to live at Broomhill, Cannock to begin with, but soon moved to Bank Street, Heath Hayes. From the birth places of their children it would appear that Edward moved from job to job. Albert was the oldest, born at Leacroft in 1882. George was born at Heath Hayes in 1885 and Blanche was born at Cannock in 1887. Then it was back to Leacroft for the birth of Ernest in 1888 and back to Heath Hayes for the birth of Cecil in 1891. Lily was born at Norton Canes in 1895, as was William Thomas in 1897 and Mabel in 1899. Then it was back to 171, Wimblebury Road, Heath Hayes for the birth of Henry in 1902. The boys all found work down the pit and in 1911 Cecil was working as a horse driver and William was an underground labourer at the Coppice Colliery, Heath Hayes. On the 29th April, 1915 William enlisted with the Royal Army Medical Corps at Hednesford and was sent to Aldershot. However, on the 17th June, 1915, William transferred to the 1st Battalion, Northamptonshire Regiment. He was at Gillingham when he was confined to barracks for five days for stealing apples from an orchard and damaging fruit trees. On the 29th September, 1915 the Battalion sailed for France, and William joined his Battalion in the field on the 4th October, 1915. On the 28th December, 1915 at the age of 18, William was killed in action. After the war, William's body was not recovered and he is remembered on the Loos Memorial to the Missing in France.

Lance Corporal Harold Henry Bird
22524

Joseph Henry Bird a 22 year old miner rock blower from Pensnett, Staffordshire married 19 year old Jane Wale from Brierley Hill, at Stourbridge, Worcestershire in 1894. Their first child, Harold Henry was born at Kidderminster, Worcestershire in 1897 and their second child Alice Gertrude was born in the same town in 1899. The family then moved to Brownhills, where Arthur John was born in 1902, and then went on to Aldridge where Herbert Horace was born in 1905. Next was Walsall Wood where Doris Mary was born in 1908 and Lilian Sarah in 1911, before the family moved to live at 19, Lyndhurst Road, Heath Hayes. Harold was a drummer with the Heath Hayes Boy Scouts Group and was a member of the Heath Hayes Primitive Methodist Church. He worked as a miner at the Coppice Colliery, Heath Hayes. On the 28th January, 1915 Harold enlisted with the 4th Battalion, Grenadier Guards, being sent to France late in 1915. On the 1st December, 1917 Harold was killed in action at the age of 23. He was described as a "gallant soldier". After the war, Harold's body was not found and he is remembered on the Cambrai Memorial to the Missing at Louverval in France. A memorial service was held at the Primitive Methodist Church for Harold. Harold's father served in the Military Police at Aldershot during the war.

Private Frederick Broome
G/62970

On the 16th February, 1890 Walter Broome a 23 year old coal miner from Worcestershire, married Priscilla Spencer from Walsall at St. Luke's Parish Church, Cannock. The couple were living at Heath Hayes, and their first child, James, was born here in 1891. Walter was born in 1893, Samuel in 1896, Frederick in 1899 and Edwin in 1903. In 1901 the family was living at Hednesford Road, Heath Hayes but by 1911, they had moved to Hednesford Road, Norton Canes. The boys had all started work down the pit by the outbreak of the Great War, but in 1917 Frederick was conscripted into the Army, initially with the North Staffordshire Regiment, before being transferred to the 7th Battalion, London Regiment, and being sent to France in July, 1918. On the 28th August, 1918, Frederick was killed in action at the age of 19. His body was buried at Suzanne Military Cemetery Number 3, near Albert on the Somme. On the 8th April, 1920, James Broome asked for Frederick's medals to be sent to him at Railway Street, Norton Canes.

Private Eli Bott
23528

For details about Eli Bott see the entry on the same soldier under Hednesford.

Private Isaac Brown
19281

John Henry Brown, a 19 year old miner from Boney Hay, Staffordshire married Muriel Ellen Grant, aged 17 from Lichfield in that city in 1889. They set up home at Rugeley Road, Burntwood and it was here that John Isaac was born in 1891. Also living with them were George and Susan Grant, Muriel's parents and her sister Jessie. By 1901, the family had moved to live at High Street, Norton Canes. The family had grown with the births of Leonard, Herbert and Ernest, all born at Boney Hay and Nathan, born at Norton Canes. Ernest died in 1902, the same year that his sister Elsie was born. Gladys was born in 1907 while the family were still living at Norton Canes, but Jack was born in 1910, just after the family had moved to live at 39, Wimblebury Road, Heath Hayes. Isaac, Leonard and Herbert had all started work as horse keepers down the pit, Isaac working at the Wimblebury pit of the Cannock and Rugeley Colliery. On the 17th April, 1915 Isaac enlisted with the Royal Army Medical Corps, being sent to Aldershot on the following day. On the 23rd May, he transferred to the Northamptonshire Regiment, joining the 1st Battalion. He was sent to France on the 29th September, 1915 and served until the 28th December, 1915 when he was killed in action at the age of 23. Isaac's body was not found after the war and he is remembered on the Loos Memorial to the Missing in France. Isaac was killed alongside his best friend Private William Thomas Archer.

Lance Corporal Charles Harrall Clayton
19095

In 1878 at Stafford, George Clayton a 22 year old labourer from Stafford married Sarah Ann Harrall from Hopton, Staffordshire. In 1881 the couple were living at Hopton, and it was here that Edwin and Louisa were both born. The family then moved to 3, Kenerdine Street, Stafford where they were lodging with Eliza Gask, a 28 year old widow and her three children. At Stafford, Edward, Harry and Charles were born. George was now a farm labourer. In 1901 the family had

6. Heath Hayes

moved to live at Moreton Street, Chadsmoor, where George was working as a banksman on the pit top, as was Edwin. Harry was a horse driver below ground, whilst Charles was at school. By 1911, only Charles was still living with his parents, and they had moved to live at 2, Cross Row, John Street Chadsmoor. On the 25th December 1912, at St. Luke's Parish Church, Cannock Charles married Elsie Poxon, with the couple moving to Heath Hayes. It was here that Leslie was born in 1914 and Charles was born in 1915. Charles enlisted soon after the birth of his second son, joining the 16th Battalion, Northumberland Fusiliers, and he was sent to Gallipoli on the 13th September, 1915. From there he served in Egypt, and then the battalion was sent to the Western Front. On the 27th February, 1918, this hard working and popular NCO was killed in action at the age of 26. After the war, Charles' body was not found and he is remembered on the Tyne Cot Memorial to the Missing near Ieper in Belgium.

Gunner Robert Coates
251189

Enoch Coates, a coal miner from Devizes, Wiltshire married Mary Ann Cockayne, from Norton Canes, Staffordshire at Wolverhampton in 1867. Their first child, George was born in Norton Canes in 1868, before the family moved to live at Carlton in Lindrick, Nottinghamshire where Ada was born in 1870, although sadly she died just a year later. Emily who was deaf and dumb was born at Carlton in 1872, and then the family moved to Mexborough in Yorkshire, although Mary Ann went back to Norton Canes for the birth of Samuel in 1879. Enoch junior was born at Mexborough in 1882, before the family moved back to the Midlands to Wimblebury Road, Heath Hayes, although it would appear that Enoch and Mary Ann had separated as he was living on his own with Emily, Samuel and Enoch. George who was now married had also moved to live on the Wimblebury Road. Intriguingly, Robert was born at Heath Hayes in 1898, and was perhaps the son of Emily. Enoch senior was described as his grandfather. Enoch senior died at the age of 73, and in 1911, Emily, Enoch and Robert were living with Mary Ann at 3 House, 3 Court, Short Acre Street, Walsall. Mary Ann was working as a charwoman, Emily as a domestic servant, Enoch was a stallman coal miner, with Robert employed as an errand boy. Also living with them was John Coates, a 21 year old colliery horse driver born at Walsall. Robert was conscripted in to the Army in 1918, joining the Royal Field Artillery. He died, probably from influenza at the age of 21 on the 17th January, 1919. He is buried in Heath Hayes churchyard.

Private William Cockayne
9465

William Cockayne was born at Leeds, Yorkshire in 1898, and was the second son of Samuel and Jane Cockayne. This couple had married at Cannock in 1890, although they both originated from Walsall. Their first child, Annie was born in the town in 1891, before the family moved to Yorkshire. While they were living in Leeds, Samuel was born in 1895, followed by William and then Ada in 1899 and Elizabeth in 1901. At that point the family were living at 2, Somerset Street, Leeds. Jane died and the family moved to live at Bank Street, Heath Hayes. On the 12th April, 1909 Annie married Harry Bott at St. Luke's Parish Church, Cannock, with the couple moving to live on the Cannock Road, Heath Hayes. However, in early 1911, Samuel died at the age of 52. Samuel junior and Ada moved in with Annie and her husband, whilst William lodged with the Smith family at Newlands Lane, Heath Hayes. By this time he was engaged as a haulage boy at the Fair Lady Colliery. William also joined the 2nd North Midland Field Company, Royal Engineers at Norton Canes, which was a Territorial unit. Just before the outbreak of the Great War, although only 16, William joined the 2nd Battalion, South Staffordshire Regiment, and on the declaration of war, the Regiment was sent to France on the 12th August, 1914. On the 28th October, 1914 William was killed in action at the age of only 17. His body was buried by Sergeant A.F. Saxton of the Royal Berkshire Regiment, although at the end of the war, William's body was not found. William is remembered on the Ieper (Menin Gate) Memorial to the Missing in Ieper city centre in Belgium.

Private Thomas Henry Dyke
84565

John Dyke, a 19 year old coal miner from Wolverhampton married Sarah Jane Mason, also 19, from Bilston at Cannock in 1891. The couple's first child, William was born the following year at Heath Hayes. The family was living at 18, Hednesford Road, and it was here that Thomas Henry or Harry was born in 1896. He was followed by John in 1900, Mary in 1902, Daisy in 1906 and Violet in 1908. The family also had a lodger, Benjamin Mason, Sarah's brother living with them in 1911. It would appear that Harry joined the Army in 1916, under the Derby Scheme, initially joining the Royal Army Service Corps, but he later transferred to the Machine Gun Corps. He was serving in this unit when he was

6. Heath Hayes

killed in action on the 10th August, 1917 at the age of 20, during the Battle of Passchendaele. After the war his body was not identified and Harry is remembered on the Ieper (Menin Gate) Memorial to the Missing in Ieper city centre in Belgium.

Private Samuel Evans
40057

David and Ellen Evans were married in 1871. David came from Newtown in Wales and his wife came from Birmingham, Warwickshire. Having married the couple settled down in Lancashire and William was born at Carnforth in 1874. At this time David was an engine driver at an iron works. The family moved back to Staffordshire briefly and Edward was born there in 1876, before they moved north again, with Henry born at Carnforth in 1879 and David junior born at Barrow in 1881. They then moved to Chapeltown, Yorkshire where Joseph was born in 1884 and then they settled back at Carnforth and it was here that Walter was born in 1885 and then to Barrow for the births of Mary in 1887, John in 1888 and Emma in 1890. Albert was born at Barrow in 1892, Jane in 1894 and Samuel in 1896. By 1901 the family had moved again, this time to Burton-on-Trent in Staffordshire, where David senior was working as an iron fitter's labourer, while David junior, Joseph and Walter were all working as colliery labourers. By 1911, the family had moved to live at 316, Hednesford Road, Heath Hayes. Albert and Samuel were both horse drivers in a colliery and in 1910, Thomas Abel had been born. Samuel joined the Hednesford Territorials and when the Great War began, he joined the 1/5th Battalion, South Staffordshire Regiment, before transferring to the 10th Battalion, Worcestershire Regiment. He was sent to France and was killed in action on the 31st October, 1916 at the age of 20. At the end of the war, Samuel's body was not found and he is remembered on the Thiepval Memorial to the Missing on the Somme in France.

Lance Corporal Walter Evans
8199

Walter Evans was the older brother of Samuel. He was born at Carnforth, Lancashire in 1885 and worked as a coal miner. When the family moved to Heath Hayes, Walter joined the Hednesford Territorials and joined the 1/5th Battalion, South Staffordshire Regiment on the outbreak of war. Walter was sent to France on the

5th March, 1915 and served until the 13th October, 1915 when he was killed in action during the charge at the Hohenzollern Redoubt during the Battle of Loos. At the time of his death, Walter was 30 years of age. After the war, Walter's body was not identified and he is remembered on the Loos Memorial to the Missing in France.

Private Oliver George Eccleshall
12533

In 1887 at Birmingham, Warwickshire George Eccleshall a brass founder's warehouseman from Birmingham, aged 20, married Florence Rathbone, also aged 20 and from Birmingham. She was the daughter of John Rathbone, the manager of an iron foundry. The couple lived at 8, St. Martin's Row, Birmingham with the bride's widowed father and her brother William, a mineral water maker. It was here that Oliver was born in 1890, with his shortlived twin sister, Florence. In 1901 the family had moved to Court 5, Great Charles Street, Birmingham. George was now a warehouse clerk, and the couple had added to their family with the births of Thomas in 1898 and May in 1899. Herbert was born in 1906, John in 1907, Florence in 1908 and Violet in 1911 and they had moved again to live at 12, Friston Street, Birmingham. There is no strong evidence to link Oliver to Heath Hayes, but he joined the Army in 1914, enlisting with the 9th Battalion, Devonshire Regiment and he was sent to France on the 27th July, 1915. Oliver was killed in action at the age of 25 on the 30th September, 1915. His body was not found after the war and Oliver is remembered on the Loos Memorial to the Missing in France.

Lance Corporal Richard Foster
21488

In 1890, Henry Foster, a 24 year old coal miner from Great Wyrley, Staffordshire married the 19 year old Eliza Burrows from Bilston. The couple set up home at Bank Street, Heath Hayes. In 1891, their first child, Albert was born, followed by Richard in 1893, Florence in 1896, Frank in 1898 and Ethel in 1900. By 1911, the family had moved to 79, Gorsemoor Road, Heath Hayes and another daughter, Doris, had been born in 1908. The family also had a lodger a 19 year old coal miner named Samuel Evans. By this time both Albert and Richard had started work as coal miner horse drivers and Frank was working as a coal miner

6. Heath Hayes

fitter. Richard joined the Army on the 2nd January, 1915, enlisting with Grenadier Guards and he was sent to France on the 5th October, 1915. He served at Ieper and in 1916 was wounded during the Battle of the Somme, being sent back to hospital at Portsmouth. On his return to the Western Front, he again served on the Somme, at Ieper and at Arras before he was wounded for a second time. Upon recovery in 1920, he was discharged, but died from his wounds shortly afterwards, and was buried at St. John's Churchyard, Heath Hayes.

2nd Lieutenant Edwin Thomas Gwyther

William James Gwyther, a 30 year old teacher from Clifton, Gloucestershire married 23 year old Louisa Amelia Gillingham, from Ealing, Middlesex who was also a teacher at Chertsey, Surrey in 1865. The couple moved to live at Monmouthshire where their first child, Louisa was born in 1867. The family then moved to live at Weston-super-Mare, Somerset where Elsie was born in 1871, and Frederick in 1872. A further move saw the family living at Retford, Nottinghamshire, where Laura was born in 1874, and then to Leeds where John was born in 1875. The next move was to Wimblebury Road School, Heath Hayes and it was here that Charles was born in 1878 and Edwin in 1880. In 1891, the family was living at Bank Street, Heath Hayes, and by this time William had given up teaching and was working as a colliery clerk. His wife continued to teach, and Laura had also begun work as a pupil teacher. John was working as a locomotive engine cleaner, with Charles employed as a grocer's assistant. Edwin and his sister Mary, born at Heath Hayes in 1885, were still at school. In 1896, John decided to join the Army, enlisting with the 1st Battalion, South Staffordshire Regiment. Three years later, his father died at the age of 64. In 1901, the family were still at Bank Street, Heath Hayes, with Louisa Amelia still teaching and she had been joined in the profession by Louisa Emma and by Edwin. By 1911, Edwin was employed as an elementary school teaching assistant at Wimblebury Road School, and was making a reputation as a local sportsman, both as a footballer and cricketer. He played cricket for Cannock and Rugeley and Gentleshaw and became Captain of Heath Hayes where he played as a wicket keeper/batsman. Edwin was also the Secretary of the Cannock Chase Cricket League. Edwin joined the Army in December 1916 and served as a Private in both the South Staffordshire and Notts and Derbys Regiments before he was offered a commission in July 1917, joining the 6th Battalion, South Staffordshire Regiment as a 2nd Lieutenant. On the 28th August, 1917 at St. Peter's Parish Church, Hednesford Edwin married Agnes Hall. He left for France again shortly afterwards. On the 8th June, 1918 Edwin Gwyther died from gas poisoning at the age of 37. His body was buried at Etaples Military Cemetery in France.

Private John Henry Gwyther
4878

John Gwyther was the older brother of Edwin and was born at Leeds, Yorkshire in 1875. Unlike many of his sisters and brother and his parents who went into teaching, John opted to work first of all as a locomotive engine cleaner, before joining the 1st Battalion, South Staffordshire Regiment in 1896 at the age of 21. He fought in South Africa during the Boer War between 1899 and 1902, holding both the King's and Queen's medals for that campaign. In 1911, he was at Whittington Barracks, Lichfield, having transferred to the 2nd Battalion. When the war began, John was serving in South Africa, but on the Battalion's return to England he was posted to France on the 4th October, 1914. Just 25 days later, during the retreat from Mons, John was killed in action at the age of 39. After the war, his body was not found and John is remembered on the Ieper (Menin Gate) Memorial to the Missing in Ieper city centre in Belgium. John was the first soldier from Heath Hayes to die in the Great War.

Lieutenant William Charles Hand

In 1881, at Walsall, Staffordshire Samuel Hand an 18 year old coal miner from Brownhills, Staffordshire married Ann Amelia Franklin, aged 21 from Bloxwich. The couple set up home at Wimblebury Road, Heath Hayes and it was here that their first child, Edwin was born in 1884. He was followed by his brother William Charles in 1885 and sister Amelia in 1890. By 1901, the family had moved to live at Bank Street, Heath Hayes, and two more children had been born, Ellen in 1894 and Bertha in 1898. Edwin had started work as a coal miner's loader, and William was a pupil monitor. By 1911, William had married Mary Ann Crozier at Bridlington the previous year with the couple living at 127, Bank Street, Heath Hayes. He became a school master at Wimblebury Road School, and was also a good cricketer, playing for Heath Hayes Unity, and he succeeded Edwin Gwyther as Secretary of the Cannock Chase Cricket League. William was also a Committee Member of Hednesford Town Football Club. William volunteered to join the Army in 1916, enlisting with the Leicestershire Regiment and being sent to France on the 25th August, 1916. On the 30th October, 1917 William was commissioned as a 2nd Lieutenant with the South Staffordshire Regiment, later being promoted to

6. Heath Hayes

Lieutenant. In April, 1918 William was severely wounded and was taken to hospital in London. He received treatment and was discharged from the Army on the 26th May, 1919. In August, 1921, William attempted to begin teaching again, but was forced to stop due to ill health. He was admitted to the Military Hospital in Birmingham for further treatment but died there at the age of 36. William was buried at St. John's Churchyard, Heath Hayes with full military honours.

Sapper Aaron Hathaway
136290

Aaron Hathaway was born at Cannock in 1887. He was the fifth son of Aaron and Rebecca Hathaway, who both hailed from Dudley, Worcestershire. They had lived in Dudley for a number of years as a couple and their first four children were all born there, James in 1880, John the following year, Charles in 1883 and Arthur in 1895. The family then moved to live on the Heath Hayes Road, Wimblebury and it was here that Aaron junior was born and Alice in 1889. By 1901, they had moved to live at Chapel Street, Heath Hayes, where the four eldest boys were all working down the pit, while Aaron was an office boy at a colliery. Another child, Ethel had been born in 1897. In 1911, the family was still living at 54, Chapel Street, but only John, Alice, Ethel and Aaron were still at home. John was now a coal miner hewer like his father while Aaron junior was a coal miner's loader. Aaron later became a fireman at Littleton Colliery. Also living with them was John Priest, aged 19, who is described as an adopted son. On the 20th October, 1915 Aaron enlisted in the Army, joining the Tunnellers and Headers Company of the Royal Engineers. He was sent to France on the 13th November, 1915, and was remustered with the 173rd Tunnelling Company on the 15th May, 1916. He was on leave from the 22nd November, 1916 until the 2nd December. Aaron received 14 days under open arrest for being absent from roll call on the 29th July, 1917. On the 17th December, 1917 Aaron died from wounds at the age of 30. Aaron was buried at Bleuet Farm Cemetery, near Ieper in Belgium.

Driver William Holford
100840

William Holford was born at Hednesford in 1878, although it is not clear as to who were his parents. In 1881, he was living at Rainbow Street, Sedgley with Robert and Fanny Stroyd, his grandparents and Amy Chumbly, their 18 year old step daughter. In 1891 the 13 year old was living at Cecil Street, Chadsmoor with William and Caroline White, also described as grandparents, Geoffrey Rotchell, their 27 year old stepson and Amy Holford, William's 16 year old sister. In 1906, William got married and in 1911, he and his wife Jeanette were living at 114, Stafford Street, Heath Hayes with their three children, Eva born at Dorchester in 1907, Doris, born at Cannock in 1909 and William born at Heath Hayes in 1910. William volunteered for the Army, probably in 1915, joining the Royal Field Artillery and being sent to serve on the Western Front. William was badly wounded and discharged from the Army on the 8th October, 1916. His health was deteriorating and after a four year battle, William died on the 15th October, 1920 at the age of 42. He was buried with the help of the local branch of the National Federation of Discharged and Demobilized Soldiers and Sailors. The Last Post was played and over 40 people attended his funeral and dropped their buttonholes into the grave.

Lance Corporal Albert Jeffrey
18173

In 1881, a 26 year old Police Constable, John Jeffrey, born at Dinton, Buckinghamshire married Mary Cotton, aged 24. She was from Willenhall, Staffordshire and the marriage took place at Dudley. Their first child, Mary was born at Kingswinford in 1884, before the family moved to Ford Row, Hednesford, where George was born in 1886, followed by Lucy in 1888 and John in 1890. May was born in 1896 and Albert in 1898, before the family moved to Cannock Wood where Ivy was born in 1903, and then they moved to live at Gorsemoor Road, Heath Hayes. John senior was now retired from the police force, but still had to work as a pit labourer. John junior was a labourer for the London and North Western Railway, while Albert was a colliery labourer, before becoming a shunter at Mid-Cannock Colliery. Albert enlisted in 1916, joining the 2nd Battalion, Coldstream Guards and he was sent to the Western Front, later that year. Albert was killed in action on the 31st July, 1917, on the first day of the Battle of Passchendaele, at the age of 19. He was described as the "best, cheeriest and most dependable man in the platoon". After the war, Albert's body could not be identified and he is remembered on the Ieper (Menin Gate) Memorial to the Missing in Ieper city centre in Belgium.

Lance Corporal Walter Lloyd
23210

Walter Lloyd was born at Heath Hayes, Staffordshire in 1890, and he was the youngest child of Samuel and Mary Elizabeth Lloyd. Samuel was from Wolverhampton and his wife came from Darlaston. Their first child, Mary Ann was born in 1870, followed by Matthew in 1871. Samuel junior was born at Brownhills in 1873 and John was born there in 1878. The family then moved to Ansley, Warwickshire where Job and Selina were born in 1880. They then moved to Heath Hayes, where Ernest was born in 1886, Frederick in 1888, Elizabeth in 1889 and Walter in 1890. On the 15th July, 1899, Mary Elizabeth was killed at Cannock Station on an excursion from the Fair Lady Colliery, and Samuel married Louisa Jordan at St. Peter's Parish Church, Hednesford on the 3rd November, 1900. In 1901, the family was living at Hednesford Road, Heath Hayes, where Job and John were both working in a colliery. In 1911, Walter was boarding with the Buckley family at 26, Bank Street, Heath Hayes and he was working as a coal miner's loader, and on the 15th October, 1911, he married Elizabeth Buckley at St. Luke's Parish Church, Cannock. Their only child, Walter was born at Cannock in 1912, before the family moved to Bloxwich. On the 3rd March, 1915, Walter enlisted with the 3rd Battalion, Grenadier Guards and was sent to France later that year. He was wounded on the Somme in July, 1916 and came home to recover, returning to France on the 26th August, 1917. On the 21st November, 1917 Walter was killed in action during the Battle of Cambrai at the age of 27. His body was not found after the war and Walter is remembered on the Cambrai Memorial to the Missing at Louverval in France.

Private William Henry Longdon
27591

In 1890, at Lichfield, John Thomas Longdon married Elizabeth Davies. He was a 21 year old coal miner from Brownhills, Staffordshire and his wife, who also came from Brownhills, was 19. The couple moved to a house at Catshill, Shenstone, where they lived with Elizabeth's 60 year old widowed mother. It was here in 1890, that their first child, John Thomas was born. By 1901, the family had moved to live at Cannock Road, Heath Hayes, although two more children had been born before they made the move. Ethel was born in 1893 and William in 1895. Jessie was born at Heath Hayes in 1899, but sadly died in 1904. In 1911, the family was living at 59, Bank Street, Heath Hayes. Maud had been born in

1907 and Carmi Alfred in 1910. John and William had both started work by this time, John as a coal miner loader and William as a coal miner driller. William joined the Army in 1916, enlisting with the 1st Battalion, Royal Warwickshire Regiment, after initially being placed with the South Staffordshire Regiment. He served on the Western Front until the 15th April, 1918 when he was killed in action at the age of 23. William's body was buried at St. Venant-Robecq Road British Cemetery at Robecq, near Bethune in France.

Private Noah John Lysons
G/63009

In 1891, at Cannock, Staffordshire Job Lysons married Clara Sophia Davies. They lived with her parents at Norton Canes and it was here that their first child, Francis was born in 1893. He was followed in 1898 by his brother Noah. Just two years later, Clara died at the tragically young age of 31. On the 25th December, 1903 Noah Davies, Noah Lysons uncle, married Charlotte Elizabeth Parker at St. Luke's Parish Church, Cannock. They set up home at Gorsemoor Road, Heath Hayes and began a family. John was born in 1905, William in 1907, Fanny in 1909 and Florence in 1911. Francis and Noah Lysons lodged with them too. In 1918, Noah was conscripted into the Army, being placed initially with the North Staffordshire Regiment, but then being transferred to the 7th Battalion, Middlesex Regiment. He was sent to fight in France in August 1918, but on the 27th August, he was killed in action by a shell, at the age of 20. Noah's body was buried at Suzanne Military Cemetery Number 3, near Albert on the Somme in France.

Lance Corporal Hubert Millard
45020

James Millard, a 23 year old puddler from West Bromwich, Staffordshire married Jane Titley, aged 19 from Oakengates, Shropshire at Penkridge in 1874. In 1881, they were living at Mill Lane, Darlaston and had had two children, Amelia born at Bloxwich in 1878 and Florence, born at Wyrley in 1880. The family then moved to Wales, where James found employment as a coal miner. In Wales, James, Ethel and Ada were born, before they moved back to live at Wimblebury, where Eliza was born in 1890. By 1901, the family had moved to live at Stafford Street, Heath Hayes. In the meantime, Alfred had been born in 1893, Clara in 1895, Violet in 1897 and Hubert in 1898. James junior was now working as a coal miner like his father. In 1911, the

6. Heath Hayes

family was living at 57, Stafford Street. Alfred had started work down the pit as a coal miner loader, and Hubert was still at school. The family had also adopted Gladys May Baker who had been born at the Cannock Union Workhouse in 1908. Hubert began work as a colliery clerk, but on the 19th February, 1917 he was called up for service, attesting at Stafford. He was posted to the 86th Training Battalion at Hornsea, where he received two days confined to barracks on the 29th May, 1917 for being absent. On the 27th October, 1917, he was sent to Boulogne and from Etaples, he was posted to the 13th Battalion, Durham Light Infantry. He served with the Battalion until the 5th October, 1918 when he was killed in action at the age of 20. Hubert's body was buried at Beaurevoir British Cemetery between Cambrai and St. Quentin in France.

Lance Corporal Albert Edward Morris
1257

In 1892, Levi Morris, a 21 year old coal miner from Norton Canes, Staffordshire married Annie Saunders aged 22 from Heath Hayes, Staffordshire at Cannock. Their first child, Albert Edward was born at Heath Hayes in 1894 and the family lived at 68, Cannock Road, Heath Hayes with John Colton, a 24 year old lodger who worked as a colliery manager's clerk. In 1911, the family was still living at the same address, but Alfred had been born in 1902, Oliver in 1905 and Adelaide in 1909. Albert was now earning his living as a horse driver at the Fair Lady Colliery at Heath Hayes, but later became a blacksmith at the same colliery. In April, 1911, Albert enlisted in the 2nd North Midland Field Company, Royal Engineers, which was a Territorial Force, proving to be a good shot and indeed, he won the cup for marksmanship in 1911. On the 5th August, 1914, Albert joined his unit and after training was sent to France on the 27th February, 1915, having just been appointed a Lance Corporal. He died from wounds on the 27th April, 1915 at the age of 21, having been shot in the back whilst supervising a working party. Albert's body was buried at St. Quentin Caberet Military Cemetery, near Ieper in Belgium. Lieutenant Patrick Welchman said of Albert, "I regarded him as my pluckiest NCO".

Private William Thomas Marriott
40072

In 1889 at Lichfield, Richard Marriott, a 20 year old coal miner from Aldridge, Staffordshire, married Maria Bailey, aged 18 from Walsall Wood. The young couple moved in with the bride's parents at Church Street, Ogley Hay, and it was here that William was born in 1890. By 1901, the family had moved to live at Hednesford Road, Norton Canes, and two more children had been born, Florrie in 1893 and Bertha in 1895. By 1911, Richard and William had set up a coal hauliers business, covering the Norton Canes/Heath Hayes area. In 1916, William enlisted with the Army, firstly joining the South Staffordshire Regiment, but then transferring to the 10th Battalion, Worcestershire Regiment. He was sent to serve on the Western Front and on the 27th July, 1917 he was killed instantaneously by a shell, at the age of 26. William's body was buried at Voormezeele Enclosure Number 3, near Ieper in Belgium. He was described by an officer in the Battalion as a "gallant fellow, we will all miss him very much. It will be a great consolation to you that he died doing his duty".

Lance Corporal Samuel Oakley
12071

Samuel Oakley was born at Dudley, Worcestershire in 1884. He was the third son of Daniel and Mary Oakley, who both came from Dudley. Their eldest child, Daniel junior was born at Dudley in 1876, followed by Minnie in 1877, and Thomas in 1880. Sarah was born in 1881, next came Samuel and he was followed by Beatrice in 1887. The family lived at 15, Hall Street, Dudley and a lodger, George Lilley a coal miner also lived with them. In 1895, Daniel senior died at the end of the year, and in 1901 Samuel had started work as a labourer in an iron works, while Beatrice was an apprentice dressmaker. Minnie Price, a one year old from Dudley had been adopted, and George Lilley was still lodging with the family. In 1906, Samuel married Amy Elizabeth Allen, a girl from Hednesford. The couple lived at Netherton for a time and it was here that William was born. The family then moved to Warwickshire where Benjamin and Edith were born, and then to New Bilton, Rugby for the birth of their fourth child, Samuel. On the 9th September, 1914 Samuel enlisted in the Army, joining the 6th Battalion, Dorsetshire Regiment. He was sent to France on the 13th July, 1915, and on the 1st December, 1915 he was admitted to 53 Field Ambulance suffering from laryngitis, but after 7 days he was returned to his unit. However, on the 22nd December, 1915 Samuel was admitted to 10 Casualty Clearing Station with a severe skull wound caused by shrapnel. He died later the same day at the age of 30. His widow and children moved back to live at 38, Bank Street, Heath Hayes. Samuel's body was buried at Lijssenthoek Military Cemetery, near Poperinghe in Belgium.

Able Seaman Michael Patrick O'Brien
Bristol Z/3909

Michael O'Brien was born at Limerick, Ireland on the 23rd July, 1892. His parents were John and Johanna O'Brien who ran the Birdhill Boys' National School at Limerick. It was therefore no surprise that Michael should follow them into the teaching profession. He made his way to England and secured a job as a teacher at Wimblebury Road Boys' School, Heath Hayes. Michael was also involved in running a Boy Scouts Troop in the village. On the 15th May, 1916, Michael joined the Royal Navy Volunteer Reserve, training on HMS Victory, before joining HMS Excellent and then HMS President. Michael was serving on the SS Edlington on the 15th March, 1917 when the vessel was sunk off the Italian coast and went down with many casualties. Michael was drowned on that day at the age of 24. Michael is remembered on the Plymouth Naval Memorial.

Private William Thomas Owen
4574

In 1906, at Lichfield, Staffordshire William Owen, a 22 year old coal miner from Kidderminster, Worcestershire married Maud Brown, aged 21, from Brownhills, Staffordshire. The couple lived at Commonside, Brownhills and it was here that Gladys was born in 1906, Maudie in 1908 and William in 1910. William was the third son of John and Annie Owen. John came from Bewdley, Worcestershire, his wife from Dudley, and he made his living in the carpet weaving industry for which Kidderminster was world famous. In 1891, the family was living at 3 Back, Cross Street, Kidderminster and Annie and Margaret, the two eldest children both worked as carpet spinners. By 1901, the newly widowed Annie had moved to live at Pier Street, Walsall Wood, where Alfred, John and William worked in the coal mining industry. William and Maud moved to live at Stafford Street, Heath Hayes before the outbreak of the Great War. Shortly afterwards, William enlisted in the Army, joining the 1st Battalion, Royal Warwickshire Regiment at Nuneaton, suggesting that his wife was not in agreement. He was sent to France on the 4th May, 1915 and served on the Western Front until the 30th April, 1916 when he was killed in action at the age of 32. William's body was buried at Bienvillers Military Cemetery, near Arras in France.

Guardsman Thomas Parker
12339

Thomas Parker was the eldest son of William and Sarah Parker and was born at Broseley in 1880. William was a coal miner from Broseley, Shropshire, and it was at Madeley, Shropshire that he married Sarah Jane Owen in 1878. The family moved to live at Wimblebury in 1885 and it was here that Edward was born in 1885, Sarah in 1887 and George in 1889. Thomas then moved to London and it was at Chelsea in 1903 that he married Flower Plumley. The couple already had a daughter, Dorothy, born at Chelsea in 1902, but the family soon moved back to Heath Hayes, and it was here that May was born in 1905. Violet was born in 1907, the birth taking place at Burrington, Somerset which was where Flower's family lived. Thomas was born at Heath Hayes in 1910, William in 1911 and Gertrude in 1914. When war broke out, Thomas was one of the first to enlist, joining the 1st Battalion, Scots Guards and he was sent to France on the 28th December, 1914. Just one month later on the 25th January, 1915, Thomas was killed in action at the age of 36. After the war Thomas' body could not be identified and he is remembered on the Le Touret Memorial to the Missing in France.

Private George Potts
17779

George Potts was the second son of Samuel and Mary Potts, and was born at Hednesford in 1887. His father was a coal miner from Willenhall, and his mother was also born there. The couple were married at Wolverhampton in 1877, but moved to live at Chase Terrace where Samuel junior was born in 1882. The family then moved to Hednesford where George, Mary, Minnie and Amy were born, before moving to Glover Street, Wimblebury where Betsy and Ada were born. Like most people at the time, the boys worked in the local collieries. George worked as a miner at Cannock and Rugeley Colliery, and on the 28th March, 1910, he married Elizabeth Earp at St. Peter's Parish Church, Hednesford. The couple lived at 131, Wimblebury Road, Heath Hayes, with their first child, Jack being born in 1911, and their second child, Harriet being born in 1915. George volunteered for the Army in 1915, joining the 7th Battalion, South Staffordshire Regiment and he was sent to Gallipoli on the 5th December, 1915. From there he went to Egypt and then to the Western Front. George was killed in action on the

9th June, 1917, at the age of 30. His body could not be found after the war and he is remembered on the Ieper (Menin Gate) Memorial to the Missing in Ieper city centre.

Private Edward Powell
12201

Edward Powell was born at Stafford in 1877 and was the fifth son of William and Emily Powell. William was a shoemaker from Stafford while his wife, born at Ashton-under-Lyne, Lancashire, also worked in the shoe trade at Stafford, as did their eldest child, William junior. Edward decided that the shoe trade was not for him, and he worked as a farm servant, before becoming a coal miner. He finally moved to Heath Hayes in 1911, living at Lyndhurst Road, while his brother William also lived in the village on the Wimblebury Road where he continued to make shoes. On the 26th December, 1912, Edward married Bertha Morris, also from Heath Hayes at St. Luke's Parish Church, Cannock. The couple continued to live at Heath Hayes, and it was here that their two children, Emily and Florence were born in 1913 and 1914 respectively. When the Great War began, Edward volunteered shortly afterwards, joining the 2nd Battalion, Cheshire Regiment. He was sent to the Western Front on the 6th March, 1915 and served until the 17th May, 1915 when he died from wounds at the age of 38. Edward's body was buried at Boulogne Eastern Cemetery in France.

Sapper James Rowley
136292

In 1873, James Rowley, an 18 year old coal miner from Brixton, London married 19 year old Mary Ann Langley from Bridgnorth, Shropshire at Lichfield. The couple set up home at Chasetown, Staffordshire and it was here that their first child, Levi, was born in 1876. The family then moved to Hednesford where Florence was born in 1877, Andrew in 1879 and James in 1881. They were then living at East Cannock Buildings, as James was working for the East Cannock Colliery, and a servant, Marie Jolly was living with them. By 1891, they had moved to live on the Hednesford Road, Heath Hayes, where Herbert was born in 1883, Winifred in 1885 and Elizabeth in 1887. Levi and Andrew had started work with their father as miners at the Coppice Colliery. In 1901, they had again moved to Chapel Street, Heath Hayes where Ethel was born in 1892, Maggie in 1894 and

Samuel in 1896. James had started work as a loader at Coppice Colliery and Herbert was a blacksmith at the colliery. On the 19th May, 1907, James married Florence Hannah Foster at St. Luke's Parish Church, Cannock. James was 26 and his bride was 21. They set up home on the Cannock Road, Heath Hayes, with Henry Foster, Florence's 68 year old father living with them. It was here that James junior was born in 1908, Ethel in 1910, and Herbert in 1911, before the family moved to live at Newlands Lane where Levi was born in 1913 and William in 1914. James volunteered for the Tunnellers and Headers Company of the Royal Engineers and was sent to France on the 9th November, 1915 and served with the 175th Tunnelling Company until the 7th March, 1916 when he was badly wounded by shrapnel in the hip. James was taken to a Base Hospital at Le Touquet, but he died there the next day at the age of 35. James' body was buried at Le Touquet-Paris Plage Communal Cemetery in France.

Private Bert Roper
48209

For details about Bert Roper see the entry on the same soldier under Hednesford.

Private Henry T. Robinson
61179

Henry Robinson was born at Heath Hayes, Staffordshire in 1899. He was the fourth son of Samuel and Jessie Robinson. Samuel was a coal miner from Brownhills, Staffordshire and he had married Jessie Palmer at Cannock in 1885. The couple set up home on the Heath Hayes Road at Wimblebury, and their first child, Martha, was born in 1888, followed by William in 1890. By 1901, the family had moved to live at 115, Hednesford Road, Heath Hayes, and it was here that Samuel junior was born in 1892, Maggie in 1894, John in 1896, Lizzie in 1897, Fred in 1901 and Lucy in 1904. By 1911, William, Samuel and John had joined their father as colliery workers. Henry also became a coal miner and worked at the Coppice Colliery, Heath Hayes until he was conscripted on the 19th April, 1918. He joined the 3rd Battalion, North Staffordshire Regiment and was sent to their base training depot at Heaton-upon-Tyne. On the 21st October, 1918, Henry was admitted to the 1st Northern General Hospital at Newcastle-upon-Tyne with double pneumonia. He fought against the illness for ten days before dying at 10.10 am on the 31st October, aged 20. Henry's body was returned to Heath Hayes and was buried with full military honours at St. John's Churchyard, Heath Hayes.

Guardsman John Henry Shirley
21961

William Shirley, a 24 year old coal miner from Tamworth, Staffordshire married Clara Elizabeth Thacker at Cannock in 1882. The couple moved to live on the Wimblebury Road, Heath Hayes, and in 1885 their first child Mary was born, followed by Florence in 1887 and William junior in 1890. James was born in 1892, John Henry in 1894, Arthur in 1896 and Richard in 1898. By 1911, Ferdinand had been born in 1902, Clara May in 1904, Rhoda in 1905 and Hannah in 1910. John was a Boy Scout and was a drummer with the organization. James and John were horse drivers at the Coppice Colliery and Arthur was a pit labourer. John became a Doggie or foreman at the colliery, which was a job with some responsibility. On the 18th January, 1915 John enlisted in the Army, joining the 2nd Battalion, Grenadier Guards. He was sent to France on the 27th October, 1915 and served until the 26th September, 1916 when he was killed in action by shellfire at Lesboeufs on the Somme at the age of 22. After the war, John's body could not be identified and he is remembered on the Thiepval Memorial to the Missing on the Somme in France.

Guardsman Arnold Smith
18010

In 1889, at Cannock, Staffordshire, William Henry Smith, a 19 year old coal miner from Brownhills, Staffordshire married Harriet Louisa Jones, aged 16, from Bilston, Staffordshire. The couple lived at Walsall Road, Cannock and their first child, named after her mother was born in 1890. Sadly, Harriet was born, in the harsher language of the time, an imbecile. The family then moved to live at Leacroft Lane, Great Wyrley and it was here that William Louis was born in 1892. He was followed by Arnold in 1896, John Bernard in 1898, and Lilian May in 1900. Florence Bott, a 16 year old domestic servant from Penkridge was also staying with the family. Tragically, later in 1901, William's wife died at the age of 29. The family then moved to live at 113, Bank Street, Heath Hayes, where William Louis, Arnold and John Bernard found employment as coal lathe labourers at the Fair Lady Colliery. Soon after the outbreak of war, Arnold volunteered for the Army, joining the 1st Battalion, Grenadier Guards and he was sent to serve on the Western Front on the 16th March, 1915. He served until the 25th September, 1916 when he was posted as missing in action. It was later presumed by the Army that he had been killed on that day at the age of 20. After the war, Arnold's body could not be identified and he is remembered on the Thiepval Memorial to the Missing on the Somme in France.

Private John Bernard Smith
17051

John Bernard Smith was the younger brother of Arnold Smith. He too was born at Great Wyrley, in 1898 and like his brother, worked as a coal lathe labourer at the Coppice Colliery, (Fair Lady) Heath Hayes. John joined the Army in 1916, probably responding to the Derby Scheme and perhaps to his brother's death the year before. He enlisted with the 6th Battalion, King's Shropshire Light Infantry and was sent to France later in 1916. He served on the Western Front until the 20th June, 1917 when he was killed in action at the age of 19. John's body was buried at Favreuil British Cemetery, near Bapaume in France.

Private Samuel Stevens
196694

Samuel Stevens was the ninth son of John and Rebecca Stevens. He was born at Heath Hayes in 1891. His parents had married at Wolverhampton in 1866; John was a coal miner from Great Bridge, Staffordshire and his bride, Rebecca Upperdine came from Wolverhampton. To begin with, the couple lived at Albion Place, Tipton and then moved to Cannock, living on the Hednesford Road, Cannock, before moving again to live at 64, Hednesford Road, Heath Hayes. John, the eldest child was born at Great Bridge, with Henry, Charles, and Benjamin all born at Cannock. The rest of the eleven children were born at Heath Hayes. Samuel suffered from epileptic fits from birth. His brothers all worked in the mining industry. John Stevens died at the age of 56 at Cannock in 1900, and in 1911, only his widow Rebecca and her two sons Levi and Samuel were still living at home. Levi was a coal miner loader and Samuel, despite his epilepsy was a colliery surface banksman. On the 12th June, 1917, Samuel was conscripted into the Army, joining the 297th Company, Labour Corps. He was sent to York Barracks and on the 21st July, 1917 had an epileptic fit. He was examined and it transpired that he had had fits at varying intervals, from 3 per day to 1 in 3 weeks. After a fit he became mentally dull and unresponsive, stammering and uncertain. On this basis, Samuel was discharged as being medically unfit for service and sent home. However, on the 4th February, 1918 Samuel died at the age of 27. His body was buried with full military honours, a gun carriage carrying his body, with his bayonet, sword and union flag on the coffin. The Durham Light Infantry provided both a military band and the buglers who played the Last Post. The Reverend W.H. Fletcher conducted the service at St. John's Parish Church, Heath Hayes.

Corporal Richard James Timmins MM 40527

Isaiah Timmins, a coal miner from Kingswinford, Staffordshire married Emma Nock, from Blackheath, Staffordshire at Dudley in 1881. Their first child, Mary Ann was born at Blackheath in 1884, with Richard James following in 1887, born at Kingswinford. The family then moved to live at Hednesford Road, Heath Hayes and it was here that William was born in 1889. Isaiah junior was born in 1893, Arthur in 1898 and Eli in 1900. By this time, Richard had begun work as a coal miner at the Fair Lady Colliery. By 1911, the family had moved to live at 38, Bank Street, Heath Hayes. Richard was still living at home, as was Isaiah junior and Arthur, both of whom were horse drivers down the pit. Mary Ann had married Thomas Savage at Cannock in 1901. She too was living with her parents with her three children, and William Nock, Emma's 73 year old father was also living with them, although he was still working as a bricklayer's labourer. Richard was a Scoutmaster with the St. John's Troop and was also a member of the Cannock Fire Brigade. Richard was an enthusiastic member of St. John's Church. On the 27th May, 1912, Richard married Annie Elizabeth Marriott at St. Luke's Parish Church, Cannock. They set up home a few doors away from Richard's parents at 33, Bank Street, and it was here that their only child, James was born in 1913. When the Great War broke out, Richard volunteered for service with the 2/5th Battalion, South Staffordshire Regiment, and was sent to France on the 24th August, 1915. He was then transferred to the 2nd Battalion, Lincolnshire Regiment, and promoted to Lance Corporal, winning the Military Medal for bravery in May 1917. On the 14th August, 1917, Richard was killed in action at the age of 30. Richard's body was not identified after the war and he is remembered on the Ieper (Menin Gate) Memorial to the Missing in Ieper city centre in Belgium.

Lance Corporal John Tooth
107442

John Tooth was born at Brereton, Staffordshire in 1895. His mother was Rosanna Tooth, the youngest daughter of John and Harriet Tooth, who was only 14 at the time of the birth. He was brought up by his mother and his grandparents at 71, Glovers Hill, Brereton. However, in 1901, Rosanna married Harry Bott at Lichfield. He was a Heath Hayes miner and the couple moved to live at 234, Hednesford Road. Their first child, Harry junior was born in 1902, followed in quick succession by Frances Harriett in 1904, Rosanna in 1906 and Edith Annie in 1908. John Tooth was also living with them and was working as a coal miner horse driver. John joined the Staffordshire Yeomanry, which was a territorial unit, but in 1916, he joined the 21st Battalion, Machine Gun Corps (Infantry). John served on the Western Front until the 27th May, 1918, when he was killed in action at the age of 23. John's body was buried at Sissonne British Cemetery, near Laon in France.

Private Harry Bertram Yardley
345051

Harry Yardley was born at Chase Terrace, Staffordshire in 1895. He was the second son of John Henry and Harriett Yardley. His father was a coal miner from Oakengates, Shropshire and his mother came from Bramshall, Staffordshire; the couple having married at Cannock in 1883. When they married, John was a railway engine driver and they lived at New Street, Chase Terrace. It was here that their first child Florence was born in 1884, followed by Annie in 1886, Eleanor in 1888 and Edwin in 1890. Gertrude was born in 1894 and Olive in 1899. In 1901 the family were living at Baker Street, Burntwood, where John had become a bank pressman at a colliery. By 1911, the family had moved to live at Gorsemoor Lane, Heath Hayes. John was now a colliery overman on the pit top, and Edwin was a colliery carpenter, while Harry was a colliery labourer. In 1916, Harry volunteered for the Army, joining the 2/8th Battalion, Manchester Regiment. He served on the Western Front until the 9th October, 1917 when he died from wounds received the previous day during the Battle of Passchendaele. At the time of his death, Harry was aged 22, and he was buried at Nine Elms British Cemetery, at Poperinghe, Belgium. A memorial service was held for Harry and Harry Bird at the Primitive Methodist Church.

6. Heath Hayes

Corporal Ernest Yates
11389

Joseph Yates, a coal miner from West Bromwich, Staffordshire, married Leah Harper from Short Heath, Staffordshire at Walsall in 1882. Their first child, Edith had been born at Bloxwich in 1881, and their second, Joseph was also born at Bloxwich in 1883. The family then moved to live at Wimblebury, where Benjamin and Rosannah were born in 1886, Ernest in 1887 and Leah in 1889, followed by Thomas in 1890. Benjamin Harper, Leah's retired father was living with them, as was her deaf and dumb brother, Thomas. By 1901, the family had moved to live at Bank Street, Heath Hayes, with both Joseph junior and Benjamin working as coal miners. Rachel had been born in 1892, Alice in 1893 and Elsie in 1900. Thomas Harper was still living with the family. In 1911, they were living at 46, Chapel Street, Heath Hayes. Ernest was now working as a banksman, and Elizabeth had been born in 1909. On the 7th April, 1912, Ernest married Clara Turner at St. Luke's Parish Church, Cannock. They moved to live at 90, Stafford Street, Heath Hayes and had two children. In 1914, shortly after the outbreak of war, Ernest joined the 2nd Battalion, South Staffordshire Regiment and was sent to France on the 25th May, 1915. Ernest rose to the rank of Corporal, but on the 14th September, 1916 he was badly wounded in the arm. He was sent back to a Base Hospital at Boulogne, but died from a haemorrhage on the 19th September at the age of 29. Ernest's body was buried at Boulogne Eastern Cemetery in France.

Captain Walter John Shaw DCM

Walter Shaw was born at Heath Hayes, Staffordshire in 1879. He was the third child of John and Sarah Shaw. His father was a coal miner, born at Great Wyrley, Staffordshire, whilst his mother came from Banbury, Oxfordshire. In 1871, they were living at Norton Canes, where Emma Louisa had been born in 1867 and Eliza in 1870. In 1881, the family was living at Stafford Street, Heath Hayes, and Albert had been born there in 1873. In 1889, Sarah died at the age of 49, and on the 2nd February, 1891 John married Emma Reynolds at St. Luke's Parish Church, Cannock. In 1898, Walter decided to join the Army, enlisting with the 2nd Battalion, King's Shropshire Light Infantry. He was sent to fight in the South African War and was awarded the Distinguished Conduct Medal. He remained on the Reserve List, and on the 3rd December, 1910, Walter married

Kate Elizabeth Howard, at St. Luke's Parish Church, when he was working as the manager of the Royal Army Training Corps at the Shropshire Regiment Head Quarters. With the outbreak of the Great War, Walter volunteered for service with the 7th Battalion, South Staffordshire Regiment and was promoted to Sergeant. He was sent to Gallipoli on the 20th July, 1915 and was wounded at the landings at Suvla Bay. On recovery he was given a commission and was attached to the Labour Corps as a 2nd Lieutenant, before returning to his Regiment as a Lieutenant. Walter saw service on the Somme, and was promoted to Captain, before he was severely wounded and invalided out of the Army. Walter then underwent treatment at various hospitals and institutions, before returning to Heath Hayes, where he lived with his sister Eliza and her husband Alfred Cooper on the Cannock Road, Heath Hayes. On Tuesday, 8th March, 1927 at the age of 48, Walter Shaw finally succumbed to his injuries. He was buried at St. John's Churchyard, Heath Hayes.

Chapter 7

NORTON CANES

Sapper Harry Adams
1293

In 1894, at Wolverhampton, Staffordshire, Harry Adams, a 25 year old Police Constable from Mucklestone, Staffordshire married Sarah Elizabeth Whitehouse, aged 27. Harry was then posted to Leek, in the north of the county and it was here that Harry junior was born in 1896. Harry then moved to live at Dilhorne, Staffordshire where Reginald was born in 1897, George in 1899 and Gertrude in 1900. The next move was to Norton Canes, where the family took up residence at Lilac Cottages, Norton Green Lane. By 1911, Harry junior was working as a mechanic hauling engineman, although he later became a blacksmith's striker, whilst Reginald was working as a clerk. On the 5th January, 1912, at the age of 17, Harry joined the 1st/2nd North Midland Field Company, Royal Engineers. When war broke out, he was called up on the 5th August, 1914, and was sent to France on the 27th February, 1915. Harry served until the 13th October, 1915, when he was killed in action during the Battle of Loos, aged 19. After the war, Harry's body could not be found and he is remembered on the Loos Memorial to the Missing in France.

Sapper William Ewart Bates
1369

James Bates, a coal miner from Lichfield, Staffordshire married Louisa Hackett, from Brownhills, Staffordshire at Cannock in 1888. The couple moved to live on the Hednesford Road, Norton Canes, and it was here that their first child,

William Ewart was born in 1890, followed by Samuel in 1891. John James was born in 1893, Florence in 1897 and Hilda in 1900. By this time the family had moved to live at High Street, Norton Canes. By 1911, William Ewart was a coal miner driver, Samuel was a hewer's loader and John was a motor driver. William too joined the 1st/2nd North Midland Field Company, Royal Engineers, and was called up just after the start of the war, being sent to France on the 1st March, 1915. William served until the 14th October, 1915, when he died from wounds incurred the previous day during the Battle of Loos. William's body was buried at Fouquieres Churchyard Extension, near Bethune in France.

Sergeant Josiah Cooper Birch
1721

Josiah Birch was born at Norton Canes, Staffordshire in 1886. He was the second son of George and Maria Birch. George was a farmer and the family lived at Commonside, Norton Canes. Josiah began his working life as a coal miner horse driver, but on the 3rd February, 1911, he decided to leave England and head for Australia. In Australia, he became a farmer, and yet on the 15th January, 1915, Josiah enlisted in the 4th Battalion, Australian Imperial Forces. He was sent to Gallipoli on the 31st May, 1915, promoted to Lance Corporal, but then contracted influenza and was sent to Egypt to recover, being assigned to guard duty at Suez. Josiah was then sent back to Aldershot, to the School of Instruction, before rejoining the 4th Battalion in France on the 12th August, 1916, being promoted to Sergeant on the 30th August. He then had a recurrence of influenza and was in hospital from the 24th September, 1916 until the 14th October. On the 6th November, 1916, Josiah was killed in action at the age of 30. Josiah's body was buried at Bulls Road Cemetery, Flers on the Somme in France.

Private Herbert Harry Bott
16348

In 1876 at Hitchin, Hertfordshire, Joseph Bott, a farmer from Shenstone, Staffordshire married Emily Ingrey from Ashwell, Cambridgeshire, the daughter of John and Emily Ingrey. In 1881, the couple were farming 92 acres at Cranebrooke Farm, Shenstone and they had had four children, Gertrude born in 1878, Edgar born in 1880, Ernest born in 1881, and Alfred born in 1883, all at Shenstone. Emily's mother was living with them, as was Emily's sister, Naomi, who was working on the farm as a domestic servant. By 1901, the family had moved to farm at Little Wyrley, Norton Canes and it was here that Laura was born in 1885, Nellie in 1887, Herbert in 1889, Elsie in 1892 and Evelyn in 1897. Edgar, Ernest and Alfred were all helping their father run the farm. By 1911, Joseph and Emily had moved to farm Hammerwich Hall. Only Herbert was helping his father run the farm, with Elsie and Evelyn helping their mother run the house. In 1914, after the outbreak of war, Herbert enlisted with the 2nd Battalion, South Staffordshire Regiment, being sent to France on the 1st June, 1915. He was wounded twice while serving, but on the 28th September, 1918, Herbert was killed in action at the age of 29. Herbert's body was buried at Noyelles-sur-L'Escaut Communal Cemetery Extension, near Cambrai in France.

Private Wilfred Cliffe
7411

Wilfred Cliffe was the fourth son of Joseph and Susan Cliffe. He was born at Norton Canes in 1887. His father, Joseph was a coal miner born in the village, his mother coming from Lichfield. In 1881, the family was living at Hednesford Road, Norton Canes, and it was here that Herbert, their first child had been born in 1878, followed by Alfred in 1880. The family stayed in the same house and by 1891, Emma, William, Wilfred and Joseph junior had been born. In 1901, they had moved to live at Chapel Street, Norton Canes. Alfred was working as a travelling draper; Emma was a pupil teacher, William a bricklayer's labourer and Joseph junior, an office messenger. Mabel had been born in 1895, but Wilfred was lodging at 13, Ellesmere Road, Shrewsbury, where he was working as a journeyman baker. Shortly after this, Wilfred decided to join the Army, enlisting with the 1st Battalion, South Staffordshire Regiment, and in 1911, he was a Lance Corporal with the Battalion and was serving in Gibraltar. After completing his service, Wilfred was placed in the Army Reserve. In 1910, he married Lilian M. Whiston at Plymouth and the couple had one child. The family returned to live at Norton East, and Wilfred worked as a miner at the Conduit Colliery in the village. With the outbreak of war, Wilfred was recalled to the Colours and was sent to France in August, 1914 with the 2nd Battalion, South Staffordshire Regiment. On the 6th September, 1914, Wilfred was killed in action at Vailly at the age of 27. His body was buried at Vailly British Cemetery in France. A memorial service was held at the Primitive Methodist Church in Norton Canes, with the Reverend E.F. Martin taking the service.

Bombardier Ernest Cooper
68022

In 1877, a 17 year old agricultural labourer from Frocester, Gloucestershire, named William Cooper, married Alice Price, aged 20, from Burghill, Herefordshire, at Ledbury. Their first child, William was born at Colwall, Herefordshire in 1880, followed by his sister Alice, born at Coddington, Herefordshire in 1881. George was born in 1884, before the family moved to Yardley, Worcestershire, where Henry was born in 1886. From there they moved to Rudge, Shropshire, where Ruth was born in 1887, and then they went to Norton Lane, Wimblebury. It was here that Arthur was born in 1890, followed by Joseph in 1892, Beatrice in 1893 and Ernest in 1897. By 1901, the family was living at School Lane, Norton Canes, where Henry worked as a boat loader on the canal wharf. William was now employed as a farm waggoner. In 1911, the family had moved to live at 166, Grange Road, King's Heath, where William had found a job as a carter. Ruth was working as a machinist, while Beatrice was employed as a cardboard cutter. Ernest was 14 and had no job. On the outbreak of war, Ernest volunteered for the Army, joining the 34th Brigade, Royal Field Artillery. He was sent to France on the 16th August, 1914, which would suggest that he had joined a Territorial unit before the war and had received basic training in gunnery, although he was under age. Ernest served until the 9th October, 1917 when he was killed in action, during the Battle of Passchendaele at the age of 20. Ernest's body was buried at Bard Cottage Cemetery, near Ieper in Belgium. After the war, his parents emigrated to live at Tauranga, New Zealand.

Private John Henry Fisher
7762

George Fisher, a coal miner from Grimley, Worcestershire, married Hannah Bishop, from Drayton, Worcestershire at Bromsgrove in 1884. The couple set up home at Charford Road, Bromsgrove, and it was here that their first child, Nellie, was born in 1885. She was followed by the birth of John Henry in 1886, Charles Austin in 1889, Florence in 1890 and Grace in 1891. The family then moved to live on the Walsall Road, Cannock and it was here that Alice was born in 1893, Jane in 1894, Martha in 1899 and George junior in 1900. By this time, John had started work as a horse driver in a local colliery. Shortly afterwards, the family moved to live at High Street, Norton Canes. John decided to join the Army, enlisting with the 1st Battalion, South Staffordshire Regiment, and seeing service at Gibraltar and South Africa. When the Great War began, the Battalion made its way from Pietermaritzburg to England, before arriving in France on the 20th October, 1914. The Battalion went into action, and on the 7th November, 1914, John was posted as missing in action. His worried parents asked for information about their son, and received a reply from Sergeant F. Thomas in May 1915. He told them that John had been killed by a shell on that date. John's body was never found after the war and he is remembered on the Ieper (Menin Gate) Memorial to the Missing in Ieper city centre in Belgium. At the time of his death, John was 28 years of age.

Private Charles Austin Fisher 18995

Charles Austin Fisher was the younger brother of John Henry. He too had been born at Bromsgrove, Worcestershire in 1889, and worked as a general labourer after the family had moved to Norton Canes. In 1905, Charles joined the Army, enlisting with the 2nd Battalion, South Staffordshire Regiment. To say that Army life was not to Charles' liking is an understatement. Between 1905 and 1910, his record was a catalogue of one misdemeanour after another, from absence, desertion, drunkenness, theft, assault, insubordination and losing clothing by neglect. In 1910, Charles was transferred to the Wiltshire Regiment, with a character assessment of "good"!! Despite being given a second chance, the problems continued; with more desertion, drunkenness, insubordination, urinating on a colleague's bedding, and losing all service entitlements. Finally, even the British Army had had enough, and Charles was dishonourably discharged on the 15th January, 1914. He returned to Norton Canes, where he found employment as a coal miner. Amazingly, with the outbreak of war, Charles volunteered for service. By an incredible coincidence, he enlisted with the 4th Battalion, Worcestershire Regiment on the same day that his older brother was killed in action in France. Charles was sent with the Battalion to Gallipoli on the 12th July, 1915 and was killed in action on the 6th August, 1915 at the age of 26. Charles' body was never found, and he is remembered on the Helles Memorial to the Missing in Turkey.

Driver George Gough
958

John Gough, a 25 year old general labourer, born at Chasetown, Staffordshire married Eliza Bedward, aged 29, at Wolverhampton in 1890. The couple already had one child, William, born at Norton Canes in 1889, and a second son, John junior was born in 1891. In 1899, John senior died at the age of 34, leaving his widow with three sons to look after, George having been born at Norton Canes in 1894. By 1911, the family was living on the Brownhills Road, Norton Canes where William worked as a pony driver at the Conduit Colliery. John was working as a screen labourer at the same pit, and George was also employed there as a ropeman. George joined the 1/2nd North Midland Field Company Royal Engineers, which was a Territorial force whose Drill Hall was based in Norton Canes. Thus when war broke out in August, 1914, George was drafted into the unit as a full time soldier. He was sent to France on the 1st March, 1915, serving until August, 1915 when he was badly wounded in the shoulder and spine. George was invalided back to England where he was treated for his wounds at Gosforth Military Hospital, Northumberland. It was here that George died from his injuries on the 9th December, 1915 at the age of 21. His body was returned to Norton Canes, where it was buried at St. James' Churchyard with full military honours, the Leicestershire Regiment providing a firing party of 60 soldiers, and buglers to play the Last Post.

Private William Grantham
G/62990

William Grantham was born at Norton Canes, Staffordshire in 1898, being the second son of William and Emma Grantham. William senior, was a coal miner from Shenstone, Staffordshire, and in 1891 at the age of 25, he had married Emma Jane Hurmson, aged 23, from Tipton, Staffordshire at Cannock. They moved to live at Nevill's Buildings, Norton East Road, in Norton Canes. Their first child, Harold was born there in 1896, followed by Ethel in 1897, William in 1898, Richard in 1900, Rhoda in 1901, Doris in 1903 and May in 1907. By this time the family had moved to live at Chapel Street, Norton Canes. Harold worked as a baker's assistant, whereas William junior found employment at the Coppice Colliery, Heath Hayes and he moved to live at Norton Green Lane. William was called up in 1917, and after his basic training was transferred from the North Staffordshire Regiment to

7. Norton Canes

the 7th Battalion, Middlesex Regiment. He was sent to France in the summer of 1918 and served there until the 8th September, 1918 when he was posted as missing in action, at the age of 20. William's body was found and he was buried at Epehy Wood Farm Cemetery, Epehy, between Cambrai and Peronne in France.

Sapper Herbert Grice
112724

Herbert Grice was born at Norton Canes, Staffordshire in 1899. He was the second son of Joseph and Martha Grice. Joseph was a coal miner from Darlaston, Staffordshire, while his wife came from Norton Canes. In 1901, the couple and their children were living with Joseph's parents, Samuel and Sarah Grice at Conduit Cottages, Norton Canes. At his point, they had four children; Ada born at Norton Canes in 1888, Joseph born in 1890, Sarah born in 1894 and Bertie born in 1899. In 1911, the family had grown and had moved to live at Walsall Road, Norton Canes. Minnie had been born in 1903, Lester in 1906 and John in 1908. Joseph junior was working as a boat loader on the colliery wharf. Despite being under age, Herbert volunteered in 1915 for service in the newly formed Tunnellers and Headers Company in the Royal Engineers. He was sent to France at the age of only 16 on the 7th September, 1915 and he was killed in action just three months later, on the 18th December, 1915, serving in the 179th Tunnelling Company, Royal Engineers. After the war, Herbert's body was never found and he is remembered on the Thiepval Memorial to the Missing on the Somme in France.

Private Joseph Charles Hancox
204431

In 1892, at Cannock, Staffordshire, Joseph Hancox, a 21 year old coal miner from Norton Canes, married Harriett Harvey, one year his senior, from Brownhills, Staffordshire. The couple set up a home at High Street, Norton Canes, and their first child, Eliza was born in 1893. She was followed by Bertha, born in 1895, Joseph Charles, born in 1897, Harold, born in 1899, and Rose, born in 1900. Betsy was born in 1905, Daisy in 1908 and Roland in 1910. By 1911, Bertha was working as a general servant, while Joseph was a coupler in a colliery. Joseph later found employment at the Coppice Colliery, Heath Hayes, and worked here until September 1917, when he enlisted in the 5th Battalion, Lincolnshire Regiment, being sent to France in December 1917. Joseph was badly wounded and captured in March, 1918 and was operated upon whilst a prisoner of war. Due to the seriousness of his injuries, Joseph was repatriated to England for further operations, and died at Rugeley Military Hospital on the 24th December, 1918 at the age of 21. His body was buried with full military honours at St. James' Churchyard, Norton Canes.

Private Harold Hancox
203940

Harold Hancox was the younger brother of Joseph Charles and was born at Norton Canes in 1899. Like his brother, he became a coal miner and worked in the mines until 1917, when he decided to enlist in the 4th Battalion, South Staffordshire Regiment, being sent to France on the 10th October, 1917. In May, 1918, Harold was posted as missing, believed captured, but this was amended to being killed in action on the 25th May when his body was found. At the time of his death, Harold was 19 years of age. Harold's body was buried at Jonchery-sur-Vesle British Cemetery, near Reims in France. On the Memorial Window at St. James', Norton Canes, Harold is named as Josiah Hancox.

William Harrison

Sadly, William Harrison remains just a name on a memorial window. There is nothing to link this man to Norton Canes, or to identify his service with the armed forces between 1914 and 1918.

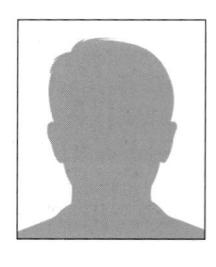

Private Thomas Heath
681264

In 1890, at West Bromwich, Staffordshire, Thomas Heath, a 24 year old iron worker from Tipton, married Eliza Bullock, aged 22, and also from Tipton. They moved in with Eliza's parents and siblings at 44, Aston Street, Tipton, and it was here that their first child, Mary Ann was born in 1890. Thomas was also born at Tipton on the 25th September, 1892, before the family moved to Walsall. It was here that Florence was born in 1895, followed by Phoebe in 1897. The family then moved to live at Hednesford Road, Norton Canes, where Thomas senior had taken a new job as a railway plate layer. Two more children were born while the family was living at Norton Canes, James and Arthur. On the 1st November, 1906, Thomas aged 14 and Mary Ann, aged 16 sailed to Montreal, Canada. They were followed in March, 1907 by the rest of the family, with the exception of Thomas senior. Thomas found work as a labourer and he married a local girl named Clara and they set up a home at 146, Harvie Avenue, Toronto, with the rest of the Heath family living at 214, Nairn Avenue, Toronto. Thomas enlisted in the 170th Battalion, Canadian Expeditionary Force on the 22nd February, 1916, arriving in England on the 31st October, 1916. He was transferred to the 169th Battalion, Canadian Infantry, before coming down with adenitis, which meant a spell in hospital, followed by a period of convalescence. It was during this time that Thomas went back to Norton Canes, and among other things, visited his old school. On recovery, Thomas was sent to France on the 10th August, 1917, being sent first to the 3rd Infantry Battalion, and then to the 9th Infantry Battalion, joining them on the 9th September, 1917. Just over a month later, on the 31st October, 1917, Thomas was killed in action at the age of 25. Thomas' body was buried at Dochy Farm New British Cemetery, near Ieper in Belgium.

Driver Walter Herbert
1097

In 1873 at Eton, Buckinghamshire, James Frederick Herbert, aged 20 from Stoke Poges, married the 18 year old Mary Ann Pullen, also from Stoke Poges. Some eight years later, they were living at Pudding Bag Street, Norton Canes, where James was employed as a coal miner. The couple had had four children at this point, Alice born in 1875, Louisa born in 1876, Alfred born in 1877 and Lily born in 1881. On the next census, the family had grown somewhat with the births of Minnie (1883), Amy (1884), Flora (1887), Edith (1889) and James Frederick junior (1890). The family had also moved to live at High Street, Norton Canes. By 1901, the family had taken up residence at Poplar Street, and Ethel (1892), Walter (1894), Bertha (1896), and Maria (1898) had increased the family still further. Interestingly, Thomas Herbert aged 15 appears on the census for the first time. In 1911, only James Frederick junior, Walter, Bertha and Maria were still living at Poplar Street with their parents. James and Walter had joined their father down the Conduit Colliery, James as a pony driver and Walter as a roadman at Number 11 Pit. Walter joined the local Territorial Force, the 2nd North Midland Field Company, Royal Engineers, and on the 6th September, 1914, he signed up for the duration of the Great War. After completing his basic training, Walter was sent to France on the 27th February, 1915. However, on the 30th April, 1915 he developed pleurisy and was invalided home, firstly to the Military Hospital in Birmingham and then to the Convalescent Hospital at Eastbourne. He returned to France on the 1st August, 1915, rejoining his unit on the 12th September. Walter served until the 16th August, 1916 when he died from his wounds during the battle of the Somme at the age of 22. Walter's body was buried at Warlincourt Halte British Cemetery, Saulty on the Somme.

Private Robert Hiden
17160

In 1877, Moses Hiden, a 25 year old agricultural labourer from Armitage, Staffordshire, married 51 year old Jane Beck. The couple lived in Mavesyn Ridware, along with Jane's brother William who was a shoe maker. Just two years later, Jane died and within a year, Moses had remarried, choosing Ann Ball as his second wife. She was 29 at the time of their wedding in 1880, and in 1881 they were living at 7, Mavesyn Ridware, along with their newly born daughter Mary Ann and William Beck. By 1891, the family had moved to live at Old Road, Armitage and the family had grown somewhat. Sarah had been born at Cannock in 1883, Fanny at Brereton in 1886, William at Hill Ridware in 1888 and Moses junior in 1890. In 1901, they had moved to live in a house attached to Hatherton House, Longford Lane, in Cannock. Robert had been born at Hill Ridware in 1892 and his younger brother Daniel was born at Cannock in 1896. In 1911, the main family had moved to live at Ball Lane, Burntwood, although only Daniel remained at home. Both Robert and his older brother Moses were working as farm labourers at Galletley's Farm at Shoal Hill, Cannock. Robert had been educated at Norton Canes School. On the 9th March, 1914, he married Emma Faith Westwood at Burntwood, with the couple living on the Chase Road at Burntwood. Robert was now working as a coal miner at the Coppice Colliery, Heath Hayes. Their only child, Ivy Edith Jane Hiden was born on 4th October, 1915. By this time, Robert had enlisted in the Army, joining the 3rd Battalion, North Staffordshire Regiment at Lichfield on the 16th March, 1915. He was transferred to the 7th Battalion of that Regiment on the 13th September, 1915 and was sent to serve at Gallipoli. From here the Regiment was sent to serve in Iraq, Robert arriving there on the 10th October, 1916. On the 25th January, 1917, Robert was killed in action at the age of 25. His body was buried at Amara War Cemetery, in Iraq.

Private George William Holloway
30915

George Holloway was born at Newton Regis, Staffordshire in 1896 and was the eldest son of John Thomas and Elizabeth Holloway. This couple had married at Tamworth, Staffordshire in 1893 and their first child, Millie was born at Newton Regis in 1894. The third child, Ethel was born at Hatton, Derbyshire in 1898 and Rosalie was born at Branston, Staffordshire in 1900. In 1901, the family was living at Branston Brook, Tattenhill near Burton-on-Trent. Nothing else is known about the family, but at some point they must have moved to live at Norton Canes. In 1916, George was called up to serve in the 8th Battalion, South Staffordshire Regiment, and he was sent to serve on the Western Front. On the 12th October, 1917, during the Battle of Passchendaele, at the age of 20, George was killed in action. His body was never found and George is remembered on the Tyne Cot Memorial, near Ieper in Belgium.

Private William James Jones
28038

In 1883, Henry Jones, a 24 year old coal miner born at Kingswinford, Staffordshire but living on the Brownhills Road, Norton Canes, married Sarah Ann Haskey at Lichfield. The newly married couple moved to a house on the Brownhills Road and it was here that their first child, Thomas was born in 1883. He was followed by Emily in 1884, and Henry in 1888. In 1892, Sarah died at the age of 34, and Henry, Thomas and Henry junior are recorded on the 1901 census as living on the Hednesford Road, Norton Canes. Also recorded on the 1901 census is William James Jones, aged five and living with his mother Emma at Broom's Row, Hednesford Road in Norton Canes. The 1911 census describes Henry Jones living with his step son, William James Jones, now a colliery door keeper, at the same address, but lodging with Emily Marshall, a 35 year old pork butcher and her older brother Edward. On the 13th February, 1915, William gave up his job as a miner at the Conduit Colliery and volunteered for the Army joining the Royal Army Medical Corps at Hednesford. On the 2nd June, 1915 he was transferred to the 3rd Battalion, Cheshire Regiment and was sent to serve in Gallipoli on the 5th September, 1915. From there he was sent to Egypt and then to Iraq where on the 8th April, 1916, William died at 16th Casualty Clearing Station. At the time of his death, William was aged 20 and his body was buried at Amara War Cemetery in Iraq.

Lance Sergeant Edward Kibble
19633

James Kibble, a 19 year old coal miner from East Leach, Gloucestershire, married Harriet Hackett at Cannock in 1887. By 1891 the couple had moved to live at Nevill's Buildings, Norton East Road and they had begun their family with the birth of Jane in 1889 and William in 1890. By 1901, the Kibbles had moved to live at Burntwood Road, Norton Canes and the family had increased considerably with the births of Lily in 1893, Edward in 1895, James in 1896, Hannah in 1899 and Harriett in 1900. Ten years later, the family was still living at the same address, and further additions had been made to the clan with Francis born in 1903, Maud in 1907, Eliza in 1909 and Thomas in 1910. James senior is described as a widow, although there does not appear to be a Harriet Kibble on the death register to coincide with this period. James senior was now a coal miner fireman, with William a pony driver. Lily was housekeeper, with Edward a coal miner ropeman. Shortly afterwards, Edward decided to join the Staffordshire Police, serving as a Police Constable at Darlaston. However, with the outbreak of war in 1914, Edward decided to enlist on the 14th October, 1914, joining the 1st Battalion, Grenadier Guards, and being sent to France on the 26th June, 1915. He served on the Western Front until 1918. In April of that year, Edward was admitted to hospital with an illness, and after recovery rejoined his unit. On the 1st May, 1918 he was badly wounded in the head by a shell fragment whilst in a dug out. Despite being taken for treatment, Edward died from his wounds the next day on the 2rd May, aged 23. Edward's body was buried at Bienvillers Military Cemetery, near Arras in France. Edward's younger brother James served with the Royal Army Medical Corps between June 1917 and May 1920.

Sergeant William Lydall
9558

Joseph Lydall, a 28 year old coal miner from Brownhills, Staffordshire but living at Heath Hayes, married Eliza Kendell, aged 21, originally from Dudley, but also resident in Heath Hayes at St. Luke's Parish Church, Cannock on the 25th December, 1891. By 1901, the couple were living on the Pelsall Road, Norton Canes and their family at this time consisted of Charles, born in 1893, Joseph, born in 1894, William, born in 1897, Elizabeth, born in 1898 and Edith, born in 1900. By 1911, the family had moved to live at 3, Birchen Cottages, Pelsall, with

Reginald having been born in 1904, May in 1906 and Nellie in 1909. Charles, Joseph and William had joined their father down the pit. In 1914, shortly after the outbreak of the war, and at the age of only 17, William joined the 2nd Battalion, South Staffordshire Regiment, being sent to France on the 25th May, 1915. He was promoted to the rank of Sergeant and served on the Western Front until the 3rd May, 1917, when he was killed in action at the age of 20. After the war, William's body was never recovered and he is remembered on the Arras Memorial to the Missing in France.

Private William Thomas Marriott
40072

In 1891, Richard Marriott, a 22 year old coal miner from Aldridge, Staffordshire was living at Church Street, Ogley Hay with his wife Maria and their 9 month old son William Thomas. At this point in their lives, the family was living with Maria's parents, Thomas and Maria Bailey. By 1901, the family had moved to live on the Hednesford Road, Norton Canes, and Florrie and Bertha had been born. Thomas Bailey, now a 68 year old widower was also living with them. 1911 saw the family at the same address, with Richard still working as a coal miner, whereas William was a 20 year old coal haulier. From his Army number, it would appear that William volunteered for service early in the war, joining the South Staffordshire Regiment, but later he transferred to the 10th Battalion, Worcestershire Regiment. He continued to serve with the Worcesters until the 27th July, 1917 when at the age of 26, William was killed in action. His body was buried at Voormezeele Enclosure No.3, a cemetery just outside the Belgian city of Ieper.

Private James Benjamin Morris
18659

James Benjamin Morris was born at Walsall Wood in 1885 and was the adopted son of James and Sarah Morris. In 1891, the Morris family, consisting of eight children, including James Benjamin, were living at Clayhanger, Staffordshire. James senior, and his eldest son, John William were both employed as coal miners. In 1901, the family had moved to live at Bullings Heath, Walsall Wood, where Sarah had set up as a shop keeper. James, James Benjamin and Samuel were all working as coal miners. In 1902, James Benjamin joined the Army, serving for nine years in both South Africa and India. In 1910, James Benjamin married Elizabeth Coyne at St. John's

Parish Church, Walsall Wood. Emily already had a child, named Albert Edward Coyne, but in 1911, the couple had a second child, named Emily Mary. A third child was born in 1912, named Sidney, before the family moved to live at Norton Canes, where another child, named James Benjamin after his father was born in 1915. By this time, James had been recalled to serve in the Army as a Reservist, serving in the 1/5th Battalion, South Staffordshire Regiment, and being sent to France on the 24th September, 1915. He served until the latter end of 1918, when in the act of rescuing a badly wounded comrade from No Man's Land, he was seriously wounded in the neck, body and legs. James was brought back to England and was taken to Manchester Military Hospital for treatment, but tragically this brave soldier died from his wounds on the 11th November, 1918 at the age of 34. His body was buried at St. James Parish Church, Norton Canes with full military honours.

Private Leonard Organ
15185

In 1891, Alfred Organ was living with his parents, John and Maria Organ, at 24, Hall Green Street in Sedgley. He was working as an iron bedstead fitter and was aged 31. Three years later, he married Ellen Griffiths at Wolverhampton. She came from Ryecroft near Walsall, and at the time of her marriage was 31 years of age. In 1901, the couple were living on the Hednesford Road, Norton Canes. Alfred was now working as a carpenter, and he and Ellen had three children, Alfred born in 1896, Leonard born in 1897 and Annie born in 1900. By 1911, the family had increased further with the birth of Elsie in 1904. Alfred senior was now a colliery surface worker, with his namesake son having become an apprentice shoe maker. Leonard was also working down the pit, as a door minder underground. The family had moved to live at Pier Street, Brownhills, although both pit workers were at 11 Pit, Conduit Colliery, at Norton Canes. Shortly after the outbreak of war in August 1914, Leonard volunteered for service in the Army, joining the 7th Battalion, South Staffordshire Regiment. He was sent to serve at Gallipoli on the 21st July, 1915, and was one of the soldiers who landed at Suvla Bay. After the evacuation from Gallipoli, Leonard served in Egypt before returning to England in 1916. It was here that he met and married Florence Daltry at Bristol, before he was sent to serve on the Western Front. Just six weeks later on the 11th September, 1916, Leonard was mortally wounded and despite being sent back to a Base Hospital at Boulogne, he died on the same day. His body was buried with full military honours at Boulogne Eastern Cemetery in France. At the time of his death, Leonard was only 19 years of age.

7. Norton Canes

Private James Penton
15298

For details about James Penton see the entry on the same soldier under Cannock.

Private Edward Powell
12201

Edward Powell was born at Stafford in 1877 and he was the fifth son of William and Emily Powell. His father was a shoe press cutter born at Hilderstone, Staffordshire and his wife worked as a shoe fitter and hailed from Ashton-under-Lyne in Lancashire. Edward did not follow his family into the shoe making trade, but instead worked as a farm servant at Seighford before enlisting in the Cheshire Regiment for twelve years, seeing service in South Africa and India. Edward came out of the army in 1911, and made his way to Heath Hayes where he found work as a colliery surface banksman. On the 26th December, 1912, Edward now aged 36 married Bertha Morris aged 26, at St. Luke's Parish Church, Cannock. The couple set up home at Broom's Buildings on the Walsall Road at Norton Canes, and it was here that their only child, a daughter named Florence Nellie Powell was born on the 6th June, 1914. When the war broke out, Edward presented himself for service again, volunteering on the 17th August, 1914, joining the 11th Battalion, Cheshire Regiment, before being transferred to the 3rd Battalion on the 10th January, 1915, as he was considered too old for General Service. However, Edward was then sent to serve on the Western Front on the 6th March, 1915. He was wounded in action in May 1915, and was sent to the 13th General Hospital at Boulogne, where he died at the age of 39 on the 17th May, 1915. Edward's body was buried at Boulogne Eastern Cemetery in France. However, there was initially great confusion, as Edward's service number had been changed he was mistaken for another soldier with the same surname.

Driver Herbert Price
488123

In 1879, Alfred Price, a 19 year old general labourer from Pembridge, Herefordshire married 18 year old Martha Baker at Dudley. Just a few months later, their first child, Alfred Edward was born at Coseley, followed by Edward in 1881. The family then moved to live at Cannock Road, Burntwood where Sarah, Charles, William and John were born. By 1901, a further move had taken place, this time to Norton Terrace, Norton Canes, and it was here that Herbert was born in 1893, followed by Clara, Percy and Sidney. In 1908, Martha Price died at the age of 49, and the widower Arthur and his family moved to live at Gidwells Lane, Norton Canes. In 1911, Alfred was working as a colliery banksman, with Alfred junior earning a living as an assurance agent. Sarah was keeping house for her family, although she was now married to Thomas Harrison, a coal miner's loader. William Price also worked as a coal miner's loader, with John and Herbert employed as colliery horse drivers at the Conduit Colliery. Percy and Sidney were still at school. Herbert volunteered for service in the Army following the outbreak of war, joining the 1/2nd North Midland Field Company, Royal Engineers. He was sent to France on the 1st March, 1915 and served until the 8th May, 1917. On this day, Herbert was on duty with the Company transport, when a shell exploded in front of the lead horses. Herbert was badly wounded and taken to a dressing station where he died from his wounds at the age of 24. Herbert's father received a letter from a Lieutenant in the Company which said that Herbert's death was deeply felt, and he was sadly mourned. Two more letters were received from Sergeant T. Sharratt and Corporal F. Yates, who had both stayed with him until the end and attended his funeral. Herbert's body was buried at Bully-Grenay Communal Cemetery British Extension near Arras in France.

Gunner Joseph Percy Proctor
175036

Joseph Proctor was a 29 year old agricultural labourer, born at Orton on the Hill, Leicestershire when he married Hannah Evans, aged 26 and who came from Sheepy Magna in the same county. The couple lived at Sheepy Magna to begin with and it was here that their first two children were born, Edith in 1887 and Florence in 1889, before the family moved to Bilstone where Charles was born in 1890. In 1901, they had moved to live at Thorpe Constantine near Tamworth, although both Harry and Joseph junior had been born at Orton on the Hill, Harry in 1894 and Joseph in 1898. Two more children, Margaret and Horace were born at Thorpe in 1902 and 1906 respectively. Joseph senior died at the age of 51 in 1907, and in 1911, his widow and family were now living at Clifton Campville, Tamworth. Hannah was earning a living as a charwoman, with Harry working as a farm labourer. Joseph was working as a cowman on the Gorse Farm at Clifton Campville, a farm run by the Carter family. In 1912, Hannah married for a second time. Her husband was a 44 year old shepherd, Albert Goodman who was living at Statfold Cottages in Tamworth. Her husband was born in Bloxwich and her father in law originally came from Norton Canes. The couple and their family moved at some point afterwards to live at Stokes Lane in Norton Canes. Joseph was conscripted into the Army in 1916, joining the 171st Siege Battery of the Royal Garrison Artillery. He was sent to the Western Front in July 1917. Just three months later, Joseph was killed in action on the 28th October, 1917 at the age of 20. Joseph's body was buried in Ypres Reservoir Cemetery in Ieper in Belgium.

Gunner Thomas Rose
62818

In 1890, James Rose, a coal miner from Longdon, Staffordshire and aged 27, married Elizabeth Whitton, aged 23 and born at Chasetown, Staffordshire. The marriage was registered at Lichfield. In 1891, the couple were living at Baker Street, Burntwood and their first child George Whitton Rose had been born just a few months before. Sadly he was to die at the age of only five. By 1901, the family had moved to live off Queen Street in Chasetown. The family now consisted of James junior, born in 1892, Arthur, born in 1894, Thomas, born in 1896, Elizabeth, born in 1898 and Gertrude, born in 1900. In 1911, the family was living at Cottage Lane, Chasetown. James senior was now working as a coal miner loader, as was James junior. Arthur and Thomas were employed as coal miner horse drivers. Elizabeth was an unemployed domestic servant, with Gertrude still at school, as were Charlotte, William Henry and Louisa. On the 4th November, 1915, Thomas enlisted in the Army. This strapping 6 footer chose to join the Royal Garrison Artillery, being sent to Fort Brockhurst at Gosport for his basic training. Thomas was not sent to France until the 13th August, 1916, joining the 49th Siege Battery, before being sent back to Base Depot. He was then posted to the 321st Siege Battery before he was wounded in the knee on barbed wire whilst diving for cover during an enemy bombardment at Shrapnel Corner, Ieper. He had to face a Court of Inquiry as it was felt by the Army that the wound might have been self inflicted, but fortunately, Thomas had a witness in the form of Bombardier Knott. After recovering, Thomas was posted to the 329th Siege Battery, serving with this unit until the 20th March, 1918, when at the age of 22, Thomas died from wounds. Thomas's body was buried at Nine Elms British Cemetery, at Poperinghe in Belgium.

Guardsman John Thomas Scott
24217

John Scott was born at Bridgtown, Staffordshire in 1891, being the eldest child of Thomas and Rose Scott. His father was a coal miner, born in Norton Canes, Staffordshire, whilst his mother came from Bloxwich, the couple having married at Cannock in 1890. In 1901, John was living with his grandparents John and Amy Stokes on the Watling Street at Bridgtown, whereas the rest of the family was living on the Brownhills Road, Norton Canes. The family had grown, with the births of Albert at Bridgtown in 1893, and Cyril, Maud and Garland, all born at Norton Canes. By 1911, the family were all living at Brownhills Road, Norton Canes. John was now aged 19 and a coal miner road repairer. Albert was a haulier down the pit, with Cyril attending the pumps underground. Maud, Garland, Mary and Joseph were all attending school, with the family completed by Dorothy born in 1909. John continued to work as a coal miner, but joined the Army in 1917, enlisting with the 1st Battalion, Grenadier Guards. He was sent to Flanders and served until the 13th September, 1918 when he was killed in action at the age of 27. John's body was buried at Vaulx Hill Cemetery, near Bapaume in France.

Private John Horace Spencer
78370

For details about John Horace Spencer see the entry on the same soldier under Cannock.

Sergeant Henry Thompson
82048

John Thompson, a 23 year old coal miner from Bilston, Staffordshire, married Sarah Matilda Evans, aged 20, and a cotton weaver from Fazeley, Staffordshire. The couple set up a home at Fazeley and it was here that their first child, John junior was born in 1879, followed in 1881 by the birth of Eliza. Henry was born in 1883, and then the family moved to live at Norton Canes on the High Street. Interestingly, Henry stayed in Fazeley, living with his paternal grandparents John and Mary Thompson. In Norton Canes, John and Sarah extended their family with the birth of Thomas in 1886 and William in 1889. By 1901, the family had moved to live at Little Norton, Norton Canes and Henry was now back with his family and working as a coal miner, as was Thomas, and of course his father. The family had also grown with the births of James in 1892, Beatrice in 1895, Arthur in 1897 and Albert in 1900. In 1911, the family was still living at Little Norton, although John Thompson was now a labourer. Henry was a coal miner, while James and Arthur were both horse drivers. In 1914, after the outbreak of war, Henry volunteered for service in the Army, enlisting with the 20th T. M. Battery, Royal Field Artillery, and he was sent to France on the 1st June, 1915. Henry served until the 6th August, 1917 when he died at the age of 34. At the time his death was unrecorded in the local papers, possibly as the family were reeling from the reported death of his older brother John. In fact it was later reported that John had become a prisoner of war. Henry's body was never found after the war and he is remembered on the Ieper (Menin Gate) Memorial in Ieper city centre in Belgium.

Private Henry Whittaker
42231

On the 2nd February, 1897 at St. James Parish Church, Norton Canes, Joseph Whittaker, a 26 year old miner married Elizabeth Cooper aged 22. Both groom and bride had been born and brought up in the village where they were married. The young couple moved in with the bride's parents, John and Mary Cooper at Fair View, Poplar Street, in Norton Canes and it was here that Henry was born in 1898, followed by his sister, Emily in 1900. By 1911, the family had grown further with the births of Joseph junior in 1903, Julia in 1907, Howard in 1908 and Bertram in 1910. Henry found employment as a coal miner at Number 11 Pit, Conduit Colliery in Norton Canes and he remained there until April 1918 when he decided to enlist in the Army, joining the North Staffordshire Regiment initially, before being transferred to serve in the 1/23rd Battalion, East Surrey Regiment. Henry was sent to France and went missing in action on the 29th August, 1918, it later being confirmed that he had died on that day. At the time of his death, Henry was 21 years old and as his body was never recovered, he is remembered on the Vis en Artois Memorial in France.

Private Samuel Whorton
81532

John Whorton, a 37 year old general labourer from Gornal, Staffordshire married the 21 year old Annie Stokes from Halesowen, Worcestershire at Stourbridge in 1885, their first child, Elizabeth being born at Old Hill, Staffordshire in 1886.

The family then moved to live at Norton Green, Norton Canes and it was here that Samuel was born in 1888, followed by William in 1890. By 1901 the family had grown and the Whortons had moved to live at Hednesford Road, Norton Canes. Alice had been born in 1893, Amy in 1896 and Harry in 1900. In 1911, John was working as a colliery surface labourer, while Fanny had set up a business as a grocer and draper on the Walsall Road, Norton Canes. Samuel was working as an insurance agent, with William employed as a locomotive stoker. A further addition to the family, Gladys was born in 1903. Samuel did well as an insurance agent and was promoted to become the assistant superintendent for Refuge Assurance. On the 4th November, 1915, Samuel enlisted in the Army, joining the Royal Army Medical Corps. He embarked for service in Southampton on the 31st May, 1916 arriving at Rouen on the 2nd June. Samuel was then posted to the 2nd Field Ambulance, serving until the 18th October, 1917 when he was sent home on leave for ten days. Samuel returned to his unit and was in France until the 18th September, 1918 when he was severely gassed. He was taken to the 141st Field Ambulance, and transferred to the 42nd Ambulance Train on the 19th September. From here Samuel was sent to the 2nd General Hospital on the 20th September, and then he was put on the Carisbrooke Castle and taken to Plymouth Military Hospital. On the 24th December, 1918, Samuel died of acute influenza at Plymouth at the age of 31. The body of the respected lay preacher was returned to Norton Canes where he was buried at St. James' Churchyard after a service at the Primitive Methodist Chapel.

Corporal William Hurmson
G/6094

Early in 1862, Adam Hurmson married Elizabeth Morris in Walsall. The couple would appear to have settled in Norton Canes and in 1881 were living at Norton Common with five children, John, Thomas, Emma, Teresa and Lizzie, and Thomas Stephenson, a lodger. By 1891, they had moved to Nevill's Buildings on the Norton East Road. The older children had left home, however, Eli, Henry, William, Melia, Samuel and Mary were all living at home. Early in 1900, Adam died at the age of 63 and in 1901, his widow was living with Harry, now aged 22 and a coal loader, William aged 19 and a horse driver, the 18 year old Samuel, a colliery labourer and Nellie. On the 4th June, 1910 William married Mary Fleet at St. James' Church, Norton Canes. In 1911, the couple were living at Norton East with their young son William Arthur. The family grew with the births of James in 1911, and Albert in 1913, And Frank in 1916. Another child, a boy was born in 1914 but died shortly after birth. In 1915 William volunteered for service, joining the 2nd Battalion, Royal Sussex Regiment and being sent to France on the 31st December, 1915. He rose to the rank of Corporal but was killed in action during the Somme Offensive on the 9th September, 1916, when he was shot in the head, most probably by a sniper. William's body was not identified after the war and he is remembered on the Thiepval Memorial to the Missing on the Somme.

Private William Thomas Morris
DM2/165342

Thomas Morris married Mary Ellen Goodfellow at Wem, Shropshire in 1893. He was a wheelwright and carpenter from Shropshire; his wife hailing from Shawbury in the same county. By 1901, the family was living at Lower Forge, Eardington near Bridgnorth; John and William Thomas having been born at Shrewsbury, while Frances had been born in Bridgnorth. By 1911, the family had moved to live on the Rugeley Road in Hednesford. William was now aged 14 and working as a tailor's cutter, whereas Frances was at school along with her sister Louisa Ellen who had been born at Bridgnorth in 1903. A lodger named Isaiah Hayward was also living with the family and was a 32 year old coal miner from Oakengates. William enlisted in 1915, initially with the Army Service Corps, but was then attached to the 12th Siege Battery, Royal Garrison Artillery. He was badly wounded in 1916 and died, aged 20, on the 3rd October, 1916, being buried at Etaples Military Cemetery in France.

By The Same Author

GASKIN

For many people the name Gaskin is synonymous with a brutal murder at Hednesford, Staffordshire in 1919.

Now for the first time, the full story of Gaskin's tragic life is told, shedding light onto a case still recalled over 80 years later.

240mm x 170mm
Paperback
Fully Illustrated
ISBN 978-1-85858-312-9
Published by History Into Print
£7.95